Semiotics for Screenwriters

Semiotics for Screenwriters

Break Down Your Favorite Movies Then Write Your Own

Michael Tierno

BLOOMSBURY ACADEMIC

NEW YORK • LONDON • OXFORD • NEW DELHI • SYDNEY

BLOOMSBURY ACADEMIC
Bloomsbury Publishing Inc
1385 Broadway, New York, NY 10018, USA
50 Bedford Square, London, WC1B 3DP, UK
29 Earlsfort Terrace, Dublin 2, Ireland

BLOOMSBURY, BLOOMSBURY ACADEMIC and the Diana logo are trademarks
of Bloomsbury Publishing Plc

First published in the United States of America 2024

Cover design: Eleanor Rose
Cover image © Normform / Getty Images

A catalog record for this book is available from the Library of Congress.

ISBN: HB: 978-1-5013-9100-2
        PB: 978-1-5013-9099-9
        ePDF: 978-1-5013-9097-5
        eBook: 978-1-5013-9098-2

Typeset by RefineCatch Limited, Bungay, Suffolk
Printed and bound in Great Britain

To find out more about our authors and books visit www.bloomsbury.com
and sign up for our newsletters.

For A. J. Greimas and Joseph Courtés.

I also wish to dedicate this to playwright Robert Patrick,
who was a great writer, a good person,
and the best writing teacher I ever had.

Contents

Acknowledgments

I wish to first thank my editor Katie Gallof for developing the book with me and for graciously offering her insights and guidance throughout the process. Also, I wish to thank Stephanie Grace-Petinos, Alyssa Jordan, and Paul King for helping with the manuscript and keeping it on track. I'd like to give a very special thanks to Merv Honeywood whose editorial insights really helped develop the concepts. Also I wish to thank Amy Brownbridge for all the work she did on the book to ensure it would be all it could be. A very special thanks also belongs to The Writers Room, an urban writing colony in New York, which creates an unrivaled atmosphere to write in, not the least of which is the support of my colleagues there. I also wish to thank East Carolina University, especially Dr. Linda Kean and Dr. Kate Bukoski, for years of support while I taught there. I wish to thank the rest of my colleagues and friends there, as well as the students I had the privilege to teach over the years, many of whom I first tried out these semiotic concepts on, and it was their enthusiasm for the system that gave me the impetus to continue developing it. Also I wish to thank Final Draft for letting me use some screenshots to show how the semiotics tools can be used with their software when writing a screenplay. Lastly, I wish to thank my amazing family and friends and, of course, my darling wife Judy Quinn, who makes it all worth it.

We outsiders or interlopers—who resist the invitation to join the discipline and to "become semioticians,"... should also feel free to bricolate *all this, that is, in plainer language, simply to steal the pieces that interest or fascinate us, and to carry off our fragmentary booty to our intellectual caves.*

Frederic Jameson

From Foreword of *On Meaning: Selected Writings in Semiotic Theory* by Algirdas Julien Greimas, viii, University of Minnesota Press 1987.

"Get it out of here!"

Bookstore manager's answer when I asked him the price of *Semiotics and Language* (a main reference book of this system).

Introduction

The Hollywood Screenwriter's Breakdown System with a Semiotics Spin

Since the beginning of time, Hollywood screenwriters and directors have used the craft of breaking down successful movies and screenplays to study why these great works have done well and then used the knowledge culled from these breakdowns to develop and write new movies. Producers, agents, and movie executives use this technique as well. I know this because as a former story analyst for Hollywood, I would often be asked to watch a movie and come up with a beat sheet of the story so the studio executive can see the essence of what made a movie work. Screenwriters and directors love to get under the hood of popular movies and learn more about what works and what doesn't so they can better their own writing and filmmaking.

The breakdown method is also what the best screenwriting systems in use today deploy, including *The Writer's Journey*, *Dramatica Pro*, *Save the Cat!*, and *Story* by Robert McKee. There's even a book I wrote years ago called *Aristotle's Poetics for Screenwriters*, which breaks down a collection of Hollywood movies using the *Poetics* as a guideline.

My semiotics for screenwriting system is built upon the tradition of the Hollywood screenwriter's breakdown method but with an analytical twist, the semiotics twist. I think of this new system I'm laying out as sort of "a ballet workout for the writing mind." And while I like to imagine that I'm inventing something unique, the reality is semiotics for screenwriting is nothing new, except perhaps that I'm vastly expanding upon the analytic system that has always been *implied* in other screenwriting systems but doing so using semiotics language.

So, in a sense, *Semiotics for Screenwriters* is a brand-new system that requires mental work and rigor to apply, but it's continuing a tradition of the Hollywood breakdown system that has been used for a long time. And I believe the rewards of applying my system will be a great boon to your writing. *Semiotics for Screenwriters* is designed to instruct you to select a collection of movies that you love and then break them down in a specific rigorous fashion, doing so in a way that your brain gets programmed with the gears of your favorite movies using *semiotics* language. Then this information will be coded in your brain as data, ready to be deployed when you work on your own screenplay. At the end of the study, I will also show you how to incorporate your semiotics data from your specimen movies right onto the Final Draft Beat Board and Outline Editor. This way, you can have your favorite specimen movies running in the background as reference whenever you need it.

You can then develop your own original screenplays from accumulated data and knowledge that semiotics has installed in your mind. And remember, since you are selecting your favorite movies based on a specific gameplan of your own design, you won't be merely "copying" the master story forms of other screenwriting systems and plugging in your story ideas into them. You'll be inventing your own original screenplays from the semiotics toolbox that this book will help install in your mind! You'll be able to think fluidly and develop originality and power in your writing using the knowledge culled from said films to shape *original* screenplays with market viability.

What is Semiotics?

Semiotics is the systematic study of sign processes and meaning making, or put another way, it's the study of how signs form "sign systems" in order for humans to be able to communicate and make meaning. It's essentially a tool of communication analysis using special terms and coded language to turn the analysis and study of various fields to which it is applied to into a science. Semiotics is a method of analysis that can be applied to *many* fields, including (but not limited to) literature, psychology, advertising, sociology, cinema, and screenwriting. And while semiotics and its attendant tools and approach use very technical sounding terms, a sign system can be as basic as letters that form the words I'm typing to create this book. Or say if you go for a drive, you'll see numbers on the speedometer; those numbers are signs and represent something, the speed you are driving at. A red light is a sign, as is a stop sign or a weathervane or a thermometer, gas gauge, numbers to select a radio station, etc.

There are different overall branches of semiotics or *movements* of semiotics as they are sometimes called. There's the American system, which was led by Charles Peirce. This system can be difficult to understand and not as immediately useful to the study of screenwriting narrative as the one I'm deploying, which is known as the Paris School. Some may call my overall approach "narratology," which is fine; perhaps narratology can be seen as an encapsulating term for all the disparate parts of semiotics and literary theory, linguistics, and narrative theory I'm pulling together for this book. That said, I believe the term "semiotics" will suffice.

The bulk of the system I'm revealing and deploying here is the system that was lurking in the pages of a bookstore find of mine; namely, *Semiotics and Language: An Analytic Dictionary* written by A. J. Greimas and J. Courtés. Because what I'm developing here relies heavily on *Semiotics and Language*, it's a natural extension to suggest my system is, as theirs is, based on classical logic and linguistics. The semiotics system I'm developing here is also influenced by the writings of Ferdinand de Saussure whose *Course in General Linguistics* is foundational to all semiotics studies. I also use some of Vladimir Propp's *Morphology of the Folktale*, which documents the evolution or *morphology* of a simple Russian folktale through 100 iterations. From this study, he derived a lot of the narrative codes that I use in this book. It's from all of these combined great works (and some related others) that I have built my semiotics system that I'm sharing with you here.

Use the Semiotics System Anywhere in your Writing Process

Semiotics for Screenwriters can show you how to enter in at any point of a brainstorming/writing process even if you have merely a spark of an idea, half a script, a "vomit draft," a log line, a synopsis, or even just a character or a solitary image. It doesn't matter what you have when you get started; in fact, you can even start with nothing, and this system will help you get started. This system can aid in helping you flesh out your story and script and help you draw out narrative threads lodged in your brain from all the film and TV watching you do, which is ultimately great fodder from which to write from if you can break it all down into information in a way that is palatable to use. You can even start with a historical reference, a philosophical idea, a situation, a beat, an event, an ending, a color, or any element you have. This semiotics system is so flexible you can enter in anywhere in your screenwriting process, use the tools and *still* arrive at a strong story.

You can even have only props you want to start with, like a sea of umbrellas on a staircase in *Foreign Correspondent*, conceived and directed by the great Alfred Hitchcock. According to Hitchcock, he started the idea for this movie by envisioning someone escaping through a sea of moving umbrellas. The moving umbrellas would serve as markers for where an escaping assassin runs after murdering a dignitary, and although we don't see the assassin escaping, we see the umbrellas shaking as the assassin bumps into each person on the stairs. Hitchcock found his way into this movie story with this unique visual action and built the story around it. The semiotics system I'm introducing you to will allow you to build an entire screenplay even with as little information as Hitchcock had when he started *Foreign Correspondent*.

Outcomes of this System—Comprehensive Beat Map for Final Draft

While the ultimate outcome of using this book is writing an exciting, moving, *finished* screenplay that gets sold and/or made by Hollywood or Indiewood, the vehicles I'm focusing you on for the purposes of this book will be the execution of an actionable comprehensive beat map/outline that can be dropped onto the Final Draft Beat Board and

Outline Editor. I started developing the original device of the comprehensive beat map with my students when I taught screenwriting at East Carolina University, and it proved invaluable to students first learning how to write scripts because it forced them to slow down and focus on the main story beats *and* the timings of each beat. The reason this is all so important is that screenwriting is a very special kind of storytelling animal. There is a fixed length that a screenplay *must* come in at for it to be taken seriously, between 90–130 pages (110 if it's a spec script). That's it! Think about it, a novel can be 1,000 pages or 200 pages. But a screenplay is a fixed length, therefore we have to truly learn how to control the timing. We do this by adding timecode information to a comprehensive beat map, all of which will eventually be dumped onto the Final Draft Outline Editor. More on this later.

Beat mapping is the key to success in my opinion; I believe if you write a good solid beat map *somewhere* before, during or after your drafting process, the scriptwriting will go more smoothly because you can work out story ideas easier and faster on the beat map and avoid the pitfall of painting yourself into story corners, which is easier to do when you start out *just* writing screenplay pages. Or you could study your collection of ideas generated from your semiotics-driven screenplay breakdowns and the subsequent comprehensive beat maps those breakdowns yield and then see what comes out when you vomit out a draft after studying your specimen movies. No matter what your workflow and writing process is, this *Semiotics for Screenwriters* system is designed to work with it.

Lastly, just in case you're becoming a little worried that the *Semiotics for Screenwriters* system might be too heady and didactic for your writing process, allow me to recall the epigraph prior to this chapter by the brilliant literary theorist and academic Frederic Jameson, who, when referring to using semiotics, states: "We outsiders or interlopers—who resist the invitation to join the discipline and to 'become semioticians' . . . should also feel free to bricolate all this, that is, in plainer language, simply to steal the pieces that interest or fascinate us, and to carry off our fragmentary booty to our intellectual caves." Well here and now, I'd like to second that sentiment by Frederic Jameson and take the opportunity to follow his passionate prescription regarding using semiotics whatever way we want to use it because our goal isn't to become semioticians, but rather to write great screenplays. Also, at this same time I'd like to, at least in my imagination, answer the irate bookstore manager who years ago yelled "Get it out of here!" at me when I inquired about the price of *Semiotics and Language: An Analytical Dictionary*. My response to him now would be: "We *are* getting it out of here. We're bringing it back to our caves and using it the way we want to use it. Now watch what we do with it!"

1

The Semiotics for Screenwriters System

Competent Observer

The most basic question we need to ask about when writing a screenplay is: Who are we writing for? Of course, hopefully we're writing for the audience who will go to the theater someday to watch the movie we wrote or stream it in their homes. Perhaps they will be attracted by seeing a trailer, or catch actors touting it on a talk show, or they'll read a review of it, or a friend will rave about it, enough so they will make it their business to see it. Either way, your potential audience is termed a *target audience*; people who watch movies of the same ilk of the kind you are trying to write. Does the target audience like a certain kind of movie, like superhero movies, romantic comedies, horror films, period dramas, Lifetime Christmas movies? Do they belong to a certain age group or demographic? Me personally, I love dialogue comedies. Can't get enough of them, but sadly they are dying. I am the sucker audience for any good dialogue comedy, or, better put, a "target audience."

But instead of talking merely about a "target audience," I would like to introduce a semiotic concept that is more useful when it comes to understanding what the nature of using semiotics to write scripts is all about. It's a superior concept to "target audience" and encompasses such but will involve much more than that. The term is called **competent observer**.

At first glance, it can seem as if it's a matter of semantics to think there is a notable difference between competent observer and a *target audience*. But there is a very important distinction between the two concepts and understanding what a competent observer is will help you get into the mindset of the semiotics system. To begin with, semiotics postulates there must be a "competent observer" for a story to be *decoded*, which means someone *puts together* the story as presented from the pieces and parts of the story:

> **Competent observer** implies that the observer has to be able to *construct meaning* from the structures that are presented to them. The "competency" comes in that said observer will be able to construct meaning from the elements put before them, but more precisely, meaning is *constructed from* combinations of words, ideas, and (in the case of movies) images and sounds, but meaning is not inherent in these separate elements themselves.

Semiotics teaches that meaning is *constructed* by the viewer/watcher/reader and is *not* inherent in words/ideas/concepts, etc. but must come together through contrast, conflict, and contradiction in someone's brain, and that's where story and meaning is created according to semiotics. You see, "competent observer" has more to do with the way meaning is created, and semiotics will teach you to break down movie story and see the individual pieces of story in a "pre-meaning" way so you can understand how meaning *is* created once those pieces are put together in a certain way by a competent observer. This understanding will facilitate your mission to learn to program your brain to build story and meaning in your screenplays. This concept is foundational to the entire semiotics system I'm laying out here for you, and it's a concept I will return to often.

Competent observer is a great starting point to begin to understand how the semiotics system works for writers. To reiterate: Meaning is not inherent in words, images, and sounds, but comes together in the mind of audience members, script readers, producers, agents, actors, etc. based on how these words, ideas, sounds, and images are structured and contrasted with each other. And before we put together words to form ideas and characters and plot lines and treatments, etc., we need to break down movies to their primary essences, break apart their structures so story and meaning are also broken down so we can then bring these back together and in doing so really learn the architecture of the movies we love. Subsequently we can then train our brains how to create our own screenplays with the same ingenious structure and flair that our specimen movies were created with.

Meaning "On the Nose" vs. Meaning Comes Together in the Mind of a Competent Observer

What does it mean if someone says your script is too "on the nose"? It means it's too literal, that the *meaning* of the story, or what is going on in the scenes, has been too easily spoon-fed to the reader/audience and they don't have to "think" at all (they don't have to construct meaning or put together the story). There's no subtext. If dialogue is too on the nose, it means that the dialogue is too literal, what's being said is exactly what is supposed to be communicated to the audience, there's no important *subtext* at play in the scenes that the audience has to realize themselves. And this writing "on the nose" makes for boring screenplays *and* boring movies not fostering audience engagement.

The critique that a script is too "on the nose" applies to other aspects of story as well. It's considered a cardinal sin of screenwriting to have dialogue that is too "on the nose," meaning scenes themselves have no "subtext" and an audience doesn't need to "construct the meaning" of what is being thought and felt by the actors. So it's well accepted in Hollywood that when meaning in a screenplay (including its story and overall information) is too easily *given* rather than *constructed* it is poor technique. The preferred screenwriting technique—namely, that a movie requires an audience to *construct* story and meaning—is proof that the principles of semiotics have always existed in Hollywood screenplay breakdown language. Of course there are differences between how Hollywood requires audiences to construct meaning and what semiotics is referring to, but I'm interested in the useful similarities in the concepts because I believe this connection between the concepts will aid your writing. Let's see how.

First off, the term competent observer implies the concept of *constructed meaning* versus meaning being "on the nose" or being completely spoon-fed to an audience. Of course, how semiotics uses the idea of competent observer is deeper than just the concept that good dramatic screenplay writing has text and subtext that must be understood by an audience. So, in order to explicate the real meaning of competent observer I'd now like to introduce the next related concept called **generative trajectory**.

Generative Trajectory—From the Surface Level to the Deep Level of Meaning

Generative trajectory is a semiotics term that has to do with how words and concepts that are "generated" on the surface of story are connected to underlying structures of meaning below the surface and together all these layers of meaning form a movie story. These levels include **the deep level of meaning** (themes) and **the narrative level** (story), which are under the iceberg, so to speak, and the tip of the iceberg (the level *above* the water that we see) is called the **surface level** of meaning, and it's here where the **elements** or "things" of story are communicated to us.[1]

1 The Surface Level (figurative level), which includes:
   – isotopies (sub-atomical particles of story in their "pre-meaning" state)
2 The Narrative Level ("story syntax"), which includes:
   – The Actantial Narrative Schema
   – The Canonical Narrative Schema
3 The Deep Level of Meaning, which includes:
   – values/transformations/themes.

Generative trajectory means that what generates emotional meaning is at the bottom of the iceberg and is delivered through to the narrative level of movie story (the middle of the iceberg) up to the surface level of a movie (images, sound, music, dialogue), which for the purposes of this book will be represented by a comprehensive beat map preceded by a canonical narrative schema summary (as a mini-treatment).

---

[1]When I used the term "meaning," I'm not using it in any philosophical or "message" kind of way. I'm merely using it to talk about information that is being communicated including story, ideas, plot, characters, and, yes, of course, thematic information. These elements are summed up by the all-encompassing term "meaning."

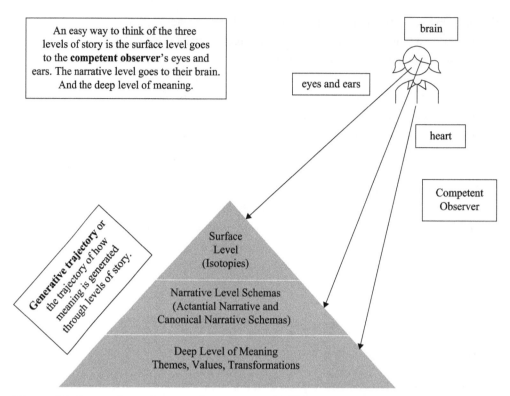

Figure 1.1 Generative trajectory of story pyramid. This serves as a visual representation of how the different layers of the narrative semiotic system are built and experienced by a competent observer.

The way I have laid out the generative trajectory of story was not done so to suggest that this is how movies are written. I've said this a million times before and will say it a million times again, many screenwriters start out having little to no idea what they are writing about and discover what they are writing about later and build on these layers of meaning as they go along. Many will forgo a traditional outline and/or treatment and merely vomit out a *vomit draft* using pure gusto and instinct and after banging out a vomit draft will later go back and shape the script based on what structure and meaning they can glean from it and then they will *find and home in on the structure and themes* they have detected the story is pointing towards. And it's in the act of determining the narrative structures and hidden themes in what *they've already written* that the semiotic method becomes particularly useful (although it's useful at *any* stage of the writing process). At some point in the writing process, screenwriters might look at their draft or pages and ruminate about all the different levels of meaning they are grappling with, which the generative trajectory teaches us *connect* through the entire story. Of course, it's unlikely screenwriters will think of what they are doing in semiotics terms, especially when they are rewriting and homing in on story and theme, but the truth is they are grappling with the exact kinds of components that semiotics can teach us a lot about.

Now let's examine each level of meaning with an eye towards how we will eventually use all the layers of the generative trajectory to break down movies, brainstorm off them, and then use the results we discover as tools to conceive, write, or rewrite our scripts.

2

Isotopies Part I

The Surface Level

Anything of surface level reality that can be written that helps to communicate "things" of story that in turn help to create the illusion of reality belongs on the *surface* level of a movie story. When I say "things" of story I mean the surface elements like ruby slippers, oil can, a photograph of Auntie Em, Professor Marvel's crystal ball, witch's broom, Good Witch's wand, Wicked Witch's crystal ball, house, yellow brick road, woods, poppy fields, Oz's castle, Dorothy, Professor Marvel, Wicked Witch of the West, Glinda, Mayor, Toto, Munchkins, flying monkeys. And if by now you haven't detected I'm talking about *The Wizard of Oz*, stop reading this book and go and watch the MGM classic immediately.

To these "things" of story I just mentioned, such as flying monkeys and Oz's castle, semiotics has given the name "**isotopy**." If isotopy sounds like it's a term borrowed directly from physics, you are correct:

> An **isotopy** in semiotics is the single most reducible atomic particle of meaning in a story.

An isotopy can be a word, a phrase, or a proper name, an expression, etc. It's a particle of meaning but more specifically it's a *narrative* particle of meaning. In fact, the term isotopy in semiotics is a narrative version of what linguistics calls a morpheme. A morpheme combines the most irreducible parts of words called semes, which form morphemes. For example, the word unbreakable is a morpheme that consists of three semes, un—break—able. Each of these three are not reducible any further; they are semes. An isotopy in narrative semiotics is an irreducible element of story but, just like atoms in physics, atoms in story must come together with other atoms to make molecules and matter.

Think of how atoms of hydrogen plus an atom of oxygen combine to make a molecule of water. Separately, neither hydrogen nor oxygen represents water, but combined in a certain configuration they form the molecule of water. A morpheme combines semes to make words or combines irreducible parts to make words. And just as atoms make molecules that make organs that make people, horses, flowers, and other *things*, an isotopy is the particle or "atom" that can be formed to make molecules of meaning that then combine to make stories.

Mind you, this "stuff of story" that the **isotopies** consist of does not only pertain to material things like ruby slippers, oil can, photo of Auntie Em, Professor Marvel's crystal ball, witch's broom, etc. It also is used to label *any* surface level isotopies that communicate reality to an audience like tornadoes, snow falling on poppy fields, etc. And there's even a special category of isotopy called "states of being," which pertain to the emotional lives of the actors (characters), and is a class of isotopies that is foundational to how movie story works because movie audiences experiencing actors living through emotional states of being in a structured movie syntax helps said audience experience a cohesive engaging narrative which is tantamount to ensuring emotional participation of said audience.

States of Being[1]

As previously stated, isotopies in movie story can be **states of being** or emotional states of the actors (characters) in a movie. In *The Wizard of Oz*, a few simple states of being are: Dorothy is melancholy when she sings "Over the Rainbow"; she is ecstatic as she dances to Oz singing "We're Off to See the Wizard"; she's frightened having to approach the Wizard; she's scared for her dog Toto's life, etc.

How Brainstorming Isotopies Trigger how Meaning is Constructed

Once you really know a movie via the technique of "breaking it down," then almost any of its atomic particles (isotopies) can help *trigger* the entire story's architecture and subsequently illuminate the design of how the story's emotional meaning works. This technique will be enhanced when you also bring into play all of the other semiotics tools I will disclose to you. These techniques of breaking down movies into isotopies of "premeaning" to see how they came together to make story and meaning will be foundational to the *Semiotics for Screenwriters* system I'll develop through this book.

Studying individual isotopies of your specimen movies will help you recognize the structure of how meaning and story comes together by a competent observer because

---

[1]States of being will be looked at on both the surface level *and* narrative level of movie story because states of being are so important to emotional meaning that I wanted you to have the opportunity to brainstorm these states as elements and as isotopies at the surface level *and* as components of narrative syntax (beats) at the narrative level. At the narrative level, "states of being" will present as part of a trilogy of "beats" labeled "pragmatic," "cognitive," and "thymic" ("thymic" is another term for the *emotional* beats of actors (characters)). We'll have a closer look at all of these three fundamental beats of story later in the narrative level because it's important to understand how story beats work in a *narrative syntax* because syntax (what follows what) is what gives narrative beats their power and emotional meaning.

you'll be analyzing individual *pieces* of a movie you know well but you'll be looking at such isotopies in their *pre-meaning* state. For example, if I say "oil can" and "yellow brick road," these isotopies don't inherently mean anything to you unless you know the movie from which they are derived, and if you do, these mere isotopies will help trigger the movie story and meaning of *The Wizard of Oz* and also activate an innate sense of how that story comes together and how the individual particles came together to create the story.

When you break down movies, you'll experience how the isotopies alone have little or less meaning apart from being conflicted or contrasted with each other to make meaning, and you'll see how the particles can *trigger* your memory of story meaning on their own. You'll also start to see how the different levels of meaning (surface/narrative and deep levels of meaning) work together. You'll learn that by brainstorming on the atomic particles of story (isotopies) you'll be able to loosely brainstorm story ideas first without writing yourself into a corner.

To get an idea of what I mean, look at Table 2.1; here's a very simple example from the timeless classic in question, *The Wizard of Oz*, which I will break down using standard semantic categories of isotopies common to this kind of semiotics narrative study: objects, places, actors (characters), events, and time.

Look at this sampling of isotopies of *The Wizard of Oz* and muse how the individual isotopies don't have full meaning of the movie story, but you can remember the movie and think of the story just by looking at the isotopic particles. If you meditate on the isotopies, many of them will allow you to hold both concepts in your mind at once: the isotopies of story in their pre-meaning state *and* how those particles come together to make the story's meaning. This exercise is the beginning technique of how to use the semiotics system to write scripts.

Table 2.1 *The Wizard of Oz* isotopies

ACTORS (CHARACTERS)*	OBJECTS**	PLACES	EVENTS	TIME
Dorothy	bike	house	tornado	day
Auntie Em	basket	yellow brick road		night
Professor Marvel	ruby slippers	cornfield		early morning
Scarecrow	oil can	woods		middle of the
Tin Man	bike	poppy fields		night
Cowardly Lion	basket on bike	City of Oz		
talking trees	photo of Auntie Em	colored horses		
Wicked Witch of the West	Marvel's crystal ball	locked storm		
Glinda (Good Witch)	witch's broom	shelter		
mayor	Good Witch's wand			
Toto	Wicked Witch's crystal			
Munchkins	ball			
flying monkeys				

* In narrative semiotics we use the term "actors" rather than characters. The reason for this will be illuminated shortly.
** The term "object" as used here (a standard semantic category of isotopies) is different from the use of object as in subject/object (one of the pairs of binary opposition of actants) in the actantial narrative schema.

Brainstorming Elements and Isotopies Using *The Wizard of Oz*

Let's assume that the movie story you are writing involves a young woman going on a journey somewhere that is far away and dangerous. You can meditate on *The Wizard of Oz*'s isotopies and get a sense of what kinds of things either aid or abet your young woman character getting to her destination (even though we might not know where she's going, why she's going, etc.). We can brainstorm random objects like a time machine, a magic car, the evil landowner's magic horse, his sword of power, first as isolated elements *without knowing how or if they fit together narratively*. But as you do meditate on these elements your unconscious will be loosely searching for a narrative syntax or a **narrative intent**.

We can look over *The Wizard of Oz*'s actors and (with the unconscious knowledge of that great movie whirling around our brain) perhaps imagine actor elements of a good landowner, evil flying robots, crooked politicians, kindly truck drivers, a supportive cyborg, an evil cyborg, etc. Same goes with events you might be inspired to dream up; perhaps you might muse on Oz's tornado and then imagine a tsunami, a meteor shower, or a nuclear explosion. But at the same time you're musing on raw elements triggered by meditating on *The Wizard of Oz*'s isotopies, you're unconsciously thinking of a narrative (and a deep level of meaning, the base of the generative trajectory iceberg) in your unconscious. But you don't have to be in control of all these layers of story yet for there are many other semiotics tools that will help you carefully build your story including how to obtain mastery over the different layers of story.

This above demonstration is merely scratching the surface and the beginning of how to use isotopies from *The Wizard of Oz* (or any movie) to brainstorm raw elements with which to write your own screenplay. But as you can see, I don't know exactly where my original demo screenplay story is going, though I have inklings that it's about a young woman on a journey to a far-flung place and there's danger lurking on the way.

It doesn't matter if you'll use all or *any* of the brainstormed raw elements you generate from studying the isotopies of your specimen movies when you write your own movie. This process will help get you thinking about your screenplay but first in a loose non-linear fashion which will provide your unconscious mind plenty of space to breathe and create. Studying isotopies like the ones present in *The Wizard of Oz* will help you meditate on your potential story *without* locking yourself into a plotline that doesn't work or backing you into any story corners. But this method can also help you get out of screenplay writing trouble by applying the technique of brainstorming raw elements in search of isotopies after you have a draft or pages and can't figure out where to go.

Something happens when you loosely brainstorm off a specimen movie's isotopies, especially one you know well . . . your unconscious starts to think about possible storylines and plot twists without locking you into any one specifically. Because if you know the plot of your specimen movie well enough, you will be simultaneously thinking about the surface isotopies of that story *and* unconsciously meditating on what underlying story they are representing. This technique will become clearer later when we break down a few movies

A writer's unconscious mind will begin to get a sense of narrative intent/narrative syntax from seeing the breakdown of the isotopic fragments.

Breaking down and observing surface level of story as isotopies: oil cans, witches brooms, flying monkeys, yellow brick roads, etc.

Figure 2.1 Isotopic brainstorming and narrative intent. Breaking down isotopies of classic movies you love and seeing the individual isotopies in a "pre-meaning" state will go a long way in helping train your unconscious of how meaning comes together and how story works.

in depth. See Figure 2.1 for a visual representation of how brainstorming surface level isotopies of classic movies can help you begin to formulate an original story.

Thinking about the surface level isotopies will also help you begin to think about the other levels of story (the narrative and the deep levels) which I will extricate later. What's more important for now is you grasp that you can have an entire brainstorming session just by breaking down movies into isotopies *and* simultaneously thinking how the parts of that movie story you love alone don't have the power of the whole *and* then thinking about what that whole is and how those parts came together, which will prime you to do great brainstorming and write your own screenplay. What I'm referring to here is a very important term we use when we talk about how the isotopies are pointing towards a story, and that term is called narrative intent. To talk about narrative intent, let's return to a potential made-up movie story I'll invent so we can start from scratch. Look at the following random elements:

Ford and Rolls Royce, cows and pigs, thunder and lighting, arm and leg.

All of these are elements that can be considered objects, except for thunder and lightning, which might be called events. You might even come up with subcategories of elements *within* the master categories of object, place, actors, etc., subcategories like "cars" (Ford and Rolls Royce), or "animals" (cows and pigs). Either way, these clusters of elements are clumped together in master semantic categories or subcategories, and in and of themselves don't suggest any narrative intent yet. They might trigger narrative intent in your brain, and that's fine. But this triggering will undoubtedly cause you to start jotting down other elements related to that narrative intent you might be conjuring up.

Perhaps you could look at the elements I cataloged above and write a movie about a farmer who weathers bad storms, the farm animals die, the farmers are destitute, and then a rich real estate developer in a Rolls Royce shows up to buy the land from under the farmers, which creates conflict in the family and a bloody standoff. But I had to *add narrative intent* to the elements and add narrative elements like a bloody standoff (which can also be considered a "beat"—more on this later).

What I'm getting at is that *technically* the items like Ford and Rolls Royce and cows and pigs are not isotopies because they don't suggest any narrative intent. Yet. So before we are sure a particle of story is really an isotopy, I'm going to refer to them as elements. It's just a technicality, but it's an important one. To further help us differentiate isotopies from elements and see how isotopies suggest narrative intent, let's look at how we plan a wedding.

Elements[2] related to planning a wedding:

- a bride
- a groom
- an engagement ring
- wedding rings
- ring bearers
- wedding dress
- favors

- band
- hall
- church
- rabbi
- priest
- bridesmaids

- food
- engagement party
- DJ
- gowns
- tuxedos
- champagne

These wedding elements, while related to the category of wedding planning and probably look like a bride and groom's impending wedding checklist, technically are *not* isotopies because they are not moving in a narrative direction; there is no obvious narrative intent. And you might retort by saying, "But a wedding is a story." No, a wedding isn't necessarily a story. Random items that belong in planning a wedding are not based on a generative trajectory of narrative meaning and aren't suggesting a story in and of themselves. Of course these elements *as is* could be part of a narrative intent, a story. But as presented here, they are not yet.

That said, let's add a few more items in the semantic category "wedding" that might help us tell a story:

- old jealous boyfriend
- angry parents
- stoned band leader
- spoiled wedding cake
- moonshine

I can bet that just by adding these new elements you can start to see how they pull in the direction of a story or suggest narrative intent and now there might be a story buzzing around your head. And as these new isotopies are written down simultaneously, a generative trajectory might be beginning to take shape in your brain, one that points to different levels of *meaning* lining up all which will help create emotional meaning in a competent observer.

You might be thinking, "Sure ... those five additional raw elements just added are of a nature which sound more like they lend themselves to story off the bat because they have conflict or suggest conflict inherently." An old jealous boyfriend is by definition conflict oriented. Moonshine is illegal. And perhaps I'm using new raw elements that have flickers

---

[2]An "element" is not really an "isotopy" yet unless it's constructing a story *or* shows narrative intent. But the catch is you'll only really know of "narrative intent" when you break down isotopies for a story that already works or, as you brainstorm elements to write your own movie, you start to see which ones create a narrative and which ones don't. This aspect of the semiotic breakdown process is challenging, but bear with it because as an overall analysis tool it proves to be very powerful.

of narrative just to show the contrast to the raw elements which don't show any intent. The new elements are potential isotopies and are helping stimulate narrative intent in part *because* they resonate with conflict and can bring conflict to the other particles and bring the other terms together with narrative intent and therefore they stand a great chance of becoming isotopies. But isotopies in and of themselves do NOT have to read with specific conflict in order to be forming a story that has narrative intent. What I mean is, you don't have to brainstorm raw elements that reek of conflict when you brainstorm. You'll develop experience with all this in greater detail when you study the breakdowns of isotopies from our specimen movies. You see, narrative intent is that connective through-line you (the competent observer) hold in your head and bring meaning to.

That said, let me tweak the original raw elements list and add to what's already there, and you can start to sense a story and see which elements might be potential isotopies (develop narrative intent):

- a very old bride
- a very young groom
- a stolen engagement ring
- wedding rings from deceased grandparents
- ring bearers that are the groom's kids from an other short-lived marriage
- black wedding dress
- favors that include marijuana rolling papers
- band that is loud and horrible
- hall in a very bad neighborhood
- church that has a funeral running late
- bridesmaids that don't want to be there
- food that tastes bad
- engagement party where fights break out
- gowns too revealing
- tuxedos that are "mod"

I was able to add modifications to the original terms and words to make them feel as if they are moving with a certain narrative intent. Yes, they are more complex sentences or *parts* of sentences rather than simple elements like "bridesmaids" and "engagement party" or even more so than "oil can" or "yellow brick road." But "oil can" and a "yellow brick road" are considered isotopies more so than "an old jealous boyfriend" because *The Wizard of Oz* items are part of an entire *system* of isotopies from the feature film *The Wizard of Oz* that when examined together have narrative intent because we know the story of *The Wizard of Oz*, including the underlying syntax those isotopies build and the narrative intent they resonate with. We are competent observers who can connect the narrative dots of the isotopies of *The Wizard of Oz*. In turn, this effort will help train our brain as to what that story is and help our story sense to grow.

Conversely, in my made-up wedding story, we are only talking about the top layer of story, the surface level of story, so even though the partial sentences *hint* at narrative intent; there isn't any real story built yet.

Now let's return to the new elements I added but let's focus on a particular semantic category, that of actors (semiotics for characters). Adding them, I can now get a sense a story beginning to suggest itself:

- old jealous boyfriend
- angry parents
- stoned band leader

Already your imagination is probably brimming with a possible story that you could write if you had to. In fact, when you think of the story ideas to connect the elements together, this method is part and parcel what you're learning about brainstorming on isotopies of classic movies; namely, what those narrative connections situated in the narrative middle part of the generative trajectory are and how the surface level of isotopies came together to create the illusion of a story.

You could start off with just the single word terms as elements and add to them later as I just did. The point is this process allows initial brainstorming without having to worry so much about how the plot fits together yet. As I write this sentence, I'm already thinking of elements of a certain kind, and I've come up with a story I would like to demo to show the principles. Remember, the key to brainstorming elements is to think of the most basic elements of the surface level of story as separate atomic particles of story before they come together to make narrative intent and meaning and become isotopies. This technique will become clearer when you learn to break down your specimen movies using semiotics and practice cataloging isotopies.

Below is an example of the surface level of a story using elements I laid out above for a wedding and fashioned into a short synopsis. Note I did *not* use all the possible elements:

Elements become isotopies on the surface level of story with some added "connectors" in our demo wedding story.

The *very old bride* is planning to marry *a very young groom* and is going to wear a *black wedding dress*. The couple plan to give out *rolling paper favors* and hold the wedding in a *bad neighborhood* to look hip. But during the engagement party everyone gets stoned and the bride starts to think the groom might not be mature enough to get married. Soon an *old jealous boyfriend* shows up and a *fight breaks out* because he claims she's made the *gown too revealing* but he's actually mad that his old flame is now being taken by a new man. The old boyfriend tries to take the very old bride away and the very young groom beats up the old jealous boyfriend, causing him to flee, and his valor helps him win the confidence of the very old bride and the wedding proceeds.

So the above demonstrates how using surface elements which inherently hint of narrative intent can help formulate the surface level of story, the "stuff" of story that we interact with when we read it or see it as a movie. The surface level of story makes the story real. The surface level is the tip of the generative trajectory iceberg that sticks out of the water. The narrative level is something below the surface level as is the *deeper* level *of meaning* which I'll talk about in later chapters.

Let's now take the method I just introduced and go a little deeper with another "made-up" story.

Brainstorming For *The Lost Dog Story*

Say I want to write a story about a dog who has gotten lost in the woods, misses his family, gets chased by gangs, cars, police, wolves, hornets, terrorists, Satan worshipers, etc. He endures storms, rain, cold, hunger, sling shots, mean kids, bears, cars, wolves, fires, etc. That's it! Those are the ideas I'm starting with, and I have nothing more yet.

And yes, these ideas read like isotopies and not mere elements because notice (not coincidentally) I've chosen items that suggest conflict (with narrative intent) because I believe that when writing it makes your life easier. Because they suggest narrative intent, they are likely to become isotopies. And you might write a mere element that never becomes an isotopy, but don't worry. That's the point of brainstorming: to start to get a sense of narrative intent, in search of an ultimate narrative syntax (story). But you may also sketch out multitudes of elements, many of which seem like automatic isotopies (have narrative intent) and not know if they are or not until you start shaping your story. This will especially become evident when we break down entire masterpiece feature films and see how, even though we know the narrative intent of the isotopies, some in and of themselves don't particularly suggest story while others will.

Back to my made-up story. Beginning with a premise that suggests conflict is a great way to go for screenwriting. I'm following my innate sense of how this story might take shape as I jot random elements down, but that said I really don't have to use every single one, not every single one will become an isotopy, or if some *seem* like isotopies but don't fit an overall narrative, that's okay too.

So to make life easy, I'm starting with a premise that is rife with conflict (story). I learned in my 15 years as a university writing teacher that it's hard to start writing with nothing. It's okay to sometimes use writing prompts. Start with something. Anything. That's a lot of how it all happens in Hollywood. There, they don't put writers in a room and say, "Think of a great movie story." A more common scenario is that a producer will have an idea to produce a movie in the current zeitgeist, something that is trending, like "talking animal stories" (*Babe*), and find a writer to write one but be specific, i.e., make it about a talking giraffe who is battling alien robot lions.

So with that thought in mind, I'm starting with a story about a lost dog. Table 2.2 shows random elements based on my potential lost dog story. I'm not worrying how they will all fit together into a narrative yet, just the way you wouldn't worry about what kind of matter

Table 2.2 Raw elements—*The Lost Dog Story*—(with an eye towards finding elements that possess or suggest narrative intent and therefore will become isotopies).Start always by using the standard narrative semiotic semantic breakdown categories (actors, objects, places, events, times) to brainstorm possible isotopies and story ideas

ACTORS	OBJECTS	PLACES	EVENTS	TIME
dog catcher	ball	woods	Christmas	day
owner	toy animal	owner's house	New Year's Eve	night
mean kids	toy snake	doghouse	dog's birthday	early morning
mean lady	bone			middle of the night
wolves	chew toy			
puppies	water bowl			
bear	doggie treats			
	meat			
	garbage			
	dog chow			
	wagging tail			
	dog collar			
	leash			
	paw			
	bone			

you were going to create if you were just assembling basic elements of the periodic table to create matter. Of course, I maintain that if a random element is generated and doesn't fit into your story, it's not an isotopy because it's not building a cohesive narrative syntax or doesn't suggest a specific narrative intent.

When I sketched out the elements in the table, I wrote them down as quickly as I could without thinking. When you brainstorm elements in search of isotopies, don't think too much; write whatever comes to mind. If you know the basic idea for your story, don't think … just write down all and any random elements as they come to you. Start to feel what narrative intent is whispering to you from the elements you are creating so they can become isotopies and form narrative intent. When you are sketching out elements as I did, you can do so thinking of a certain narrative intent or just jot down raw elements without having a clue to a story or somewhere in between. Either way, the point is to work in a non-linear fashion and not lock yourself into a story yet that will prevent you from developing a story to its maximum potential. And what this system is going to show you is how to use isotopies from your favorite specimen movies that you've broken down as a stimulating guidepost to feed your brainstorming and writing process starting with generating random raw elements.

Since you'll have broken down movies you love and isolated the isotopies of the movies' stories and then using semiotics tools put them back together seeing how the parts relate to a whole, you'll become attuned to what the narrative intent is of those particles of the classic movies you break down and how they came together on the surface level to create the illusion of a movie story.

Adding Additional "Elements" in Search of Isotopies ("Narrative Intent")

Now I'd like to return to the elements I jotted down and these combined with the basic premise of *The Lost Dog Story* and the narrative intent I see developing, I can now *add additional* elements which may become isotopies (Table 2.3) and form the surface level of a story.

Because narrative intent is more and more being *suggested* in my sketching out of elements, I can sense they are beginning to feel like isotopies. Now bear in mind I probably won't use every single element I brainstormed but that's fine. In fact, it's part of how this *Semiotics for Screenwriters* system works; you cast your net wide for raw elements, and your story brain will sense narrative intent in some of them.

Table 2.3 *The Lost Dog Story* with additional elements

	ACTORS	OBJECTS	PLACES	EVENTS	TIME
	dog catcher	ball	woods	Christmas	day
	owner	toy animal	owner's	New Year's	night
	mean kids	toy snake	house	Eve	dusk
	mean lady	water bowl		dog's	
	wolves	doggie treats		birthday	
	puppies				
Additional elements added based on original categories.	(added below) dog fight owner	(added below) water slide big steak dinner vegetable wagging tail wounded paw	(added below) unhoused woman's refrigerator box	(added below) Fourth of July	(added below) middle of the night

> You don't need to use any or all of the elements you brainstorm for your story, although you could use them all if you wanted to. The purpose of brainstorming elements in search of isotopies when sketching out a screenplay is to loosen up your thinking and help you to begin to focus on your narrative intent which will manifest in the narrative level and the deeper level of meaning and ultimately help you build a story.

Brainstorming elements you *don't* use can help anticipate a narrative intent or story direction just as much as generating ones you do use. Sometimes we learn more about what a story *is* about by learning what it's *not* about. And it's great to acquire such insight into your story at this surface level before it starts to harden in a narrative syntax.

Of course this brainstorming for isotopies technique can occur at any stage of your writing, even after you have a draft or a couple of rewrites. Seeing random elements generated that ultimately *don't* fit a story will help you shape your story because you'll be narrowing down the direction of your story as much by what you don't/can't/won't use as much as by what you do use. A random element that you brainstorm *then* reject will tell you a lot about where your story is pulling to, as it will be rejected because it doesn't fit the narrative which you're beginning to sense you're developing.

So, the elements I'm brainstorming (in conjunction with the basic premise I landed on, which is a story about a lost dog missing his family) are moving with narrative intent and that's good because a strong story/through-line (syntax) is the end goal I'm seeking. And as the narrative intent begins to surface I can comfortably begin to think about these elements as isotopies. I'm not sure if these elements will indeed become isotopies or if they will fit into a narrative, but this process has given me a sense of where the story is going as a result of the brainstorming I have done.

Now, the next phase of dealing with the brainstormed elements in search of surface level isotopies puts us in search of a narrative intent. We can now move to the next tool that will help us know what to do with the elements.

This tool and attendant method will help us come up with more elements in search of isotopies and will help us to move forward with narrative intent and start to get whispers of scenes, characters, action, twists, themes, genres, tone, emotional states of being, etc., without locking us into any particular storyline (syntax) yet or having the story "harden" and paint us into a story corner too soon. This technique is called **binary opposition**.

Binary Opposition—The Heart of the Semiotics System

Drama is conflict, right? Indeed … conflict is "the music of story" according to Robert McKee, the screenwriting seminar guru and author of *Story* (1997). Protagonist versus antagonist is the foundation of all drama. The fight, the battle, right against wrong, good against evil, life against death. We go to films to see some sort of fight or conflict play out in an exciting way such so that we can lose ourselves and our worries and get "sutured" into the story via the conflict. Or to put it more accurately, the conflict *is* the story. Of course, there are all kinds of things happening around a movie's conflict that makes us have a complete entertainment experience. There are various pleasures associated with conflicts that unfold in the stories of the movies we watch which is part of the specific pleasure of seeing movies whether it be great action sequences, an actor or actress we just love to watch, hearing great dialogue, watching gifted actors experiencing great emotions, dazzling CGI effects, or funny moments a movie delivers that make us laugh away our troubles.

All those fun elements of a movie don't work as well as individual parts without a conflict, an overarching one that unifies the entire story. Conflict holds the entire movie together; conflict is the glue. And while conflict is a great concept to use when writing a screenplay, semiotics starts with a more comprehensive term for conflict, and it's called "binary opposition."

What is a binary opposition? It means that two terms are *bound* or binded together because they are opposite from one another and the perception of one cannot exist without the other. The simplest binary opposition is good/evil. It's two terms that are polar opposites to one another but *linked* together because one cannot exist without the other, at least in terms of our perception or understanding of the concept via language. In other words, we cannot understand good without evil, life without death, hot without cold, up without down, etc.

And we can use binary opposition as both an analysis and brainstorming tool, which will help you begin to see what kind of story we are creating because it can guide you on how to clump your isotopies together to form the "molecules" of story connected or *bonded* by binary opposition. Take the very simplistic example shown in Figure 2.2.

Just as atoms of hydrogen and oxygen make a molecule of water, isotopies of story come together through binary opposition to form the building blocks of story. To turn atomic isotopies into clumps of story molecules, those clumps will be semantically related and paired. In the example below, you could look at the semantic category of owners and then using the terms of binary opposition (good vs. bad) form two polar opposites—good owners and bad owners.

But take note, sometimes the isotopies in a movie story will simply be attached to one side or the other of the controlling binary opposition terms. In other words, if you determine that the controlling binary opposition terms are good and evil, you might decide some of the isotopies you logged from a movie belong on the side of good and another set on the side of evil. More on this later.

Now that I've introduced the concept of binary opposition, I would like to expand on the use of this tool by introducing the most important component of the semiotics system: the semiotic square.

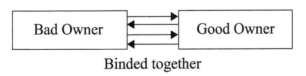

Binded together

Figure 2.2 Binary opposition. Isotopies are viewed as "bound together" to their opposite which in essence gives them the ability to be perceived. You know hot because of cold, good because of bad, life because of death, etc. This basic concept extends to and influences the entire breadth of story, narrative syntax, theme, etc.

3

Isotopies Part II
The Semiotic Square

The **semiotic square** is the single most important visual representation of the narrative semiotic system in existence. It was originally presented by A. J. Greimas in his book *Sémantique Structurale* in 1966 and was developed by him up until his death in 1992 as well as by countless others. It's the universally recognized symbol of narrative semiotics (and is used by other applications of semiotics in other disciplines). It's based on the classical logical square of oppositions. In essence it's a visual representation of the *elementary structure of all meaning*.

Here is the classical semiotic square, a representation of the semantic category of *existence* (Figure 3.1).

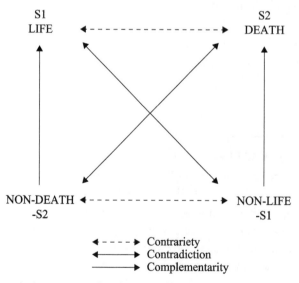

Figure 3.1 The semiotic square of existence. Traditionally this semiotic square of the semantic category of existence (LIFE/DEATH) is the one most used to introduce and demonstrate the principle of the semiotic square.

The semiotics square shows how binary opposition and its logically related corollaries as shown above can *theoretically* be used to express all meaning in language and subsequently in movie story, at least in terms of a movie story as expressed in text via a treatment, outline, beat map, or screenplay.[1]

Greimas envisioned the square to allow for variations and nuances in story analysis to act as a *constraint* to ensure everything generated from a story analysis will be based on binary opposition or in dramatic story terms *unified conflict*. Remember, conflict is the essence of dramatic storytelling, the music of story. If conflict is indeed the music of story, the semiotic square is the tuning fork of that "music."

The Semiotics Square and the Controlling Binary Opposition Terms

The semiotic square is created by figuring out the two *controlling* opposition terms in the same semantic category that can be used to guide the entire semiotic breakdown of a movie story. To do this, it's sometimes best to think *thematically* or even better to think where a movie's theme intersects with its story line to help you come up with the two controlling binary opposition terms of the movie.

I like to think of the controlling binary opposition terms of a semiotic square as *action thematic terms*. There will be other pairs of terms that I will utilize in my breakdowns and brainstorming of specimen movies but figuring out the controlling binary opposition terms is key. And remember, you don't have to know what these terms are when you start writing or even when you start to break down your specimen movies. At some point you'll want to figure the terms just as writers will at some point figure out what they are writing about, and then zero in on what they are writing about based on what they have learned their story is about—or, in other words, what they deem the theme to be.

In the above example of a semiotic square, I used the semantic category of *existence* which has the contrary poles of LIFE and DEATH listed under the heading of "S1" and "S2." In case you are wondering, S1 and S2 are merely *labels* for the two main coordinates of opposites or poles that are contrary to one another, and these poles set up the whole semiotics square. The *positions* of the poles (S1 and S2) don't matter initially; I could have just as well switched them to make S1 be DEATH and S2 be LIFE.

What goes where on the semiotic square will matter to me when I start using it to plot master story beats and their narrative trajectory, but more on that comes later. Let's return to what the square means. LIFE and DEATH are contrary, so neither needs to be true but they must be completely contrary. Both can be false, but both cannot be true. One only exists in

---

[1]Cinema semiotics as a field of study is a whole other topic separate to general narrative semiotics. It seeks to pursue the analysis of movies with the movie itself *being* the object of study, not merely the narrative of the movie. Also, there are challenges and limitations to this semiotic square system. The semiotic square project has since been developed much further from its origins and is still being developed today; much of this development is a discussion beyond the scope of this book; some developments will be discussed later on as needed. That said, for the purposes of developing mental rigor when breaking down and brainstorming specimen movies or creating your own from the wisdom you cull from such breakdowns, the basic semiotic square is a great place to start thinking about your specimen movies, your own original story, and is the best vantage point from which to begin to organize your breakdowns.

opposition to the other. In logic terms, contrary items must be diametrically opposed to one another regardless of whether they are true. This to me is why they form the main poles of any semiotic square. We don't know if either is true or false; we just know they are opposite and exist because of the other.

Next up, the contradiction axis. Notice the contradiction lines that connect LIFE and NON-LIFE and DEATH and NON-DEATH. These are contradictory connections. When items are contradictory of one another, one must be true, the other false; in other words, there must be a pure contradiction. They cannot both be true. Next, we move to LIFE and NON-DEATH and DEATH and NON-LIFE which are also considered complementary. Each of these complementarity sets *implies* the other but for our purposes each is not *the same* and these *distinctions* will help allow for variances in our analysis of semantic isotopies of films we love. In fact *all* these variances will aid us in brainstorming and creating building blocks to help us write. Finally, there is the second contrary axis on the bottom of the square the NON-LIFE vs. NON-DEATH. This axis demonstrates the same principles as the top main poles represent (LIFE vs. DEATH), but it's the *contraries* of the *contradictions* or rather they represent sort of a secondary set of contraries mirroring the main poles of contrarieties LIFE and DEATH. All of this will make more sense when you look at the creative use of this tool I deploy in later chapters.

What I just presented above about the semiotic square is merely scratching the surface of this very deep tool which has developed since Greimas invented it and is *still* being developed by semioticians to this day. It's a wonderful tool, and I use it when writing scripts all the time, but I do so with one important caveat ... I'm fully cognizant that it's a tool to serve us and *not* the other way around. To paraphrase Frederic Jameson's quote from earlier—we're not trying to become semioticians; we're stealing the pieces of it we want and bringing it back to our caves and using it as we want to.

You must always remember that when trying to use sometimes very challenging rigorous tools like the semiotic square. We're not trying to be semioticians; we're stealing parts of it we like and using it to help our screenwriting. That said, I've read deeply about the field of narrative semiotics and while I love the theoretical underpinnings of the system, there's only so far I can go without feeling like I'm lost in the semiotics rabbit hole, which can be frustrating. Therefore, I started with enough logic required for us to delve into narrative semiotics via the all-important semiotic square that is necessary to understand in order to use semiotics to write better screenplays and *not* to be semioticians. Our goal is first and always to write better screenplays by thinking about the movies we love deeply and deconstructing them in a way that trains our brain and gives us technique and fodder from which to write our own screenplays.

I also use the semiotic square as a constraint to help me keep isotopies I develop tied back to the master conflict of the movie story I'm either breaking down *or* trying to write. The master poles of the conflict are essentially what the story is built on. For each story we break down, we'll need to figure this out as well as we'll need to figure out what the master poles of conflict are for our own scripts. That doesn't mean every idea we brainstorm for our scripts must conform to this logical technique; it's just a tool to help focus us at some point in the process.

The semiotic square opens a way to build different levels of story, from the thematic level all the way through to the figurative isotopies on the surface, allowing for nuances all along the way but at the same time keeping all these story elements connected through binary opposition and to the master conflict of the story. To reiterate a point made earlier, that's sometimes why the semiotic square is labeled a "constraint." It *constrains* or delimits how you analyze elements in your story by creating binary opposition through which everything must be filtered. The constraint helps you think through screenplay elements in a way that makes everything you create in a script connected through theme or conflict or, to borrow a playwriting term, the constraints ensure there is a unity of opposites running through your story thematically and narratively. This is a very powerful tool.

Now let's look a little deeper about how to use the semiotic square to write.

Using the Semiotic Square to Write Original Screenplays

First let me start off with a quote from another very important book called *Dictionary of Semiotics*:

> Thus, in the analysis of meaning, semiotics proceeds from the recognition of differences to the definition of the relationships underpinning them. In the event, the semiotic square is no more than a visual representation of the elementary structure of meaning.
>
> (Martin and Ringham 2000: 116)

The semiotics square will help us get at the *elementary* structure of meaning or more specifically the binary opposition of meaning. Does that cover every single gradation of meaning that can possibly be represented in a movie story? It can, but it will take imagination and work to do so, which I'll address later. Greimas spent much of his final years trying to add to the semiotic square to accommodate for variances in meaning and to some extent succeeded, and the project is still ongoing. I look at this book as a continuation of this noble quest to further develop the semiotics project especially in terms of using the semiotic square to analyze and break down all meaning in story. That said, I'd like to sketch out a simple demo which depicts how the semiotic square might be used to write with. Let's talk about a vampire story we might want to create (because who doesn't want to create a vampire story these days?).

Vampire stories tend to be about life and death and the "undead," which is another way to refer to a vampire. So, let's say there's a woman who is a normal human being, call her Jill. Let's say Jill has a boring boyfriend. She has a best friend, Jane. Then she's romantically pursued by a vampire. The vampire would be considered non-death (undead). He's not alive, but he's not exactly dead. He can't die. He's eternally not alive. And say he kills Jill's friend Jane for blood. Jane is dead (she's in the S2 position.) But she comes back as a ghost, so she, too, is undead. Jill has a boring boyfriend; he's alive but he's "non-life." Take a look at how some of these elements might lay out on a semiotic square (Figure 3.2).

You can see how the master oppositions for a vampire film might be life and death and all other semantic categories of isotopies that can be generated will be connected to these master poles of conflict or more precisely the controlling binary opposition terms of S1 and S2, life and death.

A VAMPIRE STORY

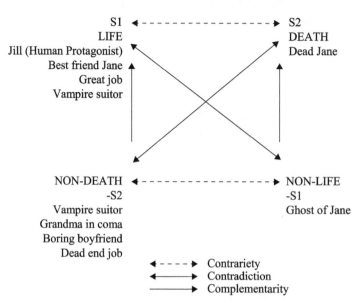

Figure 3.2 Semiotic square of *A Vampire Story*. Playing off the ubiquitous semiotic square of existence, this semantic category (life/death) easily lends itself to a traditional vampire story, a very popular subgenre of the classical horror movie.

Don't worry if, while breaking down, brainstorming, and writing, you cannot connect every plot idea back to the main poles of the controlling binary opposition terms. But you should try to consider the master poles and *all four corners* of the semiotic square as connective information to help you define the best beats to tell the story. I'll elaborate on how to do this later on, so don't worry if you aren't fluent with these concepts as of yet.

To further the use of the semiotic square of life vs. death for the vampire story, you could say that Jill is a young woman who has a boring boyfriend and is in pursuit of a normal (but dull) life. She's working a dead-end job. Or maybe she has a great job (for demonstration purposes I posted both in the square). Say Jill meets a vampire suitor who likes her, but she flees him out of instinct. She is also sad because her grandma is in a coma. Then her best friend Jane turns up dead, in a staged car accident constructed to hide the fact she was killed by a vampire. Jill seeks out a romantic relationship with the vampire. She falls in love. The vampire who starts out in the category of non-death becomes life to Jill because he makes her feel alive, in love. Jane visits as a ghost from the grave to warn Jill of the danger of the vampire boyfriend and eventually Jill realizes that to live and survive is more important than love if love means possible death by the vampire's bite.

To put the controlling binary opposition terms in perspective and bring them down to earth of everyday life, say you had hopes to become a ballerina which are not dead but are not exactly "alive" anymore. Or maybe you're in a neutral state of enthusiasm and passion for life and are not dead but not really alive. You're not leaping out of bed "alive" but not dead. And of course, this is why I used the example of the vampire story to explicate the classic "life and death" semiotic square. Both vampires and zombies are "Undead" (non-death), and vampire and zombie movies are both part of very popular genres of movies these days. Vampires and zombies are not dead per se, but they aren't exactly alive. They are undead or non-death, whichever you want to say but hopefully you can see where this is all going. As you can see, the master semiotic square for my vampire movie uses the category of existence (life vs. death) to generate a variety of story ideas, elements, and potential isotopies. I've detailed many of these elements in the semiotic square above for Jill's vampire story.

Of course you could quibble with how I use the life/death semiotic square to brainstorm the vampire story. You can swap certain elements under different poles. For example, you could say the ghost of Jane should fall under "non-death" instead of "non-life." But the secret to using this tool (as will be explicated in detail throughout this study) is that you learn to use the tool creatively. I'm being obvious in my choices generated by this semiotic square for my vampire story, but I do so to illustrate a point about how the semiotic square helps add elements that are always connected to the central conflict and/or theme, stated by the master poles of the controlling binary opposition terms. This concept of how to use the semiotic square to connect all the story's elements to the master poles of controlling binary opposition terms will become important when I break down three specimen movies in depth and brainstorm to write my demo sample movie story at the end of this book. We can use the master semiotic square to add other semantic categories to generate other isotopies of actors, places (locations), etc. And I will be teaching you how to do this not as a semiotician or a logician but in a creative way that will enhance your screenwriting. Remember, as Frederic Jameson said, we're like pirates, stealing semiotics, dragging it back to our cave and using it whatever way we want, as long as it aids our screenwriting process.

That said, I wanted to point out that semiotic square has many writing uses and can be used to look at the other levels of story, especially the deep level of meaning.

The Semiotic Square and the Deep Level of Meaning

The deep level of meaning will be a topic I'll circle back to, but I want to begin talking about it in conjunction with the semiotic square. The semiotic square can be utilized to talk about the deep level of meaning, which includes how values, themes, and transformations work in a story. Later, I'll circle back to expand on these tools, but for now I want to talk about them as they relate to the semiotic square.

First things first—what are values in a movie story? In short, values relate to the actors (characters) in a movie story and pertain to what the actors (characters) in a story *need/ want/desire*. Transformations occur when actors move significantly *closer* or *further* from what they have established they *need/want/desire* or in essence what they "value."

In real life, if I really want a new Rolls Royce and lose my job, then I'm moving *away* from being able to obtain a Rolls Royce, my explicitly stated value. Or if I want a Rolls Royce and win the lottery for one million dollars, I'm moving closer to my stated value. Now, if I rob a bank to steal money to buy a Rolls and am successful, I'm also moving towards what I value, which is being able to buy the Rolls. But something else has happened simultaneously as I've stolen the money and obtained power to purchase my dream car. I've stated through my actions that owning a car of luxury is more important than the moral implications of committing the crime of robbing a bank. In fact, I could even state this moment in my life story as a theme, *the lust of luxury goods is more important than any personal integrity and makes it worth it to be evil and rob a bank.* And while this might not be a theme stated in the most elegant sense, it gets to the point. Some themes will be stated more like traditional themes (*"love of money is the root of all evil"*); some will be stated as mere beats that represent in plain English what is happening at a key moment in plot (I rob a bank because owning a Rolls is more important than personal integrity). And while we are able to figure out what theme is stated by whether the protagonist (subject) moves closer or further from their object of value, the quest for the object of value is stated as part of the plot. Joe wants X and is getting closer or further. Or he gets it or he doesn't. Yes, I'm stating this in an overly simplistic way, but this is the foundation for values transformations and themes. And these moments that mark a protagonist's moving closer to or further from their object of value (goal) are called master story beats/themes stated.

Themes can be *stated* in a literary sense at the point of transformation; namely, those moments when actors move closer or further from their object of value. But when a moment of transformation happens in a movie (an actor moves significantly closer or further to their *object* of value), it can either be expressed as a traditional theme *"money is the root of all evil"* or perhaps not as literary and is just a mere beat, "Joe gets X." And all of this *comes together* in the mind of a competent observer.

A competent observer sees a moment of transformation in a movie story (Dorothy kills the Wicked Witch of the West by throwing water on her), and in our mind, we think, "Dorothy has won! She had the strength to defeat the evil witch." But that beat won't necessarily be perceived as a theme "stated" in the traditional sense. But sometimes there will be traditional themes stated as in the end of our first specimen masterpiece, *It's a Wonderful Life*, when George Bailey reads a note from Clarence, "Remember no man is a failure who has friends." Transformational beats can either be expressed simply as in *The Wizard of Oz* or more like philosophy as in *It's a Wonderful Life*. It depends on the individual specimen movie and how you approach the breakdown, but you need to understand both ways. I'll circle back to this idea later but wanted to introduce both of these approaches here in conjunction with how it all relates to the semiotic square so we can build on it later. This is what I mean by saying the semiotics system is more than a mere formula. It's an analytic tool.

Let's return to our vampire story and start with a question: What is valued by the lead actor (character) Jill? What does she want? She wants love. Okay, fair enough. But here is the catch that makes this system powerful to me. In the story thus far, Jill wants love but the poles by which she'll have to obtain it will move through the very poles of existence; namely, *life* and *death* as represented in the master semiotic square for the story. Life connects to *not death* which is not fully life or else it would be expressed as *life*. How does this translate to everyday existence? Did you ever feel like you weren't dead but not really alive? It can be you're deathly ill or just very depressed because your significant other dumped you. Or maybe some poor soul is in a coma, a vegetative state. They are not dead but are in state of non-life. Almost dead. This helps us move towards non-death (you're not dead but you're not exactly alive). Again, you can quibble with the specifics of how to apply the different poles of the semiotic square, but this is a *creative* brainstorming tool, not an exercise in classical logic although it uses classical logic as a framework/point of departure.

In other words, Jill can start off wanting *love* (her value) but then because she gets tangled up with a deadly vampire really winds up wanting *life* or simply to stay alive (her actual value). And yes, her *need/want/desire* will have evolved or transformed into the struggle of life vs. death in the story and every point in said story which she moves further towards life or towards death is a point of *transformation* because it's getting her closer or further from what her main value has become. And another name for these points of transformation in a story are master story beats. So what I just discussed is a taste of the deep level of meaning using the semiotic square to which I will dutifully return to later on in the book. I wished to expose it here early because it's a very deep topic. I'm introducing it now in earnest because when we return to it you'll have thought about it and I can build upon that knowledge.

Now to explore the semiotic square more explicitly in terms of helping us write a story. We'll especially examine how the controlling binary opposition terms come into play. To do so, I'd like to return to my fictional lost dog story.

The Lost Dog Story—Binary Oppositions on the Surface Level

I will start with a master semiotic square based on the premise that a dog is forced to leave his home and seeks to return to it and his beloved owners. That said, I need to come up with a

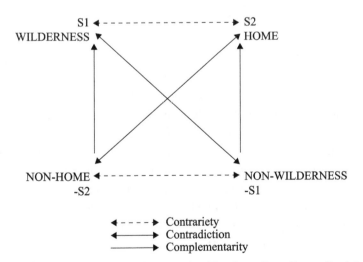

Figure 3.3 This depicts the semiotic square for *The Lost Dog Story*. Devising a master semiotic square for your original screenplay is a great brainstorming tool, helping to ensure every narrative beat that is introduced is connected to the central thematic conflict and structure of the story.

semiotic square but to do so I must think about the master controlling binary opposition terms. I utilize the premise of the story and come up with the terms wilderness and home. Bear in mind you might not come up with the master semiotic square right away; it may come to you further down the road of your brainstorming process and that's okay. This system is flexible.

Again, since the semiotic square is so important I want to quickly review how it works and what everything in it means. S1 and S2 represent the top of the square and the master controlling binary opposition terms. Wilderness/home are contrary. The dotted arrow line represents **contrariety**. -S2 that is underneath non-home is related to wilderness in a **complementarity** way. Non-home (-S2) and the solid two-headed arrow pointing to home (S2) means the terms are in **contradiction** to one another. Also remember setting up a semiotic square and deciding which side each of the contrary terms go on has nothing to do with those terms as far as their axiological significance is concerned. S1 and S2 could've been switched. That said, we'll later come to see that which term goes on which side will become important later when we discuss plot movement, especially in regards to transformations.

That said, I tend to decide what goes in S1 and S2 based on what I *predict* what the movement of the story might be. In other words, in my imagination, *The Lost Dog Story* will involve a dog going from wilderness to home so that's why wilderness is S1 and home is S2 moving left to right. This visually represents the *trajectory of the story* especially if you think of the square as a little timeline. So with the basic semiotic square for *The Lost Dog Story* established I would like to address another important aspect of how to use binary opposition terms to brainstorm raw elements and potential isotopies.

Using the Controlling Binary Opposition Terms of the Semiotic Square to Brainstorm Raw Elements and Potential Isotopies

While there are the controlling binary opposition terms for the master semiotic square for any story, there can be additional categories of binary opposition terms I use when breaking down and classifying isotopies as well as when scouting for raw elements in search of isotopies. I'll demonstrate both with *The Lost Dog Story* but would like to recall *The Wizard of Oz* to talk about these variances. These different tools will serve us because I'll then show you how we use varied categories of isotopies from breaking down *The Wizard of Oz* to help write *The Lost Dog Story*. Along those lines I used multiple kinds of binary opposition, categories like men vs. women, humans vs. animals as well as isotopies derived directly from the master controlling binary opposition terms of the movie's master semiotic square.

First, let's look at the master controlling binary opposition terms in *The Wizard of Oz*. I came up with the very simple master binary opposition terms of evil vs. good and created a master semiotic square (see Figure 3.4).

Now let's consider these two master controlling binary opposition terms (evil vs. good) and how the isotopies of the movie connect to them (Tables 3.1–3.3).

So in the below tables, you have three universally accepted master semantic categories of storytelling and a quick placement of the movie's isotopies into either sides of the

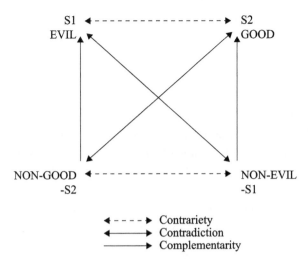

Figure 3.4 Semiotic square for *The Wizard of Oz*—"Good vs. Evil" . . . it's as basic as it gets.

Table 3.1 *The Wizard of Oz*—Actors (using the primary binary opposition terms from the movie's master semiotic square)

ACTORS

EVIL	vs.	GOOD
Wicked Witch of the West		Dorothy
flying monkeys		Munchkins
talking trees		Technicolor Horses
Wicked Witch of the West's Sister		Good Witch (Glinda)
		Professor Marvel

Table 3.2 *The Wizard of Oz*—Places (using the primary binary opposition terms from the movie's master semiotic square)

PLACES

EVIL	vs.	GOOD
Wicked Witch of the West's castle		Oz's castle
		Professor Marvel's wagon

Table 3.3 *The Wizard of Oz*—Objects (using the primary binary opposition terms from the movie's master semiotic square)

OBJECTS

EVIL	vs.	GOOD
Wicked Witch's broom		Tin Man's oil can
apples from the talking trees		snow falling in the poppy fields
Wicked Witch of the West's crystal ball		Professor Marvel's crystal ball

controlling binary opposition terms in their "pre-meaning state" before they come together and are contrasted and combined to make the whole story. Note I tried to place each of the isotopies in direct conflict with its directly opposing isotopy in the adjacent column where I could. (The Wicked Witch of the West's crystal ball vs. Professor Marvel's crystal ball, for example, are directly in binary opposition.)

But in some instances the isotopies aren't directly contrary, like the thrown "apples from the talking trees" vs. "snow falling in the poppy fields," even though they are on opposite sides of the poles. But while cataloging where isotopies are in direct binary opposition (contrary) to each other is important, it's more important to be able to place all of a movie's isotopies on either side of the master semiotic square. All of these exercises will be beneficial to writers because it's the mere act of breaking down isotopies and trying to classify which side they "belong" to that will begin to stimulate your creative story ideas as well as facilitate your ease with the semiotics tools.

Along those lines, let's look at another approach to brainstorming and classifying isotopies.

The Second Approach to Classifying Isotopies

As I said, there are multiple ways we can look at isotopies, and that is to compare them *within* other kinds of semantic categories that aren't necessarily related to the controlling binary opposition terms of the movie's master semiotic square. To do so, we use general semantic categories to log isotopies.

Table 3.4 *The Wizard of Oz*—Men vs. Women (using general semantic terms of opposition)

MEN	vs.	WOMEN
Professor Marvel		Dorothy
Wizard		Glinda
Tin Man		Wicked Witch of the West
Scarecrow		Wicked Witch of the West
Cowardly Lion		Wicked Witch of the West
		Wicked Witch's Sister

Table 3.5 *The Wizard of Oz*—Kansas vs. Oz (using general semantic terms of opposition)

KANSAS	vs.	OZ
road outside in the cornfield		yellow brick road
Professor Marvel's wagon		inside Oz's castle

You can come up with a wide variety of general semantic categories and catalog the isotopies into them in addition to pinning the isotopies to the two master binary opposition terms. And again, notice while I'm brainstorming different possible binary opposition terms in different categories to pin isotopies to, there doesn't have to be a perfectly matched contrary for each isotopy in the opposite column. For example, in Table 3.5, "Professor Marvel's wagon" isn't necessarily in binary opposition to "inside Oz's castle." But one belongs on the Kansas side, the other on the Oz side. And the two can kind of seem like they are in direct binary opposition. Again, it's the effort to think along these lines that will stimulate story ideas, not necessarily the perfection of finding exact binary opposition matches of all your isotopies.

For another example, in men vs. women, I listed the Wicked Witch of the West three times against the individual actors of the loveable trio of Oz: the Tin Man, the Scarecrow, and the Cowardly Lion. I also listed the Wicked Witch's Sister alone without a contrary but she belongs on the women's side. Keep these multiple methods of cataloging isotopies in your mind for now because they all will come into play later. With *The Wizard of Oz* as background information, let's go back to the movie I'm trying to write, *The Lost Dog Story*, and let's return the two binary opposition terms wilderness/home onto a semiotic square (Figure 3.5).

I've conceived of a master semiotic square for *The Lost Dog Story*, and right now the critical thing I need from it are the S1 and the S2 controlling binary opposition terms wilderness and home. These controlling binary opposition terms will help with the task of brainstorming raw elements in search of isotopies of story and eventually will help develop the story as I see which side to put the various raw elements I brainstorm for the potential story onto.

Again, let me reiterate, S1 and S2 are simply the positive and negative poles of the semiotic square. Labeling them positive and negative doesn't mean I'm attributing to them axiological statuses or values of good or evil to them. Such distinctions will develop in due time and will come into play later when we look at the deep level of meaning which includes themes. For the record, I choose which term to put on which side dependent on the narrative trajectory I feel the story is moving in. For *The Lost Dog Story*, I envision the dog moving from wilderness to home, and that's why I'll place wilderness in the S1 position and home in the S2 position.

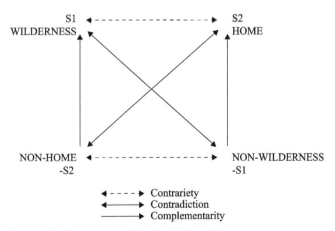

Figure 3.5 Master semiotic square—*The Lost Dog Story*.

For now, I'm interested in generating raw elements in search of isotopies. I already know my basic premise or log line for *The Lost Dog Story*. This again points up a key facet of how this *Semiotics for Screenwriters* system works: you can use it anywhere in the process of writing. That said, a clue to how I fashion it is partially based on where I think the story is moving in terms of a possible narrative trajectory of the potential story events that are percolating in my mind. To reiterate, in the case of *The Lost Dog Story*, I sense it's moving from *wilderness* to *home*. I say this because I am projecting that the lead actor (the titular lost dog) is going to have his whole value system and emotional life tied up with trying to return home.

And instead of developing uncharted raw elements in search of isotopies *then* figuring out if they can be mapped to either pole, with this story I feel compelled to start right off with the controlling binary opposition terms to help me generate raw elements in search of isotopies and also which side they belong on. So along those lines, using the two master poles of the semiotic square *wilderness* and *home*, let's brainstorm raw elements on the universal semantic categories of binary opposition.

And here are the universal semantic categories:

- Objects
- Places
- Actors
- Events
- Time

Table 3.6 *The Lost Dog Story*—Objects (Wilderness vs. Home)

OBJECTS

WILDERNESS	vs.	HOME
dirty rag		ball
grass to eat		doggie treats
tennis balls for training*		stuffed snake
human food in dumpster**		doggie food in bowl
sedative		medicine
rat poison		dog food

* Note: Not every element you toss out will have an opposition easily suggested or one that feeds into a cohesive master conflict of a story. That's okay. I forced some here, including "tennis balls for training" to oppose "stuffed snake." I asked myself, "What could possibly be a binary opposition to a dog's stuffed snake?" This made me think in terms of conflict. This led to me thinking of "tennis balls for training" and the idea that the bad owners who adopted the dog subjected him to harsh training to prepare him for dog fights. And thus the entire story idea was born. Again, the raw element I brainstormed to arrive at a story with might not remain as part of the story, but that doesn't matter . . . it got me where I needed to go. To reiterate: You might not use every raw element you think of in your final story, but it's the process of seeking them that will keep you in the mindset of story/conflict in a unified manner.

** Again, this new raw element came to me when I started to come up with raw elements to feed into either side of the binary opposition poles, indicating this process was already suggesting some scenes.

Table 3.7 *The Lost Dog Story*—Place (Wilderness vs. Home)

PLACES		
WILDERNESS	**vs.**	**HOME**
woods		owner's home
training ground of dog fights		backyards of good owners
refrigerator box		doggie bed
veterinarian's office for dog fights		veterinarian's office for good owners
rat poison trap		dog food area
dog fight ring		dog training center
dog cages		basement of owner's house
wildernesses near woods		roads near owner's house

Table 3.8 *The Lost Dog Story*—Actors (Wilderness vs. Home)

ACTORS		
WILDERNESS	**vs.**	**HOME**
bad owners		good owners
dog catcher		kind unhoused woman
newborn baby		newborn baby of friendly neighbor
sneaky cat		old dog
teeth-baring dog		friendly neighbor's dog

Table 3.9 *The Lost Dog Story*—Time (Wilderness vs. Home)

TIME		
WILDERNESS	**vs.**	**HOME**
deep dark night		sunny morning
long boring day		fun day with owners
Christmas morning alone in wilderness		Christmas morning with owners

Table 3.10 *The Lost Dog Story*—Events (Wilderness vs. Home)

EVENTS		
WILDERNESS	**vs.**	**HOME**
first dog fight		first time playing with neighbor's dogs
practice fight		playing with owner
death of homeless woman		birth of owner's baby

These are some further binary opposition within semantic categories I have brainstormed.

I'm going to take this moment to point out that just by brainstorming the initial category of Actors, through brainstorming raw elements in binary opposition such as "newborn baby," I have already generated the first story idea for my lost dog epic. The story suggesting itself, the one that is emerging from laying out elements as binary oppositions, is:

A dog is forced to leave his comfortable home because his owners have a newborn baby and are afraid to have the dog around.

Do you see how this kind of elemental brainstorming can help generate story ideas without writing yourself into a story corner from the get-go? I don't have to know anything else about the story, just a basic premise to go on. This is the first glimmer of a story that I have for this demo.

A Special Category of Isotopies—States of Being

Finally, I would like to add another isotopic category to the mix of categories we use for breaking down and brainstorming stories with, and it is specifically called "states of being." States of being are vital to any surface level of story because they point up the emotional life of the actors in a story. States of being will also be examined in the narrative level (due to their effect being predicated on narrative syntax), but we'll address this later. For now, let's brainstorm, classify, and itemize some possible states of being as raw elements that can become potential isotopies for use in the surface level of *The Lost Dog Story*:

- sad dog
- lonely dog
- happy dog
- angry dog
- excited dog
- bored dog
- confused dog
- scared dog

These states of being that I brainstormed and itemized might seem a little bargain basement, but I threw them down merely to illustrate a point. States of being will come into play at the surface level of story *and* the narrative level simultaneously. And as I said, states of being are thymic (emotional) beats which function at the narrative level of story as they are dependent on syntax (what follows what). But these thymic beats also present as isotopies on the surface level. For now, it's important for me to talk about the reason that I look at these key beats in two ways is that they are so important to making a story work, that I want us to start dealing with them upfront on the surface but also knowing they will eventually become narrative beats in syntax. Syntax is very important to understand when considering thymic beats (states of being) because syntax is structure and structure creates emotion. "States of being" will be utilized both on the surface level as an isotopy *and* on the narrative level where I'll brainstorm and create actor/narrative beats that will be influenced by the *syntax* of the story and mean more in the linear narrative, not just in terms of binary opposition on the surface level.

So, in summary, states of being are treated in two separate ways (on the surface and on the narrative level) because the states of being of the actors in a movie story are so fundamental to how a story builds and evokes emotional meaning in a competent observer. Also, states of being will handily fit into a special table of *binary opposition* with the two binary opposite poles being labeled as **euphoria** and **dysphoria**. I'll go deeper into this breakdown component later, but for now it's important to understand that states of being should be understood at the surface level of story as well as on the narrative level when we start talking about actual "beats" of story which have more to do with the syntax of where and when they occur to derive their power. The oldest saying in the world to understand why states of being derive power from narrative syntax is the mini-plot, "the queen died and then the king died because of grief." That is a narrative syntax and "grief" is a state of being which we understand because of what follows what. The king was sad his queen died and he died heartbroken. Narrative syntax.

Dysphoria vs. euphoria are the binary opposition terms or the poles to map states of being to. The euphoria/dysphoria part of the breakdown/brainstorming process serves many purposes, but an important one is helping writers plot the emotional life of actors in a story. Keep states of being in your mental toolbox for now for we shall revisit it again soon througout this study.

Along those lines, here is a basic brainstorm of possible states of being that my main actor, the dog, the titular character in *The Lost Dog Story*, might experience:

Table 3.11 Raw elements as potential states of being (isotopies)—*The Lost Dog Story*

DYSPHORIA	vs.	EUPHORIA
sad dog		happy dog
tired dog		energized dog
lonely dog		loved dog
bored dog		excited dog
hurt dog		healthy dog
angry dog		joyful dog
hungry dog		full dog

4

The Narrative Level

So while I have touched on all levels of story, until now I have been mostly focused on the surface level. I'm now going to build on the discussion of the surface level of storytelling level and will begin exploring the middle section of the generative trajectory, the narrative level. The narrative level is the *story* part of the generative trajectory iceberg that is "underneath the water," so to speak. It's the story that the audience (competent observers) are building in their minds communicated via the surface level isotopies. And this narrative level has two distinct parts, and both parts function as two completely different takes on the exact same story. And both of these matching components of the narrative level then are important and useful in our breakdowns, in our brainstorming, and ultimately in our screenwriting.

That said, at this point you may have the feeling that some of my analysis and use of samples, demos, and specimens get a little redundant because we're going over the same story territory albeit using different semiotic lenses to do so. The multitude of different kinds of breakdowns of the same story is akin to the different kinds of breakdowns an assistant director will make in order to prepare a movie for production. In this preproduction process, a shooting schedule will be created, along with a separate day out of days (DOOD) report for actor schedules, a prop list, etc., but all for the same movie. That's how this book is designed—to give you a multitude of breakdown tools to get under the hood of your specimen movies in so many different ways that by the time you're finished the movie stories will be *cognitively* mapped into your psyche; you'll know your specimen movies backwards and forwards as well as possessing the mental mechanisms and tools from said specimen movies to use to brainstorm and write your screenplay.

Both levels of narrative are important, so let's break down each one in detail, one at a time.

The Actantial Narrative Schema

The **actantial narrative schema** comes out of Greimas's work on Vladimir Propp's *Morphology of the Folktale* wherein Propp had identified 31 "narratemes" as plot building blocks. These building blocks include archetypical plot beats such as "Interdiction: Hero is warned." Or "Violation of interdiction." You might recognize a similar approach taught by *The Writer's Journey*, which deploys the use of Jungian archetypes such as the Hero Gets the

Call to Action, The Hero Refuses the Call to Action, etc. This part of the semiotics toolbox is similar to these kinds of formula-based screenplay writing systems but in my opinion is more flexible, especially given the semiotic system's non-linear approach to analyzing specimen movies and brainstorming to write.

Greimas took Propp's 31 narratemes and transformed them down to six terms or "functions" that are in play in any story. And in keeping with his whole semiotic project of binary opposition being the foundation of how all meaning is generated, he set up his functions as three pairs of binary opposition.

The results of Greimas's consolidation of the 31 narratemes yielded six **actants** of all story. The six actants or the actantial narrative schema are written as three pairs of binary oppositions:

- sender/receiver
- subject/object
- helper/opponent

These three pairs are in opposition and utilize six master plot "functions" or actants that are in essence the foundation and structure of any movie story. The three pairs of six actants are stated in binary opposition to each other and represent every possible action a movie story can have.

In looking at these six actants, it is tempting to see each actant as representing "character roles" in movie stories, and often they do represent character roles. This idea is akin to how *The Writer's Journey* talks about how in the paradigm of all fiction movie story, every movie will have a hero, a villain, a helper, shape shifters, etc. If your first instinct is to think of each actant as a character, that's fine . . . that was my instinct, too. But as I dug a little deeper into semiotics, I learned the term actant represents a more flexible and wonderful concept than just *character* or actor. In order to discuss how actants are different than mere "characters," I need to introduce another important concept from Vladimir Propp, which is the concept of story **functions**.

Actants are "Functions" and Serve as "Action Forces" Rather than Only as People

A function is a powerful term because the term implies a *doing* or having to *do something* involving action in a way that it's connected as part of the overall story mechanism. To repeat, actants serve as functions and are more like *action forces* in a story. Yes, a hero can represent a single actant such as a **subject** on a quest for an **object**. In fact, it's good for you to have the mental flexibility to be able to assign actors (characters) to actants but also to be flexible and realize this concept of actants is more expansive than just one actor per actant. Indeed, in the case of a subject, it can be assigned to a singular character and is usually associated with the movie's protagonist just the way villain can represent a single actant like an **opponent** or an **anti-subject**. But it has long been stipulated by classical dramatic theory that action forces in a story are greater than the will of individual characters.

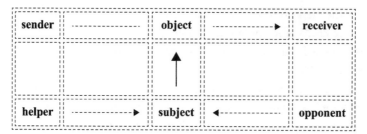

Figure 4.1 Actantial narrative schema semiotic square. We call the layout which depicts the basic mechanical operations of the actantial narrative schema a semiotic "square," but it is different than the master semiotic square previously discussed. It's starting to suggest story movement and narrative syntax. It also suggests scene structure, but more on that later.

In fact, semiotics is in many ways merely using technical language to convey classical dramatic story theory. Here is one of my favorite quotes from Aristotle's *Poetics*:

> Tragedy (serious dramatic story) is an imitation not of men but of action and life.

Aristotle, the master dramatic story theoretician, says it perfectly in the above quote, and I believe this is partially where Greimas took his theory from regarding actants. And why not; Greimas based the semiotic square on Aristotelian logic.

Actants are action forces, and there doesn't need to be a one-to-one relationship of actants to actors but there can be (and almost always is) when it makes sense. That said, look again at the special semiotic square that depicts the actantial narrative schema structure of binary oppositions of the three master pairs of actants and how the pairs are all connected in a story (Figure 4.1).[1]

This alternate semiotic square is the classical representation of the actantial narrative schema. And it's the first device we'll use to look at plot movement in time, the arrows representing the syntax of story movement in screenwriting terms.

Let's look at each pair of actants in binary opposition or story functions.

Sender/Receiver

The first pair of actants you can see in Figure 4.1 are sender/receiver. This is where a **sender** is "opposed" to a **receiver**. But the kind of binary opposition that this schema represents isn't a pure "contrary" relationship the way life and death are. It's a little more nuanced and was done so to facilitate being able to talk about linear narrative while still using the semiotics language of binary opposition. Let's look further.

A sender transmits to a receiver which causes a need or desire for the receiver to get something, need something, want something, etc. This binary opposition of the sender/receiver movement creates a subject that comes into "opposition" with an object they want, need, and/or desire to obtain. In a sense, they are in opposition to the object because they

---

[1]We will begin to see the language of the actantial narrative schema will feed directly into Hollywood storytelling and directing language, much of which is in fact derived from theater. This includes the technique of scene objectives, obstacles, etc. More on this later when we break down three specimen Hollywood movies.

don't have it yet. That is the binary opposition of this first pair of actants in terms of semiotics language.

In fact, this event constitutes that a story has been created, a narrative has been triggered. Again, a story begins when a sender sends to receiver, creating a need/want/desire, and the receiver (the subject) is formed in opposition to the object they need/want/desire to come into conjunction with.[2]

Notice I'm not necessarily attaching actors (characters) to the actants yet. I'm resisting and keeping actants in the more abstract mode of overall story action, as action forces, rather than attaching the actants directly to actors, because ultimately this discipline will give us more flexibility and help your story have more of a unified action and a more dynamic structure, ultimately relating everything back to the master controlling binary opposition terms of the entire movie.

A sender can be a person, a force (like a tornado), a desire inside a protagonist, etc. But it must be action that moves in opposition to a receiver to set up the action (sender/receiver). It doesn't have to be a good or bad force in the film; it doesn't even have to be a person. To reiterate, the sender/receiver dynamic forces a subject to be *formed* in that the subject receives a desire/need/want for an object. In Hollywood scriptwriting terms, this translates to the simple adage that the hero must have a goal, a want, a desire, or a need. But we'll see later, when we break down our three specimen movies, this simple formulaic concept via the semiotics lens provides for offers far more flexibility and can be used on the macro level to encapsulate the overall master actantial narrative schema of a movie story *or* it can provide a way to fashion individual beats, scenes, or sequences.

The primary master binary opposition of sender/receiver creating a subject in need of an object causes the beginning of a story. A subject is created only by wanting/needing/desiring an object and then is in opposition to said object in essence by not possessing the object. The sender sends to a receiver something that causes a desire, a need, or a want for an object, which makes them a subject and initiates the story. The story doesn't just roll up with this dynamic moment occurring in the backstory. It happens in the story, or as Robert McKee likes to call it, the "inciting incident."

The sender/receiver opposition initiates the story as a master beat. But sending and receiving happens throughout the story in scenes and beats. Here are some basic examples of the master sender/receiver binary oppositions in some big Hollywood movies:

- In *The Godfather*, the attempt on Don Corleone's life is a sender to Michael the receiver, receiving the mission to kill Sollozzo and Captain McCluskey to avenge his father.
- In *The Wizard of Oz*, the tornado knocks Dorothy out of Kansas to Oz, sending to her as receiver the desire to get home.

These samples from movie stories I just cited represent the master actantial narrative schemas for the movies. But as you'll see later in the breakdowns of three specimen movies, there will be many opportunities to catalog microcosms of mini-actantial narrative

---

[2]"come into conjunction with" is the semiotics way of expressing "gets."

schemas throughout the stories, and later I'll show you how to use said information to brainstorm and write your own screenplay.

That said, I believe it's important to be able to create the master actantial narrative schema at some point in our writing process. But it's equally important to be able to understand that all the micro-actants work as a microcosm *throughout* a movie connected back to the master actantial schema.

Sender/receiver is one of three binary opposition pairs of actants and part of the foundational structure of all action in a film story. Now a look at the second pair of actants, the subject/object.

Subject/Object

Although I already mentioned the binary opposition of subject/object in the above paragraphs, I want to now specifically address this second set of actants. After a sender sends to receiver, creating a need, want, desire, or goal in a receiver, a subject is created in *need* of an object.

The sender sends to receiver, creating a need, want, desire, or goal, and in turn creates a subject who needs/wants/desires an object, which is another binary opposition. Here are some classic examples of a sender transmitting a goal to a receiver making a receiver into a subject desiring, wanting, or needing an object.

1   *The Godfather*—(subject: Michael Corleone) desires to kill Sollozzo and Captain McCluskey to (save his family: object)
2   *Rocky*—(subject: Rocky) desires to last 15 rounds (to prove he's more than just another bum from the neighborhood: object)
3   *The Lord of the Rings*—(subject: Frodo) desires to destroy the one ring of power and (save Middle Earth: object)
4   *The Wizard of Oz*—(subject: Dorothy) desires to (return home: object).

These are a few examples of the subject/object opposition in some classic movies. But notice analyzing the opposition of the terms of actants is not as simple as it is with figuring out the controlling terms of a movie's master semiotic square, the terms that occupy the S1 position and S2 positions like life/death. Actants are "active," the root of the term being "to act," and this is in contrast to the *static terms* of life and death. Analyzing actants on the narrative level involves looking at events that move forward in a timeline, or a syntax. This follows that. This happens, then that happens, etc. That's why these binary oppositions are considered on the narrative level; you must talk about narrative syntax to highlight them. There is binary opposition but in a different more narrative way, as actants manifest as events or movement on a timeline. Hence sequential movement is baked into the concept of the binary opposition of actants.

We have moved into the narrative level, and this means each subject becomes a subject once they are in pursuit (need/want/desire) of a goal or object. Yes, Michael Corleone was Michael Corleone *before* he was sent and received the need to kill Sollozzo and McCluskey to save his family. And Dorothy was Dorothy *before* she is whisked away to Oz in a flying house. But Michael and Dorothy *became* subjects upon receiving from the sender, which in turn created their need/want/desire and put them in pursuit of an object.

A subject is formed once a receiver develops a need, an object or goal, want, desire, etc. and *then* a story is begun. The need/want or desire can be for someone a subject is attracted to, or a desire to return home, or to stay alive, or to get money, or to kill your uncle who killed your father (according to the ghost of your father), get cured, find peace, destroy the meteor, etc. The sender/receiver movement is the binary opposition whereby a subject (semiotics speak for a "protagonist") is in need of an object, which in Hollywood screenplay speak is merely the "goal." A cliché about story in Hollywood is that most screenplays are centered around desire. That is how the brain of the audience (competent observers) works. They are interested in characters with strong desires (wants/needs/objectives/goals). If this seems too simplistic, that's to be expected, and this semiotics system will give you tools to work *with* and *against* this principle of storytelling at the macro- and micro-beat level. Semiotics will help you develop originality and nuance while still building with and against these principles of storytelling. And note, while knowing this concept alone won't get you a great screenplay, it's the easiest, oldest adage in the book, "Your hero has to want something." And want/desire/need playing out goes for the entire story, individual scenes, beats, etc. It's also the foundation of what a scene is in classical acting/directing terms; namely, the question that an actor might ask a director, "What does the character *want* in this scene?" And if a character *wants* something in a scene, you also have to know as a writer, what the opposition to that want is? What is the obstacle? The fight? This is what movie story is all about, and semiotics will teach you to be able to use these tools in macro- and microcosm ways working with and against this principle.

And yes, there are times in arthouse films that the protagonist seems to be a passive subject rather than an active hero in pursuit of a goal. But in arthouse films often there are goals, wants, and needs going on, but they are sometimes just subverted. Great arthouse filmmakers know the rules and how to break them. In offbeat classic films, perhaps the distinction may be one of style rather than of substance. What I mean is, films that don't follow a hero wanting something strongly are usually working against the principle of the protagonist needing a desiring subject in pursuit of an object. In semiotics theory, we strive to explore the principles of how the human story brain works in order to become deft at captivating it. And merely having a character and a strong goal (subject/object duality) is only the beginning of a strong story. It's the comprehensive system that semiotics has to offer you that you can use to flesh your story out, one which will separate you out from the pack.

In summary of this second pair of actants, a sender sends to a receiver, creating a subject (protagonist) who wants to obtain the object of desire, and you have the beginning of a story. But we need more conflict to build a complete story, and this leads us to the next of the three pairs of actants.

Helper/Opponent (Anti-Subject)

The next pair of binary oppositions in the actantial narrative schema are the actants called the helper/opponent (anti-subject) pairs. A **helper** is anyone (or anything) who helps the subject obtain the object of desire. An opponent is anyone who blocks or hinders that subject in pursuit of that object. Same goes with an anti-subject. Both opponents and anti-subjects are obstacles preventing the subject from coming into "conjunction" with their object of desire.

But there is a primary difference between an opponent and an anti-subject: All anti-subjects are opponents but sometimes an opponent is merely an opponent and *not* an anti-subject. An opponent may only oppose the subject (protagonist) and not care if the subject obtains the object of desire. For example, in *The Wizard of Oz*, Dorothy wants to get home. The Wicked Witch of the West wants to kill her to get her ruby slippers. The Wicked Witch of the West is a clear-cut antagonist *and* an opponent at the same time who wishes to destroy Dorothy and inadvertently stop her from getting home. But the scary living trees in the forest that throw apples at Dorothy on her trek to Oz are mere opponents and interfere with Dorothy's quest to get home (via stopping her from getting to Oz). The apple-throwing living trees aren't anti-subjects. They are mere opponents. They don't seem to care about Dorothy's overall goal of getting home. Same goes with Frodo encountering Shelob, a monstrous spider in *The Lord of the Rings*. Shelob is not trying to stop Frodo from destroying the one ring of power. It is just a giant spider that is menacing. Sauron, the evil king, is trying to conquer Middle Earth and is diametrically opposed to Frodo. He is an anti-subject.

So, the opponent/anti-subject works in opposition to the subject, achieving the object of desire either directly (anti-subject) or indirectly (opponent). But the opponent/anti-subject is also in opposition to the helper. This is why the actantial narrative schema occurs on the narrative level; it involves action moving through time, in a syntax.

That is why there is the more complicated-looking semiotic square depicting the movement of the sender/receiver, subject/object, helper/opponent. The helper and opponent oppose each other, and one helps the subject as the other hinders or seeks to destroy the subject. All of it is considered a binary opposition in semiotics language.

The three pairs of binary opposition (sender/receiver, subject/object, helper/opponent) are both opposed each to their pair *and* are in opposition along a narrative trajectory in a completely unique way. Study this actantial narrative because it's the key to entry into the narrative level in semiotic theory.

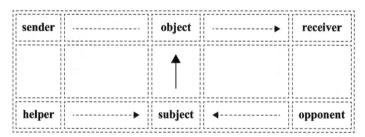

Figure 4.2 Actantial narrative schema. This schema is the beginning of dramatic "movement" as the arrows clearly depict. A "sender" sends to a receiver which constitutes an event is happening.

That said, I would like to use the semiotic square of the actantial narrative schema to brainstorm actants in our demo story, *The Lost Dog Story*. As always with brainstorming using semiotics tools, I don't have to use all or any of what I come up with. But at this juncture, it's important to emphasize the difference between brainstorming at the actantial narrative schema level vs. the surface level of elements in search of isotopies, meaning we're starting to move in a narrative direction.

Returning to our demo story we are trying to develop, *The Lost Dog Story*, let's brainstorm a couple of ideas using the three axes of the actantial narrative schema. Remember, at this stage, I don't want my story to harden; I want to keep it loose so the creative ideas (and an eventual story structure) can flow, and a strong dramatic story can blossom in my brain and on the page and eventually in the mind of readers, actors, producers. Remember the semiotics system is meant to work on a writer's unconscious, which will help stories dance around your brain and take shape there, and these story ideas will come out when you brainstorm and write; the result of your rigorous analysis and breakdown of movies you love using the semiotics method.

Remember at this phase of the process of brainstorm and writing *The Lost Dog Story*, I am pivoting off of some of the work I already did in gathering up random elements in search of isotopies on the surface level, which lead to me playing with some of these raw elements in binary opposition against the master controlling semiotic square. This gave me clues of narrative intent and ultimately led me to be able to shape a story idea. And even though I found many ways of using the six actants throughout the story in macro *and* micro ways, we always need to first think of the master actantial narrative schema as the primary setup of the story, essentially the story's premise. And then we can have all the ancillary micro-actants be connected to *the* master actantial schema. Below, in Figure 4.3, I have built an actantial semiotic square that is set up using the main premise (or master actantial narrative schema) of the main plot; in this case, it's about a dog named "Scrappy," the subject with the object of returning home. From that starting point, using this controlling actantial narrative schema, I'm able to brainstorm other potential actants. As you can see in this example, the schema is practically self-sufficient in terms of being a guideline to generate ideas to help shape a story.

To recap, actants are referred to as story functions in semiotics. While technical sounding, the term "function" is designed to help us distinguish actants from mere actors/characters per se and think of them as action forces. That's why we don't necessarily assign actants to characters (even though there often seems to be a one-to-one relationship of actant to characters).

Case in point: The Bad Owners start out as helpers in that they are supposedly potential good Owners offering to give Scrappy a new loving home. But after they take Scrappy away they change to opponents when we discover they lied about their intentions with Scrappy and will use him for dog fights, specifically to become cannon fodder to be killed by their lead dog Mad Dog McKill, putting Scrappy's health and life in peril and *furthering* him from his object or goal of returning home. So, in essence, the new Owners shift from helpers to opponents. This is just one example why (in theory) you don't want to necessarily start writing by assigning actants to actors although it's understandable why it's easy to do so. You should do so with the awareness that an actant is an *action force*, not a person. And yes,

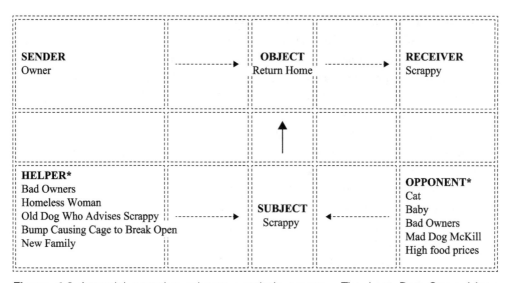

Figure 4.3 Actantial narrative schema semiotic square—*The Lost Dog Story*. Many different actantial narrative schemas can be drafted for any story when you consider the microcosms of actants against the macrocosm of actants outlined in the master actantial narrative schema above. That is why it's important to figure out what the master actantial narrative schema might be for your story at some point in your writing process.

* The helper/opponent opposition allows for the most flexibility/variance in a story. *The Lost Dog Story* doesn't really start with an *anti*-subject, or a villain who is *diametrically opposed* to the subject Scrappy and his goal of returning home to his family. But there are many opponents standing in his way of this goal and eventually the Bad Owner who captures him for dog fights becomes an anti-subject.

actants are usually embodied by a single actor but viewing actants as action forces in a movie story is beneficial.

Actants can have more than one actor perform their respective actions. To reiterate, this principle is very much like the shapeshifter archetype prescribed in *The Writer's Journey* system, which talks about how a deceptive character will evolve from a helper to an opponent (or the opposite). Actants stand for *action* that happens in binary opposition (sender/receiver, subject/object, helper/opponent), and these actants get attached to, performed by, and/or carried out by mostly actors/characters who appear to us via the surface level of story. But technically, actors/characters are not part of the "story" per se; they are part of the surface landscape that helps communicate the story to the audience through the opposition of the actants.

Now a quick summary of the actantial narrative schema is now in line: Six actants form all the action of a story and exist in binary opposition but manifest as events that happen in time. The sender sends to the receiver something that creates a need/want/desire and hence creates a subject and such need/want/desire is the subject's object, and this subject/object dichotomy is a binary opposition. This event marks the beginning of a story. Helpers and opponents work to either support the subject in coming into conjunction with their object or against the subject in this quest and are a mere unintentional hinderance. Or a story may have an anti-subject, an actant that is diametrically opposed to the subject's quest for its object, and are true antagonists or what is commonly referred to as "the villain."

These are the main actants at work in the narrative level in the actantial narrative schema communicated via actors on the surface level. It's useful to create a master actantial narrative schema at some point in your process and then use it to generate smaller instances of micro-actants, all of which can then be fed into a treatment to develop beats, scenes, and sequences.

Also to reiterate a key concept, a story will often tend to have one main character carry specific actantial functions throughout the entire movie story. And the master actantial narrative schema can allow for the ultimate object of desire to alternate in a narrative syntax. A subject (protagonist) can sometimes change in the course of a movie (although it's startling when it does). Think of Janet Leigh, the subject (protagonist) of Hitchcock's *Psycho*. Though she's the protagonist/subject of *Psycho*, she is killed off an hour into the film, and her sister (Vera Miles) takes over as the new subject. It's rare to see this happen in a movie, but it was startling to audiences when it *did* happen; namely, that the star was killed off so early on. And this strategy worked because no one expected Janet Leigh (a big star at the time of the movie's release) to get killed halfway through. Hitchcock played with the traditional story expectations in conjunction with the Hollywood star system and he used the expectations the audiences brought to the movie based on their knowledge of Leigh and the star system to shock them.

Now I would like to explore the second half of the narrative level of story. It's equally important and very powerful. It's called the canonical narrative schema.

The Canonical Narrative Schema

The **canonical narrative schema** constitutes the other half of the narrative level in semiotics theory, and it's the one schema that presents the most like a formula-based screenwriting method. Because of its form-based structure, it is similar in method to what is outlined in *The Writer's Journey* and *Save the Cat!* Those systems are great, but I prefer the semiotics method because it's more flexible and rudimentary and hence to me more readily useful to break down great movies with, and then brainstorm, build, and develop a story from the knowledge you cull from these processes.

Deconstructing the terminology behind the title of this schema might help us launch into a discussion of this part of the workflow. A "canon" is a collection of works, in our case movies, that a culture has agreed are important to revere and study until something from said canon is deemed unfit or unworthy then it's delisted or cancelled or falls out of favor and loses critical relevance. "Canonical" implies that the collection of movies that have been selected follows a general set of principles that are common to all the stories in the collection and was intended for a common target audience (a collective competent observer).

The term canonical to me implies that the method of analysis in question is more based on observing a collection of works and finding patterns in them rather than detecting actual binary opposition as is the case when we use the actantial narrative schema method to deconstruct a movie story.

For example, for our particular "canon," we'll analyze Hollywood films from the late 1930s through to the present. We're interested in commercially (and critically) successful films. An experimental film by the late great Stan Brakhage would not fit into this canon. There are some French New Wave films (which I love) that also might not fit into this canon, although they would certainly be closer than Stan's experimental ditties and I can use narrative semiotics principles to study the French New Wave entries as well. Also, I might want to use the Hollywood canon to compare the French New Wave canon to as well, since that entire movement is very related, the latter *being* somewhat of an offshoot of the former.

So, there is a commonality to the collection of movies we're going to be looking at; they are all successful narrative Hollywood films from the talking era. Again, the canonical narrative schema is the closest thing to other popular formula-based screenwriting systems (*The Writer's Journey*/*Save the Cat!* to name a few). And by using this canonical "lens" when we select and break down specimen movies, we can observe narrative patterns of these classics and hence learn to better write our own screenplays. This schema will also be the one which we use to build a more traditional treatment with, which can start as a great foundation when writing your own movie as all the other tools and breakdown elements can point to this component.

The canonical narrative schema is an excellent analysis/brainstorming/breakdown tool and will help lead us to the structural brass ring we're seeking, which is writing well-crafted story-driven screenplays. It is the next layer of narrative form that, when working in conjunction with the actantial narrative schema, begins to point more specifically towards plotting or in semiotics terms "narrative syntax" (this follows that).

The canonical narrative schema is a little bit more involved and has two sections to it. The first section has four parts:

- The contract
- The qualifying test
- The decisive test
- The glorifying test

These four components are deemed the structure of the canonical narrative schema, which I'll break down item by item. But before I do that, I like to add another layer to the narrative level via the canonical narrative schema, what I like to call story beats, semiotic style, of course!

These story beats are called specifically:

- pragmatic beats
- cognitive beats
- thymic beats

I'll illuminate more about each of these three kinds of story beats later, my ultimate aim being to seamlessly work them into the greater discussion about the narrative level in conjunction with the canonical narrative schema. These three beats will be used mainly as labels to demark and delineate the various kinds of key moments that happen in specimen movies, especially transformative moments which are core to a story's effect on an audience (competent observer).

Now let's look at the canonical narrative schema and each of its components starting with:

The Contract

Remember, according to the actantial narrative schema, the first thing that happens to launch a story is a sender sends to a receiver, which creates a need for something, or a want or desire for something. This sets up the subject/object binary opposition and officially a story is kicked off. Helpers/opponents appear that either help the subject obtain the object of need/want/desire or *oppose* them in the quest for the object or they can even be an anti-subject (in that what the anti-subject wants is diametrically opposed to what the subject wants). In *The Wizard of Oz,* the subject Dorothy wants to get home and the anti-subject Wicked Witch of the West wants to kill her to get the ruby slippers off of her feet. Dorothy is not getting home if she's dead in Oz. While I just outlined key events in the actantial narrative schema on the other level of narrative, something else is happening. At the same time the sender sends to a receiver something and creates a need/want/desire, not only does this create a subject (protagonist) who wants an object (and hence begins a story), it also establishes a **contract**.

When the contract begins, the subject moves into the story *promise* or story "bind," which is a commitment to pursue a specific action to obtain the desired object of want/need/desire. Even if the hero is passive and isn't moving too strongly towards an object, this is a principle of storytelling that must be worked *with* or *against* as is the case of so many great arthouse movies, foreign films, etc.

> I love the term **contract** because it has a "master plot" sound to it. I like to think the term contract not only lays out what happens in the story, but it also is a "deal" made between the movie and the audience: a contract is established that will be a promise of a certain mode of action and story that will be consistent. The contract establishes what story is going to be told, the genre, mode, tone, etc.

The contract is the big purposeful moment in the front part of a movie story, and it speaks to where a story gets locked into a narrative trajectory. Once the "contract" is established, it's difficult to break it without upsetting the audience. Hence the brilliant use of the legalistic term "contract." The contract[3] will run throughout the entire length of the story . . . and it establishes the terms of the story "deal" *being* struck.

The contract is created, and the subject is in need/want/desire for an object or goal. In *The Lost Dog Story,* when the Owner gives Scrappy away to the dog-fighting couple, a desire

---

[3]A veteran story editor in Hollywood told me one of the reasons it's hard for beginner writers to break into episodic television is it's hard to sell the idea that they could complete an entire extended episodic series that has a complete through-line (a *contract* that begins in the beginning and is connected throughout all the episodes) and can run its course until the end.

is established in that Scrappy wants to come back home. A contract is established: to get home. That is the master stroke of the contract but in reality, Scrappy's desire to get *back* home is a desire that is *connected* back to Scrappy's original desire to *stay home* and live upstairs peacefully with the baby, etc. It's important for me to deconstruct and delineate how the contract might work in *The Lost Dog Story* because often the contract in a movie story will *evolve*. Later on I'll demonstrate how the actual contracts of classic movie stories develop, but it's important to understand at some point early in the plot there's a definite contract that is established and it's clear to the audience (competent observer) that this event has occurred. It can sustain a whole movie or be a mere starting point for a developing contract, but more on this later.

In narrative semiotics, the contract happens on the *cognitive* dimension of story which means this … the players involved usually know they are involved in a contract or have some awareness of what the contract is and what the terms are. If they don't, it's done so to work against this principle.

The terms of the contract can develop as in *Angel Heart* when Harry Angel (Mickey Rourke) thinks he's signing on to find Johnny Favorite, but the actual contract develops into something very different and scary. The point is the contract is capable of *evolving*, but it must do so in a cogent way. You have to study specimen movies and see how this tool is used in the great works you will choose to study.

The contract is the promise of the story to follow, triggered by a sender sending a receiver and creating a desire or want or need for an object (and setting up the subject/object opposition). It's a beautiful term for us as storytellers, and here's why: A contract establishes in the mind of the protagonist (in the "cognitive" dimension of the actor/character) a need to take certain action. This need sets up the entire movie story. But there is a special added feature I'd like to disclose here about a contract.

The Contract is Made *also* with the Movie's Audience

I like to think of the contract as not only a narrative incident that establishes the need/ want/desire of the subject (protagonist) for an object, but it is this moment in the story that establishes a contract in the mind of the competent observer (audience), which means that after this plot point, the thrust of the story action isn't going to radically change or the story would be breaking the contract with the audience as well. It's my belief that the contract establishes the promise of a trajectory of a certain plot, as well as the genre, tone, goal of the protagonist (as subject). The contract, along with the need/want/desire of the subject (protagonist), can evolve, but if it evolves, it must do so cogently and in a connected manner. It must present as a unified action. The next set of tools related to the contract will help with this ambition. And how it can evolve will be related to the next series of actions that will occur in a story that will be a playing out of the contract.

Modes of Action—What Happens after the Contract

Let's now talk about what happens after the establishment of the contract in a story. First, think about what a contract in real life means: Someone has agreed to do something usually within a certain time frame in exchange for something else (usually money). In storytelling, it's the "do something" which the signing of a traditional contract initiates that I want you to focus on because as a concept it relates to a story "contract." Alternately, the contract in a story promises related story action will be delivered in the story as a result of the subject pursuing their object. This pursuit will establish what are called "modes of action" which will constitute the action of the story. These modes of action set up the need for the subject to develop competency and execute either a:

1 *being able to do something, or a*
2 *knowing how to do something.*[4]

In *The Godfather*, Michael Corleone as a receiver's contract is created when the sender which is expressed as the need to avenge his father after his attempted murder translates into: Michael must kill Sollozzo and Captain McCluskey. But before doing so, he has to *know* (learn) *how to do so* in order to *be able to do so*. Michael Corleone learns how to shoot a gun, how to effectively kill someone, what to do after the execution, etc. In *The Wizard of Oz*, the contract is created when the tornado is a sender sending Dorothy as a receiver into Oz and she must figure out how to get home. She has to learn how to get home (a **knowing how to do something**) by finding Oz with her friends and has a **being able to do something** which amounts to her eventually killing the witch (her anti-subject).

Frodo in *The Lord of the Rings* has the contract of having to destroy the ring of power and must journey to do so. He has to develop competency which manifests in him performing well in all the trials and tribulations he experiences en route to destroy the ring of power, his *being able to do so*. In *Rocky*, the titular character Rocky experiences the sender Apollo Creed offering him a shot at the heavyweight boxing crown and Rocky as receiver takes on the challenge. He sets off on his *being able to do something*, which is train enough to be able to beat Apollo Creed in the boxing match.

These narrative elements can develop and evolve during a story provided they do so in a logical coherent way. This is what makes the semiotic system more flexible and not merely a formula. Your use of these tools will be enhanced by your breakdown abilities. My study of the specimen movies will demonstrate how these kinds of modes of action (*being able to do something/knowing how to do something*) are unique in every movie and just like the actants of the actantial narrative schema, these elements in a story can evolve and be used in microcosm ways for individual scenes as well as for the master story structure as we'll see in the specimen breakdowns. They can *evolve*, but they do so in a connected way that is

---

[4]As narrative semiotics evolved, these modes of action have also been added to, but for simplicity's sake these two modes of action cover it all.

dramatically logical and satisfying. Again, there are no "rules" but principles I'm sharing culled from my observations of classic specimen movies and applying a semiotics analysis to them.

To reiterate this concept, a contract may develop in a movie story, and if it does it should do so in a connected fashion from point A to point B. You won't fare well if you introduce a *new* contract simply because you couldn't figure out where to take the initial one.

For example, the full development of the contract in *Rocky* becomes crystal clear when Apollo Creed offers Rocky a shot at the heavyweight crown. And this happens in the dead middle of the movie, around 50 minutes in (not at McKee's inciting incident point 10 minutes in). But this technical initiation of the contract (while ostensibly the concrete "contract" of the movie) is connected back to the actual overall contract which was established when Rocky was thrown out of Mickey's gym by Mickey because Mickey complained to Rocky that Rocky was a bum wasting his talent. And *this* beat occurs at the McKee inciting incident time of around 10 minutes in. The earlier beat of Rocky *being* thrown out of the gym is the technical establishment of the "contract" because Rocky's desire evolves from wanting to win the fight to just lasting 15 rounds to prove he was more than just another bum from the neighborhood. (see Table 4.1). In essence Rocky wants to prove to Mickey too that he's not the loser Mickey accused him of being in the early scene where he's thrown out of the gym (the movie's inciting incident/or the beginning of the contract).

That said, Mickey throwing out Rocky from the gym didn't cause Apollo to offer Rocky a shot at the crown. But this early beat or inciting incident is the real beginning of the contract and will be connected to what evolves to be the actual contract in terms of how the emotional meaning of the complete contract of the movie will impact the audience.

To illustrate what I mean, Table 4.1 explains how the actual contract in *Rocky* plays out.

> A movie story's contract should in some way be automatically thought of as initiating at McKee's inciting incident point, usually around 10 minutes in. But again, as we can see in the diagram below, a contract in a movie story can evolve and be complex and multifaceted provided it is cogently connected. This insight will be explored more when I break down three masterpieces at the end of this book and also when I develop an original treatment and outline using this system.

Table 4.1 Development of contract in *Rocky*

Rocky is thrown out of gym (10 minutes in). The actual "contract" of the movie is established, which is Rocky wants to be more than a bum.	Rocky is offered a shot at the crown, and he wants to win. Technical contract (50 minutes in).	Rocky decides he only wants to last 15 rounds to prove he's more than a bum from the neighborhood. Contract is completed (69 minutes in).
←	Contract	→

So, to reiterate, a contract kicks off a story. The contract requires the protagonist (subject) to develop competency to achieve the object of desire. In *The Godfather*, when Michael Corleone gets the contract to avenge his father's murder attempt and save his family, he doesn't just grab a gun and start shooting. He must practice, get up the nerve, talk about the plan. He must develop a "being able to do" and a "knowing how to do." Dorothy doesn't just receive from the sender of the tornado the contract to get home and then she immediately gets back home. She must go through an entire series of adventures before she does, and, along with her three cohorts, together they all must develop competencies expressed as multiple "being able to do" and "knowing how to do" modes of action (they need to develop brains, heart, and courage) as the four travelers to Oz merge into a composite protagonist.

Incidentally, the achievement of the goal (or a subject coming into conjunction with its object) isn't what we go to the movies to see. We gather to see movies to experience the playing out of the contract and the modes of action as we watch subjects in pursuit of that goal, or we enjoy the execution of the contract, etc. We go to movies to experience all the attendant pleasures these actions around the subject (protagonist) pursuing their object (the goal) and execution of the contract brings. This is precisely why it's important to do the drudgery work of actually breaking down your beloved specimen movies because therein you'll see what the pleasures of movie story really are; it's not just the story, it's a lot of surface elements which communicate the other layers of story explicated in the generative trajectory pyramid, such as the theme, etc., all of which get played out in an entertaining way on screen. More on this later.

So, the contract will kick off as a subject/object opposition revealing a subject who in order to obtain their object of desire must develop competencies to obtain it. These competencies are labeled a *being able to do something* and/or a *knowing how to do something*. But the canonical narrative schema doesn't just stipulate that a subject needs to develop competencies en route to conjunction with the object. The canonical narrative schema lays out a series of *three master tests* that constitutes the plot, and these three tests shape the overall narrative trajectory of the story. The three master tests will dictate the overall plot but, just as there are microcosms of actants in a story that connect back to the story's master actantial narrative schema, there are microcosms of these three tests in any story reflecting back to the story's master canonical narrative schema, and these microcosoms can be used to build beats, scenes, and sequences.

But for now, let's go macro and look at the three master tests and the three story beats that are connected to them.

The Three Master Tests and the Three Story Beats Connected to Them

Each of the heroes in the films mentioned above (and all the specimen films we will analyze later) have a contract established early on which makes the hero/protagonist a subject be in pursuit of an object of need/want/desire in some way shape or form. The contract sets up the story and creates a subject who, in order to get what they want, needs to develop a *being able to do something* (**pragmatic beat**[5]) and/or a *knowing how to do something* (**cognitive beat**) to obtain the object of desire or fulfill a need or goal or want. We call these "competencies" simply because a certain competency needs to be developed to fulfill the contract's mission/goal/need/want or desire.

To illustrate this in play, let's return to *The Lost Dog Story*. Scrappy is cast out from his original Owners, so his contract becomes he wants to return home to them. He is adopted by New Owners but soon learns that the New Owners are dog fighters and he must go into a dog fight and kill another dog in order to survive. After the fight where he kills Mad Dog McKill, he flees the evil couple (now labeled "Bad Owners") after his cage breaks open, and he then winds up in the woods. He now needs to *learn how to survive* on his own in the wild. In fact, he already is *learning how to survive*; he found the instinct to kill Mad Dog McKill (the opposing dog in the dog fight) in a kill-or-be-killed mode. I just mentioned several instances of a *being able to do something* and/or a *knowing how to do something*, so let me itemize a few of them here:

1   Scrappy needs to learn how to stay alive in the dog fighting ring and kill the evil dog.
2   Scrappy needs to learn how to escape his cage.
3   Scrappy needs to learn how to survive and eat in the wilderness.
4   Scrappy needs to learn how to return home.

All these *modalities of action* are indeed very formidable and strong. But they in and of themselves are *not* a plot. Semiotics theory offers a more concrete method to express these modes of action and construct a plot using the canonical narrative schema's[6] three master tests of story that make up the canonical narrative schema:

- The qualifying test
- The decisive test
- The glorifying test

Let's look at each of them in detail.

The Qualifying Test

The contract sets up a need for a subject to develop competencies which are called a *knowing how to do something* or a *being able to do something* in order for the subject to obtain their object of need/want/desire. These competencies will be developed via a series of three "tests." Tests are the perfect way of describing plot action because the word itself reflects what dramatic story is all about. In fact, the age-old terms of protagonist and antagonist contain the root word "agon," ancient Greek for "contest."

---

[5]Pragmatic and cognitive beats are merely describing specific kinds of events on the narrative level. These, along with thymic beats (emotional beats), are critical to understand, so I wanted to introduce them here early to facilitate this part of the discussion but will elaborate on them a little later.

[6]The canonical narrative schema provides for some distinct master plot segments that can be thought of as the master tests, but this plot building tool can be reused to derive related smaller micro-tests along the way that will enable us to build scenes that are all connected back to the three master tests and the *contract*. More on this later when I break down three specimen movies beat by beat.

The idea of drama as a contest is probably the most basic way of looking at dramatic storytelling. That goes for even the artiest independent film where often the strife and struggles of the protagonist may all be internal and the protagonist might seem passive. But rest assured in the best indies, somewhere there is a fight or a struggle going on. Without the protagonist having to perform in some kind of test (even if they are subtle and nuanced), the filmmakers risk losing the audience.

To reiterate: A sender transmits to a receiver, creating a need for action, and a contract is established creating a subject in pursuit of an object. This creates a need to *be able to do something* and/or a *knowing how to do something*, modes of action that must occur in order for a contract to be fulfilled and the object obtained. And these modes of action will begin with the qualifying test.

The **qualifying test** is the first test that is established once the contract is initiated, and the modalities of action are set up to be played out in the master tests of the canonical narrative schema. Once the contract commences, the subject/object binary opposition is established and a story has begun and the qualifying test will begin. It is this first test which will *qualify* the subject to be able to pursue the **decisive test** in pursuit of the object of need/want/desire. The qualifying test precedes the decisive test which of course will contain the climax. The qualifying test allows the subject the right to proceed on the journey towards the decisive test (and **glorifying test** which is trickier to explain but when you realize what it means it's actually a perfect term for the part of the action it delineates). The simplest example of a qualifying test is in *The Godfather*. Michael Corleone's family is under siege after an attempt is made on his father's life. Michael must rise up to save the family, and the qualifying test to "qualify" him to be able to move in that direction is manifest in him killing Sollozzo and Captain McCluskey in the Italian restaurant.

In *Rocky*, the qualifying test happens when Rocky is training for the big fight and fails to make it up the steps after a jog. Later, he jogs and makes it up the steps in the big "training" sequence. The whole training section of *Rocky* where Rocky trains leading up to the big fight is a qualifying test, but it's Rocky's ability to finally make it up the steps that constitutes the *heart* of this important qualifying test and what seems like its conclusion successfully executed by the subject Rocky. But the qualifying test has one more crucial beat.

After training and right before the fight, Rocky confesses to his girlfriend Adrian that he doesn't think he can win the boxing match against Apollo Creed because Creed is just too good. Rocky then states he's decided he just wants to last 15 rounds. He conveys that this lasting 15 rounds will prove he was more than just a bum from the neighborhood (a powerful cognitive beat). *Now* the qualifying test is complete. The fact that Rocky's qualifying test extends throughout multiple sequences and definitively concludes once he announces he's changed his objective from wanting to win the fight to lasting 15 rounds is a stroke of storytelling genius.

The beauty of using these tests is that they can both represent master movements of plot sections, and they may be used in creative ways to create scenes, beats, and sequences throughout. The master qualifying test in *Rocky* I just described is extended for a large chunk of the film over time. It contains a *being able to do something*, which is Rocky training to win the boxing match against Apollo Creed, and then later it contains a *knowing how to do something,* which is Rocky realizing he can't win and just wants to last 15 rounds. Mind you, it's likely Sylvester Stallone (and most great screenwriters) probably achieved all of these brilliant demonstrations of semiotic principles intuitively at first. But I am here to deconstruct and codify what they are doing either consciously or unconsciously (or some combination of both) and give you a way of using the codes of semiotics at work in movie narrative as information to analyze movies and then learn to write with the knowledge such analysis affords you.

The semiotics breakdown and brainstorming method allows you to learn about how these tests were used in movies you love so you can set up your plot with the contract and the three master tests across both the entire plot, and also in microcosm smaller tests (aka scenes and beats) as I just demonstrated in *Rocky*. You can reuse these tests in little ways throughout the story provided they connect back to the master tests and form a unified story action.

Of course, you can break any "rule/principle" if you know what you're doing and do it to make the story stronger. To be effective in breaking rules, it's best to analyze movies you love first to understand how they work before experimenting with trying to break ground in story form and structure.

In *The Lost Dog Story*, the contract is established once Scrappy is cast out of his original Owners' home and decides he wants to come back to that home to live. The qualifying test entails Scrappy, in order to achieve the goal of returning home, must first learning to survive in the wilderness. This master qualifying test will continue until the last third of the story.[7] And this manifests concretely in that the strongest beat of the qualifying test takes place in the kill-or-be-killed practice dog fight with Mad Dog McKill, a fight Scrappy is thrust into when the new Bad Owners take control of him. Though it's sad for him to have to kill another dog, the fact that he gets through it and prevails sets up his right to proceed to the journey towards returning home and onto the final two tests, the decisive test and the glorifying test. Note though the "qualifying test" in a sense may have climaxed by Scrappy killing Mad Dog McKill, there will still be echoes of the qualifying test of whether or not he can survive when he wanders the wilderness in search of shelter and food which all occurs after the dog fight scene.

Scrappy's "being able to do" and "knowing how to do" all culminate in him simply being able to survive in the wild (the high point being him killing a dog in a dog fight) so he can meet some "decisive test " that will finally determine if he's going to return home and a glorifying test where we and Scrappy bask in the emotions generated by the story's outcome. As you'll see in the demo treatment of *The Lost Dog Story*, the qualifying test which plays out through a long stretch of story has a climax early on, a climax which doesn't occur at the decisive test's end. This strategy is akin to how a contract might start at the inciting incident but develop and evolve later in the movie as is the case in *Rocky*.

Now on to the decisive test.

---

[7]Of note here, writing this part of the qualifying test for *The Lost Dog Story* has caused me to already brainstorm ideas for a powerful thymic (emotional) beat of a story, triggered by thinking Scrappy must kill a dog to survive. He carries this with him and is forever a little sad knowing he had to kill a brother dog, and this stays with him as a thymic (emotional) element through the rest of the story.

The Decisive Test

The decisive test is exactly what it sounds like. It's the final scene, sequence, climax where it's determined whether the subject (protagonist) achieves a "conjunction" (or disjunction) with their object (or in plain English, does the subject/hero get what they need/want/desire or do they not). In *Rocky*, the decisive test is the big boxing match against Apollo Creed at the end. It's what the entire story builds to. But as we saw earlier, the movie *Rocky* sets up a new object which is instead of him thinking he can win the fight, Rocky strives towards, evolving to the new goal of merely lasting 15 rounds to prove he's not just another bum from the neighborhood.

Back to *The Lost Dog Story* and what the decisive test will be. Earlier, before I drafted a treatment based on the actantial narrative schema, I tried to randomly come up with a decisive test on the fly.

The Lost Dog Story—decisive test:

Scrappy is adopted by a family from an urban city and goes on a camping trip with them and their raft capsizes, and he saves the family from drowning. This helps them determine to keep the dog.

Sounds more like a qualifying test.

Maybe.

Here's another stab at a possible decisive test:

Scrappy gets adopted by a family in the poor section of the city, and there are all kinds of rough dogs in the neighborhood that he has various run-ins with and even some turf fights (mini-qualifying tests). But finally, Scrappy settles in with the new family, and when home invaders break in, he must risk his life and takes a bullet to save his New Owner. He does and lives and that's the decisive test.

I like the second one better and worked it into the canonical narrative schema demo treatment (soon to follow). But remember, the initial contract and qualifying test set up a need to *be able to do something* and/or a *knowing how to do something* to *qualify* Scrappy to be able to partake in the decisive test which will ultimately determine if Scrappy could return home to his original Owner's house. This decisive test, where he takes a bullet from thieves for his New Owners, is a development from the original object of Scrappy (return home to his original Owners). His "returning home" is actually finding a new home. But it's a development that works—it's not from left field, it is organic and grows out of the story and out of the original contract of Scrappy which is his desire to return home.

To get to this decisive test, Scrappy needs to be able to survive, and he needs to learn how to live in the wilderness, fend off enemies, etc. (his qualifying test) in order to prepare himself for the decisive test, which is saving his new family (and ultimately claiming a new home).

After this movie's climax (Scrappy saves his new family from home invaders), we are now ready for the final test, the glorifying test.

The Glorifying Test

We now arrive at the glorifying test. This is the final test in a movie, and before going any further, let me just state upfront: The glorifying test is more abstract than the qualifying and decisive tests. The glorifying test is where the audience has a chance to take in and process the *meaning* of the hero (subject) having obtained or not obtained the object or need/want desire as initially set up by the contract. It allows the audience (competent observer) to process this result and experience the attendant emotions. In classical dramatic theory, this section of the film is called the denouement.

Glorifying tests are important. There have been maybe one or two occasions when I came out of a movie and felt unsatisfied due to how it wrapped up, especially if I wasn't given enough time to reflect upon the ending and feel what I was supposed to feel. That's why Aristotle marked the denouement as an important piece to follow the climax and conclusion of a dramatic story.

Semiotics theory classifies this final section of the movie's story the glorifying test, which is the same as its denouement. There is a *cognitive* competence that must be achieved for this test to be fulfilled and it's this: The protagonist must recognize what has happened and experience it as good or bad to allow us to be able to experience those same emotions. But remember, rules and principles of storytelling are meant to be broken. And as it is with all "rules/principles" of movie story, you can work with it *or* against the "rule/principle" as can be demonstrated by analyzing the end of *Goodfellas*. During this movie's denouement/ glorifying test, the lead character Henry Hill (played to perfection by the late Ray Liotta) is seen after plastic surgery in his bathrobe outside of his witness protection home and his voice-over expresses dismay because now he gets horrible food in the new region, and this seems to be all he cares about. He is oblivious to the fact that he's lucky to still be alive given his recent criminal escapades, especially in light of the fact that he became a traitor to his mob associates. This ending clearly signifies Henry Hill hasn't learned anything! There's no recognition or discovery.[8] There's no *cognitive* anything. In a sense, the

Table 4.2 Classical dramatic structure. Perhaps it might help to see a suggestion of how the canonical narrative schema might lay out against the classical tragic structure and the Hollywood movie structure:

	COMPLICATION		**DENOUEMENT**
Contract	Qualifying test	Decisive test	Glorifying test
ACT 1	ACT 2	ACT 3	

[8]Aristotle's *Poetics* talks of how, at the end of a play, the hero should experience a *recognition* and *discovery* that is linked to a *reversal of fortune*. But there is no recognition, no discovery leading to the glorifying test segment of *Goodfellas*. And it's the perfect ending. Remember the joke about the show bible for the TV show *Seinfeld*, which purportedly had the overarching guiding principle: "No hugs, no learning."

glorifying test is not a glorifying test. He hasn't really understood what just happened in his life and is just complaining about the food in the witness protection program. But Scorsese knew what he was doing; he is using the glorifying test moment in the film to work *against* the tendency to demonstrate what the hero has learned by the whole journey of the story, and in the case of *Goodfellas* the hero has learned nothing. Again, Scorsese is working against the principle of the need for a glorifying test at the end of a story; breaking the rule, so to speak.

The glorifying test also connects back to Aristotle's *Poetics* in that Aristotle teaches us that the best dramatic stories involve a hero who has a *reversal of fortune* (fortune which goes from good to bad fortune instantly), a climactic moment which is linked to a discovery made by the hero (a major cognitive beat of the hero). The most famous example of this is in Greek tragedy when Oedipus in *Oedipus Rex* realizes he killed his father and married his mother, and he is the source of the plague of Thebes. His fortune has changed and he blinds himself, but he has the revelation/and discovery that he was the culprit all along and has a deep emotional reaction (**thymic beat**).

At the end of a story a hero's fortune can change instantly, it literally can *reverse* in a second. Think of an interception in football. Your team has a receiver in the end zone waiting to catch the game-ending touchdown. The quarterback throws it, but it's intercepted and run back by the opposing team to end the game. That's what a *reversal of fortune* is. But in dramatic theory, via the *Poetics*, a *reversal of fortune* is linked to a recognition and a discovery. Something happens in the brain of the hero at that moment; they have a recognition, they learn or *discover* something. In other words, a major cognitive beat occurs.

It's during a movie's glorifying test that the recognition and discovery leads to a cognition, and it's processed and the true emotional meaning of the story is laid bare. And it was all kicked off by the contract or *inciting incident* as McKee calls it.

In *The Lost Dog Story*, I'll make up a glorifying test on the spot here. Scrappy saves his family in the poor section of the city and takes a bullet from an invader, and they are grateful. His previous Owners see the story on the news and go to the family to try and get him back. The new family refuse them and keep Scrappy. Scrappy realizes (cognitive beat) this is his new home and Scrappy realizes (cognitive beat) it's more important that he stays with the poor family that needs him rather than in the cozy rich Owner's house. As previously mentioned, the glorifying test is usually linked to a *reversal of fortune/discovery*, which is namely Scrappy has finally found a home with the new poor Owners and his fortune is reversed and thus discovers (cognitive beat) that he's more needed there, a recognition which comes at the exact time he realizes the new home has become his. Scrappy has achieved his original goal (return home), but the meaning of what home is has evolved to be a new home with new Owners.

The Glorifying Test is Not a "Test" in the True Sense

By now you may have figured out that the glorifying test is not quite a "contest" (agon) the way the qualifying test/decisive test are actual contests. As with all things semiotic, the creators of this terminology are striving to ensure the narrative system they are laying out appears unified and cohesive and the terminology all works together. That said, the glorifying test is indeed a mode of action linked up to the contract and the other two master tests in a very specific way. In *Rocky*, the glorifying test occurs when the beaten, bloodied Rocky finds Adrian at the end after the fight and he begins to yell for her and ultimately professes his love for her. It's where the meaning of the film is received by the audience, a meaning which started when the first contract was created; namely, Mickey throws out Rocky and accuses him of being a bum and having wasted his talent. And the meaning of *Rocky* completing this glorifying test, which is basking in the glorying of realizing he's more than a bum from the neighborhood, and that Rocky became more than just a bum from the neighborhood in that he found the love of one great woman.

So, you can see all of these tools and concepts don't necessarily constitute neat easy-to-use formulas or rules for movie writing; you must use them as concepts to study and analyze and break down movies you love and then see how these powerful principles which you cull from masterpieces you examine can train your brain.

In *The Wizard of Oz*, Dorothy wakes up and *realizes* she always *was* home and magical Oz was merely her having a dream while she was unconscious from the tornado and she is surrounded by love (her glorifying test). In *The Lost Dog Story* demo I'm creating, the glorifying test will be when Scrappy's original Owners come back for him and he barks at them, deciding he wants to stay with the New Owners, the poor urban family who need him more and recently adopted him, and the New Owners shower him with love and affection which he recriprocates.

Before I launch into a demo treatment of *The Lost Dog Story* from the perspective of the canonical narrative schema, I would now like to add a very important component to this level of narrative; namely, the three primary story beats that occur in any movie story. I've mentioned them earlier and have been hinting at them all along, but now I'd like to formally introduce them.

The three beats of movie story are:

- pragmatic beats
- cognitive beats
- thymic beats

For informational purposes, a "beat" in screenplay and movie story language is an event where something happens that is of importance, a pivotal point in the story.[9] It's similar to a line in an outline, but what distinguishes it from any plain old outline line is that a beat is something significant that happens in the story that is a marker for either the action, the mental life of the protagonist, or the emotional life of the story's subject (protagonist). And what makes something that happens "significant" is simply having to do with whether the

---

[9]Unfortunately, to make our lives even more complicated, there are multiple meanings to the term "beat" in a movie or screenplay. Sometimes a "beat" can just mean a pause, meaning, "take a pause" as in "Joe takes a beat." But this is *not* to be confused with a story beat, which means something significant happens and in the case of semiotics, significant in terms of the hero's movement through the canonical narrative schema and whether they are getting closer or further from their object via their performance of the three tests of story.

event gets a subject closer or further from coming into conjunction with their object of need/want/desire.

Story beats help to form a well-rounded story that has different levels of things going on in the text and subtext that helps make the actors feel real to us. And it's not simply an actor going for a goal (object) that allows us to experience the illusion of reality via a story . . . it's that the actors are experiencing attendant emotions and having related thoughts and recognitions en route to moving towards or away from said object. That's what the three story beats provide for; they round off a story in the action, the thoughts, and finally the emotions of the actors so that it gives the illusion of it possesing three dimensions and is something a competent observer can wholly and actively participate in.

What's more important about what story beats actually are for our purposes is that they are based on the same kinds of beats that Hollywood has always used, but semiotics postulates slightly technical labels for the beats as outlined above. And sometimes a single moment in a movie can contain all three beats happening simultaneously, which is in my opinion some of the best moments in movie history (more on this later).

For now, let's look at each beat in a little detail.

Pragmatic Beat

A pragmatic beat is simply an action but one that has significance in the narrative syntax. As with all things semiotic, it's not just important to be able to isolate and catalog each beat but understand where and how the beat fits into a whole. I'll be itemizing many of these beats within the canonical narrative schema discussion because this particular schema is most about sequencing and syntax, and it's important to get a feeling for story beats *in sequence* starting with the pragmatic ones.

Here are some examples:

In the master qualifying test of *The Godfather*, Michael Corleone shoots Captain McCluskey and Sollozzo at the Italian restaurant.

Now I can subdivide this beat from *The Godfather* into smaller beats:

- Michael Corleone retrieves the gun from the bathroom at the Italian restaurant.
- He sits at the table.
- He pretends to talk.
- He pulls out the gun.
- He shoots Captain McCluskey and Sollozzo.

But it's the actual beat "he shoots Captain McCluskey and Sollozzo" that *changes* the narrative trajectory of the story, *that's* why we classify that event as a "major story" beat. Michael taking that action is a big step towards him being able to save his family. This also applies to cognitive *and* thymic beats in that while there may be many small ones, it's the events that move a protagonist closer or further to their desired object that we mark as major beats. But how each of the three beats work in a movie story is unique, so let's examine the next one in detail: the second kind of story beat, the cognitive beat.

Cognitive Beat

A cognitive beat is merely a beat where an actor has mental activity and realizes something, thinks something, learns something, remembers something, understands something, etc., but something of substance in terms of the narrative syntax of the (story), specifically whether they are moving closer or further from their object of need/want/desire as established by the contract. In *Rocky*, Rocky realizes he can't win the fight against Apollo Creed; he only wants to last 15 rounds to prove he's more than just a bum from the neighborhood. In other words, while the cognitive beat doesn't necessarily change the plot (he's still going to fight Apollo), it *changes* how we view the decisive test and what the meaning of it all is. He merely wants to go the distance; he knows he can't win. And this all occurs as an *internal mental action* which he then comments upon by telling Adrian, his girlfriend. But this cognitive beat is just as important as any physical and/or emotional action.

Remember the cognitive beat involves actor thought, so it might not occur as or with a physical action specifically or happen in conjunction with any specific action at the time it happens. But it's related overall to the contract and the *three* tests. For example, in *Rocky*, the contract of the story evolves into Rocky wanting to last the 15 rounds to prove he's more than just a bum from the neighborhood. But it's at that point, where he realizes he can't win and has that *thought*, that cognitive beat, that rounds off the contract (wanting to be more than a bum from the neighborhood) which sets up the decisive test.

But in *Rocky*, the cognitive beat of Rocky realizing he can't win but merely wants to last 15 rounds is not just setting up the decisive test; it's setting up what the *emotional meaning of the decisive test will shake out to be.*

Another famous cognitive beat occurs in another absolute masterpiece of a movie, *The Rules of the Game*, whereby one of the lead actors in the story, Octave, played by the director Jean Renoir, looks at himself in the mirror and finally realizes he is just an old man. He is too old to be playing the game of chasing around women in the hunting lodge and certainly can't run off with one much younger than him. Until then he had been in denial about who he was, but he now realizes he's just an old man in this astonishing cognitive beat, and this causes him to abandon his plan to run off with Christine and instead encourages the younger man to leave with her, culminating in the plot's final scenes.

In *The Wizard of Oz*, at the end, after Dorothy wakes up and realizes all the men she knows were characters in her dream, this is a great cognitive beat and becomes the foundation of the glorifying test in that movie, realizing she always had the power to get herself back home and is loved there.

Now onto my favorite story beat, the thymic beat.

Thymic Beat (States of Being)

A thymic beat is one that involves the emotional life of an actor. It is a special beat; in fact, it's so important that I give it double duty and break it down first as an isotopy on the surface (figurative) level in binary opposition, throwing the thymic beats against two binary opposition poles (dysphoria and euphoria), and again on the narrative level so I can understand these beats in syntax. Syntax is key to the thymic beats working because they are dependent upon what preceded narratively and tend to derive their power from a story's structure. But in general, thymic beats are good to log on the surface level of story as isotopies because it's a great way to start to analyze and brainstorm on the emotional life of actors in the movies we love to feed our own writing. Of note, thymic beats also carry the label "states of being," an important concept I'll return to throughout this study.

To me there are many examples of thymic beats in movies I could use and I'll break them down more succinctly when I look at the specimen movies I analyze later in the book. A classic one is in *The Godfather* when Michael Corleone is feeling his heart rattle as he's contemplating murdering Captain McCluskey and Sollozzo. This rumbling of his heart is depicted by the subway noise underneath the restaurant. This is a very strong emotion experienced by Michael. Another example of a thymic beat is at the end of *Rocky* when Rocky is emotionally screaming for Adrian.

Another important aspect of thymic beats is to realize and observe that often the best moments in movie story occur when all three beats occur together (pragmatic, cognitive, thymic). It's my belief that these kinds of combined beats can allow for the most powerful moments in movie story. A great example occurs at the end of *Rocky*: Rocky cries screaming for Adrian, looking for her. His pragmatic action is looking for her, his cognitive beat is realizing that the love for her is what is important, and his thymic beat is the emotion he feels and subsequently expresses as he yells for her, an example of all three beats working in conjunction yielding one of the great moments of cinema.

Now, I'd like to move onto the next section of analysis and breakdown, referred to as the deep level of meaning.

5

The Deep Level of Meaning

Alfred Hitchcock, a great master director, is known to have once said that we should tell the best story possible and then things like theme (and everything related to theme) will develop.

What does this mean? Is theme even important? Is it just an add-on, an afterthought, a secondary consideration? Is it entirely meaningless? And what does semiotics have to say about theme?

Answer: Of course theme is important. How important? Perhaps that's the wrong question. Maybe a better question is: How does theme fit into our semiotics toolbox? And the flipside of that question: What does theme mean to moviegoers? The short easy answer is ... not very much. No one that I know (including me) says, "Honey let's check the showtimes ... I really need to see a good theme in the theater tonight." Nor do I sit down to write a script and say, "I want to write about XYZ theme." Normally I'll just have a story idea, or a premise, or a character, a situation ... you get it ... you're probably the same. Most writers I talk to are similar ... they write and write and write and then figure out what they're doing in the rewrites. Understanding theme is a big part of that "figuring out what you're doing," and knowing how theme works in story can help you sculpt and shape your story to be competitive.

A younger me might have said, "Themes are what the story is about." Or "The theme is what you are writing about." Sounds good, but it's not so simple. You might write a story to impact an audience a certain way and there's a theme that suggests itself as the best way of doing so. But this theme is not necessarily what the story is "about," or at least it's not what impacts said audience in a certain desirable way. And I'm not just being semantical, themes are part of the levels of storytelling at the base of the generative trajectory iceberg, the deep level of meaning, so yes, ultimately theme is what a story is "about," but it's not necessarily what gives movie story its power. The truth is what gives movie story its power is *all three levels of story* working together (the surface level/the narrative level/the deep level of meaning), and theme fits right into bottom level of the pyramid.

And while few writers start off wanting to "state a theme," a theme must be stated or if one is *not* stated, this is a principle or rule that must be broken effectively. I'm fully convinced that one of my favorite movies of all time, *Stranger Than Paradise*, doesn't have a theme. Nothing is stated. It's about nothing (even before *Seinfeld*). But for some reason this trait (being themeless) is done so in a way that you feel like its creator, Jim Jarmusch, consciously or unconsciously *knew* what he was doing in this regard, and it works ... the lack of theme helps give the movie its completely original and unique vibe. It's an existentialist treat aided by its conspicuous lack of theme (and lack of plot, story, etc.). Being void of a theme works for that movie.

So what does theme mean to the semiotics project for screenwriters? Well, allow me to play devil's advocate and contradict myself for a second ... theme means a lot. At least to the breakdown aspects of your study process and even your brainstorming, writing, and rewriting workflow. In fact, I have found that what identifying themes can do is help speed up the writing process and bring the whole story into a unified focus. And just like there is a master actantial narrative schema that the story is built on and related micro-actants that combined comprise a story, along with a master canonical narrative schema with a contract and three master tests and *related* smaller tests, there is usually a central theme and other related mini-themes circling around the master theme that gets played out in a movie story. The micro-themes that play out in a movie story generally contain the DNA of the master theme, so to speak.

And the micro-themes that are connected to the master theme are just like little actants connected to the master actantial narrative schema and smaller tests connected to the master canonical narrative schema. Again, as in all things analytical, it's not that we're trying to devise the theme or themes or message of the movie as we write to it, but it's important to understand what themes have been presented in the great movies you have chosen to analyze and be aware at some point of the theme and themes you are uncovering in your breakdown, brainstorm, and writing processes. And ultimately once you figure out your master theme it and all the connected micro-themes should be in sync with the rest of the story.

Again, let me be crystal clear: You might start drafting without knowing a theme you want to express; probably most screenwriters don't. In fact, I'm going to state right here: A theme is not necessarily stated by the writer, it's stated by the work itself, and the writer has to recognize and use it as a guidepost to rewrite and tweak the narrative. Recognizing themes to rewrite help you to tighten up the script and finish.

In fact, I'd go as far as to say you can get in trouble wanting to write to express a theme or a message. But the semiotics breakdown, brainstorm, and writing method requires that you deconstruct your favorite works to understand how theme works in them and use this knowledge to help you with that aspect of your writing.

Return to the Generative Trajectory

Earlier I discussed the generative trajectory of story and how theme rests at the base of the pyramid, within the deep level of meaning bottom third, indicating that this level of a story is what a movie story is about, along with the attendant values and transformations attached to theme. For ease's sake, allow me to repeat the pyramid right here (Figure 5.1).

Values, themes, and transformations happen in real time triggered by something that happens in the syntax of the story; namely, an object of value is gotten closer to (or further from) being realized by a subject via one of the three story beats, and this event is marked as a transformation in the story. There are many transformation points in a movie story, and I've given these key points the label of a master story beat/theme stated. Now let me be clear, this term is a catch-all phrase because while all good movie stories have master story beats,

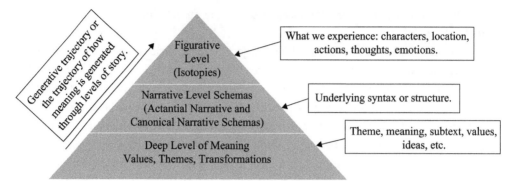

Figure 5.1 The generative trajectory pyramid. Now is a good time to review this visual representation of the generative trajectory so we reorient ourselves as to where theme (deep level of meaning) fits it and we can build on this concept to learn to develop values, themes, and transformations in movie story.

not all of them necessarily "state themes." You have to know about both kinds of storytelling, ones that "state themes" and ones that don't seem to (although you could project a theme onto almost any story). Sometimes (as you'll see in the specimen movies I break down), you'll just log a "plain English" sentence as a "theme" delineating what happened in a story beat, and that's sufficient. For example, in *Lost in Translation*, when the couple meet near the pool and decide to "go out," it's a major story beat/theme stated, and I merely call it "they make the first date." There's no philosophical or literary theme that is actually "stated" but making the "first date" with the love of your life is significant. This is in contrast to, say, in *It's a Wonderful Life*, when George Bailey is able to keep the Building and Loan solvent before 6:00 p.m. and I label the mini-theme stated at this moment as "If you plead for what is right with the community they will act in interest of the community." We'll elaborate on this later when I break down three specimen movies, but that's the basic concept.

As much as themes matter, I caution you to realize that writers can get into trouble trying to "say something" when they start writing. That said, it's good to study themes that are at play in the movies you love because the knowledge can serve as a guidepost when you break down, brainstorm, and write, especially in regard to recognizing what themes you've perhaps begun to put in play and subsequently making sure your story (and its attendant themes) are in sync with each other. Knowing what you are writing about thematically at some point will help you fashion a satisfying emotional journey for your audience and help you keep the overall unified tone in your story.

Themes are important for sure. But in some ways, theme, or overall meaning or what the film has to "say," is not as important as you may think. You'd notice it more if theme and meaning are *not* clear or present in a movie or if these elements are handled sloppily or contradict each other, or if they present as part of an overall disorganized tone for the movie.

Theme and meaning must be there and handled well to provide a well-rounded entertainment experience for an audience, but these items are not as important as making sure an audience experiences a deep *emotional meaning* from your story. So when you're breaking down your specimen movies, let the information of theme pass through your conscious mind and then drop into your unconscious, where you'll store this information ready to be accessed when you brainstorm and write.

You want to eventually be writing about something (theme), but don't lead with this intention (unless of course that is your process). Understanding how to break down movies and brainstorm themes can help with this goal because you'll perhaps through study grow to feel unconsciously in control of this tool. Tell the best story possible as the great Hitchcock said; themes develop as we go along.

Now let's take a closer look at the workings of the "deep level of meaning," or the thematic level.

Master Story Beats/Themes Stated (Values, Transformations, and Themes)

In our semiotics toolbox, the concept of themes is part of a larger connected framework of concepts which includes: values, transformations, and themes.

These three elements are all interrelated and are situated at the bottom of the iceberg of the generative trajectory and form the basis of the thematic and emotional meaning in a movie story. Shortly, we'll explore how all three of these items work together, but for now, let's look at them individually.

First, let's look at values.

Values

I realize I touched on the subject of values in an earlier section about the semiotic square, but it's a complex topic, so I wanted to whet your imagination first and then circle back to it as I am now. In a movie story, "values" are related to what the subject (actor) wants/needs/desires in the story. In *Rocky*, Rocky grows to want to last 15 rounds against Apollo Creed to prove he was more than just another bum from the neighborhood. That's what Rocky wants. That's the object he's seeking, to last 15 rounds to prove he's not a bum, and this makes him a subject (subject/object=story). To state it as such, that he wants to be more than just a bum from the neighborhood, isn't stating a theme in the traditional literary sense such as "Money is the root of all evil" states an actual literary theme. But in semiotic narrative terms, Rocky stating he wants to be more than a bum is stating a theme, but, more importantly, it's stating what he values and hence what is at stake, and this shapes our sense of "theme" in *Rocky*.

So inherently, what I'm driving at is that theme in semiotics is directly related to what the subject (Rocky) *wants/needs/desires*. And this might be stated in a very quotation-like fashion *or* something close or it might be expressed as a simple want (he wants to be more than just another bum). In *Rocky*, Rocky starts wanting to the win the fight but then states he realizes (cognitive beat) he merely wants to last 15 rounds so he'll know he's more than a bum. He's seeking self-respect. The way he claims he's going to achieve being more than a bum is simple: last 15 rounds against Creed. *But* the way he finally achieves being more than just another bum is more complex and develops; he trains to fight, he lasts 15 rounds, then in the glorifying test of that movie, after he lost the fight but lasted the 15 rounds, he and Adrian profess love for each other emotionally. Being more than a bum is more than just lasting 15 rounds. It's also *being* a well-rounded man who is able to be in a loving relationship with a woman. Those events *combined* add up to Rocky coming into conjunction with his object of not being a bum from the neighborhood. And to state all of this in a traditional theme like "Love is the most important thing in life," or "Anyone can succeed with hard work" is not as important as understanding what Rocky's value is and how he is transformed because he achieves his objective, his thing of value.

Of note here, another great screenwriting system, *Save the Cat!*, teaches the principle that early on the "theme must be stated" so the audience knows what the movie is about and gives the audience a lens to see all the story's action through. I like this concept from *Save the Cat!*, but in the semiotics project, we're seeking for a method by which a theme might be explicit or it might be buried in the deep level of meaning and not necessarily explicitly stated. This is what I mean by saying that using semiotics to write with is not like using a simple formula writing method. Semiotics requires you to learn the tools and be able to think with them. And this system, while rigorous, gives you a lot of flexibility. I'll demo both approaches (explicit themes and implicit ones) later when I deconstruct the specimen movies.

The thing of value for Rocky is for him to *know* (cognitive beat) when the bell for the 15th round rings and he's still standing; then he'll know he's no longer a bum. And all along the movie's plotline there are key moments or beats of transformation that are markers that move him *towards* or *away* from that goal he seeks, and these are called master story beats, (pragmatic, cognitive, thymic), and each time one master story beat occurs it reverberates with the music of the main theme as a mini-theme connected to a master theme. And it's important in our breakdown of specimen movies that we learn to collect and study what those master story beats/themes stated/transformation points/values are because they are the heart of story. I'll catalog them in the comprehensive beat map, and I'll also make a master story beat cheat sheet.

Sometimes it's easier to label the master story beats as traditional literary themes stated; other times it's not as easy. You need to be able be fluent with both approaches.

In the case of our mini-demo of using *Rocky*, I opted for using traditional literary type thematic statements as an example of how such themes can connect back to the master theme in *Rocky*. These occur at the key transformational moments in the movie. That's why I call them master story beats/themes stated because they occur at critical times in the storyline in terms of the subject moving closer or further from their object and these give the movie's story its bounce . . . its "swing" (if I may borrow a term from jazz music).

Master Story Beats/Themes Stated

Here is a basic table of master story beats from *Rocky* (see Table 5.1). They all have to do with whether or not Rocky (the subject) is going to achieve his object, which is become more than a bum from the neighborhood.

Table 5.1 Master story beats/themes stated—*Rocky*

MASTER STORY BEAT	BEAT TYPE	THEME STATED
Rocky is thrown out of the gym by Mickey. **Contract initiated**	pragmatic	Wasting God-given talent is a sin.
Rocky is offered a shot at the crown— **Contract deepens**	pragmatic	The Gods will offer you a shot at greatness occasionally.
Qualifying test begins Rocky fails to jog up the steps.	pragmatic	To achieve greatness is harder than it seems.
Rocky changes his goal from wanting to win the match to wanting to "go the distance." **Contract fully executed** **Qualifying test ends**	cognitive	Sometimes in life you have to be realistic.
Decisive test begins Rocky tags Creed and knocks him to the mat.	pragmatic	With hard work and determination anything is possible.
Creed tags Rocky, knocks him to the mat but he gets up.	pragmatic	Winning is harder than it seems.
Mickey tells Rocky to stay down but he gets up.	cognitive	With hard work and determination anything is possible.
Bell for end of 15th round rings signaling the fight is over, and Rocky is standing, and he lasted 15 rounds.	pragmatic	With hard work and determination anything is possible.
Decisive test ends Rocky loses by decision.	pragmatic	Even if you do everything you can to win sometimes you fail.
Glorifying test [*] Rocky and Adrian profess love for each other.	thymic	Love is more important than anything.

[*] You might wonder: Does the glorifying test really begin here, or is this moment in *Rocky* still part of the decisive test? And the answer is . . . it's not an exact science, but rather these tools are meant to force you to think about the narrative structure semiotically and apply thought and rigor to the structure of movie stories you break down so you can then use this culled wisdom to brainstorm and write your own movie.

These mini-themes stated above can add up to a long, convoluted sentence like "to not be just a bum from the neighborhood, you have to really try, and if you do, you can succeed but being successful isn't just about your career like boxing; it's about love." Yes, perhaps my efforts to present the master story beats in *Rocky* as actual "themes" might feel a little overwrought, but I'm doing so to illustrate a point. It's good to be able to at some point at least practice how to state an actual traditional theme that connects your entire story thematically, but there are times when it's not obvious or even possible with certain works. This is what I mean when I say the *Semiotics for Screenwriters* system is not really a formula. It's an analytic and brainstorming toolbox, but you have to know the variables of all the approaches it will allow you in order to fully appreciate and utilize its power. That said, I'd like to point out here that *Rocky* derives its power from the audience knowing

Rocky wants to be more than a bum from the neighborhood (his object of value) and that he achieves this objective by lasting 15 rounds and finding the love of a woman. The power doesn't come from the movie's story "stating" neat literary-like themes.

The master story beats/themes stated reflect the essence of the heart of the story; namely, that Rocky achieves his objective of being more than a bum from the neighborhood by lasting 15 rounds and finding love. The master story beats/themes stated as I listed them above are in the same tonal universe as the master theme of *Rocky*, which is to prove he's more than a bum from the neighborhood (a fulfillment of the contract). In general, all the micro-themes can be seen to be tonally (and by extension ideologically) related to each other. In fact, one common criticism of bad writing is the script is "tonally off." Sometimes this can occur when the "themes stated" clash and create dissonance, which in essence is noise created due to clash of what the movie is "saying."

There's no rule book on how to start to determine what the master story beats/themes stated in a movie story are. A good place to start is the contract and the subject's (protagonist's) object, or what the need/want/desire that kicks off the story is. The contract tends to serves a guidepost as to what the values of the story are and hence the theme or themes.

To reiterate, the table of the master story beats/themes stated in *Rocky* marks points of transformations regarding whether or not the subject/protagonist (Rocky) is getting closer or further from his object on not *being* a bum from the neighborhood. And while there are many story beats in this or any movie, the key *transformative* ones are special and give the movie its "bounce."

Now, on to a very important way to look at master story beats/themes stated.

Using the Complete Semiotics Square to Develop Master Story Beats/Themes Stated

The master story beats/themes stated table (Table 5.1) maps out values, transformations, and themes of *Rocky*. Now I'd like to demonstrate to you how you might more easily detect master story beats when you break down your own specimen movies and then finally use said information when writing your own movie. It involves using all four corners of the semiotic square.

First, let's look at the plotting of *some* of the master story beats/themes stated of *Rocky* as I've laid out on the movie's master semiotic square (see Figure 5.2). Now I'd like to discuss where some of the master story beats fall onto the four corners of the semiotic square of that movie and the explanation of the placement of each master story beat and why this is so important.

To start this analysis, I need to create the semiotic square for *Rocky*. To do so, I needed to come up with the controlling binary opposition terms that encapsulate that movie, ones that will ultimately help me map the transformations of the story and how these transformations build emotional meaning for a competent observer. The controlling binary opposition terms I came up with for *Rocky* are loser vs. winner.

ROCKY

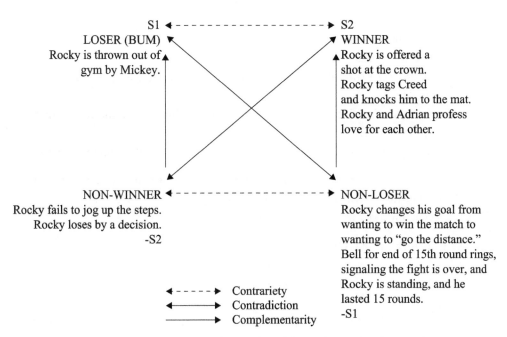

Figure 5.2 Semiotic square—*Rocky.* To understand how I use the full semiotic square to analyze some of the master story beats of *Rocky,* perhaps it's worth you viewing *Rocky* to fully understand how this technique of placing master story beats applies to this Hollywood masterpiece. *Rocky* is a virtual miracle in turning a fairy tale into reality (using the different kinds of master story beats shown) and hence making the story a great cinematic experience because cinema works best when it reflects reality being essentially a photographic (realistic) medium.

After figuring out loser vs. winner will occupy S1 and S2, I then was able to plot out the rest of the semiotic square, including what -S1 and -S2 terms would be and then proceed to form all six relationships of the story logic of *Rocky* as depicted by its semiotic square. Notice how creating four terms in the four corners of the square then allow me to take some of the master story beats/transformations of *Rocky* and plot them under one of the four headings. (I'll explain how I got there and what it all means shortly.)

For now, take a look at the semiotic square for *Rocky* and the placement of master story beats on it. Note: I only selected a few beats to place on the square for presentation purposes.

Now allow me to demonstrate how the semiotic square of *Rocky* helps me catalog its master story beats, transformations, and themes by first noticing how I placed some of master story beats under obvious terms "loser" or "winner," respectively S1 and S2,

- **S1 transformational beats**
  LOSER
  Rocky is thrown out of the gym by Mickey. (Wasting God-given talent is a sin.)

Creed tags Rocky, knocks him to the mat but he gets up. (Winning is harder than it seems.)

- **S2 transformational beats**
  WINNER (beats that are opposite LOSER)
  Rocky is offered a shot at the crown. (The Gods will offer you a shot at greatness, occasionally.)
  Rocky tags Creed and knocks him to the mat. (With hard work and determination, anything is possible.)
  Professes love for Adrian and she says it back. (Love is more important than anything.)

Easy enough. But our aim here is to utilize all four corners of the master semiotic square. Along those lines notice the bottom part of the Rocky semiotic square, -S1 and -S2, and where I placed a few more master story beats:

- **-S2 transformational beats**
  NON-WINNER (complementarity of "LOSER")
  Rocky loses by a decision. (Even if you try everything you can to succeed often you fail.)
  Story logic for this beat: The explanation of the placement of this master story beat under "NON-WINNER" (a complementarity of "LOSER") is that Rocky losing by a decision is losing the fight so he's a non-winner but he didn't lose his overall goal which was to last 15 rounds to prove he was more than just another bum from the neighborhood. And we're able to map this transformational beat to NON-WINNER instead of merely "LOSER" and hence deploying the whole semiotic square.

Again another example of using all four corners of the semiotic square of *Rocky* is below:

- **-S1 transformational beats**
  NON-LOSER (complementarity of WINNER)
  Rocky changes his goal from wanting to win the match to "wanting to go the distance." (Sometimes in life you have to be realistic.)
  Bell for end of 15th round rings signaling the fight is over, and Rocky is standing, and he lasted 15 rounds. (With hard work and determination, realistic goals are achievable.)
  So both of these transformational beats listed under NON-LOSER are about Rocky becoming realistic about his object (goal) and him obtaining his object of going the distance (lasting 15 rounds) which doesn't constitute winning but he's not losing either (NON-LOSER).

Again, Rocky changing his goal from winning the match to merely "wanting to do the distance" and then him going the distance lasting 15 rounds but losing by a decision isn't exactly him winning, but it's certainly "NON-LOSER" in terms of the construct of the story and Rocky's object to be more than just another bum from them neighborhood.

Perhaps a quick summary of the logical construction of the semiotic square of *Rocky* is in order starting with the top, the contrarian terms, LOSER vs. WINNER, that occupy the S1 and S2 positions of the square, respectively. This binary opposition of LOSER vs.

WINNER in *Rocky* underscores the foundation of how humans perceive reality through binary opposition. And the LOSER/WINNER pair in *Rocky* function in the same way as do the other typical binary opposition terms used to depict the underpinnings of all perception; namely, how you can't know HOT without COLD, UP without DOWN, and everyone's favorite, you can't perceive LIFE without DEATH. But as we've seen demonstrated above, the other corners of the semiotic square come into play to allow for some variations between simple binary oppositions, and by using the *entire* semiotic square and all four corners, it affords nuances to the task of breaking down and decoding meaning in a movie story and hence helps us map *reality* and allows movie story to depict reality. This is what the entire semiotic square helps reveal to us and then helps us brainstorm and write with.

In *Rocky*, the master story beats I assigned to these top poles LOSER vs. WINNER (S1 and S2) are easy to understand. For example, it's easy to understand how the master story beat "Rocky is thrown out of the gym by Mickey" falls neatly under the "LOSER" term. However, it requires a little more mental work to understand where all the master story beats fall on the *entire* semiotic square and how working in concert all four corners of the square help explain our perception of a nuanced picture of reality in *Rocky*. Take the other two poles of NON-WINNER and NON-LOSER of the square. These -S1 and -S2 corners of the semiotic square in *Rocky* help further codify the events in that movie story specifically in relationship to the movie's values, themes, and transformations. Below is another example.

The NON-WINNER section is where I codified two major story beats/themes stated of the story, "Rocky fails to jog up the steps" and "Rocky loses by a decision." Not "making it up the steps" isn't exactly losing but it's not winning as is "losing by a decision" is not winning but it's not exactly losing (according to how Rocky defined winning). The same goes for the opposite or the contrary of NON-WINNER, which is NON-LOSER, where I place two master story beats, "Rocky changes his goal from wanting to win the match to lasting 15 rounds" *and* "Bell for end of 15th round rings, signaling the fight is over, and Rocky is standing, and he lasted 15 rounds." These two-story beats don't constitute winning, but they are not losing and hence why they are labeled under NON-LOSER.

Greater Truths Revealed Through the Entire Semiotic Square

As we have just seen, all four corners of the semiotic square afford us nuances to deconstruct master story beats/themes stated. This is what is meant by stating that the semiotic square is a visual representation of the elementary structure of meaning (and by extension a *visual expression of the structure of our perception of reality*), especially when we use all corners of the semiotic square to map out master story beats in a movie story.

All four corners of the semiotic square of *Rocky* allow us to decode and depict what makes *Rocky* work because its major story beats/themes stated depict *reality* not fantasy, and all four corners demonstrate the nuances of how *reality* manifests in that movie, which has been referred to as a "Cinderalla" story. In fact, a simple mini-thematic binary opposition encapsulating *Rocky* can be stated as "fantasy vs. reality" or winning the fight vs. lasting 15 rounds. We'll delve more into this method of using the entire semiotic square to plot transformations and themes for three specimen movies later, and then this study will culminate with using the principles to develop a feature screenplay treatment and comprehensive beat map ready to be dropped onto Final Draft's Outline Editor. For now, I'd like to expand on how these important principles of how to use the semiotic square to help us analyze and write master story beats utilizing the mini-demo I've been developing for this study, *The Lost Dog Story.*

Values, Themes, and Transformations in *The Lost Dog Story*

I'd like to continue to explore values and transformations as master story beats/themes stated, and simultaneously develop some additional breakdown and brainstorming tools. To do so, allow me to recall *The Lost Dog Story* and its master semiotic square (Figure 5.3).

In order to devise ideas for scenes for this story that are connected to values, transformations, and themes, I first start with the controlling poles of the square S1 and S2, wilderness vs. home, and then the rest of the square -S1 and -S2 non-wilderness vs. non-home, to brainstorm ideas for master story beats/themes stated, aka transformations.

Using the master semiotic square for *The Lost Dog Story*, let's see if I can plot some key transformations that will signal themes (themes which are "stated" when a subject [protagonist] moves towards or away from their object of value). It's these key moments that the complete semiotic square can be deployed especially to depict the logic as to how I arrived there. This kind of analysis is useful when studying specimen movies and brainstorming your own. Remember, I use this (and all the semiotics tools) in a creative way. The following toolkit (Figures 5.4 to 5.17) is *not* a study of formal logic, but it's an example of how to creatively use all four corners of the semiotic square to brainstorm master story beats. Note, I also take each plotting of the master story beats/themes stated on a case by case basis, beat by beat.

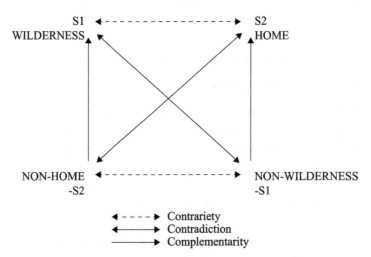

Figure 5.3 Semiotic square for *The Lost Dog Story.*

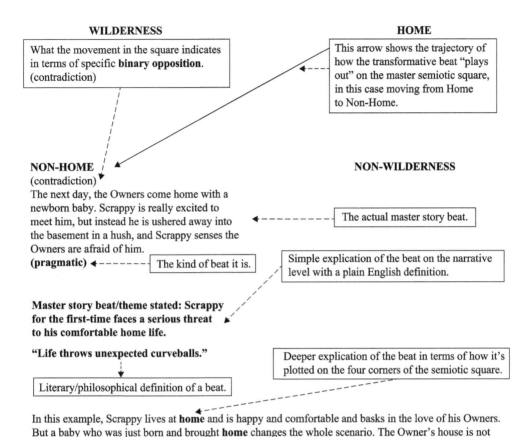

WILDERNESS

What the movement in the square indicates in terms of specific **binary opposition**. (contradiction)

HOME

This arrow shows the trajectory of how the transformative beat "plays out" on the master semiotic square, in this case moving from Home to Non-Home.

NON-HOME
(contradiction)
The next day, the Owners come home with a newborn baby. Scrappy is really excited to meet him, but instead he is ushered away into the basement in a hush, and Scrappy senses the Owners are afraid of him.
(pragmatic) ◄------- The kind of beat it is.

NON-WILDERNESS

The actual master story beat.

Simple explication of the beat on the narrative level with a plain English definition.

Master story beat/theme stated: Scrappy for the first-time faces a serious threat to his comfortable home life.

Deeper explication of the beat in terms of how it's plotted on the four corners of the semiotic square.

"Life throws unexpected curveballs."

Literary/philosophical definition of a beat.

In this example, Scrappy lives at **home** and is happy and comfortable and basks in the love of his Owners. But a baby who was just born and brought **home** changes the whole scenario. The Owner's house is not **home** anymore. *But* it's not the **wilderness**. But it's **non-home**, contradictory to what **home** is.

Figure 5.4 *The Lost Dog Story*—Master story beat 1 (with legend). Master story beats via semiotic square—this first master story beat analysis begins to show how to use all four corners of the master semiotic square for *The Lost Dog Story* and also serves as an opportunity to introduce and explain all the moving parts of this complex but powerful tool.

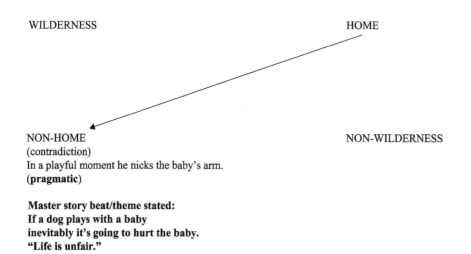

NON-HOME
(contradiction)
In a playful moment he nicks the baby's arm.
(**pragmatic**)

Master story beat/theme stated:
If a dog plays with a baby
inevitably it's going to hurt the baby.
"Life is unfair."

For this example, **home** is **non-home** because there's a new baby (a new "Owner" in the form of a baby) who is easily bruised and complains a lot. **Home** has become foreign and problematic for Scrappy, expressed as **non-home** and contradictory of **home**, but it's not quite **wilderness** yet.

Figure 5.5 *The Lost Dog Story*—Master story beat 2

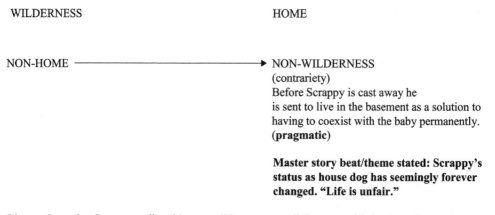

NON-WILDERNESS
(contrariety)
Before Scrappy is cast away he
is sent to live in the basement as a solution to
having to coexist with the baby permanently.
(**pragmatic**)

Master story beat/theme stated: Scrappy's
status as house dog has seemingly forever
changed. "Life is unfair."

It's **non-home** but Scrappy realizes it's **non-wilderness** as well (in a sense it's in contrariety to the **non-home**). It's his own now and he can feel comfortable and safe in his domain down there so it's **non-wilderness**.

Figure 5.6 *The Lost Dog Story*—Master story beat 3.

WILDERNESS   HOME

NON-HOME ◄──────────────────────────────── NON-WILDERNESS
(contrariety)
Scrappy is blamed for the baby's bassinette being
knocked over.
(pragmatic)

Master story beat/theme stated:
While life had seemed good for Scrappy,
it's just really not fair now. "Life is unfair."

Once again **non-wilderness** has become **non-home** (contrariety) for Scrappy.

Figure 5.7 *The Lost Dog Story*—Master story beat 4.

WILDERNESS   HOME

NON-HOME ──────────────────────────────► NON-WILDERNESS
                                          (contrariety)

Scrappy is a *sad dog* to leave, but at least now he realizes
he has a new loving home and plans to make the best
of it for the time being until he can figure out how
to get back to his original Owners.
(pragmatic/cognitive/thymic)

Master story beat/theme stated: Scrappy is a
survivor. "Make the best out of what life gives
you. If life gives you lemons, make lemonade."

Again this is another **non-home** to **non-wilderness** scenario whereby Scrappy is leaving his **home** but he's
not going to be in the **wilderness**.

Figure 5.8 *The Lost Dog Story*—Master story beat 5.

WILDERNESS
(contradiction)
Scrappy is thrown in
a basement with many
caged dogs and quickly
learns from them that the
New Owners
who adopted him are
running a dog fighting business
and plan to use Scrappy
as practice meat for the older star
killer dog Mad Dog McKill to practice.
(**cognitive/pragmatic**)

**Master story beat/theme stated:
Scrappy realizes he was naïve about the
world. "Life has unexpected twists."**

NON-HOME

HOME

NON-WILDERNESS

Scrappy, who at least thought he landed in a **non-wilderness** situation, has learned he is being handed over to dog fighters as practice meat for Mad Dog McKill, his first sense of being "in the **wilderness**," a contradiction from **non-wilderness**. **Wilderness** is not just a physical place; it's a mindset, a spiritual reality. And since **non-wilderness** exists in contradiction to **wilderness**, this is a major transformation and getting into the depths of the story.

Figure 5.9 *The Lost Dog Story*—Master story beat 6.

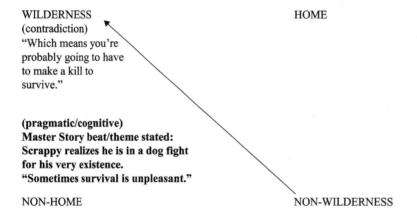

WILDERNESS
(contradiction)
"Which means you're
probably going to have
to make a kill to
survive."

(**pragmatic/cognitive**)
**Master Story beat/theme stated:
Scrappy realizes he is in a dog fight
for his very existence.
"Sometimes survival is unpleasant."**

NON-HOME

HOME

NON-WILDERNESS

Again, Scrappy realizes he must kill another dog to survive and this realization represents the furthest move from what was at least **non-wilderness** to **wilderness**, a clear contradiction.

Figure 5.10 *The Lost Dog Story*—Master story beat 7.

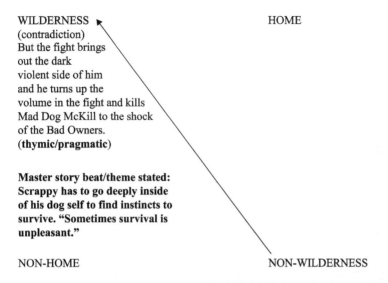

WILDERNESS
(contradiction)
But the fight brings
out the dark
violent side of him
and he turns up the
volume in the fight and kills
Mad Dog McKill to the shock
of the Bad Owners.
(thymic/pragmatic)

HOME

**Master story beat/theme stated:
Scrappy has to go deeply inside
of his dog self to find instincts to
survive. "Sometimes survival is
unpleasant."**

NON-HOME   NON-WILDERNESS

Again, Scrappy must kill Mad Dog or he'll be killed. This buys him time until he can escape. Living with the Bad Owners was certainly not **home**, but it was **non-wilderness** and to have to kill Mad Dog McKill, a brother dog albeit an evil one, makes Scrappy feel as if he's already in the **wilderness**, a contradiction to his current situation of living with the Bad Owners.

Figure 5.11 *The Lost Dog Story*—Master story beat 8.

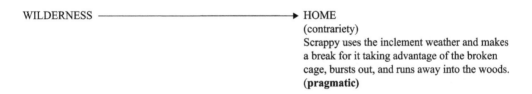

WILDERNESS ————————————————▶ HOME
                                                   (contrariety)
                                                   Scrappy uses the inclement weather and makes
                                                   a break for it taking advantage of the broken
                                                   cage, bursts out, and runs away into the woods.
                                                   (pragmatic)

**Master story beat/theme stated:
Scrappy moment to moment is learning to
survive. "Occasionally you catch a break.
Seize the day."**

NON-HOME   NON-WILDERNESS

Scrappy escaping from the broken cage and then running away feels like the most **home** since he was taken away by the Bad Owners. Even though, again, he is not really moving towards **home**, he has momentum towards returning **home**. This escape and freedom and possibility of **home** comes in a burst in direct contrariety to the **wilderness** of the S1 position, hence I label it as **wilderness** to **home**.

Figure 5.12 *The Lost Dog Story*—Master story beat 9.

WILDERNESS   HOME

NON-HOME ————————————————————▶ NON-WILDERNESS
                                              (contrariety)

While resting he processes through the fight
with Mad Dog McKill and realizes he had
no choice. But it still makes him a *sad dog* and
an *angry dog* that he was forced to have to kill
a dog. He accepts it and falls asleep.
(cognitive)

Master story beat/theme stated:
Scrappy begins to contemplate his own life
in a way he never did and thinks about his
recent actions. "It's okay to defend yourself
to survive."

Saying that Scrappy "accepts" he had to kill another dog to survive is in contrariety between **non-home**
and **non-wilderness** because he's "free" but not "**home**" but not really in the "**wilderness**" because he is
moving towards **home** with hope.

Figure 5.13 *The Lost Dog Story*—Master Story Beat 10.

WILDERNESS   HOME

————————————————————▶
NON-HOME   NON-WILDERNESS
                                              (contrariety)

He realizes because he's a killer dog now he
probably shouldn't go back to the original
Owners because they have a baby now, so he
lets go of the dream of returning home and sets
his sights on adjusting to life on the streets. He
lets go of his dream of returning to his original
Owners and going home.
(cognitive)

Master story beat/theme stated:
Scrappy is learning to accept reality.
"It's best to make peace with reality."

This, to me, is **non-home** leading as contrary towards **non-wilderness** because he's accepting his fate
and learning to make the streets as a version of **home** but also beginning to accept it's not really **home**.

Figure 5.14 *The Lost Dog Story*—Master Story Beat 11.

WILDERNESS

HOME
(complementarity)

NON-HOME

NON-WILDERNESS
Scrappy summons the same emotions he used
to kill Mad Dog McKill and chases away the
would-be crooks and saves the family but not
before taking a bullet.
(thymic/pragmatic)

Master story beat/theme stated:
Scrappy is reacting and using strength
and courage he didn't realize he had.
"Sometimes you are stronger and braver
than you think."

We're moving from **non-wilderness** (which is the New Owners' house), which is not his real **home** but it's
non-wilderness. The transformation movement is he summons emotions as if he were **home** because he has
protected his new family as Owners so it's essentially complementary. Scrappy moves towards his overall
object which is getting **home**.

Figure 5.15 *The Lost Dog Story*—Master Story Beat 12.

WILDERNESS

HOME
(complementarity)
Scrappy decides the New Owners need him
more, and he growls at the original Owners to
discourage them from taking him. They try to
ignore Scrappy's growls and go to touch him,
and he snaps at them.
(cognitive)

Master story beat/theme stated: Scrappy's
sense of where he belongs has evolved. "Go
where you are most needed."

NON-HOME

NON-WILDERNESS

Scrappy now is at **home** because he is defending his right to stay with his New Owners and doesn't
want to go back to his original Owners. He is **home** now. This moves from **non-wilderness**
(in New Owners **dwelling** which is **non-wilderness**) and moves to the complementarity (to **home**).

He has taken an act of bravery, which will engender true love from his New Owners and his need to reject the
original Owners; they need him more and he needs them more.

Figure 5.16 *The Lost Dog Story*—Master Story Beat 13.

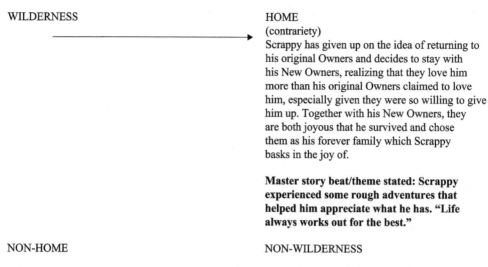

WILDERNESS

HOME
(contrariety)
Scrappy has given up on the idea of returning to his original Owners and decides to stay with his New Owners, realizing that they love him more than his original Owners claimed to love him, especially given they were so willing to give him up. Together with his New Owners, they are both joyous that he survived and chose them as his forever family which Scrappy basks in the joy of.

Master story beat/theme stated: Scrappy experienced some rough adventures that helped him appreciate what he has. "Life always works out for the best."

NON-HOME   NON-WILDERNESS

While you might be surprised to see the movement from **wilderness** (contrariety) to **home**, it's just a creative twist, a reflection on Scrappy realizing that since his original Owners were so willing to give him away, which in essence was the true **wilderness** and now he is in his true **home**.*

* Perhaps this beat plotted on the semiotic square might spawn a new original scene; namely, the original Owners take Scrappy back home but it's not home (it's the wilderness) because they rejected him in the first place. He then has to escape and make his way back to the New Owners (which is home).

Figure 5.17 *The Lost Dog Story*—Master Story Beat 14.

In Summary—Using the Entire Semiotic Square to Brainstorm Master Story Beats

So, as demonstrated with this simple demo story, by using all four corners of the semiotic square (S1, S2, -S1, -S2), I plotted the story's master story beats, also known as key transformations, ones that can be used to build *The Lost Dog Story*. You will see that the exercise of breaking down specimen movies using the entire semiotic square will facilitate your ability to brainstorm and write your own movie. Of course you might need to have a treatment or a draft of your script before you can figure out master story beats as such. You'll find your own workflow and how to utilize the semiotic tools with some practice.

Master Story Beats/Themes Stated "Cheat Sheet"[1]

A further step I like to do when breaking down specimen movies (or sometimes when I'm writing my own script) is to come up with a master story beats/themes stated "cheat sheet." It's a one-sheet whereby I can glance at the key story beats in a movie and in a snapshot see the magic moments in that movie that makes it work. These master story beats give a movie its "swing," it's movement, it's great moments, etc.

Table 5.2 shows how I outline what these master transformations depict, the themes they state, and the kind of beat they are.

Table 5.2 Master story beats/themes stated cheat sheet—*The Lost Dog Story*

BEATS	MASTER STORY BEATS/THEMES STATED
The next day, the Owners come home with the newborn baby. Scrappy is really excited to meet him but instead is ushered away into the basement in a hush and Scrappy senses the Owners are afraid of him. *He is a sad dog.* (pragmatic/thymic)	**Scrappy for the first-time faces a serious threat to his comfortable home life.** **"Life throws unexpected curveballs."**
In a playful moment, Scrappy nicks the baby's arm. (pragmatic)	**If a dog plays with a baby, inevitably it's going to hurt the baby.** **"Life is unfair."**
Before Scrappy is cast away, he is sent to live in the basement as a solution to having to coexist with the baby permanently. (pragmatic)	**Scrappy's status as a house dog has seemingly forever changed.** **"Life is unfair."**
Scrappy is blamed for the baby's bassinet being knocked over. (pragmatic)	**While life had seemed good for Scrappy, it's just really not fair now.** **"Life is unfair."**
Scrappy is a *sad dog* to leave but at least now he realizes he has a new loving home and plans to make the best of it for the time being until he can figure out how to get back to his original Owners. (thymic/cognitive)	**Scrappy is a survivor.** **"Make the best out of what life gives you. If life gives you lemons, make lemonade."**
Scrappy is thrown in a basement with many caged dogs and quickly learns from them that the New Owners who adopted him are running a dog-fighting business and plan to use Scrappy as practice meat for the older star killer dog Mad Dog McKill. (cognitive/pragmatic)	**Scrappy realizes he was naïve about the world.** **"Life has unexpected twists."**

---

[1] I like to list the master story beats/themes stated on singular "cheat sheet" so as writers you can look at the cheat sheet for the great specimen movies you break down in a snapshot.

"Which means you're probably going to have to make a kill to survive." (pragmatic/cognitive)	**Scrappy realizes he is in a dog fight for his very existence.** "Sometimes survival is unpleasant."
But the fight brings out the dark violent side of him and he turns up the volume in the fight and kills Mad Dog McKill to the shock of the Bad Owners. (thymic/pragmatic)	**Scrappy has to go deeply inside of his dog self to find instincts to survive.** "Sometimes survival is unpleasant."
Scrappy uses the inclement weather and makes a break for it taking advantage of the broken cage, bursts out and runs away into the woods. (pragmatic)	**Scrappy moment to moment is learning to survive.** "Occasionally you catch a break. Seize the day."
While resting, he processes through the fight with Mad Dog McKill and realizes he had no choice. But it still makes him a *sad dog* and an *angry dog* that he was forced to have to kill a dog. He accepts it and falls asleep. (cognitive)	**Scrappy begins to contemplate his own life in a way he never did and thinks about his recent actions.** "It's okay to defend yourself to survive."
He realizes because he's a killer dog now he probably shouldn't go back to the original Owners because they have a baby now, so he lets go of the dream of returning home and sets his sights on adjusting to life on the streets. He lets go of his dream of returning to his original Owners and going home. (cognitive)	**Scrappy is learning to accept reality.** "It's best to make peace with reality."
Scrappy summons the same emotions he used to kill Mad Dog McKill and chases away the would-be crooks and saves the family but not before taking a bullet. (thymic/pragmatic)	**Scrappy is reacting and using strength and courage he didn't realize he had.** "Sometimes you are stronger and braver than you think."
Scrappy decides the New Owners need him more and he growls at the original Owners to discourage them from taking him. They try to ignore Scrappy's growls and go to touch him and he snaps at them. (cognitive)	**Scrappy's sense of where he belongs has evolved.** "Go where you are most needed."
Scrappy has given up on the idea of returning to his original Owners and decides to stay with his New Owners, realizing that they love him more than his original Owners *claimed* to love him, realizing they didn't love him, especially given they were so willing to give him up. Together with his New Owners, they are both joyous that he survived and chose them as his forever family, which Scrappy basks in the joy of. (cognitive/thymic)	**Scrappy experienced some rough adventures that helped him appreciate what he has.** "Life always works out for the best."

Some of you may wish to write a traditional style treatment using the semiotics tools and language to get a feel for how they might apply in an entire story flow. Therefore, I've attempted as much below for *The Lost Dog Story*. Note: I will not use all of the semiotic related ideas I generated in the previous analyses, just where I think using such items might be the most informative. Later, when I break down three specimen movies, I use all the tools beat by beat to demonstrate how to do a comprehensive analysis of a specimen movie. Also let me point out that a lot of usage of the tools in a treatment might seem a little obvious, but it's all done to illustrate a point.

The Lost Dog Story Composite Treatment— Semiotics Style

Legend for Composite Treatment

- Master story beats/themes stated are in **bold** and are derived from the above analysis where I generated the master story beats/themes stated using all four corners of the semiotic square.
- "States of being" are noted in ***bold italics***.

Scrappy lives with his Owners in a nice quiet home in suburbia. His Owners are childless, so he's essentially like their child. He loves them and they love him, and he has free rein of the house, including the backyard. He enjoys belly rubs, steak dinners, and hanging out with his Owners when they read or watch television. It's an idyllic life. ***He is a happy dog.*** Then one day something changes. One Owner's belly gets bigger, and Scrappy senses she's carrying a child, and he's happy and on board in terms of accepting this new addition to the family. He gives his Owner with the big belly extra attention and protection. Initially, nothing changes in how the Owners treat him. Then one day the Owner with the big belly leaves. **The next day, the Owners come back with the newborn baby. Scrappy is really excited to meet him but instead is ushered away into the basement in a hush, and Scrappy senses the Owners are now afraid of him.** ***He is a sad dog.***

The Owners moving Scrappy to the basement is a sender to Scrappy the receiver, making him the subject with the object of returning to the upstairs of the house and proving he's okay around the baby. A helper is his own motivation and his love for his Owners, including the baby, and his Owners' love of him is a helper. An opponent to Scrappy continuing to enjoy living with his Owners is all the bad press about pit bulls, and his Owners' inexperience raising children.

At first, the Owners seem to be overreacting imagining Scrappy will harm the baby even if accidentally. Scrappy spends all day by himself in the basement and cries. ***He is a lonely dog.*** But then the Owners go to the basement and see that Scrappy is sad and realize they love him too, and Scrappy feels it. ***He feels like a loved dog.*** They decide to give Scrappy a chance to live with the baby in peace. Scrappy senses what is going on and a contract is created in that Scrappy becomes the subject and his object is to prove he can live in harmony with the baby. And this contract comes with a qualifying test, asking the central dramatic question,[2] "Will Scrappy be able to live in the house with the baby and not hurt it?" There will be a *being able to do something* in the form of Scrappy being able to prove he can play with the baby and be around it without harming it. He *knows how to do this* in that he'll never use his teeth when he plays with the baby.

The qualifying test is Scrappy must prove he can live with the baby and not harm it. Everything is fine, and Scrappy loves the baby and licks him a lot, but then in a playful moment, nicks the baby's arm when the baby catches it in Scrappy's teeth by accident. It's a tiny nick but the baby screams and cries, and this causes distress in the Owner and his wife, who have had trepidations all along about having Scrappy be around the baby for fear he'll harm it.

Scrappy has failed his first qualifying test despite the fact that it was an accident that the baby nicked its arm on Scrappy's teeth. **Before Scrappy is cast away, he is sent to live in the basement as a solution to having to coexist with the baby**. Soon Scrappy spends all day down there forbidden from coming upstairs. He is a **bored dog**, his first day down there he cries, but while his Owners hear it, they refuse to give in and let Scrappy back up. They feel it's safer for the baby if Scrappy stays down in the basement as they are inclined to playing it completely safe. This demotion to having to live downstairs is a sender to Scrappy the receiver, causing him to become a subject in need of an object, that object simply being Scrappy's desire to get back upstairs and prove he's worthy of living in the main house safely with the baby. Again, a helper for Scrappy is his own determination. His opponent is his Owners' fears.

Scrappy is a **sad dog** because he used to have free run of the house, but he accepts living in the basement as he gets to see his family occasionally and even sees the baby, in supervised sessions, of course, but those sessions make him a little happier because he still feels protective of the baby. Scrappy's patience is a helper in his cause to be able to return to living upstairs. This all sets up the next qualifying test, which will be a test to see if Scrappy will be able to find a way upstairs and prove he's harmless. He must prove competency and accomplish a *being able to do something* (get upstairs) as well as a *knowing how to do something* (prove he's harmless).

One day, Scrappy happens to be upstairs when the Owners are distracted as they are hosting a baby shower. Scrappy is an **excited dog** to be back upstairs, and he plays with people; even his Owners pet him and don't seem to mind he's upstairs. While his Owners are distracted, he notices the family cat walking into the baby's room and now Scrappy is also a **worried dog** due to the fact that the cat is probably up to no good, especially when it comes to the baby. The ever vigilante Scrappy, always eager to prove his value as a guard of

---

[2]It's always a good idea to state the three tests as "Central Dramatic Questions" with a question mark in it. In other words, the central dramatic question of *The Lost Dog Story* at this juncture is "Will Scrappy be able to prove he can live with the new baby without harming it?" Of course the real central dramatic question that will become the main one that dominates the entire story is "Will Scrappy be able to make it home?"

the baby (so he'll be allowed back upstairs full time), goes into the room to investigate and watches as the cat (an opponent) knocks over the baby's bassinet and proceeds to scramble out of the room undetected. The baby wails but is unharmed. However, the Owners come in and blame Scrappy, who is still in the room and looks guilty. They see the bassinet on the floor and become angry at Scrappy. **Scrappy is cast away. He is sent to live in the basement permanently without any upstairs privileges. This extreme measure is an attempt at a solution to allowing Scrappy to coexist with the baby**. However, as the Owners ponder the situation, they view the action of knocking over the baby's bassinet as the last straw … it is now unacceptably dangerous to the baby's well-being to keep Scrappy anywhere in the home. The cat was an opponent but not a pure anti-subject because the cat was *not* trying to get rid of Scrappy, which would make him a full-blown anti-subject, meaning he was diametrically opposed to what the subject (Scrappy) wanted (to stay home with his Owners). He is merely being a cat, and his actions add up to opposition (opponent) to Scrappy's goal to stay with his Owners.

This accident of the baby's bassinet being knocked to the ground by the house cat (but done so in a way that the event looks like Scrappy did it) becomes a sender to the receiver/Owners, creating in them a new object, a desire to get rid of Scrappy and find a good new home. Scrappy is a ***sad dog and an angry dog***[3] contemplating the unfairness that the cat inadvertently set him up to look like the cause of the baby's bassinet falling down.

This last incident of the baby's bassinet falling down is a sender to the Owners the receiver, making them the subject with the object of finding Scrappy a good new home. The male Owner puts a want ad in *Craigslist* and receives inquiries from people interested in dogs who promptly show up to meet Scrappy. They are all potential helpers to Scrappy staying home in that many of them are oddballs causing the Owners to lean towards perhaps *not* giving Scrappy away and keeping him albeit reluctantly. Finally, friendly potential New Owners show up in the form of a couple who seem sincere and dog loving. They also seem good as far as their ability to interact with Scrappy and he seems okay with them. They are a married couple, Bill and Barbara, and they proclaim with joy that they want to be New Owners of Scrappy. They are both opponents and helpers in this way—first they are offering the original Owners a way to get Scrappy out of their house with a clear conscience, but they are also opponents to Scrappy staying home. And they will be new helpers in a sense because they plan on giving Scrappy a new loving home.

Scrappy is a *sad dog* to leave but at least now he realizes he has a new loving home and plans to make the best of it for the time being until he can figure out how to get back to his original Owners. The original Owners are a sender to Scrappy a receiver, creating in him a desire to return to his original home. A new subject/object opposition is set up—Scrappy (subject) wants to return home (object). But Scrappy realizes he will have to follow through and live with the New Owners for a while until he can figure out how to get back home, so in a sense he is a new subject with a new object, trying to make the new

---

[3]This is an example of using a binary *state of being* (angry dog) which isn't "answered" by its contrary (joyful dog) until the very end. It doesn't matter if all or any of the *contraries* are used or when they are used, but it is good to know what they are when brainstorming.

arrangement work. Scrappy realizes (a new qualifying test) that he is faced with both a new *being able to do something* and a new *knowing how to do something*, which is to prove to the New Owners he's worth keeping around until he can figure out how to get back to his original Owners.

The New Owners take Scrappy, who is a ***sad dog***, and promise to give him a good home. As the New Owners drive away, Scrappy senses something is wrong. He smells a lot of different dogs in their car. When the New Owners arrive at their home, **Scrappy is thrown in a basement with many caged dogs and quickly learns from them that the New Owners who adopted him are running a dog-fighting business and plan to use Scrappy as practice meat for the older star killer dog Mad Dog McKill**. The New Owners have quickly turned from helpers (in the sense that Scrappy was willing to accept a new loving home) to opponents (they are anything but home and threaten his very existence). They can also be considered anti-subjects because while they may not necessarily be diametrically opposed to Scrappy getting home in principle, they are trying to have him killed. Either way, they are opponents to his overall goal; namely, his desire to live at home with Owners who love him.

The New Owners, whom we'll now label as Bad Owners, throw Scrappy into a cage and onto a cargo truck of other caged dogs destined for dog fights. The other dogs laugh to themselves, remarking they think "Scrappy" is only going to last a month in the dog fights and they seem insensitive to Scrappy's coming fate. Scrappy is merely meant to be cannon fodder for the meaner, tougher dogs. Scrappy is surrounded by cages of talking dogs (talk which to the outside world seems like dogs barking), and soon there emerges the voice of an Old Dog, who tells Scrappy that the only one way to survive is to escape. Scrappy is all for it. This Old Dog is a sender to Scrappy a receiver, setting up Scrappy as a subject/object; namely, that Scrappy wants/needs/desires to escape and get back to his original Owners' home and live the comfortable life he was living with them. But for now, his urgency is merely to escape the life of dog fights, so this becomes his new object. The Old Dog also serves as a helper to Scrappy.

Scrappy tries to talk to the other dogs, who taunt him and continue to yell (bark) at Scrappy, accusing him of being too soft and predicting that he is going to die right away in the dog fights because he cried when they first met him and lamented about missing his comfy bed and his steak dinners and belly rubs and trips to the beach. The other dogs all laugh and howl at Scrappy's sad complaining. He is a ***sad dog***. The other dogs are opponents in that they are making him upset and undermining his will to live.

Scrappy talks to the Old Dog about how he can execute an escape plan that the Old Dog advocated so he can make it home to his original Owners. The Old Dog tells Scrappy, "You have to survive until an opportunity comes to make a break. **Which means you're probably going to have to make a kill to survive**. Best it happens in your first fight against Mad Dog McKill. Kill him, and it will buy you some time because they'll put you into an elite training program." Scrappy complains, "I've never killed anything . . . except maybe a few snakes for my master." The Old Dog replies, "They have you marked for a quick death by Mad Dog McKill. It's either you or him. I can't be around to guide you. Get out while you can. Kill

Mad Dog McKill." Scrappy has learned that killing Mad Dog McKill in his first dog fight might be what he needs to survive, his new object, albeit a tough one to contemplate executing. The Old Dog is a sender to Scrappy the receiver, making him the subject with the object of killing Mad Dog McKill to escape. He has a new qualifying test, which is to kill Mad Dog McKill in order to buy some time so he can find an opportunity to escape. It will require a *being able to do something*, in this case being able to kill another dog in a fight.

The Bad Owner goes to feed the Old Dog, who out of nowhere suddenly goes to viciously bite the Bad Owner and the Bad Owner shoots the Old Dog dead. Scrappy realizes the Old Dog was *planning* to get aggressive so he'd be killed as he'd had enough of the dog-fighting life. But he wanted to at least share with Scrappy one bit of advice: escape while you can. The Old Dog was a helper to Scrappy and his will to escape and a helper to help Scrappy begin his journey home.

Scrappy goes into a fight with Mad Dog McKill, which is just practice for Mad Dog McKill, so Scrappy is laughed at by the other dogs watching (opponents) because he's fighting Mad Dog McKill (opponent). Scrappy starts out the fight losing and feels certain that he's going to die. **But the fight brings out the dark violent side of him and he turns up the volume in the fight and kills Mad Dog McKill, to the shock of the Bad Owners.** Scrappy has succeeded in a major qualifying test and is a step closer to having bought time to be able to escape and return to his original Owners. But it came at a price ... he lost a little of his soul.

Scrappy is a ***sad dog*** and feels terrible about having killed a fellow dog even though it was kill or be killed. He goes back to his cage in the truck, and the Bad Owners are happy with his kill and feed him steak on the way home, a sign to the other dogs that Scrappy is now the lead dog and will go into elite training and not have to fight for months. Scrappy thinks back to what the Old Dog told him about needing to kill Mad Dog McKill to survive and realizes that's why the Old Dog recommended Scrappy kill Mad Dog McKill; it would buy him time. He would go into training as a result of killing Mad Dog McKill; he wouldn't have to fight for some time.

On the ride home, the Bad Owners are impressed by Scrappy and discuss plans for his dog-fighting career, estimating he might last a few years as the new lead dog. A helper shows up in the form of an unusually bumpy car ride. Scrappy's cage gets knocked and rattled to a point where the latch breaks when the car hits a bump and flies up in the air and lands in a way that the latch is snapped against another cage. When the Bad Owners park at the dog-fighting training compound, they unload the cages. It's cold and rainy out (helper), causing it to be difficult for the male Bad Owner's visibility. **Scrappy uses the inclement weather and makes a break for it taking advantage of the broken cage, bursts out and runs away into the woods and escapes.** The male Bad Owner shoots at him but misses him. Scrappy has escaped into the woods and is free but is now completely alone in the wilderness where he must learn to survive (a new *being able to do something/knowing how to do something*). He is the "lost dog."

Scrappy wanders around the woods hungry, tired, and cold. He smells a dumpster and finds it on the outskirts of the woods. After sifting through some trash bags on the floor near the dumpster he smells out a discarded chicken dinner and eats a meal. Soon he feels a sharp twinge in his rear and turns to see a Young Boy has shot him with a slingshot. The Young Boy cocks the slingshot back and is aiming at his eye. The Young Boy is an opponent to Scrappy's object of getting home in that he's trying to kill him or damage Scrappy's body and ruin his navigation and survival skills. The Young Boy is a sender to Scrappy a receiver as well, making Scrappy the subject with the simple object to escape violence. He runs back into the woods and escapes the Young Boy.

Scrappy wanders around the woods and is a cold and *lonely dog*. He sleeps one night in a pile of leaves and is okay for the night. **While resting, Scrappy processes through the fight with Mad Dog McKill and realizes he had no choice. But it still makes him a** *sad dog* **and an** *angry dog* **that he was forced to have to kill a dog. He accepts it and falls asleep.**

Scrappy meets an unhoused woman (a helper), who sees Scrappy in need of food and shelter and lets him stay inside of her refrigerator box with her and take shelter. She feeds him from the little bit of food she has and is kind to him and rubs his belly and becomes a new temporary Owner. Scrappy has nice doggie dreams of his original Owner, which serves to reinforce his original object (return to his original Owners and original home). The unhoused woman dies of old age one night. Scrappy tries to revive her but can't. He mourns his deceased friend. He falls asleep in the refrigerator box. He has more dreams of his original Owners that are pleasant and warm (his object of desire).

But then the dream changes to his memory of killing Mad Dog McKill in the dog fight. Scrappy awakens and **realizes because he's a killer dog now he probably shouldn't go back to the original Owners because they have a baby now. So he lets go of the dream of returning home and sets his sights on adjusting to life in the wilderness. He lets go of his dream of returning home to his original Owners.**

Scrappy falls back asleep again with a new resolve to make the best of life and he wakes up scared because in the dream the earth began shaking and it seemed angry at him. He realizes the actual ground below him is moving as he is slammed against the walls of the refrigerator box. He scrambles to run up to the top but is thrown to the bottom of the box as it tilts upwards. He realizes the box is being dumped into a garbage compactor and thus is faced with a new qualifying test, which presents as a *being able to do something*; namely, survive certain death by a garbage compactor. Just when the refrigerator box lodges into the compactor, it catches on a tree branch (helper), allowing Scrappy enough time to leap out and land on the floor, where he proceeds to scramble to safety.

Eventually Scrappy wanders into a poor section of town and is adopted by a poor family that treats him well and loves him. The new family are helpers to Scrappy in that he believes they will eventually be a resting place, buying him time until he can find his way home (object) to his original Owners. He has a new sender to which he is a receiver; namely, that the family being nice to him is a sender to him the receiver, making him a subject with the object of showing gratitude and as long as he's living there be committed to protecting the family, realizing this is the surest path to him returning home.

In the new family's home, Scrappy begins to have variations on the "good life" he lived in the original Owner's home. For example, instead of sitting by a warm fire, he now sits by the radiator. He gets to eat scraps off the table that aren't steak but there's chicken and hamburger and it's still delicious. He doesn't get to play in a big backyard anymore, but he plays in the park with other dogs and with his new temporary (in his mind) family that in some ways is more fun. His New Owners love him and treat him well and seem to need him. Scrappy realizes that if they need him he has some staying power there. And he doesn't want to return to the wilderness.

There is a new opponent to Scrappy staying with his New Owners, however, and it's simply the outrageously high cost of his dog food bills. The New Owners' kids cry and lament they don't want to lose their new dog because they love him, but the parents retort they simply cannot afford him anymore. They plan to bring him to the pound. The night before they bring him, there is a new opponent in the form of an attempted break-in to their home. This is the decisive test which will determine if Scrappy can stay in the New Owners home (and subsequently find a forever home, his real object). **Scrappy summons the same emotions he used to kill Mad Dog McKill and gets the courage to chase away the would-be crooks and saves the family, but not before taking a bullet.** They rush Scrappy to the animal hospital, nervous and sad he's going to die, but Scrappy is saved by the vet. Scrappy has passed the decisive test, protecting his New Owners in a major way that qualifies him to live there forever.

The New Owners are on the news talking about Scrappy's heroic save of his family and how he took a bullet for them. They get sad as they praise Scrappy (thymic) because they still can't afford him. Viewers of the news program as helpers send in enough money so the New Owners can afford to feed and take care of him for life. The family decides they are going to keep Scrappy, using the newfound money donated by news viewers to feed him. The decisive test is now complete in that Scrappy has a forever home with New Owners even though it's a modification of his original goal to return to his original Owners.

Meanwhile, the original Owners have seen the newscast about Scrappy saving the family and recognize him and marvel in his heroics. They decide they want him back. The original Owners are the subject with the object of getting Scrappy back, and they set out with a new mini-contract to retrieve him, offering the New Owners a lot of money, a mini-qualifying test to see if they can convince the New Owners to give them back Scrappy and achieve their decisive test of getting Scrappy back home and then achieve their own mini-glorifying test of enjoying his love again.

When the original Owners show up and try and claim Scrappy and offer money to get him back, Scrappy recognizes them but he decides the New Owners need him more. He growls at the original Owners to discourage them from taking him. They try to ignore Scrappy's growls and go to touch him and he snaps at them. Their tests to retrieve him have failed, and the original Owners see Scrappy with his new family and get emotional but have to leave him there. Scrappy has found his new forever home. In essence, this event becomes a new decisive test for Scrappy and has evolved from his original decisive test (to return home). This real overall decisive test has been won, manifest in resolution that he will live in the joy and comfort of his new loving forever family.

Scrappy has given up on the idea of returning to his original Owners and decides to stay with his New Owners, realizing that they love him more than his original Owners

claimed to love him. Scrappy acknowledges they didn't love him, especially given they were so willing to give him up. Together, Scrappy and his New Owners are both joyous that he survived and chose them as his forever family, as Scrappy basks in the joy of the love of his new forever family. This proves to be his glorifying test of the story. *He is a joyous dog.*

6

The Breakdown of Three Specimen Movies

I have chosen to break down three specimen movies, including a traditional Hollywood movie (*It's a Wonderful Life*), a female directed/female protagonist movie with an "indie" vibe (*Lost in Translation*), and finally something from contemporary Black Cinema (*Get Out*). They are all masterpieces, and I encourage you to see every one of them (along with *Rocky* and *The Wizard of Oz*) to be able to appreciate the full depth of this study.

Eventually when in pursuit of your own semiotics guided writing practice, you'll want to select at least three specimen movies of your own to break down. Perhaps as a prescription on how to do so, consider the simple formula I used to select the three specimen movies of this study: Choose one classical movie you love (*It's a Wonderful Life*), then pick one specimen movie close to the one you're trying to write (*Lost in Translation*), which for me is "close" to the demo I created to test the tools of the book (*Through the Night*, see Chapter 7). And finally, select a movie that is completely different—perhaps even a different genre like *Get Out*—preferably one like *Get Out*, which utilizes the **semiotic square of veridiction**, an additional semiotic writing tool and by extension another analytic technique that I'll discuss later.

Specimen #1– *It's a Wonderful Life*

Traditional, White, Patriarchal Hollywood Cinema

TITLE: *It's a Wonderful Life*
GENRE: Comedy, Drama
SUBGENRE: Fantasy
SCREENWRITERS: Frances Goodrich, Albert Hackett, Frank Capra
Based on "The Greatest Gift" by Philip Van Doren Stern
DIRECTOR: Frank Capra
LOG LINE: A man dreams of living an adventurous life but is thwarted by having a family and helping his community, and he sees, through his guardian angel, what life would've been like without him, and that his life is worth living.

The Surface Level—Cataloging Isotopies[1]

In analysing *It's a Wonderful Life*, I was surprised by the sheer number of isotopies I was able to log from it. It's a very "busy" movie. It's particularly instructive for me to glance at some of the isotopies and think about the plot and individual scenes as a whole, in conjunction with me contemplating a mere isotopy of the movie. In general, I tend to study the isotopies of a specimen movie first as I try and ascertain the semiotic square for said movie, which has proven to be a good workflow for me.

So, while the cataloging of isotopies can seem tedious, it's a very important exercise to do in order to understand the isotopic particles and how they form the dynamic story of your specimen movie on the surface level of story. Hopefully, you already know the movie *It's a Wonderful Life*, so when you peruse its rich wealth of isotopies, you can start to see how the story is evoked by them and in doing so come to a greater understanding of what story is (the narrative level) and how meaning is delivered (the deep level of meaning).

Table 6.1 Isotopies (Objects, Places, Time, Events/Holidays)—*It's a Wonderful LIfe*

OBJECTS	
Christmas card "One Horse Open Sleigh"	winter hats
Christmas card credits with Santa and director Frank Capra's credit	shovel "sleds"
	wish machine in drugstore
Bedford Falls sign	glass divider in Gower's drugstore
talking star cluster	Gower's booze bottle
angel's wings (never seen)	shoelaces
small megaphone	loose change to buy shoelaces

[1]For *It's a Wonderful Life*, I'll also take the opportunity to set up and explain all the components of the specimen breakdowns and then continue to deliver the next two specimens without the same explication as it can be inferred from this first one and applied to the other two.

bows in girls' hair
cash register
fountain drink dispenser, glass, scoop
chocolate ice cream
National Geographic magazine
shredded coconut
ice cream spoon
Gower's cigar
war telegraph of Gower's son's death
jar of poison
pill boxes
photo of Gower's son
pills on floor
jar of poison
sign "Ask Dad, he knows"
strings on fingers as reminders
Potter's wheelchair and blanket covering his
    legs
Peter Bailey sign on door
old analog phone
George's bleeding ear
freeze frame of adult George Bailey
small luggage
old secondhand suitcase with George's name
    on it
street outside Bailey building
Violet's dress
Ernie's cab
shaking chandelier
broom
pies Harry carries
George's dinner
Bedford Falls High School Class Of 1928 party
    sign
cup prize for Charleston contest
button to open swimming pool
key to unlock swimming pool button
swimming pool
#3 football shirt borrowed for George
white robe borrowed for Mary
wet clothes
rock
old Granville House (as object NOT place)
pipe
newspaper
the moon
hydrangea bushes
automobile
legal documents
black mourning armband
loan document
portrait of Peter Bailey
accountant's hat
travel guide

corsage
train
bags
popcorn
photo cameras at Bailey house
Uncle Billy's hat
cigarette and match
sound of train whistle
newspaper
train ticket
stick
Mary's house's mailbox
mirror Mary checks her hair in
drawing of "George Lassos the Moon"
Victrola
record of "Buffalo Gals"
fence gate to Mary's house
George's wristwatch
tiny model house
train tickets
wedding flowers
bridal bouquet
wedding rice
umbrellas
wedding car/"Just Married" sign
wedding champagne gift
stack of cash for honeymoon
gate to Bailey Building and Loan building
booze bottle
sweat rag
sign: "All you can take with you is that which
    you've given away."
customer bankbooks
"Own Your Own Home" sign
police sirens
ledger for loans
basket with 2 dollars in it
safe
wedding cigars
bridal suite sign
chickens turning in fireplace
Time To Retire "Get a Fisk" poster
exotic vacation travel posters
candlelight dinner
record player turning the chickens on a spit
Martini moving truck
Martini's furniture
goat
wood sign "Welcome to Bailey Park"
loaf of bread
container of salt
bottle of wine
city real estate planning maps

(*Continued*)

Table 6.1 *Continued*

OBJECTS

intercom
mink stole
Wainwright's limo
Wainwright's chauffeur
George's old car
expensive cigar
expensive lighter
wallpaper
wallpaper tool
sign "Checking Station Recruit Reception
    Center"
sewing machine
plastic hoods for planes
draft notices
tank
Army rifle and uniform
multitude of planes with paratroopers jumping
exploding planes
flying bullets
sign for Tires/Gasoline
air raid whistle and costume
stacks of newspapers
wheelbarrows of scrap metal
rubber tires in rubber drives
sign outside of church calling for special prayers
    as requested by President Harry Truman
newspapers with front page of news showing
    President decorating Harry Bailey
black band around George's arm
bank examiner's briefcase
stack of $8,000 for deposit
fountain pen
trash can
cash to Violet
mess of papers in Uncle Billy's office
Merry Christmas sign in George's living room
Janie's piano
baby's mask
Christmas tree star
tinsel
muffins from the oven
Zuzu's flower
petals from Zuzu's flower
glass of water for flower
tree George crashes into
bridge (also PLACE)
water under bridge (also PLACE)
tollhouse keeper's light
clothesline in tollhouse
cups of tea
wet clothes
Tom Sawyer novel

seat that tollhouse keeper falls off of
tollhouse door that blows open
cash register with bell ringing
Pottersville sign
Harry's tombstone 1911–1919
Burt's gun
piece of staircase that comes off
telegram from Sam Wainwright
adding machine
ringing bell on Christmas tree
kid's baseball gear
old automobile
horse-drawn carriage
dance bid card

PLACES

Christmas card snowy landscape
wintery Christmas scene street
Gower Drugs
Martini's bar
auto garage
George's mother's house
George's house
outer space
black screen when Clarence looks at George's
    past life
iced lake
hole in the iced lake
sunny street
Bailey Building and Loan building
luggage store
high school gymnasium
walk to Mary's house
old Granville House
train station
street outside Bijou theater
Mary's house
Mary's living room
Sam Wainwright's office
Potter's home office
in front of Martini's house
Martini's new block
sewing center USO
train for soldiers
Sam Wainwright's plastic factory
military recruitment scene outside County Court
    House
recruiting military officer
North Africa Second World War battlefield
paratrooper air raid over France
Remagen Bridge
outside a Navy airplane

Office of Price Administration (World War Two)
window of man's bedroom
outside newspaper building
dumping grounds
streets outside Capitol building in DC
inside Catholic church
bank
bank teller window
George's office
Uncle Billy's house
Zuzu's bedroom
inside Martini's bar
tollhouse
Pottersville
Nick's bar (was Martini's)
outside Nick's bar in snow
main street of Pottersville with bars, billiard
    halls, etc.
burlesque club in Pottersville
"dime-a-dance" hall
inside Ernie Bishop's Pottersville cab

320 Sycamore in Pottersville
Ma Bailey's Boarding House
cemetery formerly Bailey Park
Pottersville Public Library
bridge
water under bridge
talking star clusters

TIME
10:45 p.m. "Earth Time"*
waiting 200 years to win wings
1919 (when George was 12)
December 24th
morning before Christmas 10:00 a.m. Bedford
    Falls time

EVENTS/HOLIDAYS
Christmas
Harry's high school graduation
    party
George and Mary's wedding

---

* Earth Time, most probably Eastern Standard Time, is considered "Earth Time" even though there are 24 time zones on planet earth.

Table 6.2 Isotopies (Actors)—*It's a Wonderful Life*

ACTORS

Joseph the angel
Lead angel (as talking star cluster)
Clarence
Young George Bailey
Young Harry Bailey (George's brother)
Marty
Young Mary
Young Violet
Annie (Bailey housekeeper)
Ma Bailey (George's mother)
Peter Bailey (George's father)
Uncle Billy Bailey
Bailey dog
high school graduation party orchestra
Mr. Partridge (high school graduation party
    MC)
Sam Wainwright
Marty Hatch
Freddie Othello
man on porch
Dr. Campbell
Mr. Potter
Potter's bodyguard
Jimmy the Crow
Ernie Bishop

Cousin Tilly
Cousin Eustace
Ruth Dakin Bailey
Violet's boyfriend
crowd listening to George talk to Violet
Mrs. Hatch (Mary's mother)
Sam Wainwright
wedding guests
mob on bank run
Miss Davis
Charlie
Tom
Ed
Ernie Bishop
neighbors moving Martini
Giuseppe Martini
Mrs. Martini
Martini's children
Red Cross nurses
soldiers on train
officers visiting Sam Wainwright
soldiers storming Remagen Bridge
crowd at Office of Price Administration
man in window
kids helping with paper drive

(*Continued*)

Table 6.2 *Continued*

men moving metal scraps	crowd around Mary
kids rolling tires for rubber drive	kids running on Martini's new block
churchgoers	Jane Wainwright
squirrel	real estate salesman
Mrs. Welch	nurse
Mr. Welch	baby Bailey
Nick	soldiers marching to enlist
tollhouse keeper	cop arresting violent Violet in Pottersville
barrellhouse piano player	bank examiner
Nick's bouncer	Eustace
panhandling Gower	Horace the bank teller
mean Nick bar owner	man whose great grandfather planted tree
angry Violet in Pottersville	man in truck who almost hits George
cops in Pottersville	churchgoers on VE day
ghost of Clarence the angel	recruiting military officer
Ma Bailey in Pottersville	Potter's secretary
old maid Mary	kids: Janie, Tommy, Pete, Zuzu

Cataloging the isotopies in *It's a Wonderful Life* allowed me to easily come up with the "master semiotic square," including its controlling binary opposition terms. Knowing the movie as well as I do, I'm astonished that by merely glancing at the isotopies, so much of the movie's story is easily evoked. In essence, you can say the isotopies are rich in narrative intent, but that is because I'm extracting them from a whole movie with a great story, so the narrative intent I derived from them is something I hold in my brain (competent observer) and can "bring it together" instantly by looking at an isotopy of the story. It's via this concept and technique that I'm training my story brain to write my own stories. For an example, take a simple isotopy from the table of "objects" like "a scoop of ice cream." There's nothing in that isotopy which particularly points to the *It's a Wonderful Life* story, especially if a reader doesn't know the movie's story. However, I've seen the movie often, and when I think of that isotopy of the ice cream scoop, I'm led to think about Young George Bailey dishing it up to Young Mary as he cockily talks about his big dreams, all of which evoke the entire story, theme, and meaning. In other words, this single isotopy is rich in narrative intent. But you must be a competent observer to bring it together; it's in this action you can sense the story, the narrative intent. In this way, the concept of "narrative intent" is rather paradoxical. You really see it in isotopies when you know the story they are pointing to but nevertheless they are still pointing to a story.

Give it a try; if you know *It's a Wonderful Life* well (as anyone who owns a television does), look at any of the isotopies and take note how easy it is to use one or all of them as individual particles in their "pre-meaning" state to then think of the whole story. But remember, an isotopic particle is merely just a particle. This knowledge of narrative intent in the particles of the isotopies is a great lesson to behold.

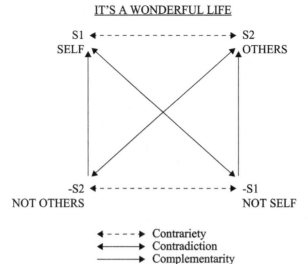

Figure 6.1 Master semiotic square—*It's a Wonderful Life.*

Oppositions of Isotopies of *It's a Wonderful Life*

Now it's time to see if we can apply different binary oppositions to *It's a Wonderful Life* regarding its isotopies I've cataloged. I see this process as having two different methods, both contributing to our overall breakdown and brainstorming initiative. First, of course, I need to establish the controlling binary opposition terms of the movie's semiotic square. I determine the terms self vs. others to be the most effective terms for this movie. The reason for this is simple: Early in the movie, George Bailey makes noises about wanting to travel, work exotic jobs in far flung locations, etc., which would amount to George serving himself (self). The "others" side of the equation is George's community and family, which he, in the end, winds up serving, and it is in recognizing the value of this path that the entire movie's meaning comes into focus.

First, I need to simply recatalog the main isotopies in the standard semantic categories of object, place, events, time and actors but do so using the movie's master semiotic square and its controlling binary opposition terms (self) vs. (others), the S1 and S2 of the story.

Logging Isotopies to Either Side of the Controlling Binary Opposition Terms of the Master Semiotic Square

Now I will see first what different categories of isotopies can be *associated* with either side of the master controlling terms, self and others. The isotopies themselves will not necessarily be in binary opposition (more on this later), but they can be associated with either side of the different binary terms controlling the movie story. In some instances, I was able to have isotopies also in direct binary opposition on the opposite side (as will be demonstrated shortly).

Overall, what's important about this phase of the study is to learn to use the semiotics tools to think through a specimen movie and learn about narrative intent via binary opposition.

But note, what's on one side of the columns (self) and directly to its right the other side of the columns (others) isn't necessarily in direct binary opposition to one another per se. I just cataloged and placed what relevant isotopies I thought "belonged" on one side of the table (or binary opposition term) and the same with the isotopies I place on the other side. My cataloging of isotopies of *It's a Wonderful Life* and distributing them to either side of the movie's controlling semiotic square via its opposing binary opposition terms has led me to recognize there is a need for a secondary semiotic square to capture what happens in the third act of the story. This in no way negates the significance of the master semiotic square and its main binary opposition terms (self vs. others), but this technique allows for me to break down the movie a little further, affording me additional information to help fully capture and comprehend the beautiful architecture of this movie.

Table 6.3 Isotopies in binary opposition based on master semiotic square (Objects)—*It's a Wonderful Life*

OBJECTS**

SELF (GEORGE)	vs.	OTHERS (COMMUNITY)*
cash register		Christmas card "One Horse Open Seigh"
fountain drink dispenser, glass, scoop		Christmas card credits with Santa with director
chocolate ice cream		Frank Capra's credit
National Geographic magazine		Bedford Falls sign
shredded coconut		talking star clusters (also PLACE)
secondhand suitcase with George's		angel's wings (never seen)
name on it		wish machine in drugstore
Bedford Falls High School Class Of 1928		glass divider in Gower's drugstore
party sign		Gower's booze bottle
#3 football shirt borrowed for George		shoelaces
white robe borrowed for Mary		loose change to buy shoelaces
wet clothes		bows in girls' hair
small megaphone		ice cream spoon
winter hats		Gower's cigar
shovel "sleds"		war telegraph of Gower's son's death
Ernie's cab		jar of poison
pies Harry carries		pill boxes
photo cameras at Bailey house		photo of Gower's son
shaking chandelier		pills on floor
cup prize for Charleston contest		jar of poison
old Granville House (as OBJECT *not*		sign "Ask Dad, he knows"
PLACE)		strings on fingers as reminders
the moon		Peter Bailey sign on door
travel guide		old analog phone
train ticket		George's bleeding ear
Violet's dress		freeze frame of adult George Bailey
expensive lighter		small luggage
expensive cigar		old secondhand suitcase with George's name on it
Potter's wheelchair and blanket covering		street outside Bailey building
his legs		broom

George's dinner
button to open swimming pool
key to unlock swimming pool button
swimming pool
rock
pipe
newspaper
hydrangea bushes
automobile
legal documents
black mourning armband
loan document
portrait of Peter Bailey
Jimmy the Crow (also as ACTOR)
accountant's hat
corsage
train
bags
popcorn
Uncle's Billy's hat
cigarette and match
sound of train whistle
newspaper
train ticket
stick
Mary's house's mailbox
mirror Mary checks her hair in
drawing of "George Lassos the Moon"
Victrola
record of "Buffalo Gals"
fence gate to Mary's house
George's wristwatch
tiny model house
train tickets
wedding flowers
bridal bouquet
wedding rice
umbrellas
rain
wedding car/"Just Married" sign
wedding champagne gift
stack of cash for honeymoon
gate to Bailey Building and Loan building
booze bottle
sweat rag
sign: "All you can take with you is that which
    you've given away."
customer bankbooks
"Own Your Own Home" sign
police sirens
ledger for loans
basket with 2 dollars in it
safe
wedding cigars
bridal suite sign

(Continued)

Table 6.3 *Continued*

OBJECTS**		
SELF (GEORGE)	**vs.**	**OTHERS (COMMUNITY)**
		chickens turning in fireplace
		Time To Retire "Get a Fisk" poster
		exotic vacation travel posters
		candlelight dinner
		record player turning the chickens on a spit
		Martini moving truck
		Martini's furniture
		goat
		wood sign "Welcome to Bailey Park"
		loaf of bread
		container of salt
		bottle of wine
		city real estate planning maps
		intercom
		mink stole
		Wainwright's limo
		Wainwright's chauffeur
		George's old car
		wallpaper
		wallpaper tool
		sign "Checking Station Recruit Reception Center"
		sewing machine
		plastic hoods for planes
		draft notices
		tank
		army rifle and uniform
		multitude of planes with paratroopers jumping
		exploding planes
		flying bullets
		sign for Tires/Gasoline
		air raid whistle and costume
		stacks of newspapers
		wheelbarrows of scrap metal
		rubber tires in rubber drives
		sign outside of church calling for special prayers as requested by President Harry Truman
		newspapers with front page of news showing President decorating Harry Bailey
		black band around George's arm
		bank examiner's briefcase
		stack of $8,000 for deposit
		fountain pen
		trash can
		cash to Violet
		mess of papers in Uncle Billy's office
		Merry Christmas sign in George's living room
		Janie's piano
		baby's mask
		Christmas tree star
		tinsel

muffins from the oven
Zuzu's flower
petals from Zuzu's flower
glass of water for flower
tree George crashes into
bridge
water under bridge
tollhouse keeper's light
clothesline in toll house
cups of tea
wet clothes
Tom Sawyer novel
seat tollhouse keeper falls off of
tollhouse door that blows open
cash register with bell ringing
Pottersville sign
Harry's tombstone 1911–1919
Burt's gun
piece of staircase that comes off
telegram from Sam Wainwright
adding machine
ringing bell on Christmas tree
kid's baseball gear
old automobile
horse-drawn carriage
dance bid card

* Note: Most objects fall on the side of "others." This is how this movie is designed . . . it's heavy on set-up and exposition in the first two acts, building towards the brilliant third act, which postulates that George never existed or in semiotics terms, when George is in absentia (absent).

** In these charts, I place isotopies on the side of the terms from the semiotic square I believe them to be associated with. Therefore, "side by side" on this chart doesn't mean they are specifically in binary opposition item by item but in general belong to one side of the controlling binary opposition terms or its opposite.

Table 6.4 Isotopies in binary opposition (Places)—*It's a Wonderful Life*

PLACES*

SELF	vs.	OTHERS
sunny street		black screen when Clarence looks at George's past
iced lake		life
hole in the iced lake		outer space
Gower Drugs (when George was a kid)		Gower Drugs with George as an adult
old Granville House		old Granville House when Mary is making it home
George's Mother's house		Mary's house
		Mary's living room
		Zuzu's bedroom
George's office		Sam Wainwright's office

(Continued)

Table 6.4 *Continued*

PLACES*		
SELF	**vs.**	**OTHERS**
Bailey Building and Loan building high school gymnasium Uncle Billy's house in front of Martini's house Potter's office street outside Bijou theater		
Office of Price Administration (World War Two) train for soldiers military recruitment scene outside County Court House sewing center USO		Sam Wainwright's plastic factory North Africa Second World War battlefield paratrooper air raid over France Remagen Bridge outside a Navy airplane outside newspaper building dumping grounds for scrap rubber streets outside Capitol building in DC

* For isotopies of place, I found it easier to find direct binary oppositions as demonstrated above. For example, starting with the first three instances above ("sunny street, iced up lake, hole in the iced up lake"), these can be seen as directly contrary to the "black screen which appears when Clarence looks at George's past life." George's Mother's house is in direct binary opposition to Mary's house, etc. I do the best I can to make direct binary oppositions with isotopies where possible; within the semantic category of place, it's easier as demonstrated above. Again, the outcome of this exercise is to think deeply through your specimen movies.

Table 6.5 Isotopies in binary oppositions (Actors)—*It's a Wonderful Life*

ACTORS		
SELF	**vs.**	**OTHERS**
Sam Wainwright Harry Bailey Mr. Potter*		George
Sam Wainwright's wife Harry Bailey's wife Violet		Mary

* Specifically when Potter offers George a lucrative deal to cross over to his side.

Secondary Category of Binary Opposition Terms for *It's a Wonderful Life*[2]

Now that we know the controlling terms of the master semiotic square for *It's a Wonderful Life* are self and others, I would like to introduce a related secondary category of binary opposition terms that will help me analyze the story; namely, the terms present/absent.

This new pair of binary opposition terms is related to the self/others master terms but pertains specifically to Act 3, which is a prolonged decisive test for the story. I devised these two additional terms based on George Bailey getting his wish and seeing what life would be like if he never existed.

Table 6.6 Isotopies in binary opposition—Objects (Present/Absent)—*It's a Wonderful Life*

OBJECTS

PRESENT	vs.	ABSENT
Zuzu's petals		Zuzu's petals not in his pocket
George's bloody lip		George's not bloodied lip
tree George smashed into with wound		tree not wounded
George's car		car not there
restored Granville Home (George and Mary's house)		dilapidated run-down Granville house

Table 6.7 Isotopies in binary oppositions—Places (Present/Absent)—*It's a Wonderful Life*

PLACES

PRESENT	vs.	ABSENT
Bedford Falls sign		Pottersville sign
Martini's bar		Nick's bar (was Martini's)
		outside Nick's bar in snow
main street of Bedford Falls with movie theater, Building and Loan building		main street of Pottersville with bars, billiard halls, etc.
		burlesque club in Pottersville
		"dime-a-dance" hall
inside Ernie Bishop's cab (Bedford Falls)		inside Ernie Bishop's cab (Pottersville)
George and Mary's house after restoring it		320 Sycamore in Pottersville (old Granville house)
George Bailey's childhood home		Ma Bailey's boarding house
Bailey Park		cemetery formerly Bailey Park
		Pottersville Public Library

[2]Sometimes inventing a secondary category of binary opposition terms can facilitate a breakdown, as is the case with the very idiosyncratic "third act" of *It's a Wonderful Life*. Remember, regarding *Semiotics for Screenwriters*, there are no hard and fast rules . . . it's what you deem is necessary and useful to make the best analytic breakdown of your specimen movie that will be your guiding overarching principle of how to use these tools.

Table 6.8 Isotopies in binary opposition—Actors (Present/Absent)—*It's a Wonderful Life*

ACTORS		
PRESENT	**vs.**	**ABSENT**
Mr. Gower		panhandling Mr. Gower
Nick		mean Nick bar owner
nice Violet		angry Violet in Pottersville
Burt the cop singing for George's honeymoon		Burt the cop in Pottersville
Ma Bailey		Ma Bailey's in Pottersville
Mary at her house		old maid Mary
friends of George trying to help him at bar		Nick's bouncer
crowd around George and Mary at the high school dance		crowd around old maid Mary as she screams
crowds who laugh at George discouraging Violet wanting to date him		crowd around Violet as she screams being chased out of a "dime-a-dance" hall

Table 6.9 Isotopies in binary opposition—Events/Celebrations (Present/Absent)—*It's a Wonderful Life*

EVENTS/CELEBRATIONS		
PRESENT	**vs.**	**ABSENT**
Christmas Eve, Bedford Falls		Christmas Eve, Pottersville

Special Binary Oppositions within General Semantic Categories

My wish is to see if any of the isotopies present specifically in binary opposition within a range of different general semantic categories beyond the two controlling terms of the master controlling semiotic square. Again, I'm extending my breakdown and cataloging of the movie's isotopies with this additional lens based on my instincts. Finding different ways of breaking down isotopies can force us to think hard about the movie's isotopies and their narrative intent, and subsequently allow us to absorb the movie's narrative mechanisms.

The first term I would like to itemize is the special isotopic category which is time/ durativeness. There are several mentions of different "times" in the movie, and the contrast between the two ideas of time are striking, as this points up to the mechanism of how the narrative works in that the third act of the movie which culminates in a "magical time" of George seeing the world *without* him (absent). This stark contrast between real time (earth) and Clarence the angel's time (heaven) helps set up the logical possibility of the magical third act time of a world without George in the mind of the audience. See the tables below.

Table 6.10 Isotopies in binary opposition (other semantic categories)—*It's a Wonderful Life*

OPPOSITION OF TIME/DURATIVENESS		
HEAVEN (DURATIVENESS)	**vs.**	**EARTH (TIME)**
waiting 200 years to win wings		10:45 p.m. Earth Time.
		1919 (when George was 12)
		December 24th (Christmas Eve)
		1911–1919 (written on grave)
		end of the Second World War

Table 6.11 Isotopies in binary opposition (other semantic categories)—*It's a Wonderful Life*

PLACES		
OUTDOORS	**vs.**	**INDOORS**
outer space		Nick's Bar
frozen lake		
main street of Bedford Falls		

Table 6.12 Isotopies in binary opposition (other semantic categories)—*It's a Wonderful Life*

STREETS	vs.	OUTSIDE
streets of Bedford Falls		outside Mary's house

Table 6.13 Isotopies in binary opposition (other Semantic Categories)—*It's a Wonderful Life*

HEAVENLY	vs.	EARTHLY
stars		water under bridge

Table 6.14 Isotopies in binary opposition (other semantic categories)—*It's a Wonderful Life*

PARENTAL DOMESTIC DWELLING	vs.	MARITAL DOMESTIC DWELLING
Mary's parlor		George and Mary's home

Table 6.15 Isotopies in binary opposition (other semantic categories)—*It's a Wonderful Life*

ACTORS

YOUNG	vs.	OLD
Young George		adult George
Young Harry		adult Harry
Young Mary		adult Mary/old maid Mary
Young Violet		adult Violet

Table 6.16 Isotopies in binary opposition (other semantic categories)—*It's a Wonderful Life*

MEN	vs.	WOMEN
George		Mary
Harry		Violet
Potter		Ma Bailey
Uncle Billy		Mary's mother
Pa Bailey		Harry's wife

These are just a sampling of possible additional special binary opposition categories I can conjure up *within* general semantic categories of opposition. There can be many more, but you get the idea; it all helps you deconstruct and understand how the story works.

Isotopies—States of Being

As stated previously, I track states of being on the surface level as well as on the narrative level because states of being are powerful in terms of ascertaining how movie story comes together and works, hence the "double treatment." States of being evoke (and portray) the emotional life of the characters, so it's good to view them as isotopic particles (pre-meaning) and as well as on the narrative level because the effect of states of being are predicated on narrative syntax (what follows what).

States of being should be examined at both the surface level of a specimen *and* then at the narrative level because the surface level is the first opportunity you might have to look at disconnected emotional building blocks of a movie and then the narrative level allows you insight into the cause *and* effect power these states of being derive by the syntax of the narrative. In other words, an actor's emotion is created in the mind of a competent observer by what has followed from the preceding scenes in conjuction with the current scene where emotion is being experienced. Or as William Goldman liked to say, "Screenplays are structure." It's the structure that generates emotional beats, aka states of being and only structure can make them work.

States of being, as I mentioned earlier, represent a crucial element of movie story because they are the foundation of the *emotional life of the characters*. States of being are a unique isotopy because unlike most of the other isotopies (objects, places, actors), which represent the "things" of story, and the next set of isotopies (events, time), which aren't material "things" but nevertheless do feel tangible as "things" of story. By contrast, states of being are emotional states and hence represent a more abstract form of isotopy and perhaps can be viewed as even a tad more subjective than other kinds of isotopies.

So in keeping with the magic of all the isotopic breakdown processes, the process of tracking and logging states of being on the surface level of your specimen movies will stimulate your unconscious and help you gather understanding of narrative intent as materials to formulate rich stories and dynamic characters in your own screenplays. You'll also get double duty from decoding states of being when you analyze them again on the narrative level, tracking *how* their power is generated by the syntax of the story's structure.

As usual, I capture the raw isotopies first *then* see how I can log them to unique binary opposition category of euphoria/dysphoria. First, a look at the raw states of being in *It's a Wonderful Life*. (Note: This list represents my first impression of states of being in the movie. Later on, when I'm writing the different components for this specimen, I might have tweaked or evolved them. I believe we should capture raw states of being when breaking down a movie just the way we capture raw isotopies.)

States of Being —*It's a Wonderful Life* (First Pass)

- *Prayerful concern and love for George.*
- *Clarence is excited that he can get his wings.*
- *Young Mary expresses love until the day she dies for George.*
- *Mr. Gower is drunk and distraught with death of son.*
- *Mr. Gower realizes via Young George his mistake that he put poison in the pills he dispensed and embraces Young George crying.*
- *George is excited when he first sees adult Mary.*
- *Mary is excited when she first sees adult George.*
- *They are having exhilarated fun dancing the Charleston at the gym.*
- *The crowd is exhilarated watching George and Mary dance near the edge of the pool.*
- *George is excited to tell Mary about getting out of Bedford Falls with big plans.*
- *Mary is concerned about George's father's stroke.*
- *Uncle Billy is angry at Mr. Potter for wanting to dissolve the Building and Loan.*
- *George passionately dismisses Potter's attempt to dissolve the Bailey Building and Loan.*
- *George is distressed he can't leave for college and must take over from his father and run the Building and Loan in order to preserve it.*
- *George and Uncle Billy are happy about Harry's marriage to Ruth.*
- *George is concerned as he contemplates what it means that his brother is married and has a job offer.*

- Violet is distressed about George's "date" idea.
- Mary is frustrated and angry at George for rejecting her and smashes the "Buffalo Gals" record from the record player.
- As George and Mary listen to Sam on the phone, George smells her hair, and they both get turned on.
- George expresses anger about not wanting to get married.
- Mary cries over George's anger about not wanting to get married.
- George and Mary kiss and embrace and profess their love after George got angry.
- The crowd is exhilarated after George and Mary's wedding at church.
- George expresses joy when discussing his honeymoon plans in Ernie's cab.
- George is happy that Miss Davis only needs $17.50.
- George and co-workers are exhilarated they didn't have to close their doors before 6 p.m., and then he realizes he forgot about Mary.
- George and Mary kiss, and have a romantic bonding moment.
- Mary and George embrace as she emotionally expresses that she wished for the old Granville house to be their new home.
- Burt annoyedly bops Ernie on the head for kissing him after singing.
- Giuseppe Martini is overjoyed about his new house acquisition.
- George is frustrated he can't drive down to Florida with Sam Wainwright and kicks the door.
- George is nervously excited having learned Mary is pregnant.
- George angrily berates Uncle Billy for losing the $8,000 deposit.
- George begs Potter to loan him the $8,000 dollars to cover the lost money.
- George emotionally hugs his son on Christmas Eve and has a mini-breakdown.
- George angrily almost smashes broken piece on staircase.
- George berates Zuzu's teacher Mrs. Welch on phone for letting Zuzu walk home with her coat open.
- George berates Mr. Welch for his wife's actions of letting her student Zuzu walk home with her jacket open.
- George angrily knocks down a model bridge he had built in his living room.
- George emotionally prays to God for help.
- Mr. Welch angrily yells at George after punching him in a bar.
- George is about to jump off the bridge to commit suicide.
- Clarence jumps in first, screaming for help, and George dives in to save him.
- Nick angrily berates Clarence for his drink order.
- George angrily berates Clarence for telling him he has a gift by having a chance to see what the world would be like without him.
- Violet screams violently as she's dragged into custody by police.
- George frantically yells out for his wife and children at the old, dilapidated Granville house.
- George desperately tries to convince Burt and Ernie that he knows them, recalling when they sung for him on his wedding night.

- *Burt yells in pain as Clarence bites his hand.*
- *George fearfully contemplates his mother not knowing him and learns that Uncle Billy is now in an insane asylum.*
- *George emotionally pleads to Clarence about Mary's whereabouts.*
- *Clarence emotionally yells to George disclosing Mary's whereabouts.*
- *George emotionally pleads with Mary trying to make sense of what is going on.*
- *Mary screams fearfully as a response to George pleading with her.*
- *Mary screams and almost passes out.*
- *Burt the cop shows up, George angrily punches Burt, who fires at him as George runs away.*
- *George makes an emotional plea to Clarence to put things back to normal and that he wants to live again.*
- *George angrily threatens to hit Burt again.*
- *George is ecstatic when he realizes Burt knows him, his mouth is still bleeding, and he has Zuzu's petals, all signs point to he's back to existing.*
- *George ecstatically yells hello to his old town Bedford Falls.*
- *George runs and happily yells "Merry Christmas" to townspeople.*
- *George runs and happily yells "Merry Christmas" to familiar old buildings.*
- *George happily yells "Merry Christmas" to Mr. Potter.*
- *George returns home and happily greets the bank examiner and authorities at his home.*
- *George emotionally kisses the broken piece on the staircase.*
- *George emotionally embraces his children.*
- *Mary emotionally reunites with George.*
- *Mary emotionally prepares George and family for the community with money coming in.*
- *Townspeople happily give George money.*
- *Crowd is ecstatic over telegram from Sam Wainwright advancing George $25,000.*
- *The bank examiner there to arrest George tears up the warrant for his arrest happily.*
- *George winks to the sky and congratulates Clarence.*

States of Being—Euphoria vs. Dysphoria

I now will proceed to log these states of being into the unique binary opposition category of euphoria vs. dysphoria. Of note: I'm placing the various states of being on one side or the other (euphoria vs. dysphoria) attempting to match each one to its direct contrary on the other. That said, these contraries are not always a perfect match in terms of both the states of being working in *exact* binary opposition to the one on the opposite side. Some will exist as stand-alone (but still listed under their proper binary opposition term) without necessarily having a contrary binary opposition *state of being* on the immediate other side. Remember, as always, the purpose of performing these specific breakdowns is to force you to think about the emotional journey of the actors and how the emotional beats of the actor's journey exist pre-meaning first (as isotopies) and then in a narrative syntax from whence they derive their full power and contextual meaning. Incidentally, this technique is a great brainstorming tool for understanding how to control the tone of your movie as well.

Table 6.17 States of being in binary opposition—*It's a Wonderful Life*

EUPHORIA	vs. DYSPHORIA
• *Clarence is excited that he can get his wings.*	• *Prayerful concern and love for George.*
• *Young Mary expresses love until the day she dies for George.*	• *George emotionally pleads with Mary trying to make sense of what is going on.*
• *George is excited when he first sees adult Mary.*	• *Mary screams fearfully as a response to George pleading with her.*
• *George and Mary kiss and embrace and profess their love after George got angry.*	• *Mary screams and almost passes out.*
• *George is nervously excited having learned Mary is pregnant.*	
• *George passionately dismisses Potters attempt to dissolve the Bailey Building and Loan.*	• *George begs Potter to loan him the $8,000 dollars to cover the lost money.*
	• *George is distressed he can't leave for college and must take over from his father and run the Building and Loan in order to preserve it.*
	• *George is concerned as he contemplates what it means that his brother is married and has a job offer.*
• *They are having exhilarated fun dancing the Charleston at the gym.*	• *Mary is frustrated and angry at George for rejecting her and smashes the "Buffalo Gals" record from the record player.*
• *The crowd is exhilarated watching George and Mary dance near the edge of the pool.*	
• *George and Uncle Billy are happy about Harry's marriage to Ruth.*	• *George expresses anger about not wanting to get married.*
• *George and Mary kiss and embrace and profess their love after George got angry.*	• *Mary cries over George's anger about not wanting to get married.*
• *George expresses joy when discussing his honeymoon plans in Ernie's cab.*	• *Burt annoyedly bops Ernie on the head for kissing him after singing.*

- *Giuseppe Martini is overjoyed about his new house acquisition.*

- *Mary and George embrace as she emotionally expresses that she wished for the old Granville house to be their new home.*

- *George and Mary kiss, and have a romantic bonding moment.*

- *George and co-workers are exhilarated they didn't have to close their doors before 6 p.m.*

- *George makes an emotional plea to Clarence to put things back to normal and that he wants to live again.*

- *George is ecstatic when he realizes Burt knows him, his mouth is bleeding, and he has Zuzu's petals, all signs that he's back to existing.*

- *George ecstatically yells hello to his old town Bedford Falls.*

- *George runs and happily yells "Merry Christmas" to townspeople.*

- *George runs and happily yells "Merry Christmas" to familiar old buildings.*

- *George happily yells "Merry Christmas" to Mr. Potter.*

- *George returns home and happily greets the bank examiner and authorities at his home.*

- *George emotionally kisses the broken piece on the staircase.*

- *George emotionally embraces his children.*

- *Mary emotionally reunites with George.*

- *Other townspeople happily give George money.*

- *Crowd is ecstatic over telegram from Sam Wainwright advancing George $25,000.*

- *George desperately tries to convince Burt and Ernie that he knows them, recalling when they sung for him on his wedding night.*

- *George frantically yells out for his wife and children at the old, dilapidated Granville house.*

- *George angrily berates Uncle Billy for losing the $8,000 deposit.*

- *George is on the verge of suicide contemplating jumping into the water.*

- *George emotionally prays to God for help.*

- *George angrily berates Clarence for telling him he has a gift by having a chance to see what the world would be like without him.*

- *Burt the cop shows up, George angrily punches Burt, who fires at him as George runs away*

- *George berates Zuzu's teacher Mrs. Welch on phone for letting Zuzu walk home with her coat open.*

- *George berates Mr. Welch for his wife's actions of letting her student Zuzu walk home with her jacket open.*

- *George emotionally hugs his son on Christmas Eve and has a mini-breakdown.*

- *George angrily knocks down a model bridge he had built in his living room.*

- *Mary screams fearfully as a response to George pleading with her.*

- *Mary screams and almost passes out.*

This ends our breakdown and brief analysis of isotopies in *It's a Wonderful Life*. What I noticed when collecting the isotopies and placing them into either side of the controlling terms (self/others) or logging them to secondary terms (present/absent) or finally when I logged the states of being into either the euphoria or dysphoria columns is that I became more and more aware of how the entire movie is set up to make the final movement (George's decisive test) where George experiences life without him existing as powerful as it can be in that he realizes (as a competent observer in his own story piecing everything together) that he has lived a good life.

Now on to the narrative level.

The Narrative Level of *It's a Wonderful Life*: The Actantial Narrative Schema

My first pass at the master actantial narrative schema depicts Clarence the angel as a *shadow* protagonist who is charged with saving George from suicide.

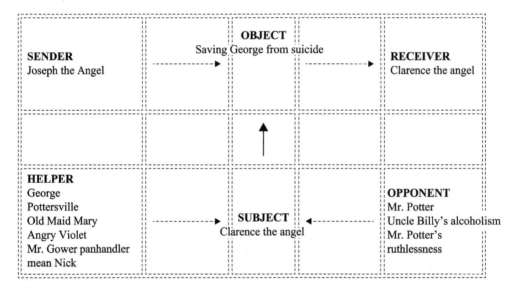

Figure 6.2 Actantial narrative schema 1—*It's a Wonderful Life*. The three different actantial narrative schemas for this movie will basically track the narrative syntax of the story's structure. Often one schema per movie will suffice . . . however, for this movie I felt the need to generate multiple ones, perhaps because of the protagonist/shadow protagonist (George/Clarence the angel) structure.

Since Clarence is merely a *shadow* protagonist to George, who will become the *actual* protagonist, a second master actantial narrative schema is in order and depicted below.

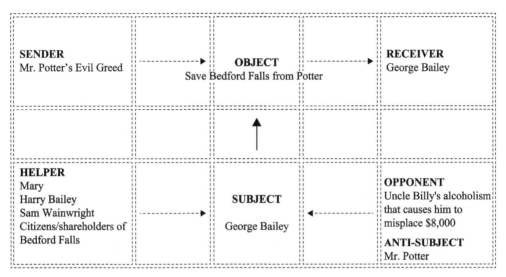

Figure 6.3 Actantial narrative schema 2—*It's a Wonderful Life*.

A third actantial narrative schema (Figure 6.4) covers the third act of the movie where Clarence allows George to "not exist" (be absent) and see what life would've been like without him. George as protagonist/Clarence as shadow protagonist agendas merge.

The fact that I could easily devise three unique actantial narrative schemas for *It's a Wonderful Life* demonstrates that semiotics is *not* a formula, it's a *method* to analyze movie story with in a way that will provide you with excellent brainstorming fodder for your writing. Each movie you break down will have its own needs, quirks, and nuances, and some will have very special breakdown requirements, as we'll see when we look at *Get Out*. The language of the semiotics system and the tools it offers remain the same for each movie, but the methods and insights derived from the individual specimen movies will yield different brainstorming materials for your writing.

Now, on to the canonical narrative schema. *It's a Wonderful Life* is a unique structure in that there is a technical (shadow) protagonist (Clarence the wingless angel) and an *actual* protagonist, George Bailey. Together, they create a shared protagonist. And just as their agendas merged to generate additional actantial narrative schemas, the canonical narrative schema summary will reflect this unique shared protagonist structure as well.

Canonical Narrative Schema Summary—*It's a Wonderful Life*

The first contract occurs when Clarence, George Bailey's guardian angel, is charged with stopping George from committing suicide because George has failed in his life, both to protect his community and family from the evil Mr. Potter and escape home and live a life of adventure. Clarence negotiates a promise to get his "wings" if he succeeds in saving George from suicide—his first contract.

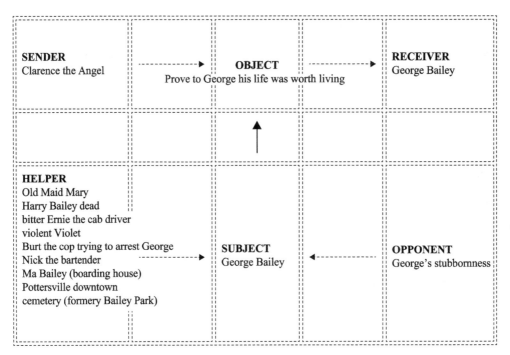

Figure 6.4 Actantial narrative schema 3—*It's a Wonderful Life*

Clarence, a dual protagonist with George, spends the first two-thirds of the movie as an omniscient observer of George, allowing George to eventually "take over" as the actual protagonist. Understanding this "dual protagonist" nature of the movie is key to understanding the schema. As an actual protagonist, George's first contract ever since he was a young boy was his dream to leave town and go out into the world and live a life of adventure. But as we trace adult George's story, we learn his qualifying test to escape town is failing. George meets the beautiful Mary at a school dance, and they partake in the Charleston contest, have a fun fall in the swimming pool, and walk home together singing. George shares his dreams of escaping his hometown with her. They both throw rocks at the old Granville house, smashing windows and making a wish. Their dueling wishes will come to represent the two poles/forces that pull George in two directions; one to leave and live a life of adventure; the opposite pole being his eventual desire to marry Mary, build a life in Bedford Falls, and serve his community. When his father suddenly dies, George's dream of going to college then escaping Bedford Falls is thwarted by having to take over and run the family business, allowing his younger brother to go to college first. When Harry comes back from college, years later, he's married and his wife's father has set Harry up with a career, again thwarting George's plans to get out of town. All of these events can be seen as qualifying tests to leave home, which George is failing.

George visits Mary at her house reluctantly and is angered by his own attraction to her because she represents him settling down, never getting to escape his home. He embraces her first angrily then with passion, which leads to them getting married. In essence, marrying Mary is the last blow to George's original contract, of him escaping town to a life of adventure. His qualifying test, to merely escape home to set up his decisive test to live a life of adventure, is in danger of failing. He won't be able to ever leave home if he marries Mary. His new contract has emerged; namely, to stay in town, build a family with Mary, and serve his community, especially by protecting them from being taken over by evil Mr. Potter. But his failure to execute and play out his original contract to escape Bedford Falls still haunts him and will psychologically spring up throughout the movie, fully reverberating throughout the story, especially in the third and final act when George views what life would've been like if he never existed via the magic of Clarence the angel's powers.

Along these lines, George's first new qualifying test occurs when he and Mary are en route to their honeymoon, and they spot a bank run in progress. George now has a *being able to do something*, which is keep the Building and Loan open until 6:00 p.m. and give every customer the money they need, or else Potter will shut it for good. George and Mary use their honeymoon money to bail out the Building and Loan and save the community from selling out to Potter. They are able to keep the bank open until 6:00 p.m. George has passed his unintentional qualifying test of saving the community from Potter, which will set him up for the ultimate decisive test later to save the community from Potter for good.

This decisive test to save the community from Potter comes when the drunk Uncle Billy accidentally drops the day's deposit of $8,000 ($146,000 in today's money) in Potter's newspaper and later can't recall where he might have misplaced it. This mistake sets up the Building and Loan for criminal charges for misappropriation of funds and eventual closure for good. George is faced with a decisive test of needing to *be able to* retrieve the $8,000 and save the town again, but he fails to find it or raise the money, and that is when he decides to kill himself, with the hint that his life insurance policy will provide for his family.

But right before George can jump in the river, Clarence (who has landed on earth) prepares to step in. Clarence (the dual protagonist with George), who earlier was charged with saving George from suicide (Clarence's decisive test), will first start with a qualifying test; namely, to keep George from drowning in the river. As we'll see, the real decisive test will be Clarence proving to George that his life was worth living. So now Clarence has a *being able to do*, which is to save George from suicide that starts as a qualifying test played out when Clarence jumps in the river and pretends to be drowning so George forgets about killing himself and dives in to save Clarence. Later, when they are drying out, Clarence moves onto his real decisive test, which is convincing George that life without him would've been very bad for his wife and community. He does this through magically making George absent from existence, from ever having been born.

George and Clarence go back into the town and encounter all the people George knows. George sees that the entire community has changed and not for the good. Many people in his community as well as his wife are affected by George's absence from existence, which George experiences as he and Clarence revisit his town. The town has been taken over by evil Mr. Potter and the friendly townspeople have become mean. Mr. Gower is a drunken unhoused man, Uncle Billy is dead, and Mary is an old maid who never married. She screams when George tries to appeal to her as his wife. George realizes that he did have a good life, he did have a positive effect on his community, and his existence mattered, and he wishes to exist again (be present) and wants all to go back to normal. All of the encounters George has with people he knows and seeing how much worse off they are without him serve as qualifying tests to prove to George his life was worth living, which culminates in the decisive test of George recognizing his life was worth living when he sees Mary never married and without children. George pleads with the angel Clarence to put everything back to normal.

Clarence grants him his wish; everything is back to normal, and George (and Clarence) have passed the decisive test of George recognizing his life has had tremendous impact on his community and his wife and family. Clarence has succeeded in his own decisive test with the shared protagonist George, which was first to prevent George's suicide but it evolved into proving George's life was worth living. The two protagonists' contracts and objects have merged, and they become a fused single subject (shared protagonist). The beauty of this transformative story moment is that George is no longer concerned about whether or not he'll be held accountable for the missing money; his decisive test is recognizing his life was worth living, merging with Clarence's decisive test to prove to George the same.

All that follows is George lives through a glorifying test running around town expressing his love for everything and everybody ecstatically. His friends deliver the money he needs to cover the missing $8,000, including Sam Wainwright, who wires in $25,000. George has succeeded in saving his community but also in realizing it's worth it to have lived the wonderful life he is living. George's glorifying test is manifest when he, his family, and his community sing "Auld Lang Syne," which is capped off when a bell on the Christmas tree rings, signifying Clarence got his wings and also signifiying both he and George are simultaneously living their shared glorifying test.

Comprehensive Beat Map for *It's a Wonderful Life*

Following is a beat-by-beat timeline (Table 6.18) with relevant story beats captured and sketched out along with timecode. These beats include master story beats/themes stated in **bold** and states of being beats (which may or may not be master story beats/themes stated) in **bold italic.** The two master schemas, the actantial narrative schema and the canonical narrative schema, will be traced as story beats throughout as well as microcosms of the master schemas with an eye towards how they connect back to the master schemas.

The three types of story beats (pragmatic, cognitive, and thymic) will also be cataloged in an adjacent column. You'll notice I don't make schema notes for *every* beat, only ones I deem necessary to help give you a sense of how to generate a comprehensive beat map that will be a useful tool for your own writing. I also list the movie's timecode (which delineates the movie's running time in hours, minutes, and seconds) for each beat/scene (easily captured on Amazon Prime Video). It's wise to practice the rigor of capturing and writing in timecode references from your specimen movie breakdowns as this information will come in handy when placing your breakdowns on Final Draft's Beat Board and Outline Editor, which will serve as a reference track to write your original movie against. More on this later.

Comprehensive Beat Map—*It's a Wonderful Life* and the Addition of Master Story Beats/Themes Stated, and States of Being

Immediately following this page, you'll find the comprehensive beat map for *It's a Wonderful Life*, a primary tool that can be a very useful analysis and brainstorming device for writing original screenplays, especially in how it will easily flow into Final Draft's Outline Editor. Now, a word about how this powerful map and its ancillary related tools are compiled. After completing a draft of a comprehensive beat map, I'll then zero in on the master story beats/themes stated and create a separate chart that I call a master story beats/themes stated "cheat sheet." It will include some (but not all) of the information from the comprehensive beat map. I'll explain more about the cheat sheet later, but the reason I bring it up now is to help you understand the importance of capturing the master story beats/themes stated up front in the comprehensive beat map. Also, for this one specimen, I will have worked some of the states of being into the comprehensive beat map, including (where appropriate) as part of the master story beats/themes stated. In the subsequent remaining breakdowns, I won't do the same as to allow you different takes on breaking down movies so you can feel comfortable developing your own style. To reiterate an earlier point, these master beats/themes stated story beats can be expressed as plain English sentences or can be stated as an actual "theme" in a literary sense. It depends on the specimen movie being broken down and what you need out of the movie's breakdown in terms of your own writing.

As regards to work flow and what process follows what, there's no one way. For example, after I figure out what the master story beats/themes stated are, I return to the comprehensive beat map and add any master story beats/themes stated additional information to the beat map. This way, I can then study the entirety of all the beats and clearly see where the master story beats/themes stated come in terms of narrative syntax of the beats.

Finally, in the last section of the breakdowns of each specimen movie, I plot the master story beats/themes stated on all four corners of the controlling semiotic square (as I demonstrated earlier in *The Lost Dog Story* demo section). This process will also serve as a way to meditate on how those master story beats/themes stated were derived using the entire master semiotics square for each movie, which will ultimately help you brainstorm your own master story beats for your screenplays.

Having the master story beats flagged in the comprehensive beat map will also help if you map your specimen script breakdown to the Final Draft Beat Board (a process I recommend trying).

Also note: For this first specimen breakdown, the comprehensive beat map will have explicatory boxes that will help you understand each of the columns and the information contained in all of them.

Table 6.18 Comprehensive beat map—Three specimen movies—Specimen #1—*It's a Wonderful Life*

TIMECODE*	BEAT	BEAT TYPE	ACTANTIAL NARRATIVE SCHEMA	CANONICAL NARRATIVE SCHEMA
	Note: Master story beats/themes stated will be in **bold** and also contain the label "Master story beat/theme stated". States of being will be in ***bold italic.***		Note: Not every beat has an actantial narrative schema note; only key ones as deemed necessary.	Note: Not every beat has a canonical narrative schema note; only key ones as deemed necessary.
1:16–1:58**	George Bailey's friends and family pray for his welfare and express ***prayerful concern and love for George.*** States of being may be part of general beats depicted in ***bold italic*** as shown above. Each box represents a scene or sequence or a group of related beats.	PRAGMATIC	Sending prayers to God, but we the audience (competent observers) receive them. Where appropriate, I will repeat information in these columns for multiple beats in other columns.	George, in crisis, sets up a loop that will be returned to at the end and will set up the eventual contract with Clarence to save George from suicide by showing him his life had worth. Where appropriate, I will repeat the information in these columns for multiple beats in other columns.
2:00–2:46	Angels discuss trying to save George and sending for Clarence the angel to help him.	PRAGMATIC		Can Clarence handle the contract of saving George?

2:47–3:54	Clarence is assigned the task of saving George, who is despairing and considering suicide, and if Clarence achieves his goal of saving George, he'll be awarded his wings. ***Clarence is excited that he can get his wings.***	PRAGMATIC THYMIC	Sending to Clarence the receiver, making Clarence the subject with the object of saving George Bailey from suicide.	Master contract established for Clarence: Save George Bailey from suicide, which will evolve into proving to George that he wasn't a failure for not leaving home to follow his dreams and instead chose to build a life with Mary and serve the community. Clarence's decisive test is laid out: To get his wings, Clarence must prevent George from taking his own life, which will evolve into a decisive test of proving to George that his life was worth living.
3:55–5:06	Clarence is granted vision into Young George's childhood where George saves his younger brother Harry from drowning in ice while sledding, which cost George his hearing. **Master story beat/theme stated: Young George saves Young Harry from drowning in ice water. "Helping others without regard for personal welfare gives life meaning."** Master story beats/themes stated are listed in **bold** (a sample is directly above this box) and will also be listed on a "cheat sheet" *and* again each one will be deconstructed against all the four points of the master semiotic square for the specimen movie in question.	PRAGMATIC COGNITIVE	Harry's near drowning is a sender to George the receiver, making him the subject with the object of saving Harry. George's benevolent nature is a helper to what will be his overall object, which is to realize his life as lived had worth. Harry is also an opponent to George's object to leave town.	Despite George's personal original contract, which is to see the world, he experiences an early qualifying test in saving Harry in what will become his new contract, which is serving others and saving the town from Potter.

(Continued)

Table 6.18 *Continued*

TIMECODE*	BEAT Note: Master story beats/themes stated will be in **bold** and also contain the label "Master story beat/theme stated". States of being will be in ***bold italic.***	BEAT TYPE	ACTANTIAL NARRATIVE SCHEMA Note: Not every beat has an actantial narrative schema note; only key ones as deemed necessary.	CANONICAL NARRATIVE SCHEMA Note: Not every beat has a canonical narrative schema note; only key ones as deemed necessary.
5:07–6:55	Young George shows Young Mary a *National Geographic* as he brags about his exploring aspirations.	PRAGMATIC	Young George's own enthusiasm for adventure makes him a sender to himself the receiver. He is a young subject with an object of seeing the world and having a life of adventure. Mary will be an opponent to this goal and a subject with her own object of marrying George and never leaving town.	George's personal contract begins with him wanting to explore the world, one which he will fail at, but his contract will morph into saving his community and coming to appreciate his life as he lived it.
6:56–7:09	Unbeknownst to Young George, Young Mary whispers in his deaf ear "George Bailey, I'll love you 'til the day I die." ***Young Mary expresses love until the day she dies for George.***	PRAGMATIC COGNITIVE THYMIC	Young Mary is a sender of a message of pure love and commitment to Young George, who doesn't hear in one ear so can't receive it; therefore, we the audience (competent observers) become the receivers.	Mary's own qualifying test will come later when she tries to get George to marry her. Her *being able to do something* is to get George to fall in love with her and marry her, which manifests later when George visits her home.
7:10–8:48	George learns that Mr. Gower's son died then sees a drunk distraught Mr. Gower put poison into prescription pills by accident. ***Mr. Gower is drunk and distraught with death of son.***	COGNITIVE THYMIC	Mr. Gower's accidentally using poison in a prescription is a sender to Young George the receiver, making Young Geroge the subject with the object of figuring out how to solve this problem.	Mini-qualifying test begins (Can George stop Gower from poisoning customer?). He has a clear *being able to do something*, figure out how to keep a customer from being poisoned.

Time	Event	Modality	Analysis	Analysis
9:01–10:24	Young George goes into a meeting with his father, who is battling Mr. Potter, who wants to foreclose on homeowners not paying mortgages.	PRAGMATIC	Young George's father is a potential helper to George but is tied up fighting Potter. Potter serves as an inadvertent opponent in that Young George's father is preoccupied with fighting him so can't advise Young George.	Mini-qualifying test of George trying to stop Gower from poisoning customer is still in play as Young George's father engages in his own decisive test to protect his community from Potter's greed.
10:27–11:24	Young George is smacked by Mr. Gower, who is mad at him that he didn't deliver the pills, but George explains he put poison in the pills, hence the reason for not delivering them.	PRAGMATIC COGNITIVE		Young George's mini-qualifying test succeeds because Gower realizes he put poison in the pills by accident. Young George's *being able to do something* (keep the poisoning of the customer from happening) devolves to him having to tell Mr. Gower about the mistake of putting poison in the pills, risking further abuse from Gower.
	Young George cries, and Mr. Gower checks the poison jar.	THYMIC		
11:25–11:38	*Mr. Gower realizes via Young George his mistake that he put poison in the pills he dispensed and embraces crying Young George out of gratitude and gets emotional.* **Master story beat/theme stated: George risks getting hit by Mr. Gower to save him. "Doing the right thing, even if it means suffering, gives life its meaning."**	COGNITIVE		Young George has succeeded in successfully completing a mini-qualifying test in risking his own well-being (a beating by Gower) to keep Gower from poisoning customers.
11:39–12:17	Angel Joseph shows Clarence adult George as he attempts to buy luggage for his world adventures in order to familiarize Clarence with where George's life has progressed to.	COGNITIVE	George's lust to travel and see the world is a sender to himself as receiver, making him a subject with the object of leaving. (Clarence stands in as a competent observer piecing this together for us the audience (competent observers)).	
	Clarence is anxious to learn if he married Mary, did he go exploring?	COGNITIVE		

(Continued)

Table 6.18 *Continued*

TIMECODE*	BEAT Note: Master story beats/themes stated will be in **bold** and also contain the label "Master story beat/theme stated". States of being will be in ***bold italic.***	BEAT TYPE	ACTANTIAL NARRATIVE SCHEMA Note: Not every beat has an actantial narrative schema note; only key ones as deemed necessary.	CANONICAL NARRATIVE SCHEMA Note: Not every beat has a canonical narrative schema note; only key ones as deemed necessary.
12:18–12:58	George is handed a big suitcase by Joe in the luggage store, purchased for him by Mr. Gower as a going-away present to help him to leave Bedford Falls	PRAGMATIC	Mr. Gower as helper is a sender and gives George luggage in support of George's personal contract, his desire to see the world (his object). George is the receiver.	George's original decisive test to escape Bedford Falls seems in play, especially in that Gower provides luggage for his trip.
12:59–13:11	George returns to Mr. Gower to thank him for the luggage and wishes for a million dollars on the "magic" cigar lighter.	PRAGMATIC		
13:12–14:15	George banters with Burt the cop and Ernie as Violet walks by, and they leer at her as she passes.	COGNITIVE PRAGMATIC	Violet's beauty is a sender to George the receiver, making him the subject with the object of "lusting" after her, feeding into his desire to see the world.	A mini "qualifying test" implied in this beat is that Violet will make herself available to George in the film, and George gently rejects her. This of course sets him up to be able to withstand the qualifying test of marriage faithfully to Mary, which will feed into what his overall contract and decisive test morphs into: to realize his life as he lived it was worth living.
14:16–15:07	George and brother Harry come down to dinner after horsing around, and Harry chases Annie the maid into the kitchen and smacks her on the rear.	PRAGMATIC		

Time	Action	Modal	Sender/Receiver Analysis	Qualifying Test
15:08–19:00	George talks to his father about his plans to see the world, go to college. His father asks him to take over the business, and George respectfully declines his father, causing his father to admit that this small town is no place for him to have to "crawl to Potter."	COGNITIVE THYMIC	George's father ultimately is a sender (and helper) to George the receiver, giving him his blessing and incentive to leave home and live out his fantasies of adventures, making George now fully the subject with the object of following his dreams of leaving home.	George's original contract to leave home is again reinforced by his dad. All systems are go to leave home for George. His qualifying test to have the means to get out of his hometown is in motion.
19:01–20:04	At the high school dance, George and the gang banter, and George sees Mary from across the room and is struck by her girl-next-door beauty, and she notices him. *George is excited when he first sees adult Mary. Mary is excited when she first sees adult George.*	COGNITIVE	Mary's beauty is a sender to George a receiver, making him a new subject with the object of falling in love with her, which will ultimately make him marry her and never leave. She will be an opponent to him leaving home, his original object.	What will become George's ultimate final contract, to save his community from Potter and come to believe his life was worth living, is kicked off on a deep level by seeing Mary and her natural beauty. She still stands as an opponent to his contract of wanting to leave, but will be key in him succeeding in the final decisive test of him learning that his life as lived was worth it.
20:05–22:00	George and Mary dance the Charleston with the crowd. *They are having exhilarated fun dancing the Charleston at the gym.*	PRAGMATIC		Mini-qualifying test in the form of an actual "contest," the Charleston contest, which will kick off George and Mary's bond.
22:01–22:50	Freddy and Othello devise a plan to open the gym floor so George and Mary will fall into the swimming pool below.	COGNITIVE PRAGMATIC	Freddy and Othello are trying to be opponents to George and Mary's romance by opening the pool and ruining the dance but it causes them to have fun and thus they become helpers to what will become George's new object of staying home and building a life and saving the community in that falling in the pool causes fun bonding for the couple.	Mini-qualifying test: Will George and Mary survive the test of the swimming pool trap as they fall in and have fun, putting them on the road to marriage?

(Continued)

Table 6.18 Continued

TIMECODE*	BEAT Note: Master story beats/themes stated will be in **bold** and also contain the label "Master story beat/theme stated". States of being will be in ***bold italic.***	BEAT TYPE	ACTANTIAL NARRATIVE SCHEMA Note: Not every beat has an actantial narrative schema note; only key ones as deemed necessary.	CANONICAL NARRATIVE SCHEMA Note: Not every beat has a canonical narrative schema note; only key ones as deemed necessary.
22:51–24:01	George and Mary are dancing up a storm and fall into the swimming pool once it's open. ***The crowd is exhilarated watching George and Mary dance near the edge of the pool.*** The rest of the crowd jumps in and dances in the water.	PRAGMATIC THYMIC PRAGMATIC	" . . . "	
24:04–25:38	George and Mary, after drying off, walk back home singing, and a quiet moment occurs when George wants to kiss her, but Mary chickens out and walks away.	PRAGMATIC COGNITIVE	Mary serves as an opponent to George's desire to leave.	While George would be perfectly happy to just "make out" with Mary, she walks away because he will be led into a new contract (to stay and marry her) instead of his original contract to leave and find adventure.
25:39–26:33	George breaks window in the old Granville house and discloses what he wished for, which is his dreams to travel and build things. ***George is excited to tell Mary about getting out of Bedford Falls with big plans.***	PRAGMATIC THYMIC	George's wish is a sender to the "universe" as receiver that he wants to leave Bedford Falls and build things.	The dueling contract (George leaves/ George stays) is expressed in George and Mary throwing rocks for different reasons.

26:34–26:46	Mary breaks a window/George asks her what she wished for, and she smiles and walks away singing.	PRAGMATIC COGNITIVE	Mary's wish is a sender to the universe (receiver). She is a new subject with the object of marrying George.	A dueling contract (George leaves/George stays) is expressed in George and Mary throwing rocks for different (opposing) reasons.
26:47–28:57	George promises to "lasso the moon" for Mary whereby she'll swallow it and moonbeams will radiate out of her hair; an old man observing from his porch encourages him to kiss her.	PRAGMATIC	George's stubborn desire to leave and find adventure translates to how he expresses his desire to "lasso the moon," etc. He is a sender to Mary the receiver, making him the subject with the object of "objectifying" her (moonbeams will radiate out of her hair). Albeit seemingly benevolent, this still sidesteps marriage to her. His lust to leave home is an opponent to what will become his ultimate object, which is to serve his community and realize his life as lived was worth it.	
27:58–29:22	Mary runs away, losing her robe, and hides naked in the bushes. George negotiates with her about how she gets her robe back.	PRAGMATIC PRAGMATIC	Mary losing her robe and being essentially naked behind the bushes is the climax of her being an object of lust, a helper to his desire to see the world.	Mini-qualifying test now with George having Mary accidentally naked in the bushes: How will he behave? Given the situation, will he protect her honor (related to the contract of staying home) or exploit the situation and attempt to see her naked (related to contract of leaving).

(Continued)

Table 6.18 Continued

TIMECODE*	BEAT Note: Master story beats/themes stated will be in **bold** and also contain the label "Master story beat/theme stated". States of being will be in ***bold italic.***	BEAT TYPE	ACTANTIAL NARRATIVE SCHEMA Note: Not every beat has an actantial narrative schema note; only key ones as deemed necessary.	CANONICAL NARRATIVE SCHEMA Note: Not every beat has a canonical narrative schema note; only key ones as deemed necessary.
29:23–29:47	Uncle Billy drives up to tell George that his father had a stroke. Mary hears it, too, and George tosses her her robe before departing with his uncle. ***Mary is concerned about George's father's stroke.***	COGNITIVE COGNITIVE	Uncle Billy is a sender to George the receiver about his father's stroke, which will make George a subject with the object of running the family business. His father's stroke is an opponent to George leaving.	This is strong fodder that George's original contract to leave will fail.
29:48–34:01	3 months after George's father's death, George argues with Mr. Potter in front of the board of the Bailey Building and Loan Corporation, trying to push back on Potter's bid to forclose on many homes and dissolve the community-based outfit. ***Uncle Billy is angry at Mr. Potter for wanting to dissolve the Building and Loan.*** ***George passionately dismisses Potter's attempt to dissolve the Bailey Building and Loan.*** **Master story beat/theme stated: George pushes back on Potter. "You must plead for what is right to protect the community."**	PRAGMATIC PRAGMATIC PRAGMATIC	Potter's greed is a sender to George the receiver, making him a new subject with the object of saving the community from Potter, who is a perennial anti-subject.	Mini-qualifying test of: How will George fare in his defense of the community against greedy Potter? His *being able to do something* comes in his making an impassioned plea to the board against Potter.

34:02–35:02	George learns the board voted down Potter's takeover bid and will keep the Building and Loan company if George takes over. **Master story beat/theme stated: George is voted to take over the board. "If you plead for what is right with the powers that be, they will act in the interest of the community."** *George is distressed he must not leave for college and instead take over the Building and Loan in order to preserve it.*	PRAGMATIC COGNITIVE	The board is sending to George the receiver charge of the Building and Loan, making him the subject with the object of helping the community over his own desires, which serves as an opponent to him leaving and seeing the world. (Note: But they are not an anti-subject, they are not diametrically opposed to him leaving, they just present a community need to him that challenges his original object to leave home.)	George succeeds in mini-qualifying test in that the board voted down Potter taking over the Building and Loan provided George leads the company. They are opponents to his own contract to leave and see the world, which is morphing into a contract to save his community. However, his original qualifying test to leave home is failing.
35:03–35:17	The angels discuss George not leaving for college and how Harry went instead of George going.	COGNITIVE	The angels constructing the narrative mirror us the audience as competent observers piecing together the narrative. The outside circumstances in terms of the needs of his community surrounding George will be senders to him the receiver, forcing him to serve others rather than self.	George's new decisive test to stay and save the community is taking shape.
35:23–35:48	George and Uncle Billy wait for Harry to return from college and George discusses international job opportunities that excite him.	PRAGMATIC		

(Continued)

Table 6.18 *Continued*

TIMECODE*	BEAT Note: Master story beats/themes stated will be in **bold** and also contain the label "Master story beat/theme stated". States of being will be in ***bold italic.***	BEAT TYPE	ACTANTIAL NARRATIVE SCHEMA Note: Not every beat has an actantial narrative schema note; only key ones as deemed necessary.	CANONICAL NARRATIVE SCHEMA Note: Not every beat has a canonical narrative schema note; only key ones as deemed necessary.
35:49–37:19	Harry arrives, and George learns Harry has gotten married and has a job offer with his wife's father's company. **Master story beat/theme stated: George takes his brother's place. "If you don't seize the day and take opportunities when you can, you'll lose out."** ***George and Uncle Billy are happy about Harry's marriage to Ruth.***	COGNITIVE COGNITIVE	Harry's marriage and job opportunity is a sender to George a receiver, making George the subject with the object to stay put and run the family business again. Harry's wife is an opponent to George leaving, his original object.***	Mini-qualifying test; namely, George is charged with still "holding down the fort" in the family business instead of escaping town, which will feed into his overall decisive test of realizing his life had worth because he protected his community from Potter.
37:20–37:45	George learns that the job Harry's father in-law offered him is a great opportunity. **Master story beat/theme stated: George realizes his brother has an opportunity. "Sacrificing for others is worth it."** ***George is concerned as he contemplates what it means that his brother is married and has a job offer.***	COGNITIVE COGNITIVE[1]	" . . . "	Same as above.

[1]While it might seem obvious that all "states of being" will be labeled as "thymic" beats, occasionally I label them as pragmatic beats or as cognitive beats, as is the case here. The reasoning behind this is simply sometimes I believe in particular movie moments the actor's cognition of what is going on is key to understanding the moment first and foremost before viewing the beat as purely "emotional" (thymic).

37:46–38:53	During the wedding celebration of Harry, George talks to drunk Uncle Billy and sends him home.	PRAGMATIC		
38:54–39:21	George, alone outside of party, hears a train whistle, looks at travel pamphlets and frustratingly throws them away.	THYMIC		George's own personal contract to leave and explore the world is rapidly deteriorating and failing, morphing into the new one to stay and save his community and marry Mary.
39:22–41:10	George's mother asks him why he's not interested in Mary, who has just come back from college. He claims she's involved with Sam Wainwright.	COGNITIVE	Mother is a "sender" to George the receiver, making him a reluctant subject with the object to pursue Mary. She's also a helper to the new object of George staying and saving the community but an opponent to him leaving.	
41:11–42:29	While wandering in town, George meets Violet, who comes on to him, and he is able to get out of it by proposing a preposterous date of climbing Mt. Bedford, swimming in the pond, etc. **Violet is distressed about George's "date" idea.**	PRAGMATIC / THYMIC	Violet's advances are a sender to George the receiver, making him the subject with the object of gently rejecting her while protecting her ego. Her come-on and availability without the seeming "strings attached" that Mary brings is a would-be potential helper to him leaving town.	Mini-qualifying test of George refusing Violet's advances, which, if accepted, would feed into him leaving and not staying (not marrying Mary, etc.). His *being able to do something* in this case is figuring out how to reject Violet gently.
42:30–44:02	Mary sees George outside her house and encourages him to come inside, and he kicks open the broken fence to do so.	PRAGMATIC	Mary is a sender to George the receiver, asking him to "come inside." Again, she is an opponent to him leaving.	George's decisive test to finally escape town will fail when he falls for Mary, setting up a new decisive test to live happily in and save Bedford Falls, which he fails to do at first, and then will ultimately experience a new contract and new decisive test that is about him realizing his life was worth living.

(Continued)

Table 6.18 *Continued*

TIMECODE*	BEAT Note: Master story beats/themes stated will be in **bold** and also contain the label "Master story beat/theme stated". States of being will be in ***bold italic***.	BEAT TYPE	ACTANTIAL NARRATIVE SCHEMA Note: Not every beat has an actantial narrative schema note; only key ones as deemed necessary.	CANONICAL NARRATIVE SCHEMA Note: Not every beat has a canonical narrative schema note; only key ones as deemed necessary.
44:03–45:52	George and Mary talk, but there's tension because they like each other but he's resisting settling down.	PRAGMATIC	Mary is a sender to George the receiver, offering herself to be a mate.	Same as above.
45:03–46:39	George and Mary argue about why he came over, and he leaves as Sam Wainwright calls.	PRAGMATIC		George tries to save his original contract to escape as he tries to reject his future mate that will tie him down to home.
46:40–46:51	***Mary is frustrated and angry at George for rejecting her and smashes the "Buffalo Gals" record from the record player.***	PRAGMATIC THYMIC		Same as above.
46:52–47:38	Sam Wainwright calls, and George returns for his hat, and Mary talks to Sam in a way that makes George notice jealously, and she puts him on with Sam.	PRAGMATIC	Mary is a sender to Sam, feigning romantic interest in him but in reality "sending" to George (receiver) ideas about her to make him jealous.	George's decisive test to escape is failing as he's led back into Mary's home and ultimately into a life-changing marriage with her tying him to home and community.
47:39–49:41	***As George and Mary listen to Sam on the phone, George smells her hair, and they both get turned on.***	THYMIC	Mary's presence is a sender to George the receiver through the smell of her hair making him a new subject with the object of falling in love with Mary.	George's decisive test to escape is failing as he's led back into Mary's home and ultimately into a life-changing marriage with her tying him to home and community.

49:42–50:12	**George expresses anger about not wanting to get married.** **Mary cries over George's anger about not wanting to get married** **George and Mary kiss and embrace and profess their love after George got angry.** **Master story beat/theme stated: George and Mary fall in love. "It's impossible to escape your destiny of whom you were meant to be with."**	PRAGMATIC THYMIC	George is angry at Mary for being an irresistible opponent to his leaving home. George succumbs to Mary and forever loses his chance to leave, she is the ultimate opponent in that regard but will be the ultimate helper in what will be his final object, to realize his life as lived was good.	George's decisive test to escape is failing as he's led back into Mary's home and ultimately into a life-changing marriage with her tying him to home and community.
50:13–51:02	George and Mary are just married, and rice is thrown at them by their guests. **The crowd is exhilarated after George and Mary's wedding at church.** They get into Ernie's cab to go on their honeymoon.	PRAGMATIC PRAGMATIC		
51:03–51:49	George and Mary in the cab gleefully discuss their honeymoon plans to Ernie the cab driver. **George expresses joy when discussing his honeymoon plans in Ernie's cab.**	PRAGMATIC THYMIC		George's original contract to "see the world" has morphed into the consolation prize of honeymoon plans to travel with Mary (which also will soon be thwarted).
51:50–52:23	Ernie, George, and Mary see a bank run on his bank.	COGNITIVE	The bank run is a sender to George the receiver, making him the subject with the object of projecting the community. His benevolence is a helper.	George's new qualifying test commences. (Will George be able to keep his doors open until 6 p.m. and save his company and protect the community from Potter?) He has a *being able to do something* (stave off a bank run).

(Continued)

Table 6.18 Continued

TIMECODE*	BEAT Note: Master story beats/themes stated will be in **bold** and also contain the label "Master story beat/theme stated". States of being will be in **bold italic**.	BEAT TYPE	ACTANTIAL NARRATIVE SCHEMA Note: Not every beat has an actantial narrative schema note; only key ones as deemed necessary.	CANONICAL NARRATIVE SCHEMA Note: Not every beat has a canonical narrative schema note; only key ones as deemed necessary.
52:24–53:42	George lets customers into the bank and learns from Uncle Billy that the bank called their loan. And they have no money.	COGNITIVE	Same as above.	George's new qualifying test commences. (Will George be able to keep his doors open until 6 p.m. and save his company and protect the community from Potter?) He has a *being able to do something* (stave off a bank run).
53:48–54:48	George learns from Potter that he took over George's bank and he's offering 50 cents on the dollar for George's customers' shares, and if he closes his doors before 6 p.m. he'll never reopen.	COGNITIVE	Same as above, plus Potter is an anti-subject in that he is trying to destroy the community financially, offering them 50 cents on the dollar for their shares. He's also an anti-subject to George's efforts to save the community.	George's new qualifying test commences. (Will George be able to keep his doors open until 6 p.m. and save his company and protect the community from Potter?) He has a *being able to do something* (stave off a bank run).
54:49–57:44	George tries to convince the crowd not to sell out to Potter. ***George is happy that Miss Davis only needs $17.50.***	PRAGMATIC THYMIC	George is a sender to the crowd the receiver, pleading with them not to sell out to Potter, making the crowd the subject with the object of not selling out. George's persuasiveness and popularity is a helper.	George's new qualifying test commences. (Will George be able to keep his doors open until 6 p.m. and save his company and protect the community from Potter?) He has a *being able to do something* (stave off a bank run).
57:45–58:37	Mary offers up their honeymoon money to the crowd for now, and George is able to give shareholders enough money to tide them over.	PRAGMATIC	" . . "	Same as above, but Mary has joined the qualifying test. She comes up with the *being able to do something* solution; namely, use her and George's honeymoon money to stop the bank run.

58:38–1:00:08	**George and co-workers are exhilarated they didn't have to close their doors before 6 p.m., but then George realizes he forgot about Mary.** **Master beat/theme stated: George saved the community from Potter. "If you plead for what is right with the community, they will act in interest of the community."**	THYMIC COGNITIVE PRAGMATIC	George's qualifying test succeeds. George was able to keep the Building and Loan open until 6 p.m., and saved his community from a Potter takeover.
1:00:09–1:02:51	As his friends scramble to get the Granville house turned into their honeymoon hotel, George arrives "home" and sees Mary has laid out an opulent dinner. A friend pretending to be a host literally pushes *George to Mary, and they kiss and have a romantic bonding moment.* *Mary and George embrace as she emotionally expresses she wished for the old Granville house to be their new home.*	PRAGMATIC THYMIC THYMIC	A mini-qualifying test by the community: to see if they can intercede and help give George and Mary a makeshift honeymoon after the couple blew their honeymoon money saving the citizens from Potter's greed. A *being able to do something* is the community's ability to stage the makeshift honeymoon.
1:02:53–1:03:48	As Burt and Ernie sing outside the window, Mary confesses she wished for this exact set-up when years ago (and earlier in the story) they broke a window at the old Granville house. *Burt annoyedly bops Ernie on the head for kissing him after singing.*	PRAGMATIC COGNITIVE THYMIC PRAGMATIC	Mary reveals what her wish was when she broke a window on the house years ago. (Her sending to the universe the receiver that she be married to George living there as they now are.) The mini-qualifying test of the community staging a honeymoon will lead to a small "decisive test" of consummating the marriage, which, of course, happens off camera and feeds into the master structure of George staying home.

(Continued)

Table 6.18 Continued

TIMECODE*	BEAT Note: Master story beats/themes stated will be in **bold** and also contain the label "Master story beat/theme stated". States of being will be in **bold italic**.	BEAT TYPE	ACTANTIAL NARRATIVE SCHEMA Note: Not every beat has an actantial narrative schema note; only key ones as deemed necessary.	CANONICAL NARRATIVE SCHEMA Note: Not every beat has a canonical narrative schema note; only key ones as deemed necessary.
1:03:49–1:04:42	George and Mary help Mr. Martini and family move out of his rental to his new home, prompting Martini to happily proclaim his joy in that he owns his own home. **Giuseppe Martini is overjoyed about his new house acquisition.**	PRAGMATIC THYMIC	George is the sender to Martini the receiver, making an object of Martini being able to obtain a home. George is a helper to Martini's quest to build a life in Bedford Falls.	
1:04:42–1:04:52	The Martini moving caravan drives Into Bailey Park.	PRAGMATIC		
1:04:53–1:05:23	George and Mary welcome the Martinis into their new home with ceremonial words and offerings of salt, wine, and bread as symbolic gestures.	PRAGMATIC		
1:05:24–1:06:33	In Potter's office, the real estate salesman shows Potter how George's Building and Loan homes are growing and taking away from Potter's rental business.	PRAGMATIC COGNITIVE	Potter is an anti-subject trying to find a way to undermine George's project to provide the community with their own homes.	Potter's decisive test is laid out; namely, how will he destroy the momentum of citizens buying homes instead of renting in his slums?
1:06:34–1:07:32	George and Mary say goodbye to Sam Wainwright and wife, who are driving down to Florida **George is frustrated he can't drive down to Florida with Sam Wainwright and kicks the door.**	PRAGMATIC THYMIC		Sam Wainwright's invitation to George and Mary to drive to Florida with him and his wife is a reminder to George of his original contract to escape town, which now has been shelved for life.

Time	Description	Modality	Analysis	Analysis 2
1:07:33–1:12:43	George is offered a lucrative deal with Mr. Potter to run his properties and at first is excited then rejects it. **Master beat/theme stated: George is offered money from Potter. "Money isn't everything, especially if it involves turning your back on the community."**	COGNITIVE PRAGMATIC	Potter is a sender to George the receiver, appealing to George's greed, and attempts to turn George into a subject with the object of desiring of Potter's wealth offer, enough to almost make George turn his back on his community. Potter is also an anti-subject to George protecting the community from Potter.	Potter's qualifying test manifests with a *being able to do something* (bring George onboard via money), which will ultimately lead to Potter's own personal decisive test of controlling the city and money of the people failing.
1:12:44–1:13:40	George comes home to his sleeping wife Mary, thinking of Potter's offer, and about lassoing the moon and Mary singing "Buffalo Gals."	COGNITIVE		
1:13:41–1:14:42	George wakes up Mary and learns she is pregnant. **George is nervously excited having learned Mary is pregnant.**	COGNITIVE THYMIC	Mary's baby is a sender to George the receiver, making George the subject with the object of now being a solid provider.	The fact that George is now an expectant parent further contributes to his failed decisive test to escape Bedford Falls.
1:14:43–1:15:08	As angels discuss how "You must have guessed by now George never left" over a montage of the children George and Mary had as she fixes up the home.	PRAGMATIC COGNITIVE	"You must have guessed by now George never left" is another instance of the angels addressing Clarence as a competent observer (standing in for the audience) constructing the narrative.	
1:15:10–1:16:49	The angels discuss the effect of the Second World War which now begins and how many of the locals went into battle and George stayed back because he was 4F due to his bad ear and helped with local tasks pertaining to the war	PRAGMATIC	Saving Young Harry early on damaged George's hearing, so George can't even leave to fight in the war, which ultimately feeds into his new object of staying and saving the community.	

(Continued)

Table 6.18 *Continued*

TIMECODE*	BEAT Note: Master story beats/themes stated will be in **bold** and also contain the label "Master story beat/theme stated". States of being will be in ***bold italic.***	BEAT TYPE	ACTANTIAL NARRATIVE SCHEMA Note: Not every beat has an actantial narrative schema note; only key ones as deemed necessary.	CANONICAL NARRATIVE SCHEMA Note: Not every beat has a canonical narrative schema note; only key ones as deemed necessary.
1:16:50–1:18:25	George shows off front page news of the President decorating his brother Harry with the Congressional Medal of Honor to his friends and business associates.	PRAGMATIC THYMIC		
1:18:26–1:19:05	George meets the bank examiner coming to examine his bank's books.	PRAGMATIC		The preliminary foundation of what will emerge as the master decisive test of George being able to save his community from Potter has begun.
1:19:06–1:19:58	At the bank, Uncle Billy gleefully grabs Potter's newspaper to gloat about the headline depicting Harry's Congressional Medal of Honor but accidentally puts the $8,000 bank deposit in Potter's paper.	PRAGMATIC	Uncle Billy's drunkenness is an opponent to George protecting his community from Potter. It's a helper to Potter as an anti-subject seeking to own the community.	Uncle Billy's drunken error of losing $8,000 accelerates George's decisive test of saving the town from Potter, which he'll mostly fail at until it becomes less important and evolves to the real final decisive test of the story; namely, will George learn to appreciate his "wonderful" life as lived.
1:19:59–1:20:27	Uncle Billy can't find the money to deposit.	COGNITIVE	Same as above.	

Time	Event	Type	Function	Analysis
1:20:27–1:21:00	Mr. Potter discovers Uncle Billy accidentally gave him the $8,000 and opens the door to the bank and spies on Uncle Billy scrambling for it.	COGNITIVE	Potter's anti-subject strategy to defeat George and take over the town has been handed to him.	Potter's own decisive test solution has literally fallen into his lap.**** he has the misplaced money from Billy that can sink George's company and thwart George interfering in Potter's domination. George has begun to fail at his new contract to protect his community and family from Potter (his decisive test).
1:21:01–1:21:07	Potter contemplates his next move now that he knows Uncle Billy misplaced $8,000.	COGNITIVE		Potter's decisive test is in play; namely, arrest and crush George, his obstacle to taking over the town. His *being able to do something* means he has to let things play out, and let the money Uncle Billy misplaced bring down George Bailey's Building and Loan corporation.
1:21:08–1:21:45	Violet shows up to talk to George. Uncle Billy returns to office to look for money.	PRAGMATIC		
1:21:46–1:22:25	In George's office, George gives Violet her money and some extra, and she is in love with him and gives him a friendly kiss.	PRAGMATIC	Violet, who was available to George romantically seemingly without "strings" attached, was always available as a helper to his object to leave. But he rejected her, and this beat punctuates Violet's mode as a possible helper for George leaving while simultaneously underscoring his moral standing.	A mini-qualifying test: Violet, who has always wanted to romantically connect with George, shows up, and he gives her a loan; she kisses him but in a friendly way. This could've turned into an affair but this final beat closes the loop on that mini-qualifying test, reaffirming George's new contract to be loyal with Mary and protect his community.

(Continued)

Table 6.18 *Continued*

TIMECODE*	BEAT Note: Master story beats/themes stated will be in **bold** and also contain the label "Master story beat/theme stated". States of being will be in ***bold italic***.	BEAT TYPE	ACTANTIAL NARRATIVE SCHEMA Note: Not every beat has an actantial narrative schema note; only key ones as deemed necessary.	CANONICAL NARRATIVE SCHEMA Note: Not every beat has a canonical narrative schema note; only key ones as deemed necessary.
1:22:26–1:23:25	George learns from Uncle Billy that the $8,000 bank deposit is missing, and Cousin Eustace confirms Uncle Billy had it at his desk before they closed up.	COGNITIVE	Potter is a complete anti-subject to George's object of protecting the community and now, what will eventually be his object, seeing that his life was worth living is under threat without any easy way seemingly out.	George's newly evolved decisive test (protecting the community from Potter) has failed, due to George trusting his drunk Uncle Billy with the company's bank deposits. A clever reversal in that George's new contract (to build a life with Mary and protect his community and to not leave home) has imploded, caused by George's own trust in Uncle Billy. George is failing his new decisive test. Soon Clarence will change the very nature of what George's decisive test will be (accepting his life is wonderful and staying behind and building a life with Mary was the best decision).
1:23:26–1:24:43	***George angrily berates Uncle Billy for losing the $8,000 deposit.***	THYMIC	George is a sender to Uncle Billy a receiver to find the money, making Uncle Billy a subject with the object of finding the lost money.	". . ."

Time	Beat	Category	Analysis	
1:24:44–1:25:57	George returns home distraught, Mary realizes something is wrong when **George emotionally hugs his son on Christmas Eve and has a mini-breakdown.**	COGNITIVE THYMIC	Losing the $8,000 is an opponent to George protecting his community and family from Potter. It also begins to remind him that he originally wanted to escape town (his initial contract). His failure to protect his community and family and the weight of having given up his dream to leave are coming together at rapid fire, now a strong sender to George the receiver, which will yield his new object to kill himself.	As George fails his new decisive test to save the community from Potter, his original failure at the decisive test (to escape town) is also echoing through all of these beats and scenes.
1:25:58–1:27:45	George interacts in a stressful tone with Mary and kids and is clearly frustrated by the missing money.	PRAGMATIC THYMIC	Currently everything about George's life is a frustrating reminder that he gave up his original dream (object) to leave town and live a life of adventure.	As George fails his new decisive test to save the community from Potter, his original failure at the decisive test (to escape town) is also echoing through all of these beats and scenes.
1:27:46–1:29:00	George checks on Zuzu, sick with a cold, and pretends to fix her flower and pockets petals that have fallen off it.	PRAGMATIC	Currently everything about George's life is a frustrating reminder that he gave up his original dream (object) to leave town and live a life of adventure.	As George fails his new decisive test to save the community from Potter, his original failure at the decisive test (to escape town) is also echoing through all of these beats and scenes.
1:29:01–1:29:52	**George berates Zuzu's teacher Mrs. Welch on phone for letting Zuzu walk home with her coat open.**	PRAGMATIC	Currently everything about George's life is a frustrating reminder that he gave up his original dream (object) to leave town and live a life of adventure.	As George fails his new decisive test to save the community from Potter, his original failure at the decisive test (to escape town) is also echoing through all of these beats and scenes.

(Continued)

Table 6.18 *Continued*

TIMECODE*	BEAT Note: Master story beats/themes stated will be in **bold** and also contain the label "Master story beat/theme stated". States of being will be in ***bold italic.***	BEAT TYPE	ACTANTIAL NARRATIVE SCHEMA Note: Not every beat has an actantial narrative schema note; only key ones as deemed necessary.	CANONICAL NARRATIVE SCHEMA Note: Not every beat has a canonical narrative schema note; only key ones as deemed necessary.
1:29:53–1:30:23	***George berates Mr. Welch for his wife's actions of letting her student Zuzu (George's daughter) walk home with her jacket open.***	PRAGMATIC	Currently everything about George's life is a frustrating reminder that he gave up his original dream (object) to leave town and live a life of adventure.	As George fails his new decisive test to save the community from Potter, his original failure at the decisive test (to escape town) is also echoing through all of these beats and scenes.
1:30:24–1:30:32	George yells at family; Mary realizes something is *really* wrong.	COGNITIVE	Currently everything about George's life is a frustrating reminder that he gave up his original dream (object) to leave town and live a life of adventure.	As George fails his new decisive test to save the community from Potter, his original failure at the decisive test (to escape town) is also echoing through all of these beats and scenes.
1:30:33–1:32:04	***George angrily knocks down a model bridge he had built in his living room.*** He apologizes to the kids and Mary, expresses frustration with his behavior, and suggests he leave.	PRAGMATIC THYMIC	Currently everything about George's life is a frustrating reminder that he gave up his original dream (object) to leave town and live a life of adventure.	As George fails his new decisive test to save the community from Potter, his original failure at the decisive test (to escape town) is also echoing through all of these beats and scenes.
1:32:05–1:32:17	Mary calls Uncle Billy to find out what is going on.	PRAGMATIC		

Timecode	Description		Analysis
1:32:18–1:35:20	**George begs Potter to loan him the $8,000 dollars to cover the lost money.** Potter's response is to promise he'll swear out a warrant for his arrest Master story beat/theme stated: **George attempts to make a deal with the devil Potter. "At some point, everyone will contemplate making a deal with the devil."**	THYMIC PRAGMATIC	George is the sender to Potter the receiver, making Potter the subject with the object of instead of helping George using Uncle Billy's mistake to finally destroy George and get him arrested.	As George fails his new decisive test to save the community from Potter, his original failure at the decisive test (to escape town) is also echoing through all of these and these scenes.
1:35:21–1:35:31	Leaving Potter's office, George climbs into his car as the door is broken.	PRAGMATIC		
1:35:32–1:36:27	George goes to Martini's bar, where George looks at his life insurance policy, and then **George emotionally prays to God for help.**	THYMIC	George is sender to receiver God, the universe, or specifically, the angels (Clarence) making Clarence the subject with the object of saving George.	This beat is fascinating because it's the culmination of the two sides of George failing, failing to protect his community from Potter (his new decisive test) and having failed his original decisive test to escape town all of which has finally morphed into the solution to kill himself to end his pain of his meager life and provide for his family through the insurance policy.
1:36:08–1:37:09	Mr. Welch hears George Bailey's name, and **Mr. Welch angrily yells at George after punching him in a bar.** They throw Welch out.	PRAGMATIC	Losing the $8,000 is an opponent to George protecting his community and family from Potter. It also begins to remind George that he originally wanted to escape town (his initial contract). Melding with his failure to protect his community and family with the weight of having given up his dream to leave are coming together at rapid fire now.	While George continues to experience the playing out of him failing the decisive test to protect his community from Potter, simultaneously being heaped on is the reminder of the futility of his life in which he gave up his own dream of leaving (his original contract). This altruism seems particularly pointless now, and he has neither his original dream or his satisfaction of saving his community.

(Continued)

Table 6.18 *Continued*

TIMECODE*	BEAT Note: Master story beats/themes stated will be in **bold** and also contain the label "Master story beat/theme stated". States of being will be in ***bold italic.***	BEAT TYPE	ACTANTIAL NARRATIVE SCHEMA Note: Not every beat has an actantial narrative schema note; only key ones as deemed necessary.	CANONICAL NARRATIVE SCHEMA Note: Not every beat has a canonical narrative schema note; only key ones as deemed necessary.
1:37:10–1:37:37	Martini and Nick help George and see he has his life insurance policy and try to convince George not to go back out as he's drunk and not in his right mind.	PRAGMATIC		
1:37:38–1:38:11	George is drunk and rams his car into an old tree and is chastised by the tree's owner. He leaves.	PRAGMATIC		
1:38:12–1:38:33	George walks on bridge and is almost hit by a truck	PRAGMATIC		
1:38:34–1:38: 53	George stands on bridge and stares at water below, contemplating suicide and preparing to jump into the water and kill himself. ***George is on the verge of suicide, contemplating jumping into the water.***	COGNITIVE THYMIC	The culmination of failing to escape his hometown and failing to protect his community and family comes together as a combined sender to George the receiver, making him the subject with the object of killing himself.	George has failed in original decisive test to escape his hometown and now his newly evolved decisive test to protect his community culminates in a combined sense of failure and frustration, making him want to kill himself, a *being able to do something.*
1:38:54–1:38:56	Clarence is on the bridge watching George, knowing George is thinking of killing himself.	COGNITIVE		Clarence's qualifying test to save George is a *being able to do something* as George is ready to jump off the bridge.

Time	Description	Category	Notes
1:38:56–1:39:43	**George is about to jump off the bridge to commit suicide.** **Master story beat/theme stated:** **George is about to end his life.** **"Sometimes you are worth more dead than alive. Sometimes life feels too frustrating and painful to go on."** **Clarence jumps in first, screaming for help, and George dives in to save him.** **Master story beat/theme stated:** **George risks his own life to save Clarence. "No matter how distraught, he is a good man will always try and help his fellow man whose life is in danger."**	PRAGMATIC THYMIC PRAGMATIC THYMIC	Clarence's *being able to do something* manifests by him jumping in so George will save him and he can buy time. A mini-qualifying test of George jumping in to save Clarence is in play, buying time getting George's suicide off the table for the moment.
1:39:44–1:41:42	Clarence discloses to the tollhouse keeper and George in the tollbooth that he's an angel.	PRAGMATIC	
1:41:43—1:43:33	Clarence tells George he's his guardian angel there to help save George and in turn earn his wings.	PRAGMATIC	
1:43:34–1:44:14	Clarence gets the idea of granting George his wish that he never had been born.	COGNITIVE	

(Continued)

Table 6.18 Continued

TIMECODE*	BEAT	BEAT TYPE	ACTANTIAL NARRATIVE SCHEMA	CANONICAL NARRATIVE SCHEMA
	Note: Master story beats/themes stated will be in **bold** and also contain the label "Master story beat/theme stated". States of being will be in ***bold italic.***		Note: Not every beat has an actantial narrative schema note; only key ones as deemed necessary.	Note: Not every beat has a canonical narrative schema note; only key ones as deemed necessary.
1:44:15–1:44:28	Clarence grants George his wish of having never been born, and the wind blows open the door. **Master story beat/theme stated: Clarence grants George his wish. "Sometimes you need to go to extremes to prove a point and help someone in need."**	PRAGMATIC	Clarence is sender to the angels the receivers to grant George's wish of seeing life without him. This will make George the subject with the new object of coming to realize his life was worth living.	The new and final master decisive test begins and will run through most of the rest of the movie: Will Clarence be able to bring a reluctant George to the realization that his life was worth living, including for him to have stayed in Bedford Falls, and that his life impacted his community and has value? Since Clarence is a shadow protagonist to George the actual protagonist and their goals (contracts) merge here, even though it's driven solely by Clarence for most of this movement.
1:44:29–1:45:29	George experiences the immediate benefits of him having never been born, including his hearing in his left ear is back, his lip isn't bleeding.	PRAGMATIC COGNITIVE	Clarence is now a helper to George the subject; together, they share the object of making George see his life was worth living.	George's hearing in his left ear is restored, signifying he is shored up to partake of the master decisive test of him seeing his life was worth living.
1:45:30–1:46:41	George goes to retrieve his car that he rammed into the tree, but the car isn't there, and then he learns the town is now called "Pottersville," not Bedford Falls.	PRAGMATIC COGNITIVE	Clarence is a sender to George the receiver with Clarence as subject with the object of making George see the manifestation of Potter's greed unchecked (eventually merging Clarence and George into shared protagonists).	George is getting to see how Potter's master decisive test would've succeeded handily without George to block him. George's new final decisive test of seeing the impact of him missing from existence, leading to him realizing his life was worth living is in play.

1:46:42–1:48:05	George learns Martini's bar is now "Nick's Bar," and Nick is mean to Clarence when Clarence tries to order an unusual drink ***Nick angrily berates Clarence for his drink order.***	PRAGMATIC PRAGMATIC	Clarence is a sender to George the receiver with Clarence as subject with the object of making George see the manifestation of Potter's greed unchecked (eventually merging Clarence and George into shared protagonists).	George is getting to see how Potter's master decisive test would've succeeded handily without George to block him. George's new final decisive test of seeing the impact of him missing from existence, leading to him realizing his life was worth living is in play.
1:48:06–1:48:13	George remarks that Nick's anger Is strange behavior for him.	COGNITIVE	Clarence is a sender to George the receiver with Clarence as subject with the object of making George see the manifestation of Potter's greed unchecked (eventually merging Clarence and George into shared protagonists).	George is getting to see how Potter's master decisive test would've succeeded handily without George to block him. George's new final decisive test of seeing the impact of him missing from existence, leading to him realizing his life was worth living is in play.
1:48:14–1:49:31	Nick overhears Clarence talk about being an angel and begins to throw them out.	PRAGMATIC	Clarence is a sender to George the receiver with Clarence as subject with the object of making George see the manifestation of Potter's greed unchecked (eventually merging Clarence and George into shared protagonists).	George is getting to see how Potter's master decisive test would've succeeded handily without George to block him. George's new final decisive test of seeing the impact of him missing from existence, leading to him realizing his life was worth living is in play.
1:49:32–1:50:32	George sees Mr. Gower come in destitute and a panhandler, and Gower doesn't recognize George, confusing George.	COGNITIVE	Clarence is a sender to George the receiver with Clarence as subject with the object of making George see the manifestation of Potter's greed unchecked (eventually merging Clarence and George into shared protagonists).	George is getting to see how Potter's master decisive test would've succeeded handily without George to block him. George's new final decisive test of seeing the impact of him missing from existence, leading to him realizing his life was worth living is in play.

(Continued)

Table 6.18 *Continued*

TIMECODE*	BEAT Note: Master story beats/themes stated will be in **bold** and also contain the label "Master story beat/theme stated". States of being will be in ***bold italic.***	BEAT TYPE	ACTANTIAL NARRATIVE SCHEMA Note: Not every beat has an actantial narrative schema note; only key ones as deemed necessary.	CANONICAL NARRATIVE SCHEMA Note: Not every beat has a canonical narrative schema note; only key ones as deemed necessary.
1:50:33–1:50:43	George and Clarence are thrown out, and Nick rings the cash register, mocking Clarence's claim that every time a bell rings an angel gets their wings.	PRAGMATIC	Clarence is a sender to George the receiver with Clarence as subject with the object of making George see the manifestation of Potter's greed unchecked (eventually merging Clarence and George into shared protagonists).	George is getting to see how Potter's master decisive test would've succeeded handily without George to block him. George's new final decisive test of seeing the impact of him missing from existence, leading to him realizing his life was worth living is in play.
1:50:44–1:52:01	George sees the bar is now "Nick's" from the sign outside and hears from Clarence he now doesn't exist and Clarence confirms he has no wallet, or papers, and he doesn't have Zuzu's petals in his pocket anymore.	COGNITIVE PRAGMATIC	Clarence is a sender to George the receiver with Clarence as subject with the object of making George see the manifestation of Potter's greed unchecked (eventually merging Clarence and George into shared protagonists).	George is getting to see how Potter's master decisive test would've succeeded handily without George to block him. George's new final decisive test of seeing the impact of him missing from existence, leading to him realizing his life was worth living is in play.
1:52:02–1:52:10	Clarence declares George has been given a great gift, "a chance to see what the world would be like without you" and ***George angrily berates Clarence for telling him he has a gift; a chance to see what the world would be like without him.***	COGNITIVE THYMIC	Clarence is a sender to George the receiver with Clarence as subject with the object of making George see the manifestation of Potter's greed unchecked (eventually merging Clarence and George into shared protagonists).	George is getting to see how Potter's master decisive test would've succeeded handily without George to block him. George's new final decisive test of seeing the impact of him missing from existence, leading to him realizing his life was worth living is in play.

1:52:11–1:52:45	George is starting to sense something is really off but accuses Clarence of being crazy and goes off to find his family.	COGNITIVE	Clarence is a sender to George the receiver with Clarence as subject with the object of making George see the manifestation of Potter's greed unchecked (eventually merging Clarence and George into shared protagonists).	George is getting to see how Potter's master decisive test would've succeeded handily without George to block him. George's new final decisive test of seeing the impact of him missing from existence, leading to him realizing his life was worth living is in play.
1:52:47–1:52:49	George sees the sign "Pottersville."	COGNITIVE	Clarence is a sender to George the receiver with Clarence as subject with the object of making George see the manifestation of Potter's greed unchecked (eventually merging Clarence and George into shared protagonists).	George is getting to see how Potter's master decisive test would've succeeded handily without George to block him. George's new final decisive test of seeing the impact of him missing from existence, leading to him realizing his life was worth living is in play.
1:52:50–1:53:31	George stumbles around Pottersville and sees it's more "Vegas" than Bedford Falls with "dime-a-dance" halls, burlesque shows, etc.	COGNITIVE PRAGMATIC	Clarence is a sender to George the receiver with Clarence as subject with the object of making George see the manifestation of Potter's greed unchecked (eventually merging Clarence and George into shared protagonists).	George is getting to see how Potter's master decisive test would've succeeded handily without George to block him. George's new final decisive test of seeing the impact of him missing from existence, leading to him realizing his life was worth living is in play.
1:53:32–1:53:44	George points to the place where the Bailey Building and Loan building used to be and learns it's not there and went out of business years ago.	COGNITIVE	Clarence is a sender to George the receiver with Clarence as subject with the object of making George see the manifestation of Potter's greed unchecked (eventually merging Clarence and George into shared protagonists).	George is getting to see how Potter's master decisive test would've succeeded handily without George to block him. George's new final decisive test of seeing the impact of him missing from existence, leading to him realizing his life was worth living is in play.

(Continued)

Table 6.18 Continued

TIMECODE*	BEAT Note: Master story beats/themes stated will be in **bold** and also contain the label "Master story beat/theme stated". States of being will be in ***bold italic.***	BEAT TYPE	ACTANTIAL NARRATIVE SCHEMA Note: Not every beat has an actantial narrative schema note; only key ones as deemed necessary.	CANONICAL NARRATIVE SCHEMA Note: Not every beat has a canonical narrative schema note; only key ones as deemed necessary.
1:53:45–1:54:00	George is confused when he sees an angry different Violet getting dragged out off a "dime-a-dance" hall into a paddy wagon. ***Violet screams violently as she's dragged into custody by police.***	COGNITIVE THYMIC	Clarence is a sender to George the receiver with Clarence as subject with the object of making George see the manifestation of Potter's greed unchecked (eventually merging Clarence and George into shared protagonists). Of particular note is the binary opposition of how Violet's life has played out minus the benevolent treatment by George, a man she was "available to."	George is getting to see how Potter's master decisive test would've succeeded handily without George to block him. George's new final decisive test of seeing the impact of him missing from existence, leading to him realizing his life was worth living is in play.
1:54:01–1:54:45	George learns more evidence that he doesn't exist as he learns from Ernie that Ernie has never seen him before, lives in a shack in Pottersville rather than in Bailey Park, and his wife left and took his kid.	COGNITIVE	Ernie is the sender to George the receiver, making him the subject with the object of convincing them that they "know" him.	George is getting to see how Potter's master decisive test would've succeeded handily without George to block him. George's new final decisive test of seeing the impact of him missing from existence, leading to him realizing his life was worth living is in play.
1:54:46–1:54:57	Ernie bangs the side of his car door to get the attention of Burt the cop, who starts to tail the cab George is in.	PRAGMATIC	Even though everybody George interacts with in Pottersville is antagonistic to him, they are helpers in terms of bringing George to his new object of seeing the value of his life.	George is getting to see how Potter's master decisive test would've succeeded handily without George to block him. George's new final decisive test of seeing the impact of him missing from existence, leading to him realizing his life was worth living is in play.

Time	Event	Modality	Analysis	
1:54:58–1:55:47	George sees the house he lives in abandoned and in disrepair, and *George frantically yells out for his wife and children at the old dilapidated Granville house.* Clarence appears and confirms they are not there, and he has no children. *George desperately tries to convince Burt and Ernie that he knows them, recalling when they sung for him on his wedding night.*	COGNITIVE THYMIC PRAGMATIC THYMIC	Even though everybody George interacts with in Pottersville is antagonistic to him, they are helpers in terms of bringing George to his new object of seeing the value of his life.	George is getting to see how Potter's master decisive test would've succeeded handily without George to block him. George's new final decisive test of seeing the impact of him missing from existence, leading to him realizing his life was worth living is in play.
1:55:48–1:56:47	Burt the cop attempts to bring George in, thinking he's crazy, and Clarence bites his hand, and *Burt yells in pain* so George can escape, then himself disappears after crying out to the angel Joseph. *Burt yells in pain as Clarence bites his hand.*	PRAGMATIC THYMIC	Even though everybody George interacts with in Pottersville is antagonistic to him, they are helpers in terms of bringing George to his new object of seeing the value of his life.	George is getting to see how Potter's master decisive test would've succeeded handily without George to block him. George's new final decisive test of seeing the impact of him missing from existence, leading to him realizing his life was worth living is in play.
1:56:48–1:57:47	*George fearfully contemplates his mother not knowing him and learns his uncle Billy is now in an insane asylum.*	COGNITIVE	Again his interaction with his mother is in binary opposition to his original interaction, which involved her pushing (helping) him to fall in love with Mary.	George is getting to see how Potter's master decisive test would've succeeded handily without George to block him. George's new final decisive test of seeing the impact of him missing from existence, leading to him realizing his life was worth living is in play.

(Continued)

Table 6.18 *Continued*

TIMECODE*	BEAT Note: Master story beats/themes stated will be in **bold** and also contain the label "Master story beat/theme stated". States of being will be in ***bold italic.***	BEAT TYPE	ACTANTIAL NARRATIVE SCHEMA Note: Not every beat has an actantial narrative schema note; only key ones as deemed necessary.	CANONICAL NARRATIVE SCHEMA Note: Not every beat has a canonical narrative schema note; only key ones as deemed necessary.
1:57:48–1:57:59	George thinks hard about what is going on, why so much about the life he knows is radically different.	COGNITIVE	All of the antagonisms/antagonists are serving as helpers to George, whose new object is to see his life as lived was a good one.	George is getting to see how Potter's master decisive test would've succeeded handily without George to block him. George's new final decisive test of seeing the impact of him missing from existence, leading to him realizing his life was worth living is in play.
1:58:00–1:58:22	George determines he'll talk to Martini to figure out what is going on.	COGNITIVE	Visual reminder (sender) that George's (receiver) presence in his hometown was important to its well-being.	George is getting to see how Potter's master decisive test would've succeeded handily without George to block him. George's new final decisive test of seeing the impact of him missing from existence, leading to him realizing his life was worth living is in play.
1:58:23–1:58:31	George and Clarence visit what was Bailey Park, only to realize it's now a cemetery	COGNITIVE	Visual reminder (sender) that George's (receiver) presence in his hometown was important to its well-being.	George is getting to see how Potter's master decisive test would've succeeded handily without George to block him. George's new final decisive test of seeing the impact of him missing from existence, leading to him realizing his life was worth living is in play.

Time	Description	Type	Notes
1:58:32–1:59:15	George cleans off Harry's grave and learns he died at 8 years old because George wasn't around to save him, and the men Harry had originally saved in turn died in the Second World War because Harry (in this world where George doesn't exist) wasn't around to save them.	COGNITIVE	George's non-existence is echoed by Harry's now "non- existence" caused by George's absence from life. This is a special helper to bring George closer to his object of realizing his life was worth living.	George is getting to see how Potter's master decisive test would've succeeded handily without George to block him. George's new final decisive test of seeing the impact of him missing from existence, leading to him realizing his life was worth living is in play.
1:59:16–1:59:52	George is starting to realize Clarence might be telling the truth and asks Clarence about Mary.	COGNITIVE	The former community of friends now turned antagonists of Pottersville have pushed George to be emotional enough to want to know what happened to Mary, so, in essence, all of these antagonists (former friends) will be ultimate helpers in bringing George closer to what will be his new final object . . . realizing his life was worth living.	George is getting to see how Potter's master decisive test would've succeeded handily without George to block him. George's new final decisive test of seeing the impact of him missing from existence, leading to him realizing his life was worth living is in play.
	George emotionally pleads to Clarence about Mary's whereabouts.	THYMIC		
	Clarence reluctantly admits Mary is an old maid and is about to close up the library.	PRAGMATIC		
	Clarence emotionally yells to George Mary's whereabouts.	THYMIC		Note: George's emotional tie to his wife Mary deepens his evolving decisive test to realize his life was worth living.
1:59:53–2:00:37	George finds Mary leaving the library, and she is an old maid and doesn't recognize him. ***George emotionally pleads with Mary, trying to make sense of what is going on. Mary screams fearfully as a response to George pleading with her.***	COGNITIVE THYMIC PRAGMATIC	The former community of friends now turned antagonists of Pottersville have pushed George to be emotional enough to want to know what happened to Mary, so, in essence, all of these antagonists (former friends) will be ultimate helpers in bringing George closer to what will be his new final object . . . realizing his life was worth living.	George is getting to see how Potter's master decisive test would've succeeded handily without George to block him. George's new final decisive test of seeing the impact of him missing from existence, leading to him realizing his life was worth living is in play.
	George's insistence that he knows her scares her, and she screams and runs away.	THYMIC		
	Master story beat/theme stated: George realizes Mary would be alone without him. **"If you never existed, the one you were meant to be with could have a bad life."**			

(Continued)

Table 6.18 Continued

TIMECODE*	BEAT Note: Master story beats/themes stated will be in **bold** and also contain the label "Master story beat/theme stated". States of being will be in ***bold italic.***	BEAT TYPE	ACTANTIAL NARRATIVE SCHEMA Note: Not every beat has an actantial narrative schema note; only key ones as deemed necessary.	CANONICAL NARRATIVE SCHEMA Note: Not every beat has a canonical narrative schema note; only key ones as deemed necessary.
2:00:38–2:01:19	George runs into a bar and screams that she's his wife, and ***Mary screams and almost passes out.*** Burt the cop shows up; George punches Burt, who fires at him as George runs away.	THYMIC PRAGMATIC	The former community of friends now turned antagonists of Pottersville have pushed George to be emotional enough to want to know what happened to Mary, so, in essence, all of these antagonists (former friends) will be ultimate helpers in bringing George closer to what will be his new final object . . . realizing his life was worth living.	George is getting to see how Potter's master decisive test would've succeeded handily without George to block him. George's new final decisive test of seeing the impact of him missing from existence, leading to him realizing his life was worth living is in play. Note: George's emotional tie to his wife Mary deepens his evolving decisive test to realize his life was worth living.
2:01:20–2:02:01	George runs back onto the bridge and ***makes an emotional plea to Clarence to put things back to normal and that he wants to live again.*** **Master story beat/theme stated: George wants to live again.** **"Seeing what life would be like without you existing will bring you to the greatest understanding of your value."**	COGNITIVE THYMIC	The entire experience of seeing life without him has been a sender to George the receiver, making him the subject with the object of wanting to exist again. George's plea to Clarence is a sender to Clarence receiver to make Clarence the subject with the object of making George exist again.	Master decisive test completed: George has been brought to not wanting to commit suicide by virtue of wanting to continue existing because he sees how things are bad without him having been around to help his community and marry Mary and that life would be bad without him.

2:02:02–2:02:49	Burt comes and asks George if he's okay, and **George angrily threatens to hit Burt again.** **George is ecstatic when he realizes Burt knows him, his mouth is bleeding, and he has Zuzu's petals, all signs that he's back to existing.**	COGNITIVE THYMIC	Burt is now a helper to George realizing it was worth it for him to be alive (his new and final object).	The glorifying test has begun. As stated previously, the recent decisive test of George protecting the community from Potter (which he has failed at) has morphed into the decisive test of George realizing his life was worth it, from which he has succeeded. So, from this point on, he is in his glorifying test mode, not caring about the consequences of the missing money.
2:02:50–2:02:58	George runs back to see his car is crashed into the tree again, and he yells in happiness. **George ecstatically yells hello to his old town Bedford Falls.**	COGNITIVE THYMIC PRAGMATIC	George's new final object (to realize his life as lived was worth living) is in full play, and the idea of saving the community and finding $8,000 isn't in the forefront anymore.	The glorifying test has begun. As stated previously, the recent decisive test of George protecting the community from Potter (which he has failed at) has morphed into the decisive test of George realizing his life was worth it, from which he has succeeded. So, from this point on, he is in his glorifying test mode, not caring about the consequences of the missing money.
2:03:00–2:03:25	George now recognizes old Bedford Falls and **George ecstatically yells hello to his old town Bedford Falls.** **George runs and happily yells "Merry Christmas" to townspeople.**	THYMIC PRAGMATIC	George's new final object (to realize his life as lived was worth living) is in full play, and the idea of saving the community and finding $8,000 isn't in the forefront anymore.	The glorifying test has begun. As stated previously, the recent decisive test of George protecting the community from Potter (which he has failed at) has morphed into the decisive test of George realizing his life was worth it, from which he has succeeded. So, from this point on, he is in his glorifying test mode, not caring about the consequences of the missing money.

(Continued)

Table 6.18 *Continued*

TIMECODE*	BEAT Note: Master story beats/themes stated will be in **bold** and also contain the label "Master story beat/theme stated". States of being will be in ***bold italic.***	BEAT TYPE	ACTANTIAL NARRATIVE SCHEMA Note: Not every beat has an actantial narrative schema note; only key ones as deemed necessary.	CANONICAL NARRATIVE SCHEMA Note: Not every beat has a canonical narrative schema note; only key ones as deemed necessary.
2:03:26–2:03:34	***George happily yells "Merry Christmas" to Mr. Potter.***	THYMIC PRAGMATIC	George's new final object (to realize his life as lived was worth living) is in full play, and the idea of saving the community and finding $8,000 isn't in the forefront anymore.	The glorifying test has begun. As stated previously, the recent decisive test of George protecting the community from Potter (which he has failed at) has morphed into the decisive test of George realizing his life was worth it, from which he has succeeded. So, from this point on, he is in his glorifying test mode, not caring about the consequences of the missing money.
2:03:35–2:04:35	***George returns home and happily greets the bank examiner and authorities at his home.*** ***George emotionally kisses the broken piece on the staircase.*** ***George emotionally embraces his children.***	THYMIC PRAGMATIC	George's new final object (to realize his life as lived was worth living) is in full play, and the idea of saving the community and finding $8,000 isn't in the forefront anymore.	The glorifying test has begun. As stated previously, the recent decisive test of George protecting the community from Potter (which he has failed at) has morphed into the decisive test of George realizing his life was worth it, from which he has succeeded. So, from this point on, he is in his glorifying test mode, not caring about the consequences of the missing money.

2:04:39–2:04:59	Mary comes home, and George embraces her with joy. **Mary emotionally reunites with George.**	THYMIC	George's new final object (to realize his life as lived was worth living) is in full play, and the idea of saving the community and finding $8,000 isn't in the forefront anymore.	The glorifying test has begun. As stated previously, the recent decisive test of George protecting the community from Potter (which he has failed at) has morphed into the decisive test of George realizing his life was worth it, from which he has succeeded. So, from this point on, he is in his glorifying test mode, not caring about the consequences of the missing money.
2:05:00–2:05:23	Mary brings George and kids into the living room to prepare for a wonderful miracle that has occurred. **Mary emotionally prepares George and family for the community with money coming in.**	PRAGMATIC	George's new final object (to realize his life as lived was worth living) is in full play, and the idea of saving the community and finding $8,000 isn't in the forefront anymore.	The glorifying test has begun. As stated previously, the recent decisive test of George protecting the community from Potter (which he has failed at) has morphed into the decisive test of George realizing his life was worth it, from which he has succeeded. So, from this point on, he is in his glorifying test mode, not caring about the consequences of the missing money.
2:05:25–2:07:01	All George's friends from Bedford Falls come into his home and dump money to pay for the lost $8,000 dollars, and George smiles at and carefully scrutinizes all the friends he encountered when he didn't exist that seem back to normal. **Master story beat/theme state: His community came through and bailed him out. "If you treat people well, they will come through for you in the end."**	PRAGMATIC	George's friends, brother and community are all helpers, pitching in to bail George out and helping him overcome his company's deficit, but also helpers in realizing his final object, that his life was worth living.	The glorifying test has begun. As stated previously, the recent decisive test of George protecting the community from Potter (which he has failed at) has morphed into the decisive test of George realizing his life was worth it, from which he has succeeded. So, from this point on, he is in his glorifying test mode not caring about the consequences of the missing money.

(Continued)

Table 6.18 Continued

TIMECODE*	BEAT Note: Master story beats/themes stated will be in **bold** and also contain the label "Master story beat/theme stated". States of being will be in **bold italic.**	BEAT TYPE	ACTANTIAL NARRATIVE SCHEMA Note: Not every beat has an actantial narrative schema note; only key ones as deemed necessary.	CANONICAL NARRATIVE SCHEMA Note: Not every beat has a canonical narrative schema note; only key ones as deemed necessary.
2:07:02–2:07:14	Ernie reads a telegram from London: Sam Wainwright is advancing George $25,000 dollars if he needs it. **Crowd is ecstatic over telegram from Sam Wainwright advancing George $25,000.** **The man there to arrest George tears up the warrant for his arrest happily.**	PRAGMATIC		The glorifying test has begun. As stated previously, the recent decisive test of George protecting the community from Potter (which he has failed at) has morphed into the decisive test of George realizing his life was worth it, from which he has succeeded. So, from this point on, he is in his glorifying test mode, not caring about the consequences of the missing money.
2:07:15–2:09:02	The celebration continues, and George finds a Tom Sawyer novel that is signed by Clarence proclaiming "Remember George:— No man is a failure who has <u>friends</u>— Thanks for the wings! Love, Clarence." **Master story beat/theme stated: George realizes he has friends and is loved. "No man is a failure who has friends."**	COGNITIVE		The glorifying test has begun. As stated previously, the recent decisive test of George protecting the community from Potter (which he has failed at) has morphed into the decisive test of George realizing his life was worth it, from which he has succeeded. So, from this point on, he is in his glorifying test mode, not caring about the consequences of the missing money.

2:09:03	A bell on the Christmas tree rings, and Zuzu proclaims, "Every time a bell rings an angel gets his wings" **Master story beat/theme stated: Clarence succeeded in getting his wings. "If you persevere, you'll eventually succeed."** *George winks to the sky and congratulates Clarence.*	COGNITIVE		Glorifying test completed.

* When breaking down and studying your specimen movies for brainstorming purposes, you want a quick reference as to where in the movie's timeline the beat in question occurs and how much time it takes to play out.

** Credits precede the story and end at 1:16.

*** This is beautifully captured when George pulls Harry's new bride to the side and asks if this new job Is a good one, and she says it's an opportunity, and her father "fell in love with Harry." George remarks, "So did you," almost disgruntled. She is a clear opponent to his initial contract; namely, his dreams of leaving town and living a life of adventure.

**** This could be considered bad dramatic structure; namely, drunk Uncle Billy misplaces $8,000 of the company's money, which is almost a deus ex machina (from Aristotle's *Poetics*, the God from the machine comes down to bring judgment and end the play instead of it ending organically from the plot). But narratively it balances out against the magic of the story given the "unfair advantage" aided to George via angels overseeing and eventually interfering on his behalf.

Master Story Beats/Themes Stated "Cheat Sheet"—*It's a Wonderful Life*

As previously stated, there are several ways to analyze master story beats/themes stated in movie story. I tend to work with two primary approaches. The first approach is to start with a log of the master story beats and write what the beat is in a plain English description, such as the beat "Young George saves Young Harry from drowning in ice water." This description is *reiteration* of what the actual beat is, a restatement in simple terms. Next to it you'll notice a "/" and then the thematic-sounding phrase "Helping others without regard for personal welfare gives life meaning." The second part of the master beat/theme stated (the "helping others" part) is stated as a traditional literary theme, sounding almost like a proverb, such as "Do the right thing for others even if it means suffering." This method of scoring master story beats (charting first the beat as a plain English reiteration of the beat *and* then writing next to it an accompanying proverb like "theme stated") is one way of handling master story beats. For some, this literary theme method may seem like overkill and moving us away from understanding the beauty of pure "story energy," which is vital to understand to be able to write strong scripts. I just wanted to lay out this approach for those who may be inclined to use it. Again, there are no rules . . . just tools.

However, there is a second way of creating them.

The Second Way of Handling Master Story Beats/Themes Stated

In some specimen movies (as you'll see in my subsequent specimen breakdown of *Lost in Translation*), I will use just the same plain English reiteration of the plot event alone to capture the master story beats/themes stated such as "Love at first sight through mutual connection" (lifted directly from the *Lost in Translation* comprehensive beat map). This is merely a restatement of the beat in simple language. I don't bother trying to add a more thematic way of expressing that master story beat; a plain English reiteration is enough. Of course, I could add a more literary thematic label to this master story beat, but I don't feel the need to in every case.

Both approaches to master story beats/themes stated are valid, and either one can be used according to your own discretion and depending on which specimen movie you are breaking down. To me, the decision of what to use when depends on the individual movie. For example, *It's a Wonderful Life* seems to reek with literary-type themes that are expressed through the master story beats, whereas *Lost in Translation* is a different case, as is *Get Out*, all which will be explicated later. You could, of course, find ways of stating the master story beats in *Lost in Translation* and *Get Out* in a more traditional literary "theme" type way, as you could simply state the master story beats in *It's a Wonderful Life* as just plain English reiterations of story beats. There aren't rules; it's whatever way works best for the specimen breakdowns you are doing in the light of what you eventually want to write being the prime factor to consider when selecting your approach to master story beats. The important takeaway when thinking about different approaches to master story beats/themes stated is these master beats constitute the main "moments" in a story and will feel thematic to an audience, regardless of whether they lend themselves to being expressed in a literary way or not.

Cheat Sheet of Master Story Beats/ Themes Stated

That said, in *all* cases of specimen breakdowns, I like to gather up my master story beats/ themes stated on a single table as a "cheat sheet" with timecode from the movie, so I can study the beats in a snapshot because these tend to be the moments in a movie that make it work. For workflow purposes, I usually first do a draft of the comprehensive beat map (see Table 6.18) *then* work the master story beats out by plotting them against the four corners of the controlling semiotic square (see Figures 6.3 to 6.18). Then, after using the four corners of the master semiotic square to really think through what the master story beats are, I'll go back to the comprehensive beat sheet and add them back in. That said it's good to have a "cheat sheet" to study just the master story beats/themes stated of your specimen movie breakdowns to give you a command of the most powerful moments in the stories you are studying.

Table 6.19 Master story beats/themes stated—cheat sheet— for *It's a Wonderful Life*

TIME CODE	BEAT (derived from comprehensive beat sheet)	MASTER STORY BEATS/ THEMES STATED	BEAT TYPE
3:55–5:06	Clarence is granted vision into Young George's childhood where George saves his younger brother Harry from drowning in ice which caused Young George to lose hearing in his left ear, a condition that would be with him for life.	**Young George saves Young Harry from drowning in ice water. "Help others without regard for personal welfare gives life meaning."**	PRAGMATIC COGNITIVE
10:27–11:24 11:25–11:38	Young George is smacked by Mr. Gower, mad at him that he didn't deliver the pills, but George explains Gower put poison in the pills, hence the reason for not delivering them. Young George cries, and Mr. Gower checks the poison jar. *Mr. Gower realizes via Young George his mistake that he put poison in the pills he dispensed and embraces crying Young George out of gratitude and gets emotional.*	**Young George risks getting hit by Mr. Gower to save him. "Doing the right thing even if it means suffering gives life meaning."**	PRAGMATIC COGNITIVE THYMIC
29:48–34:01	3 months after George's father's death, George argues with Mr. Potter in front of the board of the Bailey Building and Loan, trying to push back on Potter's bid to dissolve it.	**George pushes back on Potter. "You must plead for what is right to protect the community."**	PRAGMATIC

(Continued)

Table 6.19 *Continued*

TIME CODE	BEAT (derived from comprehensive beat sheet)	MASTER STORY BEATS/ THEMES STATED	BEAT TYPE
34:02—35:02	George learns the board voted down Potter's takeover bid and will keep the Building and Loan going, provided that George takes over.	**George is voted to take over the board. "If you plead for what is right with the powers that be they will act in the interest of the community."**	PRAGMATIC COGNITIVE
35:49–37:19	Harry arrives, and George learns he has gotten married and has a job offer with his wife's father's company.	**George takes his brother's place. "If you don't seize the day and take opportunities when you can, you'll lose out."**	COGNITIVE
37:20–37:45	George learns that the job Harry's father in-law offered Harry is a great opportunity.	**George realizes his brother has an opportunity. "Sacrificing for others is worth it."**	COGNITIVE
49:42–50:12	*George expresses anger about not wanting to get married.* *Mary cries over George's anger about not wanting to get married.* *George and Mary kiss and embrace and profess their love after George got angry.*	George and Mary fall in love. "It's impossible to escape your destiny of whom you were meant to be with."	PRAGMATIC THYMIC
58:38–1:00:08	*George and co-workers are exhilarated they didn't have to close their doors before 6 p.m., but then realizes he forgot about Mary.*	George saved the community from Potter. "If you plead for what is right with the community, they will act in interest of the community."	THYMIC COGNITIVE PRAGMATIC
1:07:33–1:12:43	George is offered a lucrative deal with Mr. Potter to run Potter's properties and is excited by the offer then rejects it.	**George is offered money from Potter. "Money isn't everything, especially if it involves turning your back on the community."**	COGNITIVE PRAGMATIC
1:32:18–1:35:20	*George begs Potter to loan him the $8,000 dollars to cover the lost money.* Potter's response is to promise he'll swear out a warrant for George's arrest.	**George attempts to make a deal with the devil Potter. "At some point, everyone will contemplate making a deal with the devil."**	PRAGMATIC THYMIC

1:38:56–1:39:43	*George is about to jump off the bridge to commit suicide.*	**George is about to end his life.** "Sometimes you are worth more dead than alive. Sometimes life feels too frustrating and painful to go on."	PRAGMATIC THYMIC
	Clarence jumps in first, screaming for help, and George dives in to save him.	**George risks his own life to save Clarence.** "No matter how distraught he is, a good man will always try and help his fellow man whose life is in danger."	THYMIC PRAGMATIC
1:44:15–1:44:28	Clarence grants George his wish of having never been born, and the wind blows open the door.	**Clarence grants George his wish.** "Sometimes you need to go to extremes to prove a point and help someone in need."	PRAGMATIC
1:59:53–2:00:37	George finds Mary leaving the library, and she is an old maid and doesn't recognize him. *George emotionally pleads with Mary trying to make sense of what is going on. Mary screams fearfully as a response to George pleading with her.*	**George realizes Mary would be alone without him.** "If you never existed, the one you were meant to be with could have a bad life."	COGNITIVE THYMIC PRAGMATIC
	George's insistence that he knows her scares her, and she screams and runs away.		THYMIC
2:01:20–2:02:01	George runs back onto the bridge and *makes an emotional plea to Clarence to put things back to normal and that he wants to live again.*	**George wants to live again.** "Seeing what life would be like without you existing will bring you to the greatest understanding of your value."	COGNITIVE THYMIC
2:05:25–2:07:01	All George's friends from Bedford Falls come into his home and dump money to pay for the lost $8,000 dollars, and George scrutinizes all the friends he encountered when he didn't exist that seem back to normal.	**George's community came through and bailed him out.** "If you treat people well, they will come through for you in the end."	PRAGMATIC

(Continued)

Table 6.19 *Continued*

TIME CODE	BEAT (derived from comprehensive beat sheet)	MASTER STORY BEATS/ THEMES STATED	BEAT TYPE
2:07:15–2:09:02	The celebration continues, and George finds a Tom Sawyer novel that is signed by Clarence proclaiming "No man is a failure who has friends—Thanks for the wings! Love, Clarence."	**George realizes he has friends and is loved. "No man is a failure who has friends."** *	COGNITIVE
2:09:03	A bell on the Christmas tree rings, and Zuzu proclaims, "Every time a bell rings, an angel gets his wings." **George winks to the sky and congratulates Clarence.**	**Clarence succeeded in getting his wings. "If you persevere, you'll eventually succeed."**	COGNITIVE

* This is the actual main theme of the entire movie, whereby all the other ones in this list can be seen to be connected to or related to, even if sometimes in a binary opposition manner.

Using the Entire Master Semiotic Square to Plot Master Story Beats/Themes Stated—*It's a Wonderful Life*

In the final section of each specimen breakdown, I will deconstruct master story beats/themes stated from another angle, plotting them against all four corners of the master semiotic square for the movie for further brainstorming and analysis. I introduced this tool earlier when I brainstormed for the demo of *The Lost Dog Story* and also used it to examine *Rocky*. I examined it earlier because it's a powerful yet complex tool.

Let me start off first by reiterating what master story beats/themes stated are. They are beats in a movie which occur at significant transformation points, meaning they mark plot points where the protagonist (subject) moves conspicuously closer (in conjunction) or further from (in disjunction) with their object of want/need/desire, or what is deemed as a value for the story. It is the tracking of these transformation points that we analyze and plot against the master semiotic square because these beats essentially control the movie, and this technique will teach us a lot how to unify the beats in terms of the story and themes.

Use all Four Corners of the Master Semiotic Square Creatively

I use all four corners of the movie's master semiotic square in a creative/analytical brainstorming way to see if it can offer insights into these transformative moments and also prepare my brain to devise new ones for an original screenplay I might be writing. Again, this part of the breakdown process is not to test your knowledge of classical logic, but it's to help force you to relate everything back to the master semiotic square and use all four corners of it creatively whenever possible. I view this as a creative breakdown exercise.

Brief "Legend" of how Master Story Beats/Themes Stated are Plotted

I decided to facilitate use of this tool to again create a simple "legend" starting with the very first master story beat/theme stated for *It's a Wonderful Life*. The same legend will apply for all of the specimen movies the book breaks down and can be used for any specimen movie you break down. It can also be used to brainstorm for your original screenplay.

For "legend" purposes, the master story beats/themes stated will be in **bold**, and the states of being will be in ***bold italic.*** Also, while I already used callout boxes to explicate the plotting of the master story beats on the semiotic square for *The Lost Dog Story*, I thought it would be a good idea to repeat the descriptions again to facilitate the breakdown process, as there are a lot of moving parts.

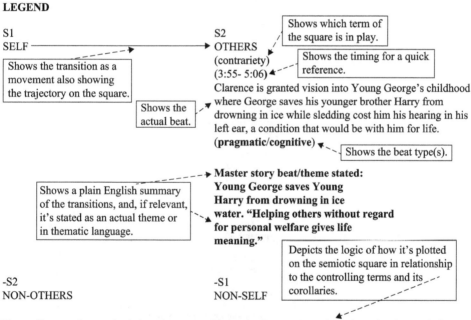

LEGEND

S1
SELF

[Shows the transition as a movement also showing the trajectory on the square.]

[Shows the actual beat.]

S2
OTHERS
(contrariety)
(3:55- 5:06)

[Shows which term of the square is in play.]

[Shows the timing for a quick reference.]

Clarence is granted vision into Young George's childhood where George saves his younger brother Harry from drowning in ice while sledding cost him his hearing in his left ear, a condition that would be with him for life. **(pragmatic/cognitive)**

[Shows the beat type(s).]

[Shows a plain English summary of the transitions, and, if relevant, it's stated as an actual theme or in thematic language.]

Master story beat/theme stated: Young George saves Young Harry from drowning in ice water. "Helping others without regard for personal welfare gives life meaning."

[Depicts the logic of how it's plotted on the semiotic square in relationship to the controlling terms and its corollaries.]

-S2
NON-OTHERS

-S1
NON-SELF

Young George takes an altruistic action to save his brother Young Harry from drowning (**others** before **self**), which causes permanent hearing loss for Young George. This doesn't hamper George's dream to leave but will help inform him later that his life had meaning when he experiences life without him (Harry would've died and not saved his fellow men in WWII). This is pure disregard for **self** for **others**, hence the movement on the square.

Figure 6.5 Master story beat/theme stated 1—*It's a Wonderful Life* (includes LEGEND). I used the first master beat of *It's a Wonderful Life* to explicate how the moving parts of this complex tool work, a reiteration of the explanation from an earlier chapter, but one I believe duly required at this juncture.

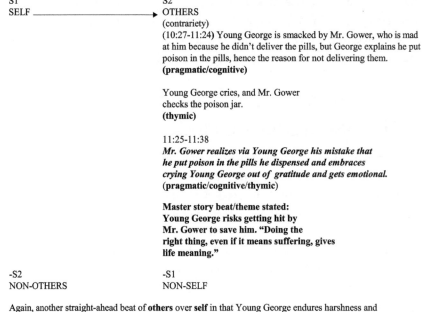

S1
SELF ⎯⎯⎯⎯⎯⎯⎯⎯⎯⎯⎯⎯⎯⎯➤

S2
OTHERS
(contrariety)
(10:27-11:24) Young George is smacked by Mr. Gower, who is mad at him because he didn't deliver the pills, but George explains he put poison in the pills, hence the reason for not delivering them.
(pragmatic/cognitive)

Young George cries, and Mr. Gower
checks the poison jar.
(thymic)

11:25-11:38
Mr. Gower realizes via Young George his mistake that he put poison in the pills he dispensed and embraces crying Young George out of gratitude and gets emotional.
(pragmatic/cognitive/thymic)

Master story beat/theme stated:
Young George risks getting hit by
Mr. Gower to save him. "Doing the
right thing, even if it means suffering, gives
life meaning."

-S2
NON-OTHERS

-S1
NON-SELF

Again, another straight-ahead beat of **others** over **self** in that Young George endures harshness and violence from Mr. Gower to make sure he doesn't poison his customer. While this doesn't hamper his dreams of escaping home, it is formative in what will become his perspective of how he impacted people. Of note: I plot the move directly from **self** to **others** because he's too young to even realize the implications of just selflessly helping others. It comes naturally.

Figure 6.6 Master story beat/theme stated 2—*It's a Wonderful Life.*

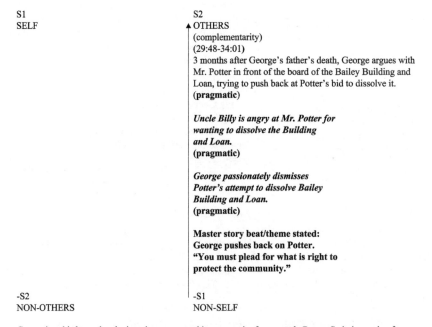

S1
SELF

S2
▲OTHERS
(complementarity)
(29:48-34:01)
3 months after George's father's death, George argues with Mr. Potter in front of the board of the Bailey Building and Loan, trying to push back at Potter's bid to dissolve it.
(pragmatic)

Uncle Billy is angry at Mr. Potter for
wanting to dissolve the Building
and Loan.
(pragmatic)

George passionately dismisses
Potter's attempt to dissolve Bailey
Building and Loan.
(pragmatic)

Master story beat/theme stated:
George pushes back on Potter.
"You must plead for what is right to
protect the community."

-S2
NON-OTHERS

-S1
NON-SELF

George is at his best when he is trying to protect his community from greedy Potter. So he's moving from **non-self** to **others** because it's not completely against his own interests in that the family business, and he has no personal stake yet because he thinks he's leaving.

Figure 6.7 Master story beat/theme stated 3—*It's a Wonderful Life.*

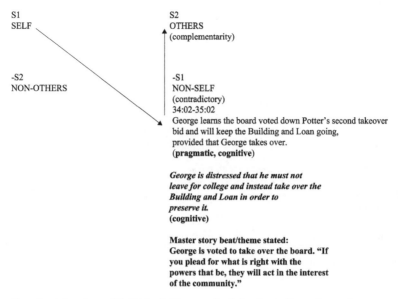

George learns the outcome of his fighting for his community; the board wants him to take over the Building and Loan Company to keep them from selling to Potter. This could be taken as an opportunity certainly not for **self**, or from **self** to **non-self** then to **others** because he's not happy about having to stay in Bedford Falls. This is why I plotted from **self** to **non-self** to **others**. His action to run the board is directly affecting his master decisive test to escape town.

Figure 6.8 Master story beat/theme stated 4—*It's a Wonderful Life.*

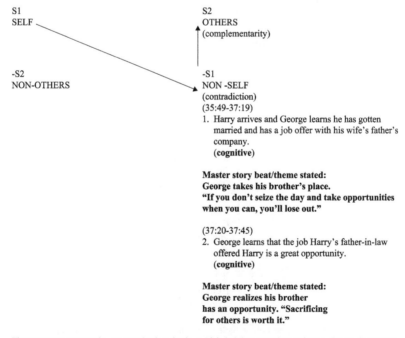

These two master story beats occur back-to-back, so I labeled them together. In beat 1, George hasn't yet failed in his initial chosen **contract** to leave home and explore the world but is unhappy about what this latest wrinkle means to his plan to escape, hence the move from **self** to **non-self**. In beat 2, George learns directly that the job is of great future benefit to his brother, hence the move from **non-self** to **others**.

Figure 6.9 Master story beat/theme stated 5—*It's a Wonderful Life.* Sometimes two master story beats are so related that I show them together, as is the case above.

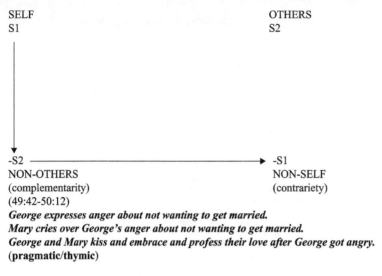

SELF
S1

OTHERS
S2

-S2
NON-OTHERS
(complementarity)
(49:42-50:12)
George expresses anger about not wanting to get married.
Mary cries over George's anger about not wanting to get married.
George and Mary kiss and embrace and profess their love after George got angry.
(pragmatic/thymic)

Master story beat/theme stated:
George and Mary fall in love. "It's
impossible to escape your destiny
of whom you were meant to be with."

-S1
NON-SELF
(contrariety)

George is on the verge of failing a qualifying test of leaving town which has to do with a being able to resist the temptation of Mary (*a being able to do*), who would ground him in Bedford Falls forever. But this beat is a transformative scene that begins his shift towards a newly evolved contract which will be to serve his community and live the life he was meant to live. This is not merely serving **others** because it involves satisfying his love life, yet it's not specifically serving **self** because it will keep him in Bedford Falls. This is why I used the movement of **self** to **non-others** and then to **non-self**. This movement underscores a key essence of the story architecture; namely, how George outright serves his community, and inadvertently and indirectly serves himself in a way that will serve his community which he'll fully realize at the end.

Figure 6.10 Master story beat/theme stated 6—*It's a Wonderful Life.*

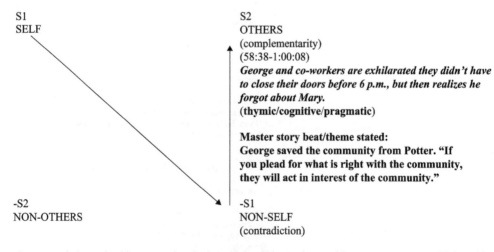

S1
SELF

S2
OTHERS
(complementarity)
(58:38-1:00:08)
George and co-workers are exhilarated they didn't have
to close their doors before 6 p.m., but then realizes he
forgot about Mary.
(thymic/cognitive/pragmatic)

Master story beat/theme stated:
George saved the community from Potter. "If
you plead for what is right with the community,
they will act in interest of the community."

-S2
NON-OTHERS

-S1
NON-SELF
(contradiction)

George again is serving his community via the vehicle of his marriage and honeymoon money, which could be said to move from **self** to **non-self** to **others**. He still has a key role in the community, employed by the company albeit he uses his own money. He is solidifying what will become his vision and final decisive test of seeing his importance in having lived, especially when he sees in his absence that Potter took over the town.

Figure 6.11 Master story beat/theme stated 7—*It's a Wonderful Life.*

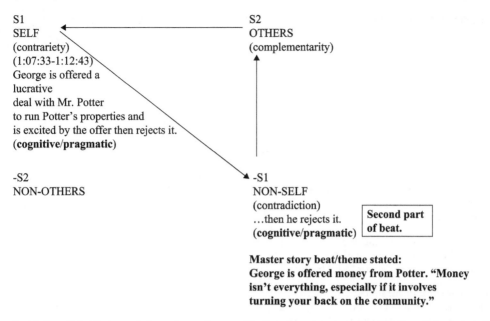

S1
SELF
(contrariety)
(1:07:33-1:12:43)
George is offered a
lucrative
deal with Mr. Potter
to run Potter's properties and
is excited by the offer then rejects it.
(**cognitive/pragmatic**)

S2
OTHERS
(complementarity)

-S2
NON-OTHERS

-S1
NON-SELF
(contradiction)
…then he rejects it.
(**cognitive/pragmatic**)

Second part of beat.

Master story beat/theme stated:
George is offered money from Potter. "Money isn't everything, especially if it involves turning your back on the community."

In this beat, I decided to split it starting at the top with George getting excited by Mr. Potter's lucrative offer to serve himself (**others** to **self**), but by the end of the deal George rejects it, and I split the beat down to the movement from **non-self** to **others**.

Figure 6.12 Master story beat/theme stated 8—*It's a Wonderful Life*. This master beat is split into two parts.

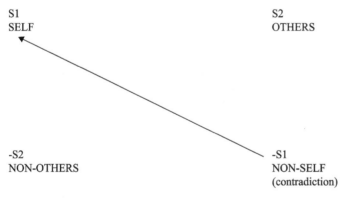

S1
SELF

S2
OTHERS

-S2
NON-OTHERS

-S1
NON-SELF
(contradiction)

(1:32:18-1:35-20)
George begs Potter to loan him the $8,000 dollars to cover the lost money.
Potter's response is to promise he'll swear out a warrant for George's arrest.
(**pragmatic/thymic**)

Master story beat/theme stated:
George attempts to make a deal with
the devil Potter. "At some point everyone will
contemplate making a deal with the devil."

George takes to begging Mr. Potter to bail him out (and lend him the $8,000), and while it can help the community, it's to save George Bailey himself. But this effort is not directly just for himself, but it's not specifically for others either. I see it as indirectly saving the community moving from **non-self** to **self** because he's saving himself. It's also a beat which moves him further from ever leaving (his original decisive test/object) and exacerbating that he did decide to stay producing the attendant frustration, with both failing the community and having failed his original dream (to leave).

Figure 6.13 Master story beat/theme stated 9—*It's a Wonderful Life.*

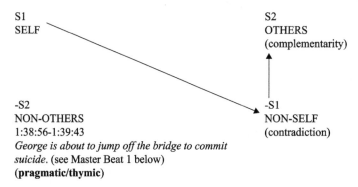

S1
SELF

S2
OTHERS
(complementarity)

-S2
NON-OTHERS
1:38:56-1:39:43
George is about to jump off the bridge to commit suicide. (see Master Beat 1 below)
(pragmatic/thymic)

-S1
NON-SELF
(contradiction)

Clarence jumps in first screaming for help and George dives in to save him.
(thymic/pragmatic) (see Master Beat 2 below)

Master story beat/theme stated:
1: George is about to end his life.
"Sometimes you are worth more dead than alive.
Sometimes life feels too frustrating and painful to go on."

Master story beat/theme stated:
2: George risks his own life to save Clarence.
"No matter how distraught he is, a good man will always try and help his fellow man whose life is in danger."

George is acting selfishly (**self**) in his own interest by contemplating committing suicide, hence the move from **self** to **non-self** (committing suicide for the insurance policy) then to **others** when he saves Clarence. This echoes the master beat/theme stated earlier when Young George acted in the interest of Young Harry's life and jumped into icy waters, damaging his hearing and grounding him home. His action to save Clarence is setting him up to evolve his final decisive test (from saving the community) to realizing his life as lived was worth it.

Figure 6.14 Master story beat/theme stated 10—*It's a Wonderful Life*. Again, sometimes two separate beats occur closely on the narrative timeline and are closely connected.

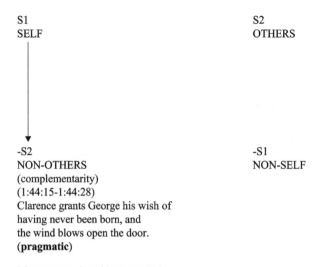

S1
SELF

S2
OTHERS

-S2
NON-OTHERS
(complementarity)
(1:44:15-1:44:28)
Clarence grants George his wish of
having never been born, and
the wind blows open the door.
(pragmatic)

-S1
NON-SELF

Master story beat/theme stated:
Clarence grants George his wish.
"Sometimes you need to
go to extremes to prove a point and help
someone in need."

In this beat, George is opting out of ever having existed, which is obviously *not* serving **others** (**self** to **non-others**) because indirectly he will remove his "service" to **others**. It's going to set him up to realize his dream of leaving (his original decisive test) and it sets up the move from failing to protect his community (his 2nd decisive test) to his final decisive test realizing his life as lived was great.

Figure 6.15 Master story beat/theme stated 11—*It's a Wonderful Life.*

S1
SELF

S2
OTHERS

-S2
NON-OTHERS ————————————→ -S1
NON-SELF
(contrariety)

1:59:53 2:00:37
George finds Mary leaving the library, and she is an old maid
and doesn't recognize him. *George emotionally pleads with Mary,*
trying to make sense of what is going on. Mary screams fearfully as a
response to George pleading with her. George's insistence that he
knows her scares her, and she screams and runs away.
(cognitive/thymic/pragmatic)

Master story beat/theme stated:
George realizes Mary would be alone
without him. "If you never existed, the one you were meant to be
with could have a bad life."

George's opting out of ever having existed is *not* serving **others** and not "serving" himself, so I depict the movement from **non-others** to **non-self**. It doesn't get him closer to leaving home (his original contract), but in an emotional way, it's a core beat because here he feels deep in his soul the consequence of his absence seeing Mary as an old maid (**non-self**).

Figure 6.16 Master Story beat/theme stated 12—*It's a Wonderful Life.*

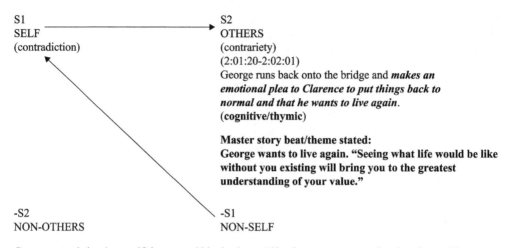

S1
SELF
(contradiction)

S2
OTHERS
(contrariety)
(2:01:20-2:02:01)
George runs back onto the bridge and *makes an emotional plea to Clarence to put things back to normal and that he wants to live again.*
(**cognitive/thymic**)

Master story beat/theme stated:
George wants to live again. "Seeing what life would be like without you existing will bring you to the greatest understanding of your value."

-S2
NON-OTHERS

-S1
NON-SELF

George not existing (**non-self**) has moved him back to **self** but in a new way, moving then from **self** to **others**. He has entered to his final decisive test, which is to see his life was worth living as is.

Figure 6.17 Master story beat/theme stated 13—*It's a Wonderful Life.*

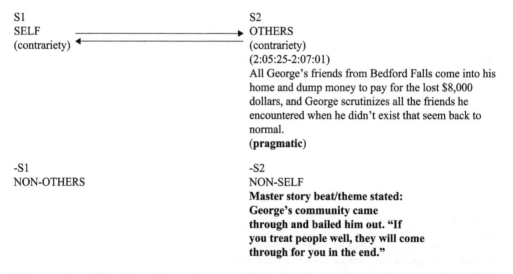

S1
SELF
(contrariety)

S2
OTHERS
(contrariety)
(2:05:25-2:07:01)
All George's friends from Bedford Falls come into his home and dump money to pay for the lost $8,000 dollars, and George scrutinizes all the friends he encountered when he didn't exist that seem back to normal.
(**pragmatic**)

-S1
NON-OTHERS

-S2
NON-SELF
Master story beat/theme stated:
George's community came through and bailed him out. "If you treat people well, they will come through for you in the end."

The move from **self** to **others**, who are the community that in turn saves him and gives him his fullest life (back to **self**), which is him fully now living and appreciating the life he actually has. His decisive test is complete (he realizes his life is great), he now is in fully glorifying test mode experiencing the glory of life as is.

Figure 6.18 Master story beat/theme stated 14—*It's a Wonderful Life.*

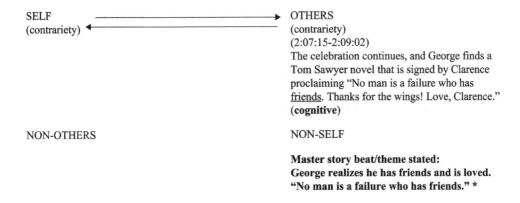

SELF   OTHERS
(contrariety)   (contrariety)
                                        (2:07:15-2:09:02)
                                        The celebration continues, and George finds a
                                        Tom Sawyer novel that is signed by Clarence
                                        proclaiming "No man is a failure who has
                                        <u>friends</u>. Thanks for the wings! Love, Clarence."
                                        (**cognitive**)

NON-OTHERS   NON-SELF

                                        Master story beat/theme stated:
                                        George realizes he has friends and is loved.
                                        "No man is a failure who has friends." *

George is now happy in his life with the recognition that he had a great life with his family and serving the community. He is in complete conjunction with the object of seeing the worth of his life, his final decisive test, and living his glorifying test of the aftermath (being showered with money to cover the missing money, signaling the unconditional support of his community). **Others** and **self** are serving each other, perfectly demonstrated by the 2 arrows that go both ways.

* This is the actual main theme of the entire movie whereby all the other related themes can be seen to be connected to or related to.

Figure 6.19 Master story beat/theme stated 15—*It's a Wonderful Life.*

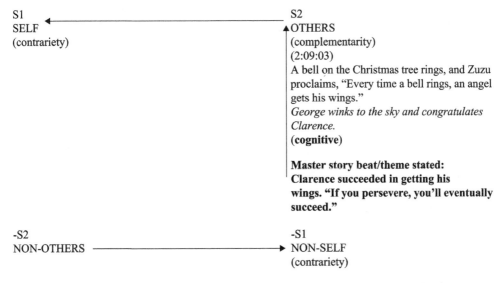

S1   S2
SELF   OTHERS
(contrariety)   (complementarity)
                                        (2:09:03)
                                        A bell on the Christmas tree rings, and Zuzu
                                        proclaims, "Every time a bell rings, an angel
                                        gets his wings."
                                        George winks to the sky and congratulates
                                        Clarence.
                                        (**cognitive**)

                                        Master story beat/theme stated:
                                        Clarence succeeded in getting his
                                        wings. "If you persevere, you'll eventually
                                        succeed."

-S2   -S1
NON-OTHERS   NON-SELF
                                        (contrariety)

George has the awareness that the ringing bell constitutes Clarence the Angel has gotten his wings, reminding him of his own journey of awareness and having moved from **non-others** (seeing life without himself existing) to **non-self** returning to life that is a life of service (completely **others**) but encapsulating himself in fulfillment (to **self**).

Figure 6.20 Master story beat/theme stated 16—*It's a Wonderful Life.*

Specimen #2—*Lost in Translation*

Female Writer/Director, Female Protagonist, "Indiewood"

TITLE: *Lost in Translation*
GENRE: Dramedy
SUBGENRES: Romantic Drama/Romantic Dramedy
SCREENWRITER: Sofia Coppola
DIRECTOR: Sofia Coppola
LOG LINE: A young, depressed woman is stuck in Japan on her husband's business trip and meets an older movie star shooting booze commercials, and they share a once-in-a-lifetime emotional romance.

The Surface Level—Cataloging Isotopies

This is a very visual movie. It's a movie style that is sometimes referred to as a "hangout" movie. I believe this movie belongs to a mini-genre of romance movies I like to call "brief encounters," based on the original masterpiece of the genre *Brief Encounter,* a 1945 British movie written by Noel Coward and directed by David Lean. *Lost in Translation* is built on the audience feeling connected to the internal loneliness and angst of the actors and being able to "read" what the internal thoughts of actors are, more so than in *It's a Wonderful Life.* That said, its isotopies are fewer but telling.

Table 6.20 Isotopies (Objects, Places)—*Lost in Translation*

OBJECTS	
female buttocks	white sheets
pink underwear	pillows
limo window	comforter
neon lights	alarm clock (4:20)
buildings of neon/Japanese writing	fax machine
billboard of Bob Harris in scotch ad (Japanese writing)	fax asking about bookcase construction
hypnotic Japanese billboard	curtains that auto open
limo	shower head too small
business cards	camera bag
gift	camera, film
letter from Lydia Harris about forgetting Adam's birthday, "I'm sure he'll understand"	film EQ dolly
	scripts for commercial
kimono robe	lights
sandals	boom microphone
TV with video on	video monitor
cigarettes, drinks	movie slate
whiskey in a glass	director's video monitor
cigar	booze bottle
beer in glass	subway map
	props

Bob's tuxedo
director's wristwatch
train sign
incense
temple drum
temple statutes
phone
lipstick
pink hanging flowers
camera, lenses, bags
sunglasses
red armband
gray knitted scarf
pink underwear
knitting needle
lit cigarette
bellhop
police car on TV show in car chase
remote control
sexy stockings
paper lamp in hotel room
sushi breakfast
Charlotte's umbrella
crowd's umbrellas
video production gear
scotch bottle filled with iced tea
two scotch glasses filled with iced tea and fake
    ice
Bob's fake suit pinned from back
light meters
makeup brush
cell phone
still camera
still camera lighting timer
photo film plate
dinner settings
open tux tie
cigar
cup of sake
suit backstitched with clamps
photo sheets
elliptical machine
gym towel
headphones
self-help CD
paparazzi's flashing cameras
screen for Kelly's talk
Midnight Velocity (name of Kelly's movie)
Ikebana display
Ikebana flower Charlotte puts in vase
remote
actors on TV playing game with noodles and
    chopsticks
Japanese action film
cigarette
lighter

pack of cigarettes
bar napkin
vodka tonic
Bob's remote
arcade video games
drums for arcade game
Rock Hero guitar
Bob's remote
John's camera case
wrapped bottles of wine
John's luggage
white bathrobes
FedEx box of rug samples
note from Bob's wife about samples, "I like
    burgundy but whatever you want"
orange camouflage shirt
inside out camouflage shirt
scissors to cut tag
tag
photon BB gun
photon BBs
bottle flung and smashed
cab
small camera
booze bottle
karaoke screen
karaoke microphone
pink wig on Charlotte
fur hat
shot glass
shoes
blanket
electronic room lock
gift box
hotel room phone
golf club
tee
golf balls
chopsticks
wheelchairs
directory for hospital
cane
X-ray delivery machine on track
X-ray of fractured toe
stuffed toy
subway map
cab
drinks at strip club
truck with billboard of Bob in whiskey ad
hotel karaoke system and mic
sweater
magazine
envelope slid under door
message from Mr. Harris, "Are you awake?"
TV with *La Dolce Vita* playing
sake in wood cups

(*Continued*)

Table 6.20 *Continued*

OBJECTS	PLACES
newspaper	hotel bed
white paper tied to trees	skyline
tiny razor blade	limo
shaving cream	barricade on street
political campaign minivan	door inside hotel room
fax from Charlotte inviting Bob out	table by window
TV set for talk show	building with video of dinosaur
Polaroid of Charlotte	building with video of woman in a mirror
Bob's hotel room bathtub	walking towards herself
towel	building with video of elephants crossing
TV show with Bob and host on it	elevator
CGI hearts on TV	lobby of hotel
table of breakfast foods eaten	skyline of Tokyo with many red airplane warning
empty champagne bottle and two flutes with a	lights
little champagne	hotel restaurant table of Charlotte and her
black lingerie	husband and business associates
"cook your own food" device on table	elevator mirror
shopping bag gift	hotel gym
sodas	lobby
menus	Charlotte's messy hotel room
fire truck	lobby outside conference room
fax from John, "I miss you, see you tonight"	window next to Charlotte's bathtub
white phone in lobby	Charlotte's hotel bed
big gift box	Bob's bed
Bob's jacket	hotel pool with exercise class
limo	arcade
political tracts	crosswalk from window
luggage cart	skyline in day
	nightclub party of Charlotte's friends
PLACES	ball with video on it
inside limo	arcade
outside of hotel	street in back of arcade
elevator in hotel	hall outside karaoke room
floor hallway	friend's apartment
Bob Harris's room	inside car
bar in hotel	skyline from inside moving car
Bob's hotel bed	looking at car window as car moves
window outside Charlotte's hotel	hallway outside Charlotte's room
Charlotte and John's bed in hotel	Charlotte's bed
Bob's shower	golf course outside of mountain
Charlotte's window	sushi restaurant
elevator when Bob and Charlotte are on	examination room
together	waiting room
set for liquor commercial	X-ray examination room
subway	street outside hospital
magazine	mountain
subway escalator	in-room golf setup
subway station near street	outside strip club
walkway to temple	hotel bar as karaoke room
temple	Bob's bed in his room
building	mountain from out of train window
Charlotte's hotel by window	inside train

train station
trees with white paper tied around them
wooden steps on lily pond outside Heian
    Shrine
street outside hotel
TV studio for Takashi Fujii
inside limo
door outside Bob's room
street

Japanese restaurant
hotel bar
elevator
sunrise skyline of Tokyo
inside limo
street outside hotel
highway to airport
street signs to airport
hospital

Table 6.21 Isotopies (Actors)—*Lost in Translation*

ACTORS

Charlotte
Bob Harris
John
city dwellers
bellhop
Ms. Kawasaki
press agent
press agent
press agent
elevator full of Japanese hotel guests and
    Bob
lounge singer
bar guests
American businessman
2nd American businessman
riders in hotel elevator including child
commercial director
Suntory client
crew for commercial
commercial director
people in train station
people on subway
people on escalator
people in subway station
people in temple
priests/monks
dancers on TV show
spokesman on TV show
actor on TV show
Bob Harris on TV show
chimpanzee
construction workers on TV show
Premium Fantasy Woman
crowd waiting to cross Shibuya Crossing
production crew
makeup woman
photographer
lounge singer
Charlotte's husband's friends
waiter
Kelly

crowd listening to Kelly talk about her movie
    and reincarnation
paparazzi taking photos of Kelly
Kelly's translator
Ikebana instructor
Ikebana students
bartender
pool class instructor
pool class students
Rock Hero player and friends
crowd in crosswalk from window
Charlie
Bambi
crowd at party
Hiroko
bartender
apartment party guests
patient with Band-Aid
hospital receptionist
hospital guests and patients
X-ray technician
old man
people in waiting room
doctor in waiting room
nurses on escalator
ladies in waiting room
orthopedic doctor
doctors and people on escalator
strippers
patrons at strip club
crowd on streets outside strip cub
hotel karaoke bartender
actors in *La Dolce Vita* on TV
passengers at train station
train station concierge
group of schoolgirls
traditional Japanese wedding party
people wandering around temple grounds
candidate and woman announcing for him in
    minivan
technical director for TV show

(Continued)

Table 6.21 *Continued*

ACTORS	
TV host	photographer
translator	female concierge
crowd on street	crowd outside hotel
waitress	woman handing out political tracts
2nd waitress	limo driver
crowd outside during fire drill	Michael Rohatin, Ph.D. self-help guru
singing piano player	on CD
concierge escort	sushi chefs
sexy businesswoman	German hotel guests

The isotopy of Time/Durativeness is a fascinating one in this movie because much of the effect of the story is built on the two lovers being trapped in a different time zone and wandering around in a certain kind of jet lag/dreamlike state that they never really get over. But they live this together. So rather than completely trying to place these isotopies of time in direct binary opposition, I prefer to catalog them and just take note of how many different variations of times there were in the story.

Table 6.22 Isotopies (Time/Durativeness)—*Lost in Translation*

TIME/DURATIVENESS

Tokyo is 16 hours *ahead* of Los Angeles (where the two actors/characters live in the story). This creates an ongoing psychological binary opposition; what the actors' current time is versus what their bodies are telling them. Below is a collection of the different times of day and next to them the "real time" for the actor/characters.

night-time vs. 4:00 a.m.
4:20 a.m. vs. 12:00 noon
middle of night vs. 10:00 a.m.
morning vs. 4:00 p.m.

Following are all the other "times" that the story of *Lost in Translation* takes place in. You can merely add 16 hours to it and imagine that the actors are living in a binary opposition in terms of their "body clock" versus the actual clock time they are on during the movie. While jet lag is briefly referenced in the story, it's felt throughout and part of the dreamy quality the movie has, important to the overall romantic feeling the story generates. The jetlag contributes to and underscores the sense of "lostness" and displacement that is key to the romance working.

Add 16 hours to the below time frames of the movie for binary oppositions of time:

early afternoon	early evening	early evening
late afternoon	evening	middle of the night
early evening	early morning	morning
evening	late morning	afternoon
morning breakfast time	early evening	late afternoon
late morning	evening	early evening
night-time	late evening	late evening
middle of the night	middle of the night	late morning
morning	early morning	noon
afternoon	noon	middle of the night
late afternoon	afternoon	evening
evening	late afternoon	morning
morning	evening	

States of Being—*Lost in Translation* (First Pass)

States of being in *Lost in Translation* are in a sense tied to the binary opposition of the two time zones that the actors are experiencing throughout the movie or at least are tainted with the overall duality of home time/jet lag time as a shadow over the entire tone of the story.

- *Charlotte's sleeplessness.*
- *Bob groggy waking up.*
- *Bob jet-lagged in elevator.*
- *Bob and Charlotte smile at each other in elevator and connect.*
- *Charlotte at temple feelingless.*
- *Charlotte cries on phone because she felt nothing in temple.*
- *Kelly is really happy to see John.*
- *John is really happy to see Kelly.*
- *Charlotte looks annoyed that Kelly has shown up.*
- *Charlotte is chastised by John for criticizing Kelly for getting a reference wrong.*
- *Bob sleepless in bar.*
- *Charlotte sleepless in bar.*
- *Bob convinces Charlotte to escape the bar, hotel, city, and country as their feelings for each other grow.*
- *John kisses Charlotte and tells her he loves her as he leaves, and she reciprocates.*
- *Bob and Charlotte have fun running away from the photon BB gun attack.*
- *Bob watches Charlotte sing "Brass in Pocket" and is smitten.*
- *Charlotte watches Bob sing "More Than This" and is also taken with him when they exchange looks at each other, signaling they are falling in love.*
- *After Bob has laid Charlotte to sleep, he touches her shoulder as he leaves, showing great affection in his face.*
- *Charlotte laughs when Bob tells her his masseuse caused him pain.*
- *Bob and Charlotte laugh as they run away from Kelly singing karaoke in the bar.*
- *Bob and Charlotte share intimate moments and sake and watch TV.*
- *Charlotte talks of being "stuck," and Bob talks about his midlife angst of being a parent and husband as he is holding her naked foot.*
- *Charlotte is disappointed that Bob had a woman in his room, and Bob is embarrassed.*
- *Charlotte is angry at Bob at lunch, and he's annoyed by her childishness.*
- *During a fire drill, Charlotte expresses to Bob that she'll miss him, and he looks at her and feels the same.*
- *Bob and Charlotte say goodbye in the bar and hold hands. Bob expresses not wanting to leave, and they are both quietly emotional.*
- *They have a light kiss goodnight in the elevator, and it's awkward but emotional.*
- *Bob and Charlotte say goodbye in the lobby of the hotel and feel sad.*
- *Charlotte has tears in her eyes when Bob chases her down on the busy street.*
- *Bob and Charlotte have an emotional final hug and a real kiss goodbye.*

The Master Semiotic Square for *Lost in Translation*

I found that thinking of terms for the master semiotic square for this movie was relatively easy. There were a lot of first potential candidates:

- Together/Separate
- Open/Closed
- Lost/Found
- Lonely/Connected
- Alone/Together

Each of these pairs of potential binary opposition terms mostly means the same thing, and at first, I was especially attracted to lost/found but thought perhaps that was a little too poetic. So, I went with the obvious choice, which is lonely/connected. This pair would encompass as much of the movie as possible, and these terms of course trigger the emotions the movie generates.

First, a look at the master semiotic square for the movie:

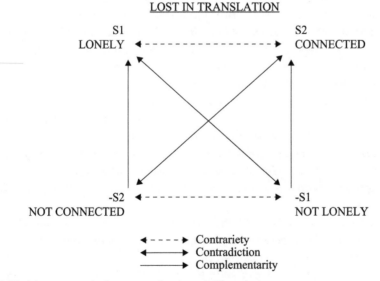

Figure 6.21 Master semiotic square for *Lost in Translation*.

Table 6.23 Isotopies of Objects in binary opposition (based on master semiotic square)—*Lost in Translation*. (Note: The individual isotopies are not in direct binary opposition on each side of the columns, but I merely used the columns to distinguish which side the isotopies go on.)

LONELY	vs.	CONNECTED
OBJECTS		

LONELY	CONNECTED
female buttocks	lipstick
pink underwear	pink hanging flowers
limo window	Charlotte's umbrella
neon lights	crowd's umbrellas
buildings of neon/Japanese writing	cup of sake
billboard of Bob Harris in scotch ad (Japanese writing)	Ikebana display
	Ikebana flower Charlotte puts in vase
hypnotic Japanese billboard	white bath robes
limo	inside out camouflage shirt
business cards	scissors to cut tag
gift	tag
letter from Lydia Harris about forgetting Adam's birthday, "I'm sure he'll understand"	photon BB gun
	photon BBs
kimono robe	bottle flung and smashed
sandals	cab
TV with video on	small camera
cigarettes, drinks	booze bottle
whiskey in a glass	karaoke screen
cigar	karaoke microphone
beer in glass	pink wig on Charlotte
white sheets	fur hat
pillows	shot glass
comforter	shoes
alarm clock (4:20)	blanket
fax machine	electronic room lock
fax asking about bookcase construction	arcade video games
curtains that auto open	drums for arcade game
shower head too small	Rock Hero guitar
camera bag shoulder	cigarette
camera, film	lighter
film equipment, dolly	pack of cigarettes
scripts for commercial	bar napkin
lights	vodka tonic
boom microphone	chopsticks
video monitor	wheelchairs
movie slate	directory for hospital
director's video monitor	cane
booze bottle	X-ray delivery machine on track
subway map	X-ray of fractured toe
props	stuffed toy
Bob's tuxedo	white phone in lobby
director's wristwatch	big gift box
train sign	Bob's jacket
incense	envelope slid under door
temple drum	message from Mr. Harris, "Are you awake?"
temple statutes	
phone	TV with *La Dolce Vita* playing

(Continued)

Table 6.23 *Continued*

LONELY	vs.	CONNECTED

OBJECTS

camera, lenses, bags		sake in wood cups
sunglasses		newspaper
red armband		white paper tied to trees
gray knitted scarf		fax from Charlotte inviting Bob out
pink underwear		
knitting needle		
lit cigarette		
bellhop		
police car on TV show in car chase		
remote control		
sexy stockings		
paper lamp in hotel room		
sushi breakfast		
video production gear		
scotch bottle filled with iced tea		
two scotch glasses filled with iced tea and fake ice		
Bob's fake suit pinned from back		
light meters		
makeup brush		
cell phone		
still camera		
still camera lighting timer		
photo film plate		
dinner settings		
open tux tie		
cigar		
suit back stitched with clamps		
photo sheets		
elliptical machine		
gym towel		
headphones		
self-help CD		
paparazzi's flashing cameras		
screen for Kelly's talk		
Midnight Velocity (name of Kelly's movie)		
remote		
actors on TV playing game with noodles and chopsticks		
Japanese action film		
Bob's remote		
fax from John, "I miss you, see you tonight"		
Bob's remote		
John's camera case		
wrapped bottles of wine		
John's luggage		
FedEx box of rug samples		
note from Bob's wife about samples, "I like burgundy but whatever you want"		

orange camouflage shirt
gift box
hotel room phone
golf club
tee
golf balls
subway map
cab
drinks at strip club
truck with billboard of Bob in whiskey ad
hotel karaoke system and mic
sweater
magazine
tiny razor blade
shaving cream
political campaign minivan
TV set for talk show
Polaroid of Charlotte
Bob's hotel room bathtub
towel
TV show with Bob and host on it
CGI hearts on TV
table of breakfast foods eaten
empty champagne bottle and two flutes with a
    little champagne
black lingerie
"cook your own food" device on table
sodas
menus
fire truck
limo
political tracts

Table 6.24 Isotopies of Place in binary opposition (based on master semiotic square)—*Lost in Translation*. (Note: The individual isotopies are not in direct binary opposition on each side of the columns, but I merely used the columns to distinguish which side the isotopies go on.)

LONELY	vs.	CONNECTED
PLACES		
inside limo		nightclub party of Charlotte's friends
pull up outside of hotel		ball with video on it
elevator in hotel		arcade
floor hallway		street behind arcade
Bob Harris's room		hall outside karaoke room
bar in hotel		inside car
Bob's hotel bed		skyline from inside moving car
window outside Charlotte's hotel		looking at car window as car moves
		hallway outside Charlotte's room

(Continued)

Table 6.24 *Continued*

LONELY	vs.	CONNECTED
PLACES		

Charlotte and John's bed in hotel		sushi restaurant
Bob's shower		sushi chefs
Charlotte's window		examination room
elevator when Bob and Charlotte are on together		waiting room
on set for commercial		X-ray examination room
set for liquor commercial		street outside hospital
subway		inside train
magazine		train station
subway escalator		trees with white paper tied around them
subway station near streets		wooden steps on lily pond outside Heian
walkway to temple		Shrine
temple		street outside hotel
building		hotel bar
Charlotte's hotel by window		elevator
hotel bed		street outside hotel
skyline		
limo		
barricade on streets		
door inside hotel room		
table by window		
building with video of dinosaur		
building with video of woman in a mirror walking towards herself		
building with video of elephants crossing		
elevator		
lobby of hotel		
skyline of Tokyo with many red airplane warning lights		
hotel restaurant table of Charlotte and her husband and business associates		
elevator mirror		
hotel gym		
lobby		
Charlotte's messy hotel room		
lobby outside conference room		
window next to Charlotte's bathtub		
Bob's bed		
hotel pool with exercise class		
arcade		
crosswalk from window		
skyline in day		
Bob's remote		
Charlotte's bed		
golf course outside of mountain		
in-room golf setup		
outside strip club		
hotel bar as karaoke room		

mountain from out of train window
TV studio for Takashi Fujii
inside limo
door outside Bob's room
street
Japanese restaurant
sunrise skyline of Tokyo
luggage cart
inside limo
highway to airport
street signs to airport
streets of Tokyo

Table 6.25 Isotopies of Actors in binary opposition (based on master semiotic square)—*Lost in Translation*. (Note: The individual isotopies are not in direct binary opposition on each side of the columns, but I merely used the columns to distinguish which side the isotopies go on.)

LONELY	vs.	CONNECTED
ACTORS		
city dwellers		Charlotte
bellhop		Bob Harris
Ms. Kawasaki		Ikebana instructor
press agent		Ikebana students
press agent		bartender
press agent		pool class instructor
elevator full of Japanese hotel guests and Bob		pool class students
lounge singer		Rock Hero player and friends
bar guests		crowd in crosswalk from window
American businessman		Charlie
2nd American businessman		Bambi
riders in hotel elevator including child		crowd at party
commercial director		Hiroko
Suntory client		bartender nightclub
crew for commercial		apartment party guests
commercial director		patient with Band-Aid
people in train station		hospital receptionist
people on subway		hospital guests and patients
people on escalator		X-ray technician
people in subway station		old man
people in temple		people in waiting room
priests/monks		doctor in waiting room
dancers on TV show		nurses on escalator
spokesman on TV show		ladies in waiting room
actor on TV show		orthopedic doctor
Bob Harris on TV		doctors and people on escalator
chimpanzee		crowd on street outside strip cub
construction workers on TV show		hotel karaoke bartender
Premium Fantasy Woman		

(Continued)

Table 6.25 *Continued*

LONELY	vs.	CONNECTED
ACTORS		
crowd waiting to cross Shibuya Crossing		actors in *La Dolce Vita* on TV
production crew		passengers at train station
makeup woman		train station concierge
photographer		group of schoolgirls
lounge singer		traditional Japanese wedding party
Charlotte's husband's friends		people wandering around temple grounds
waiter		crowd outside hotel
Kelly		woman handing out political tracts
John's assistant		limo driver
crowd listening to Kelly talk about her movie and reincarnation		
paparazzi taking photos of Kelly		
Kelly's translator		
strippers		
patrons at strip club		
candidate and woman announcing for him in minivan		
technical director for TV show		
TV host		
translator		
crowd on street		
waitress		
2nd waitress		
crowd outside during fire drill		
singing piano player		
concierge escort		
sexy businesswoman		
photographer		
female concierge		

Now I will attempt to classify states of being to either side of the binary category of dysphoria vs. euphoria, trying to find specific binary oppositions where I can. Again, to reiterate, when we look at the isotopies of states of being, this is where the movie begins to feel like a narrative. This should come as no surprise because states of being exist on the narrative level as well as on the surface level. Bear in mind, this logging process is not perfect, but it's an exercise in thinking through these key structural beats in *Lost in Translation* using the binary opposition categories of dysphoria vs. euphoria. Where it made sense, I tried to put states of being next to ones that were directly in binary opposition on either side of the columns, but, again, it's an approximation.

Table 6.26 States of being in binary opposition—*Lost in Translation*

EUPHORIA	vs.	DYSPHORIA
• *Bob is sleepless in bar.* • *Charlotte sleepless in bar.*		• *Bob groggily wakes up.* • *Bob is jet-lagged in elevator* • *Bob is drowsy and sleepy from flight.*
• *Bob convinces Charlotte to escape the bar, hotel, city, and country as their feelings for each other grow.* • *Bob watches Charlotte sing "Brass in Pocket" and is smitten.* • *Charlotte watches Bob sing "More Than This" and is also taken with him when they exchange looks at each other.* • *Bob and Charlotte have fun running away from the photon BB gun attack, signaling they are falling in love.* • *After Bob has laid Charlotte to sleep, he touches her shoulder as he leaves, showing great affection in his face.* • *Charlotte laughs when Bob tells her his masseuse caused him pain.* • *Bob and Charlotte laugh as they run away from Kelly singing karaoke in the bar.* • *Bob and Charlotte share intimate moments and sake and watch TV.*		• *Charlotte at temple feelingless.*
• *Charlotte talks of being "stuck," and Bob talks about his midlife angst of being a parent and husband as he is holding her naked foot.*		• *Charlotte is chastised by John for criticizing Kelly for getting a reference wrong.*
• *During a fire drill, Charlotte expresses to Bob that she'll miss him, and he looks at her and feels the same.*		• *Charlotte talks on phone to Lauren and expresses sadness that she was at the shrine but didn't feel anything and cries that her husband has become shallow.*
• *Bob and Charlotte say goodbye in the bar and hold hands. Bob expresses not wanting to leave, and they are both quietly emotional.*		• *Charlotte is disappointed that Bob had a woman in his room, and Bob is embarrassed.*
• *They have a light kiss goodnight in the elevator, and it's awkward but emotional.*		• *Charlotte is angry at Bob at lunch, and he's annoyed by her childishness.*
• *Bob and Charlotte say goodbye in the lobby of the hotel and feel sad.* • *Charlotte has tears in her eyes when Bob chases her down on the busy street.* • *Bob and Charlotte have an emotional final hug and real kiss goodbye.*		
• *Kelly is really happy to see John.* • *John is really happy to see Kelly.*		• *Charlotte looks annoyed that Kelly has shown up.*
• *Bob and Charlotte smile at each other in elevator and connect.* • *John kisses Charlotte and tells her he loves her as he leaves, and she reciprocates.*		

This ends our look at isotopies in *Lost in Translation*. Now, on to the narrative level.

The Narrative Level for *Lost in Translation*: The Actantial Narrative Schema

The structure of *Lost in Translation* is simple and effective. There is a fair amount of "setup" time that entails us living with the actors being alone, which creates their individual identities and their need to come together.

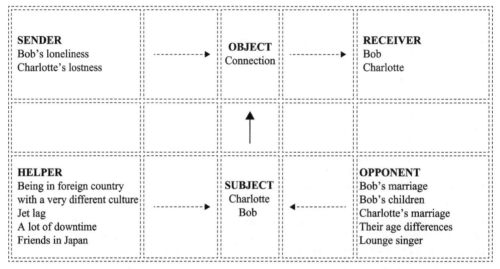

Figure 6.22 Actantial narrative schema semiotic square—*Lost in Translation*. This movie is relatively short and simple; hence the simple actantial narrative schema semiotic square.

Canonical Narrative Schema Summary— *Lost in Translation*

Bob and Charlotte are in Japan and in need of connection and intimacy which has been lost in their lives (lost in the "translation" of living). Bob is a fading middle-aged American movie star holed up in Japan to shoot booze commercials for millions of dollars. He acts in the spots touting Japanese whiskey, and he's desired for his American movie star "recognizability." On set, he endures language barrier issues with the Japanese crew, etc. Meanwhile, Charlotte is in town with her photographer husband, who is on assignment to shoot a rock band in Japan. They are newly married, and she is recently graduated from college. Early on, we see Charlotte visit a Japanese temple, and she bears witness to a religious ceremony which prompts her to later lament on a phone call to a relative that she didn't "feel anything." She cries, signifying her loneliness *and* immaturity.

Later, Charlotte endures chastising from her husband, who is critical of her smoking cigarettes, and he takes issue with her commenting on Kelly, a movie star they bumped into, and how she mocked Kelly for giving the front desk a male code name for herself at the hotel to be incognito. He complains, "Not everybody went to Yale."

Bob and Charlotte are staying at the same luxury Japanese hotel. The contract of the story begins when Bob and Charlotte "spot" see each other, first in a crowded elevator, then in the hotel bar whereby Charlotte sends him sake as a gesture of her recognition of him. Later, they meet again in the same bar, and Charlotte, bored of her husband's business meeting at the bar, walks over to Bob, and he discusses a "prison break," which would entail getting out of the bar, hotel, city, country, etc., and then asks Charlotte to be his accomplice to this itinerary, which she laughingly agrees to.

The contract (which remains unspoken) will shape up to be an agreement that the couple commits to spending time together for the short duration of their visit to Japan and also to having a fun intimate albeit sexless experience together, helping each other suspend their mutual loneliness by forming a mutual connection. This bond will be a source of intimacy and connection which is missing in both their worlds, yet all will be done with an unspoken agreement to do so without complicating their lives by adding an extra layer of sexuality to their "affair," which would make their brief time together constitute an actual infidelity and ruin the fun of their "fling."

This, of course, will involve a *being able to do something* and/or a *knowing how to do something* that will be manifest in a qualifying test, which will set up a decisive test and a glorifying test, as follows: To see if the couple can have a short experience of deep love and intimacy *without* consummating the relationship. This qualifying test comes in the form of Charlotte inviting Bob to a party with friends. There is a sense he might be too old, not hip enough, etc. He shows up in her hotel with a camouflage shirt, which he takes off in her bathroom and reverses, literally undressing in her room without moving towards sex. His *being able to do something* is manifest in that he is able to participate in the party, talk to her friends, and when someone shoots harmless photon BBs at them, he takes her out and they "escape" together, playful fun that adds to their burgeoning relationship. The two proceed to a karaoke bar together, where they take turns singing, with all the songs recognizable American rock songs, all of which directly or indirectly convey their growing emotional attachment towards each. It's the scene where they both acknowledge and recognize internally deep feelings for each other.

Later on during their stay, the decisive test formulates, which stated as a central dramatic question would be "Will this newly formed couple be able to drink alcohol and hang out in a hotel room without getting physical, which neither actor desires as it would complicate their lives and somewhat 'ruin' the innocence of their connection?" This decisive test as thus stated is carried out during one very intimate scene in which they are boozed up and lying in bed next to each other and discussing their doubts and disillusionments while Bob has his hand on Charlotte's recently injured foot, gently holding it. This gesture represents a small physical connection yet one of immense power because Bob is literally holding Charlotte's wounded limb as he is touching her life wounds, comforting her. The night concludes without the couple consummating the relationship physically but deepening their bond emotionally and hence have passed the decisive test, which is carrying out a deep intimate love affair without sex.

Having won the decisive test with nowhere else to go considering they don't want to consummate the relationship, Bob sleeps with the lounge singer, and Charlotte discovers this and becomes mad at him because he "violated" the unspoken terms of their contract; namely, not only that they wouldn't consummate *their* relationship, but they wouldn't sleep with other people in the meantime. They eventually reconcile but do so with the loom of their soon coming mutual departure from Japan and hence the end of their brief encounter. This, of course, sets up the coming ending of the narrative, the glorifying test, the momentum of which is easily sensed by the audience (competent observers). Before the glorifying test occurs, where they will make their final goodbyes, they are able to revisit the decisive test again and hold hands in the bar romantically, conspicuously not taking the affair to a hotel room as they might not be able to keep it platonic. They are basking in an in-between decisive test and glorifying test as they savor the last drops of their emotional intimacy.

The glorifying test comes at the end the next day when after they say goodbye to each other. Bob sees Charlotte from his limo and runs into the street and talks to her. She is crying, and they hug and have a real kiss, and then he embraces her, and he whispers something in her ear, something which we the audience aren't privy to, which can be a sweet romantic goodbye or a promise of greater connection and contact in the future. We, as competent observers, are left to construct what was whispered by Bob by ourselves.

Comprehensive Beat Map—*Lost in Translation*

Following is the comprehensive beat map for *Lost in Translation*. This deployment of this important tool will be a somewhat simpler approach to the previous one. States of being will not be included as originally cataloged and will be reiterated as general beats/master story beats, etc. Also, master story beats will not have any literary definition or comment attached to them (as is the case for the same in *It's a Wonderful Life*). All of this is done to demonstrate a different take on using this comprehensive beat map and any semiotic tool and to note that what's being laid out in this study is not a set of rules but a collection of powerful analysis and writing tools.

Table 6.27 Comprehensive beat map—Three specimen movies—Specimen #2—*Lost in Translation*

TIMECODE	BEAT Note: Master story beats/ themes stated will be in **bold**.*	BEAT TYPE	ACTANTIAL NARRATIVE SCHEMA	CANONICAL NARRATIVE SCHEMA
1:02–1:35	Charlotte's rear end in pink underwear faces the camera.	PRAGMATIC COGNITIVE	The image is sending to us the competent observer a direct communication from the writer/ director Sofia Coppola, who, as a female filmmaker, is able to show Charlotte's beautiful essentially naked figure without the appropriation of the male gaze, setting up the film as a female gaze love story.	The only test in play is the test of the audience as competent observers to be entrusted with this image without it provoking sexual a desire, but it is shown for its aesthetic beauty.
1:46–1:52	Over black, we hear a PA announcement, first in Japanese then translated: "Welcome to Tokyo International Airport."	PRAGMATIC	The voice on the PA is sending to us the receiver that we are now in a foreign country where everything will need to be translated and where awareness of what has become "lost" will become evident.	
2:47–3:02	Bob is drowsy and sleepy from the flight. Bob spies a billboard ad of him drinking scotch with Japanese writing, which he cannot read.	COGNITIVE	A sender to Bob the receiver, making him a subject with the object of needing connection (he is alienated from himself).	Bob's trip to Japan will carry out a literal contract to make a booze commercial (all of which will underscore dissatisfaction with where he is in life, setting up his future contract with Charlotte for connection).

(*Continued*)

Table 6.27 *Continued*

TIMECODE	BEAT Note: Master story beats/ themes stated will be in **bold.***	BEAT TYPE	ACTANTIAL NARRATIVE SCHEMA	CANONICAL NARRATIVE SCHEMA
3:13–3:58	Bob is greeted by press agents and handlers and then gets a fax from his wife Lydia that he missed his son's birthday but he'll understand.	PRAGMATIC COGNITIVE	While Bob is being welcomed to Tokyo, his wife is sending to him the receiver guilt about missing their son's birthday, setting a subject/object opposition where Bob will be more conscious of his lack of participation in his kids' lives. This alienating prodding from his wife will be a helper to make him seek the object of intimacy (albeit chaste) with Charlotte.	Establishes the contract of Bob as parent, who has a *being able to do something*, which is still proof he is in his kids' lives, but he is simultaneously failing a qualifying test in that regard. Also, the alienating "prodding" by Bob's wife underscoring his parental inadequacies will set up his eventual contract with Charlotte, to engage in a chaste romance with her as he is partially a parent figure to her as well.
3:58–4:06	Bob is jet-lagged in elevator.	PRAGMATIC	Sending/receiving to Bob himself that Bob is there to work and feels general lostness and alienation in this foreign country. Again, this, too, contributes to his enhanced desired to have a real intimate experience (a helper) while visiting there (his object).	A new contract is being established in that Bob will have to perform duties as a commercial actor and get through a qualifying test of success on his job (specifically unknown to us but we sense that it's appearing in commercials for Japanese liquor).

4:08–4:29	Bob is recognized by many hotel staff and warmly greeted.	PRAGMATIC COGNITIVE	The staff of the hotel are sending to Bob the receiver their recognition of him because of his movie acting fame and his commercial gig, which is enforcing (establishing a contract) his need to have to work while he is there.	All the business attention underscores Bob is working and will have a qualifying test soon of performing in the commercials.
4:30–4:44	Bob sits alone on his comfortable bed in a lavish suite, wearing hotel slippers.	COGNITIVE	The environment is sending to Bob the receiver a need to perform for his job. Again, this all feeds into being a helper to make him seek connection from Charlotte.	Bob's mini-qualifying test will come soon at his commercial shoot.
4:45–6:00	Bob is sleepless in bar. Bob sits in the hotel bar, smoking and drinking in a way that it seems like he drinks a lot. He's recognized by two businessmen who know his American action movies, and he lies about why he is in Japan (seeing friends).	PRAGMATIC	The two businessmen are sending to Bob the receiver a need to go incognito and develops in him a further helper to have the need for a real connection.	Bob's mini-qualifying test will come to bear soon at the commercial shoot where he'll have to perform.
6:01–6:48	Bob lies awake at 4:20 a.m. with jet lag and receives fax from his wife in LA for him to pick shelves for his study, also mentioning she's spending "quality time" with the construction crew and hopes he's having fun there.	PRAGMATIC COGNITIVE	Bob's wife as sender to Bob as receiver underscores the superficiality of their marriage and the duality of his LA time vs. his current Japanese time, helping make him a subject with the object of wanting to connect.	His wife's comments on quality time with the construction crew points to how his time in Japan will be a decisive test of the fidelity of their marriage, setting up the entire story of his soon coming chaste romance with Charlotte.

(Continued)

Table 6.27 *Continued*

TIMECODE	BEAT Note: Master story beats/themes stated will be in **bold.***	BEAT TYPE	ACTANTIAL NARRATIVE SCHEMA	CANONICAL NARRATIVE SCHEMA
6:49–6:59	Charlotte sits in her underwear on the windowsill, "floating" over the city, and hears her husband snore, underscoring their partnership has lost some sex appeal.	COGNITIVE	As Charlotte contemplates her life, she is a sender to herself as receiver, thinking deeply about where she is in life. This, too, makes her a subject with the object of needing to connect, which she will later do with Bob.	Japan will prove to be a character in the story. Her time there will be a mini-qualifying test, underscoring where Charlotte is in her life and her uneasiness with her lot, which will raise questions about what she is going to do next.
7:00–7:39	Charlotte is in bed with her husband who snores. She wakes him up: he hugs her and continues to snore, causing her not to be able to sleep.	PRAGMATIC COGNITIVE		
7:40–7:53	Bob is awakened as his room's curtains automatically open letting in sun. Bob groggily wakes up.	PRAGMATIC COGNITIVE	Bob's mission to work is sending to him as receiver, making him a subject in pursuit of the object of making commercials, which is of a lower professional status than making movies. This is also a helper, emotionally setting him up to be in need of intimacy (connection) with Charlotte.	
7:54– 8:17	Bob is too tall for the height of the showerhead.	PRAGMATIC		

Time	Event	Type	Sender/Receiver	Analysis
8:18–8:40	Charlotte watches husband leave for work.	COGNITIVE	Her being left alone is a sender to her as receiver, making her a subject with the object of amusing herself all day.	Charlotte's marriage to her husband is strained but substantial enough to oblige her to remain faithful to him, which will manifest in her coming decisive test of conducting a deep chaste love affair with Bob.
8:41–8:42	Charlotte sits on the windowsill, looking out on city.	COGNITIVE	" . . . "	She is faced with a simple qualifying test to occupy herself (symbolically moving towards her own self-actualizing which we will later come to understand).
8:43–9:11	Bob is tired in an elevator and spots Charlotte, the only other non-Asian, and she smiles at him. **Master story beat/theme stated: first sighting of the lovers.**	COGNITIVE	Their mutual interest is a sender to each other as receivers, creating a subject/ object of a need to further their experience of each other.	A mini-contract is established that will amount to a series of mini-qualifying tests testing whether they will be able to get together despite their busy comings and goings at the hotel.
9:12–12:39	Bob acts in the whiskey commercial and endures a fiery director barking directions at him that he can't understand and are translated to very simple directions.	PRAGMATIC	The director is a sender to Bob the receiver, making Bob the subject with the object of delivering what the director wants. This commercial acting work frustrates Bob, making him feel alienated and in need of connection.	Bob's mini-qualifying test of performing for the commercial is completed seemingly successfully. His "knowing how to do" was simply interpreting what the director wanted even though he couldn't understand all that he is saying.\n\nThe alienating frustration of this commercial work is setting up Bob to need to find connection while in Japan (his contract).
12:40–13:10	Charlotte takes subway.	PRAGMATIC		
13:10–13:21	Charlotte walks to shrine.	PRAGMATIC		
13:22–13:50	Charlotte visits shrine and watches religious ceremony. Charlotte is at temple as feelingless.	PRAGMATIC	Japanese priest is a sender to his temple goers (receivers), Charlotte being one of them.	

(Continued)

Table 6.27 Continued

TIMECODE	BEAT Note: Master story beats/ themes stated will be in **bold**.*	BEAT TYPE	ACTANTIAL NARRATIVE SCHEMA	CANONICAL NARRATIVE SCHEMA
13:51–15:05	Charlotte talks on phone to Lauren, expresses sadness that she was at the shrine but didn't feel anything, and cries that her husband has become shallow. **Master story beat/theme stated: You can be married and very alone.**	COGNITIVE	Charlotte admits despite the sending from the priest she couldn't receive from him. Her sadness establishes her as a subject with the object of seeking out meaning and depth in her own life.	Charlotte has failed a mini-qualifying test in having a prime opportunity to connect spiritually via a local religious service, but it had zero impact on her soul, indicating she's stuck emotionally and setting up the eventual contract for the need to connect with Bob.
15:06–15:56	Charlotte puts on makeup, relaxes and hangs pink flowers, then stubs her toe.	PRAGMATIC		
15:57–16:46	Charlotte's husband John preps his camera gear and complains about work, and Charlotte walks by in pink underwear that he ignores, and he complains about her smoking.	PRAGMATIC	The sender of the sexy pink panties that was received by us the competent observer is ignored by her husband, who seems disinterested in sex with her despite her attractiveness. It's a helper making Charlotte a subject with the object of needing intimacy with Bob.	John criticizes Charlotte for smoking (she has failed a qualifying test to uphold her health), signifying their marriage is a source of strife and criticism albeit expressed because of love and caring, helping to serve the dual role of presenting enough of a real marriage to make it risky on Charlotte's part to sleep with Bob but cold enough to have a need to connect with Bob.

16:47–17:02	Bob returns to hotel.	PRAGMATIC		
17:03–19:31	Bob watches TV in hotel and sees himself in an old TV skit dubbed in Japanese. A Premium Fantasy Woman knocks and comes in and asks him to "lip" (rip) her stockings. She pulls him down, and he resists and smashes a lamp.	PRAGMATIC	The Premium Fantasy Woman is a sender to Bob a receiver, creating a need for him to be courteous and follow through and have the fantasy with the woman, but this furthers his alienation and need for the object of intimacy.	It also amounts to a mini-qualifying test pertaining to the fidelity and sanctity of Bob's marriage being on shaky grounds and causative of making him seek the contract of connection with Charlotte.
19:32–19:37	Bob eats breakfast.	PRAGMATIC		
19:38–20:10	Charlotte walks in city.	PRAGMATIC		
20:11–20:42	Bob meets his handler and press agents and learns the "Johnny Carson" of Japan wants him to appear on his show.	PRAGMATIC		
20:43–24:17	Bob is in a still photo shoot for the whiskey company and has to perform to the photographer's desires.	PRAGMATIC	The photographer is a sender to Bob the receiver to deliver good poses.	A mini-qualifying test to see if Bob is worth the money for the commercial.
24:18–25:42	Charlotte sends sake to Bob in the hotel bar as she sits bored with her husband and clients. **Master story beat/theme stated: In a role reversal, the female sends the drink, a classic move signaling she's open to a relationship.**	PRAGMATIC COGNITIVE	Charlotte is a sender to Bob the receiver, initiating a romance and creating a subject/object. (They as subjects and as shared protagonist now have the shared object of furthering their romance.)	A new contract is initiated which is the thrust of the movie; namely, that they will pursue love during their stay in Japan, setting up a qualifying test of whether they execute an intimate chaste affair (*a being able to do something/knowing how to do something*).

(Continued)

Table 6.27 *Continued*

TIMECODE	BEAT Note: Master story beats/ themes stated will be in **bold.***	BEAT TYPE	ACTANTIAL NARRATIVE SCHEMA	CANONICAL NARRATIVE SCHEMA
25:43–25:58	Bob rides elevator and looks at himself in the reflecting doors, contemplating his age and appearance.	COGNITIVE		
25:59–26:37	Bob exercises on an elliptical machine and has a hard time controlling its speed.	PRAGMATIC		
26:38–26:55	Bob meets up with his handler and PR team.	PRAGMATIC		
26:56–28:52	Charlotte and her husband John run into Kelly, a movie star, and Kelly is flirty with John. Kelly gives John her pseudonym that she's staying under, the name "Evelyn Waugh," and, after she leaves, this prompts Charlotte to remark Evelyn Waugh is a man's name. John chastises her for being snotty.	PRAGMATIC	Kelly is a sender to John the receiver with a faint promise of a hookup. John's chastising of Charlotte makes her the subject with the object of finding connection, which she will find later with Bob.	

28:53–29:14	Charlotte listens to a self-help CD.	PRAGMATIC	Charlotte continues to be her own sender with her as receiver, establishing a need for searching for her purpose.	This will set up a contract to connect with Bob Harris, and he will help her feel good about her finding her path.
29:15–30:14	Charlotte spies on Kelly giving a press conference and talking about all her banal likes in a surfacy Hollywood way.	PRAGMATIC COGNITIVE		
30:15–31:20	Charlotte attends an Ikebana instruction in the hotel and successfully places a flower in a pot.	PRAGMATIC		
31:21–31:27	Charlotte relaxes in bathtub listening to a self-help CD.	PRAGMATIC		
31:28–31:54	Charlotte awakens in the middle of the night and puts on the TV of a Japanese game show featuring a woman trying to eat large amounts of noodles.	PRAGMATIC		
31:55–32:10	Bob watches Japanese action movies.	PRAGMATIC		
32:11–32:13	Charlotte walks in hotel hallway.	PRAGMATIC		

(Continued)

Table 6.27 Continued

TIMECODE	BEAT Note: Master story beats/ themes stated will be in **bold.** *	BEAT TYPE	ACTANTIAL NARRATIVE SCHEMA	CANONICAL NARRATIVE SCHEMA
32:14–35:28	Charlotte and Bob meet up in the hotel bar and discuss Bob's marriage, his midlife crisis, and Charlotte's not having found any direction in life yet. **Master story beat/theme stated: Two lovers begin a relationship by baring their souls to each other.**	PRAGMATIC	Their attraction to each other is a sender to them as receivers, making each a subject with the object of furthering their intimacy.	The qualifying test of the couple developing greater and greater intimacy without consummating the relationship has taken a further step.
35:29–36:06	Bob watches an exercise class in the pool, then swims.	PRAGMATIC		Bob settles down into calm behavior, a mini-qualifying test (swimming), setting him up to be able to partake in romance.
36:07–37:20	Charlotte wanders into an arcade and watches Japanese teenagers have fun playing a mixture of games.	PRAGMATIC		Charlotte also settles down into a relaxing observation of young people, a mini-qualifying test that she can exist calmly within herself and also setting herself up for romance.

37:21–37:48	In hotel room, Charlotte's husband tells her that he's meeting Kelly for drinks and, to his silent dismay, Charlotte says she wants to tag along.	PRAGMATIC	Kelly is a sender to John the receiver, flirtatiously sending him a subtle hint of possible sex.	A mini-qualifying test is set up if Charlotte can keep her husband from Kelly.
37:49–40:15	In the bar, Kelly blabs about her being perceived as anorexic, her father's capture in Cuba, and a cleanse she did, boring Charlotte, who sees Bob and talks to him, and he proceeds to tell her he's planning a "prison break," to which she replies, "I'm in." **Master story beat/theme stated: the promise of fun their relationship offers.**	PRAGMATIC	Again, their mutual attraction is a sender to themselves as receivers, setting up the subject/object opposition challenging them to find space and time to be more intimate with each other. Their marriages are opponents to a sexual romance	The mini-qualifying test of Charlotte protecting her husband from Kelly has ended, and now the master qualifying test of seeing if the lovers can partake in an emotional romance without consummating it has taken a further step.
40:16–41:12	John packs to leave and gives Charlotte two bottles of champagne. He offers for her to go with him, but she responds that he'll be working and will have a better time on her own. He professes his love for her, promising to return Sunday.	PRAGMATIC	John's departure is a sender to Charlotte a receiver to be on her own and forge her own identity while alone.	It's a mini-qualifying test to see if she can be alone and entertain herself, a *being able to do something.*
41:13–42:03	Charlotte sits on windowsill and seems to "float" over the city in a dreamlike contemplation of possibilities.	COGNTIVE		

(Continued)

Table 6.27 Continued

TIMECODE	BEAT Note: Master story beats/ themes stated will be in **bold.***	BEAT TYPE	ACTANTIAL NARRATIVE SCHEMA	CANONICAL NARRATIVE SCHEMA
42:04–42:09	Charlotte dives into the pool.	PRAGMATIC		
42:10–42:54	Charlotte and Bob, both in white robes, run into each other, and Charlotte invites him to come out and visit friends with her. **Master story beat/theme stated: the first date.**	PRAGMATIC COGNITIVE		The master qualifying test of seeing if they can deepen their relationship by spending time together has commenced.
42:55–43:24	Bob dumps a box of rug samples on the floor mailed from his wife, reading a note that she likes the burgundy but he can't tell which one is which.	PRAGMATIC	Lydia (Bob's wife) is a sender to Bob the receiver, forcing him to make decoration decisions, superficializing their relationship and making him more of a subject/object, setting him up for a need/want/desire for a deep connection with Charlotte.	Further pushing Bob towards a qualifying test of a romance with Charlotte.
43:25–44:41	Bob comes to Charlotte's room to pick her up, and she mocks his camouflage shirt, which he flips inside out in the bathroom, then she cuts tag off.	PRAGMATIC		The master qualifying test to see if they can experience ultimate emotional intimacy without sex is progressing.

44:42–46:48	Charlotte and Bob mingle at Charlotte's friends' party, and they are chased out by a bartender shooting photon BBs.	PRAGMATIC	The master qualifying test of whether they can sustain a chaste romance is furthered developed by their youthful partying.
46:49–47:12	Bob and Charlotte are chased outside by the bartender, who keeps shooting BBs at them.	PRAGMATIC	The master qualifying test of whether they can sustain a chaste romance is furthered developed by their youthful partying.
47:13–47:49	Bob and Charlotte run through another arcade and into a cab with friends waiting.	PRAGMATIC	The master qualifying test of whether they can sustain a chaste romance is furthered developed by their youthful partying.
47:50–49:07	Bob and Charlotte are at a different party of friends and are having fun and dancing.	PRAGMATIC	The youthful parties that Charlotte is pulling Bob into has the effect of a sender to the couple as receivers, repositioning them to be subjects with the object of a new young innocent love. The master qualifying test of whether they can sustain a chaste romance is furthered developed by their youthful partying.

(Continued)

Table 6.27 *Continued*

TIMECODE	BEAT Note: Master story beats/ themes stated will be in **bold**.*	BEAT TYPE	ACTANTIAL NARRATIVE SCHEMA	CANONICAL NARRATIVE SCHEMA
49:08–52:21	Bob sings karaoke, and Charlotte admires him. Charlotte in a pink wig sings "Brass in Pocket" directly at him, slightly off-key, as Bob watches and falls in love with her. Bob sings "More Than This," which expresses the plot of their short-lived romance and causes Charlotte to recognize her love for Bob. **Master story beat/theme stated: the moment you realize you are in love with the other person, and it's mutual.**	PRAGMATIC COGNITIVE THYMIC	Their mutual attraction is a sender to themselves as receivers, making their desire for each other strong, each becoming a subject with the object of connection and romance with each other.	Success of winning the master qualifying test of the couple conducting a sexless emotional romance is furthered by the warm feelings the karaoke party produces.
52:22–53:09	Charlotte and Bob have a quiet moment outside the karaoke room, where they share a smoke, and she rests her head on him. **Master story beat/theme stated: complete trust in each other.**	PRAGMATIC	Their shared unspoken commitment to carry out their "affair" without consummating it is reinforced, which is a helper to both as they don't wish to complicate their lives with adultery at this juncture.	The master qualifying test of whether or not they could engage in a sexless emotional love affair is completed successfully.

Time	Description		
53:10–54:22	Charlotte watches from cab window the sites of the city at night and then looks across and sees Bob is asleep and smiles.	PRAGMATIC	The master qualifying test of whether or not they could engage in a sexless emotional love affair is completed successfully.
54:23–56:01	In hotel, Bob carries the sleeping Charlotte to her room, tucks her in bed, closes the light and then lets himself out. **Master story beat/theme stated: caring for her without having to sleep with her.**	PRAGMATIC	The master qualifying test of whether or not they could engage in a sexless emotional love affair is completed successfully.
56:02–58:14	Bob talks to his wife on the phone and discusses the burgundy carpet sample and the party he went to and tries to get his very young daughter to eat.	PRAGMATIC	The alienation Bob has from his wife is underscored, deepening his object of needing to connect with Charlotte.
58:15–59:16	Bob golfs on a beautiful course.	PRAGMATIC	
59:17–1:00:33	Charlotte and Bob have lunch, and she shows him her toe that she stubbed, and he insists on taking her to doctor.	PRAGMATIC	

(Continued)

Table 6.27 *Continued*

TIMECODE	BEAT Note: Master story beats/ themes stated will be in **bold.***	BEAT TYPE	ACTANTIAL NARRATIVE SCHEMA	CANONICAL NARRATIVE SCHEMA
1:00:34–1:01:41	Bob takes Charlotte into the hospital, pushing her in a wheelchair, and cracks jokes, entertaining her.	PRAGMATIC	Charlotte's foot injury is a helper, giving Bob an opportunity to care for Charlotte, deepening their emotional romance. Bob's playful sense of humor is a sender to Charlotte as receiver, helping her fall in love with him. (They as the shared protagonist are the subject with the object of furthering their romance.)	
1:01:42–1:03:04	Bob waits for Charlotte, who is getting X-rayed, and banters with an old Japanese gentleman.	PRAGMATIC		
1:03:05–1:03:12	Charlotte learns that her toe is okay from Japanese doctor.	PRAGMATIC		
1:03:13–1:03:28	Charlotte exits and sees Bob holding a stuffed animal for her.	PRAGMATIC	This beat is a helper to the couple (Bob gives her a toy "gift" answering the drink she gave him yet underscoring the innocence of their romance).	

Time	Description	Type	Analysis
1:03:29–1:03:47	Charlotte sits in her room, looking at photos of her and her husband.	COGNITIVE	Since the master qualifying test of Charlotte and Bob *being able to* deepen their romance without consummating it has been successful, she's examining her marriage and thinking about it more deeply.
1:03:48–1:03:51	In his room, Bob putts and hits a golf ball.	PRAGMATIC	
1:03:52–1:05:18	Bob meets Charlotte at a strip club that Charlie invited her to. After watching naked women dance, they leave.	PRAGMATIC	The naked stripper is helping to cast carnal sexuality in a harsh light and strengthens the couple's impulse to continue to pursue the object of a chaste romance.
			The naked stripper that Bob and Charlotte view is a signal that we've begun the decisive test (if they will be able to "go all the way" with a sexless romance), cued by the blatant crass sexuality of the scene which causes discomfort and the couple to leave.
1:05:19–1:05:50	Bob and Charlotte playfully cut in and out of traffic, and they see Bob's image on a drive-by whiskey ad billboard.	PRAGMATIC	
1:05:51–1:06:34	Bob and Charlotte see Kelly performing "The Spy Who Loved Me" in the bar, and they escape without her spotting them.	PRAGMATIC	The potential sender of Kelly's possible potential affair with Charlotte's husband (to Charlotte the receiver) is gone since Kelly has remained behind and John is away, making Charlotte alone bear the guilt of engaging in potential "adultery" with Bob if she consummates the relationship with him.
			More signals that we are in the decisive test zone of the lovers reaching the zenith of their emotional affair; the couple seeing Kelly makes them self-conscious and represents they literally "have to escape" the bar as prophesized early in their affair.

(Continued)

Table 6.27 Continued

TIMECODE	BEAT Note: Master story beats/themes stated will be in **bold**.*	BEAT TYPE	ACTANTIAL NARRATIVE SCHEMA	CANONICAL NARRATIVE SCHEMA
1:06:35–1:08:02	Charlotte wakes up and receives a hotel telegram from Bob, asking if she's awake.	PRAGMATIC		
1:08:03–1:09:26	In his room, they drink sake and watch *La Dolce Vita* (*The Sweet Life*) and reminisce about their different perceptions of the first time they saw each other. **Master story beat/theme stated: deepening the baring of their souls and recognizing they both view each other as once-in-a-lifetime lovers.**	PRAGMATIC COGNITIVE	The way has been cleared for the couple to deepen their emotional love affair. Their current situation is a sender to the couple as receiver to deepen the relationship. The helper is Charlotte's husband being away for a few days and Bob's wife being away on another continent. An opponent to continue the relationship is that, if consummated, it can present a danger to their respective committed marriages and family lives.	A decisive test of them *being able to* fully experience a deep romantic emotional affair without consummating it is in play. This decisive test kicks off the last third of the movie (what can be called Act 3), with the lovers being in sync in terms of experiencing jet-lagged induced sleeplessness and their commitment to keep the affair chaste.
1:09:27–1:09:58	They continue sharing the evening, and Charlotte proclaims that they should never come here again as it would never be as much fun. **Master story beat/theme stated: deeping the specialness of their bond and time together by acknowledging it.**	PRAGMATIC	As their situation is a sender to them as receivers, making them the subjects with the object of communicating to each other the specialness of this encounter. She also is openly acknowledging the romantic nature of their relationship. Their seeming willingness to keep the relationship chaste is a helper.	The decisive test (of the deep emotional love affair) is reaching its heights, signaled especially by the line "It would never be as much fun," meaning they are sharing a once-in-a-lifetime love affair, an awareness of which they are in mutual agreement about.

1:09:59–1:14:02	Lying in bed, Charlotte and Bob share very intimate aspects of their lives. Charlotte talks about being lost professionally and in her marriage, and Bob talks about how his life changed after his kids were born, but his kids are delightful, all while he is touching her foot. **Master story beat/theme stated: completely baring their souls to each other and, despite drinking and lying on a hotel bed, not consummating the relationship.**	PRAGMATIC COGNITIVE THYMIC	Bob is a sender to Charlotte as receiver with the hope and joy of having children, making her the subject with the object of having a future family, but it's an opponent to them furthering their relationship. The decisive test concludes here with them having the perfect opportunity to consummate the relationship, but they keep it sexless despite there being physical contact, which could've progressed to sex but didn't.
1:14:03–1:14:45	Charlotte alone rides the train.	PRAGMATIC	
1:14:46–1:16:05	Charlotte walks to the shrine and witnesses a traditional Japanese wedding in progress.	COGNITIVE	The wedding is a sender to Charlotte the receiver, making her the subject with the object of preserving her marriage and Bob's marriage while continuing their "fling." It is also a sign she might be able to maintain some of the "connection" she has developed with Bob. This beat is in binary opposition to the beat of her earlier seeing the spiritual ceremony and feeling nothing. With the decisive test now concluded, Charlotte can rethink her marriage, which seems like it has a shot and is more realistic than getting together with Bob.

(Continued)

Table 6.27 *Continued*

TIMECODE	BEAT Note: Master story beats/ themes stated will be in **bold**.*	BEAT TYPE	ACTANTIAL NARRATIVE SCHEMA	CANONICAL NARRATIVE SCHEMA
1:16:06–1:17:02	Charlotte walks and ends up tying white paper to a tree (O-mikuji) a Japanese ceremony of wish making.	PRAGMATIC		The movie needs to "fill time" between the recently ended decisive test of the couple achieving maximum depth in their emotional affair and the promise of a coming glorifying test that is looming.
1:17:03–1:17:41	Bob shaves and gets called about fax.	PRAGMATIC		The movie needs to "fill time" between the recently ended decisive test of the couple achieving maximum depth in their emotional affair and the promise of a coming glorifying test that is looming.
1:17:42–1:18:29	Bob sneaks past his handler and then calls and accepts to do the talk show.	PRAGMATIC		The movie needs to "fill time" between the recently ended decisive test of the couple achieving maximum depth in their emotional affair and the promise of a coming glorifying test that is looming.
1:18:30–1:19:46	Bob shows up to do the Japanese talk show and participates in the offbeat show.	PRAGMATIC	Bob is returning to unsatisfying iterations of himself, which are alienating, making him want the object of connection with Charlotte.	

1:19:47–1:20:08	Bob sits in limo and looks at a Polaroid of Charlotte.	COGNITIVE	The photo is a sender to Bob the receiver, who now is turning towards his real life.	The decisive test completed, signaling the couple will go their separate ways, Bob is now faced with the blandness of his real life of carpet swatches and alienated wife and kids.
1:20:09–1:22:11	Bob talks to his wife and tells her he's lost, but, when pressed for clarity on that, he sidesteps it, and she questions whether or not she has to "worry" about him. **Master story beat/theme stated: He is lost in his life and marriage.**	COGNITIVE	The seemingly cold alienated nature of the call with Bob's wife is a sender to Bob the receiver, making him the subject with the object of wanting to continue the warm connected romance with Charlotte.	The decisive test completed, signaling the couple will go their separate ways, Bob is now faced with the blandness of his real life of carpet swatches and alienated wife and kids.
1:22:12–1:22:25	In sauna, Bob listens to German men banter, which he doesn't understand.	PRAGMATIC		
1:22:26–1:22:51	Bob watches himself on the offbeat TV show where the host holds a digital "heart."	COGNITIVE		
1:22:52–1:23:13	Bob sits in bar and meets the lounge singer.	PRAGMATIC		Now that the decisive test has concluded, and he and Charlotte will not consummate their relationship, Bob will be open to other opportunities.

(Continued)

Table 6.27 *Continued*

TIMECODE	BEAT Note: Master story beats/ themes stated will be in **bold**.*	BEAT TYPE	ACTANTIAL NARRATIVE SCHEMA	CANONICAL NARRATIVE SCHEMA
1:23:14–1:24:22	Bob wakes up and realizes he slept with the lounge singer. Charlotte comes to go out to lunch with him and is disappointed that he slept with the singer. **Master story beat/theme stated: He has cheated on his wife and on Charlotte and their special relationship.**	PRAGMATIC COGNITIVE	The sender/receiver of Bob having to return to his bland life back home puts pressure on him to blow off steam. Bob's promiscuity is an opponent to the lovers continuing their "chaste fling."	Charlotte is disappointed that although the couple collectively passed the decisive test and were deeply intimate without consummating the relationship, Bob "cheated" on them (and his wife) with the singer. This beat also signals the end of the story is near.
1:24:23–1:25:02	Bob receives call from his wife about his daughter's ballet recital on Sunday.	COGNITIVE	Bob's life is a sender to him the receiver that he is a subject with the object of having to return to his wife and family (and honor that original contract of his marriage to Lydia). His marriage and family life is an opponent to furthering his relationship with Charlotte.	The decisive test has concluded, the promise of a glorifying test looms.

1:25:03–1:26:35	Charlotte and Bob share lunch. She's angry that he slept with the singer, mocking his age, and he retorts by mocking her "neediness," saying she couldn't find someone to pay attention to her. **Master story beat/theme stated: They are faced with a crisis and the end of their short love affair.**	PRAGMATIC	Bob's normal life as sender to him as receiver suggests he is returning to his old habits of meaningless flings, making him and Charlotte the subjects with the object of returning to harmony in their relationship.	Charlotte is mad that although they together passed the decisive test of not consummating the relationship and not officially "cheating," he seems to have violated this by cheating on his wife.
1:26:36–1:28:03	A fire drill draws Charlotte and Bob into the lobby, where they reconcile and she asks when he's leaving and says she'll miss him, and his face shows he feels the same. **Master story beat/theme stated: They are beginning to process their inevitable parting for life and that they'll miss each other.**	PRAGMATIC COGNITIVE	The sender/receiver status of both their regular lives is calling them; they are subjects with the object of trying to make their lives work. Their regular lives are opponents to them furthering their relationship.	With the decisive test out of the way and Bob having returned to normal adulterous behavior, there's nowhere for the Bob/Charlotte chaste love affair to go.
1:28:04–1:28:59	Charlotte and Bob hold hands in the bar, and Bob says he doesn't want to leave. **Master story beat/theme stated: holding hands as lovers who are having an affair.**	THYMIC	The sender/receiver status of both their regular lives is calling them; they are subjects with the object of trying to make their lives work. Their regular lives are opponents to them furthering their relationship.	They briefly revisit the decisive test of still basking in the warm deep chaste romance without consummating it. But the promise of a glorifying test is felt, it is looming.

(Continued)

Table 6.27 *Continued*

TIMECODE	BEAT Note: Master story beats/ themes stated will be in **bold.***	BEAT TYPE	ACTANTIAL NARRATIVE SCHEMA	CANONICAL NARRATIVE SCHEMA
1:29:00–1:29:49	Charlotte and Bob wait for the elevators and have awkward goodbye kisses, then she gets on the elevator. **Master story beat/theme stated: Without ever consummating the relationship, it has to now break apart.**	PRAGMATIC	Their real lives and relationships are opponents to them staying together.	The revisited decisive test (a chaste romance) is again closed, completed for them as a couple. We sense as competent observers that the glorifying test is coming, but how it will manifest and play out is unknown and will take some time.
1:29:50–1:29:55	Bob looks out over city, thinking about getting back to LA.	PRAGMATIC		The promise of a glorifying test is coming as he basks in the lingering end of the revisited decisive test of the warm love that they were able to experience keeping the romance chaste.
1:29:56–1:30:09	Fax comes into Charlotte's room, "Miss You" from her husband.	PRAGMATIC	The sender of both their normal lives is strongly bringing them back to earth, making them receivers and subjects with the objects of figuring out how to live in their old worlds with the new knowledge of a deep love for one another.	Further impetus to have kept her affair with Bob chaste and recalling and reflecting the recently ended decisive test.

Time	Master story beat			
1:30:10–1:32:33	From lobby, Bob calls up Charlotte to say goodbye and asks her to return his jacket. She does and they say goodbye. **Master story beat/theme stated: penultimate and inadequate goodbye.**	PRAGMATIC THYMIC		
1:32:34–1:35:05	From his limo, Bob spots Charlotte and gets out and runs after her. She is tearful, and they embrace and kiss and have a real goodbye. He whispers something in her ear. **Master story beat/theme stated: the final acknowledgment that they love each other, must part, and that their love was a once-in-a-lifetime romance.**	THYMIC	Their ordinary lives act as a sender to the couple as receiver, making them the subject with the object of returning to their real dull lives but their real lives are opponents to them staying together and helpers to enhancing the overall romantic feelings the short-lived chaste romance produced.	The glorifying test of them finally kissing and therefore being open about their feelings.
1:35:06–1:36:43	Bob returns to his limo and takes a beat to process perhaps that he will never see Charlotte again. The remainder of the movie is POV images from the limo.	COGNITIVE THYMIC	Ultimately, their regular lives were a powerful sender to them as receivers, making them the subjects with the objects of maintaining those lives.	The glorifying test is fully processed by Bob, and he accepts that it's over and that he had something beautiful with Charlotte.

* For *Lost in Translation*, these master story beats will be expressed in simple "plain English" terms and not as literary themes. All the different ways that I'll present master story beats/themes stated are relevant and merely represent a creative use of this powerful tool. Again, the *Semiotics for Screenwriters* project is more of an analysis than a formula. How you use the tool depends on the movie you're breaking down, your own sensibility, and what you need out of the specimen to bolster writing your own screenplay.

Master Story Beats/Themes Stated "Cheat Sheet"—*Lost in Translation*

Following is a master story beats/themes stated "cheat sheet" for *Lost in Translation*. The first thing you may notice is it's much simpler and cleaner looking. Also, the master story beats will just be plain English reiterations of the actions being described. It's important to see this more simple approach to master story beats/themes stated because this approach might serve your style and/or the specimen movie you're breaking down and by extension the movie you might be trying to write. Also note, states of being have been absorbed into the regular beat flow without special "flagging" and have been reiterated as part of the beat map language. I didn't use the exact states of being from the initial brainstorming/cataloging session, the results of which I presented earlier in this chapter.

Table 6.28 Master story beats/themes stated—cheat sheet—for *Lost in Translation*

TIMECODE	BEAT	MASTER STORY BEAT/THEME STATED*	BEAT TYPE
8:43–9:11	Bob is tired in an elevator and spots Charlotte, the only other non-Asian, and she smiles at him.	**First sighting of the lovers.**	COGNITIVE
13:51–15:05	Charlotte talks on phone to Lauren and expresses sadness that she was at the shrine but didn't *feel* anything and cries that her husband has become shallow.	**You can be married and very alone.**	COGNITIVE THYMIC
24:18–25:42	Charlotte sends sake to Bob in the hotel bar as she sits bored with her husband and clients.	**In a role reversal, the female sends the drink, a classic move signaling she's open to a relationship.**	PRAGMATIC COGNITIVE
32:14–35:28	Charlotte and Bob meet up in the hotel bar and discuss Bob's marriage, his midlife crisis, and Charlotte's not having found any direction in life yet.	**Two lovers begin a relationship by baring their souls to each other.**	PRAGMATIC
37:49–40:15	In the bar, Kelly blabs about her being perceived as anorexic, her father's capture in Cuba, and a cleanse she did, boring Charlotte, who sees Bob and talks to him. He proceeds to tell her he's planning a "prison break," to which she replies, "I'm in."	**The promise of fun their relationship offers.**	PRAGMATIC

42:10–42:54	Charlotte and Bob, both in white robes, run into each other, and Charlotte invites him to come out and visit friends with her.	**The first date.**	PRAGMATIC COGNITIVE
49:08–52:21	Bob sings karaoke, and Charlotte admires him. Charlotte, in a pink wig, sings "Brass Pocket" directly at him, slightly off-key, but Bob watches and falls in love her. Bob sings "More Than This," which expresses the essence of their short-lived romance and causes Charlotte to recognize her love for Bob.	**The moment you realize you are in love with the other person, and it's mutual.**	PRAGMATIC COGNITIVE THYMIC
52:22–53:09	Charlotte and Bob have a quiet moment outside the karaoke room, where they share a smoke and she rests her head on him.	**Complete trust in each other.**	PRAGMATIC
54:23–56:01	In hotel, Bob carries the sleeping Charlotte to her room, tucks her in bed, closes the light and then lets himself out.	**Caring for her without having to sleep with her.**	PRAGMATIC
1:08:03–1:09:26	In his room, they drink sake and watch *La Dolce Vita* (*The Sweet Life*) and reminisce about their different perceptions of the first time they saw each other.	**Deepening the baring of their souls and recognizing they both view each other as once-in-a-lifetime lovers.**	PRAGMATIC COGNITIVE
1:09:27–1:09:58	They continue sharing the evening, and Charlotte proclaims that they should never come here again as it would never be as much fun.	**Deepening the specialness of their bond and time together by acknowledging it.**	PRAGMATIC COGNITIVE
1:09:59–1:14:02	Charlotte and Bob lie in bed and share very intimate aspects of their lives; Charlotte about being lost professionally and in her marriage and Bob how his marriage changed after his kids were born, but his kids are delightful, all while he touches her foot.	**Completely baring their souls to each other and, despite drinking and lying on a hotel bed, not consummating the relationship.**	PRAGMATIC COGNITIVE THYMIC

(Continued)

Table 6.28 *Continued*

TIME CODE	BEAT	MASTER STORY BEAT/THEME STATED*	BEAT TYPE
1:20:09–1:22:11	Bob talks to his wife and tells her he's lost, but, when pressed for clarity on that, he sidesteps it, and she questions whether or not she has to "worry" about him.	**He is lost in his life and marriage.**	COGNITIVE
1:23:14–1:24:22	Bob wakes up and realizes he slept with the lounge singer. Charlotte comes to go out to lunch with him and is disappointed that he slept with the singer.	**He has cheated on his wife and on Charlotte and their special relationship.**	PRAGMATIC COGNITIVE
1:25:03–1:26:35	Charlotte and Bob share lunch. She's angry he slept with the singer, mocking his age, and he retorts by mocking her "neediness," saying she couldn't find someone to pay attention to her.	**They are faced with a crisis and the end of their short love affair.**	PRAGMATIC COGNITIVE
1:26:36–1:28:03	A fire drill draws Charlotte and Bob into the lobby, where they reconcile and she asks when he's leaving and says she'll miss him, and his face shows he feels the same.	**They are beginning to process their inevitable parting for life and that they'll miss each other.**	PRAGMATIC COGNITIVE
1:28:04–1:28:59	Charlotte and Bob hold hands in the bar, and Bob says he doesn't want to leave.	**Holding hands as lovers who are having an affair.**	THYMIC
1:29:00–1:29:49	Charlotte and Bob wait for the elevator and have awkward goodbye kisses, then she gets on the elevator.	**Without ever consummating the relationship, it has to now break apart.**	PRAGMATIC
1:30:10–1:32:33	From lobby Bob calls up Charlotte to say goodbye and asks her to return his jacket. She does, and they say goodbye.	**Penultimate and inadequate goodbye.**	PRAGMATIC THYMIC
1:32:34–1:35:05	From his limo, Bob spots Charlotte and gets out and runs after her, and she is tearful, and they embrace and kiss and have a real goodbye. He whispers something in her ear that we cannot hear.	**The final acknowledgment that they love each other and must part and that their love was a once-in-a-lifetime romance.**	THYMIC

* To repeat, the "themes" stated are not always "stated" in a traditional literary sense, or as precepts. Sometimes (as in this above table), we catalog the beats reiterated in plain English.

The comprehensive beat map for *Lost in Translation* above yields simple master story beats/themes stated that collectively represent an excellent snapshot of a "brief encounter"-type romance, allowing us to study the reiteration of the master story beats and use them to brainstorm our own brief encounter-type story. Of course, you can go deeper and meditate on these transformative beats by plotting them against the master semiotic square for the movie. It's important to note that the treatment of master story beats/themes stated are treated very differently in *Lost in Translation* as compared to *It's a Wonderful Life* and also in contrast to how they are expressed in *Get Out*. That said, we'll still deploy the technique of plotting the master story beats against the master semiotic square for the movie.

Plotting Master Story Beats/Themes Stated on All Four Corners of the Master Semiotic Square— *Lost in Translation*

Using all corners of the master semiotic square for *Lost in Translation*, let's see if I can reverse-engineer and "plot" key transformations of the movie's story for those which occur when a subject (protagonist) moves towards or away from their object of value as defined by the actantial narrative schema. In this story, the object of value is simple—the experience of a deep once-in-a-lifetime type love affair experienced mutually without consummating it.

It's in seeking to understand how these master story beats can be mapped to all four corners of the entire semiotic square that we can really deploy the power of this semiotics system.

First, another look at the master semiotic square for *Lost in Translation*.

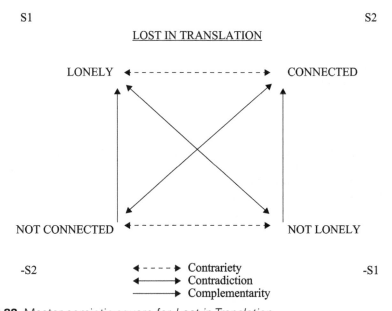

Figure 6.23 Master semiotic square for *Lost in Translation*.

Using the Entire Master Semiotic Square to Plot Master Story Beats/Themes Stated

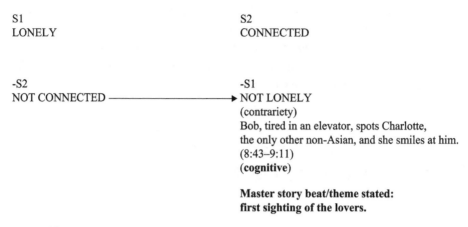

S1
LONELY

S2
CONNECTED

-S2
NOT CONNECTED ──────────────▶

-S1
NOT LONELY
(contrariety)
Bob, tired in an elevator, spots Charlotte,
the only other non-Asian, and she smiles at him.
(8:43–9:11)
(cognitive)

Master story beat/theme stated:
first sighting of the lovers.

To me, this transformation moves from **not connected** to **not lonely** because obviously the two lovers share a little glance/exchange in an elevator which doesn't constitute a full-blown connection but it's a start. And Bob is coming from work and feeling somewhat good in himself in this mini crowd (**not connected**).

Figure 6.24 Master story beat/theme stated 1—*Lost in Translation.*

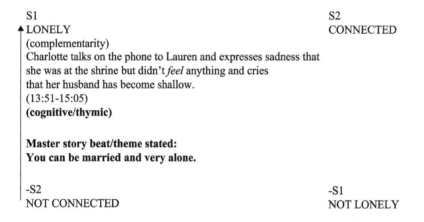

S1
▲LONELY
(complementarity)
Charlotte talks on the phone to Lauren and expresses sadness that
she was at the shrine but didn't *feel* anything and cries
that her husband has become shallow.
(13:51-15:05)
(cognitive/thymic)

Master story beat/theme stated:
You can be married and very alone.

S2
CONNECTED

-S2
NOT CONNECTED

-S1
NOT LONELY

This beat sets up Charlotte's psychological state, which will prime her to be in need and receptive to a fun brief romantic fling with Bob Harris. She is as far from feeling **connected** as she can be. She is **lonely** in every way possible, doesn't recognize her husband, etc. But she's not completely alone, so I'm plotting from **not connected** (to her husband) to **lonely**.

Figure 6.25 Master story beat/theme stated 2—*Lost in Translation.*

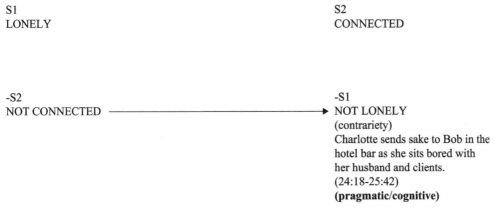

Master story beat/theme stated:
In a role reversal, the female sends
the drink, a classic move signaling
she's open to a relationship.

While this is not exactly the deep **connection** the love affair will aspire to, it's a step towards **not lonely** from **not connected**. (She is with her husband, so not completely alone for sure.)

Figure 6.26 Master story beat/theme stated 3—*Lost in Translation.*

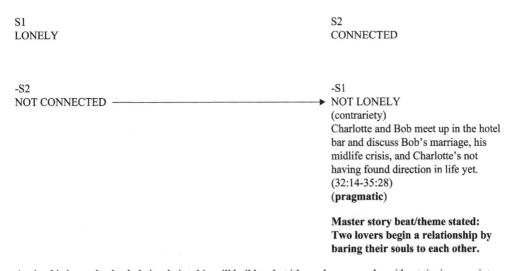

Master story beat/theme stated:
Two lovers begin a relationship by
baring their souls to each other.

Again, this is not the depth their relationship will build to, but it's as close as can be without tipping over into romance. This distinction is not merely semantics; it's real. If you look at the subtlety of the four corners of the semiotic square, it allows Sofia Coppola to *ease* into the love story, hence the move from **not connected** to **not lonely**.

Figure 6.27 Master story beat/theme stated 4—*Lost in Translation.*

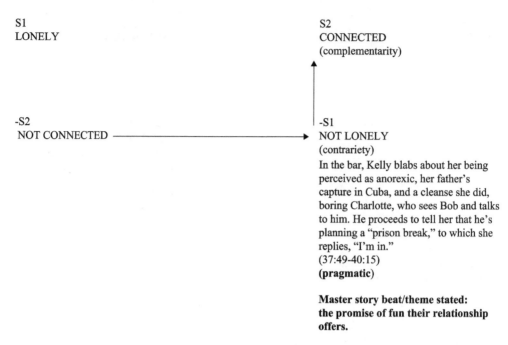

Charlotte meets Bob again in the bar, and he jokingly proposes that they "escape together" which will swing them from **not connected** to **not lonely** to **connected** and begin the acceleration of their romance. It happens almost at the midpoint of the movie. Again, all of this "painting the corners" and nuanced movement towards the goal of a perfect romance *without* consummating is remarkable.

Figure 6.28 Master story beat/theme stated 5—*Lost in Translation.*

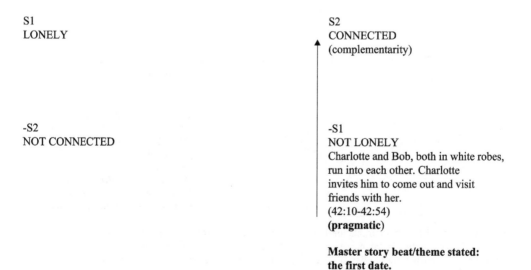

While they are both wearing white (equally matched, neutral, eliminating the male dominance), she asks him out on a date to which he accepts. We're going to be leaving **not lonely** and move directly to **connected** for a few segments, but Coppola has eased into it beautifully.

Figure 6.29 Master story beat/theme stated 6— *Lost in Translation.*

S1
LONELY

S2
CONNECTED
(complementarity)
Bob sings karaoke, and Charlotte
admires him. Charlotte, in a pink wig,
sings "Brass in Pocket" directly at him,
slightly off-key. Bob watches and
falls in love her.

Bob sings "More Than This," which
expresses the essence of their short-lived
romance and causes Charlotte to recognize
her love for Bob.
(49:08-52:21)

(pragmatic/cognitive/thymic)
Master story beat/theme stated:
the moment you realize you
are in love with the other person,
and it's mutual.

-S2
NOT CONNECTED ————————————→ NOT LONELY

-S1
NOT LONELY

The **connected** mode for both lovers is real and palatable, mutually experienced by each individual internally.
Again, in keeping with this being a female protagonist love story, it happens when she brings him to a party
of her "peers" (young people), and they dance to her music. For good measure, I'm showing the movement
from **not connected** to **not lonely** to **connected** because they are now teetering on a full-blown love affair but
with the shared object of not consummating it.

Figure 6.30 Master story beat/theme stated 7—*Lost in Translation.*

S1
LONELY

S2
CONNECTED
(complementarity)
Charlotte and Bob have a quiet moment outside
the karaoke room, where they share a smoke and
she rests her head on him.
(52:22-53:09)
(pragmatic)

Master story beat/theme stated:
complete trust in each other.

-S2
NOT CONNECTED

-S1
NOT LONELY

This moves from **not lonely** to **connected**. The object of a full-flung perfect romance without
consummating it is in reach and in play.

Figure 6.31 Master story beat/theme stated 8—*Lost in Translation.*

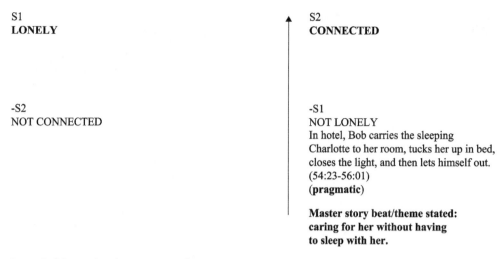

Retread of the previous beat movement from **not lonely** to **connected** because of their bond that flourishes without sex.

Figure 6.32 Master story beat/theme stated 9—*Lost in Translation.*

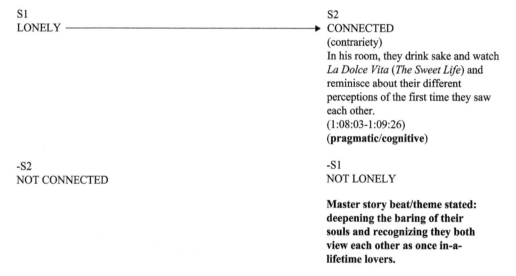

Somehow this scene, where they lie in bed and he touches her wounded foot, seems to transverse from **lonely** to **connected** because the full extent of their shared **loneliness** is completely felt here as well as the intensity of their shared object of a chaste romance. This is their decisive test in full swing.

Figure 6.33 Master story beat/theme stated 10—*Lost in Translation.*

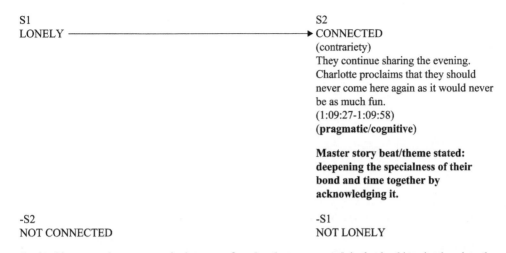

Again, this repeats the movement in the square from **lonely** to **connected**, in that by this point deep into the movie, we are starting to sense the depth of their individual **loneliness** and their deep **connection**, but also the inevitability of their having to part. The fact that she brings up not to come here again and making this place special is an awareness of the depth of their **connection** but also has hints of there being a finitude to their relationship. The decisive test is in full swing (their shared commitment to a deep chaste romance).

Figure 6.34 Master story beat/theme stated 11—*Lost in Translation*.

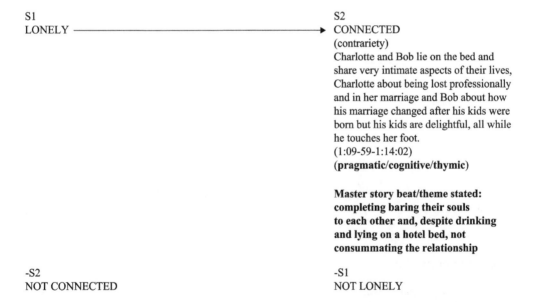

This is where the decisive test climaxes: namely, following through on a completely chaste romance. Again, to me, like the previous few beats it moves from **lonely** to **connected**. Ironically, as their love deepens, so does our awareness of their real lives, their shared mutual **loneliness** and their inability to escape their current situation.

Figure 6.35 Master story beat/theme stated 12—*Lost in Translation*.

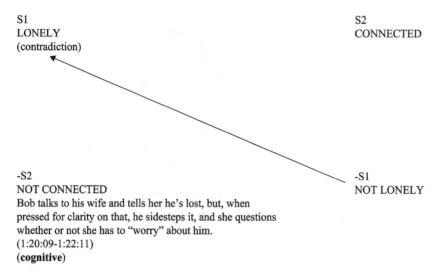

S1
LONELY
(contradiction)

S2
CONNECTED

-S2
NOT CONNECTED
Bob talks to his wife and tells her he's lost, but, when
pressed for clarity on that, he sidesteps it, and she questions
whether or not she has to "worry" about him.
(1:20:09-1:22:11)
(cognitive)

-S1
NOT LONELY

Master story beat/theme stated:
He is lost in his life and marriage.

He is lost in his life and marriage, but while he has the promise of continuing an emotional "affair" with
Charlotte, here he is literally "down to earth" in a bathtub. While he isn't **connected**, he is **not lonely**, and the
conversation moves straight from **not lonely** to **lonely** recalling all that is void and empty about his marriage.

Figure 6.36 Master story beat/theme stated 13—*Lost in Translation.*

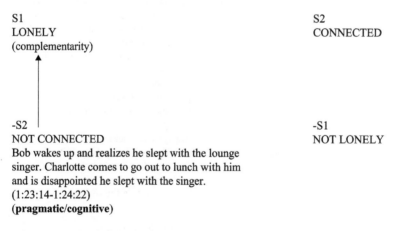

S1
LONELY
(complementarity)

S2
CONNECTED

-S2
NOT CONNECTED
Bob wakes up and realizes he slept with the lounge
singer. Charlotte comes to go out to lunch with him
and is disappointed he slept with the singer.
(1:23:14-1:24:22)
(pragmatic/cognitive)

-S1
NOT LONELY

Master story beat/theme stated:
He has cheated on his wife and
on Charlotte and their
special relationship.

He isn't **lonely** but certainly **not connected,** as the relationship with the singer is superficial. Bob and
Charlotte's mutual deal to pursue a chaste romance, their shared object, is in question despite having
already gone through the decisive test of hanging out boozed up in his hotel room without having sex.

Figure 6.37 Master story beat/theme stated 14—*Lost in Translation.*

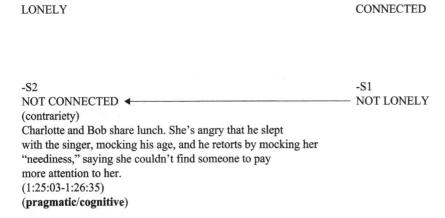

S1
LONELY

S2
CONNECTED

-S2
NOT CONNECTED ◄─────────────────────── NOT LONELY
(contrariety)
Charlotte and Bob share lunch. She's angry that he slept
with the singer, mocking his age, and he retorts by mocking her
"neediness," saying she couldn't find someone to pay
more attention to her.
(1:25:03-1:26:35)
(pragmatic/cognitive)

-S1
NOT LONELY

Master story beat/theme stated:
They are faced with a crisis and
the end of their short-lived love affair.

The crisis has caused a rupture in their deal, their shared object of a chaste romance. Since they have a bond, they are **not lonely** but not particularly connected (**not connected**). They are beginning to process their inevitable parting for life and that they'll miss each other. They are also aware of their age differences.

Figure 6.38 Master story beat/theme stated 15—*Lost in Translation*.

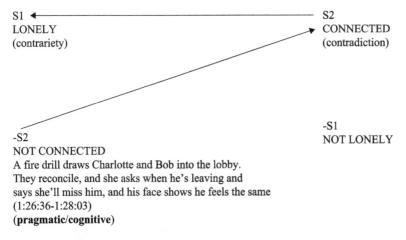

S1 ◄─────────────────────── S2
LONELY   CONNECTED
(contrariety)   (contradiction)

-S2
NOT CONNECTED
A fire drill draws Charlotte and Bob into the lobby.
They reconcile, and she asks when he's leaving and
says she'll miss him, and his face shows he feels the same
(1:26:36-1:28:03)
(pragmatic/cognitive)

-S1
NOT LONELY

Master story beat/theme stated:
They are beginning to process their
inevitable parting for life and that
they'll miss each other.

Upon accidentally seeing each other in the lobby, caused by the fire drill, they have a quick "reconciliation" and begin as **not connected** (they have had each other's company and aren't **lonely**). But the end of their hanging out, time is imminent, and in acknowledgement of the specialness of their bond and that they'll miss each other, moves to **connected** to **lonely** (the awareness of what is coming).

Figure 6.39 Master story beat/theme stated 16—*Lost in Translation*.

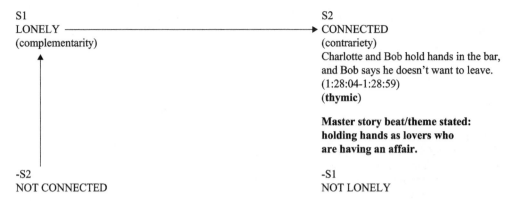

Having moved from **not connected** to **connected** to **lonely** because of the awareness of their inevitable parting, I reverse the movement back from **lonely** to **connected** because in the warm "holding hands" scene they now seem restored to the "moment" and not necessarily staring in the face of parting.

Figure 6.40 Master story beat/theme stated 17—*Lost in Translation.*

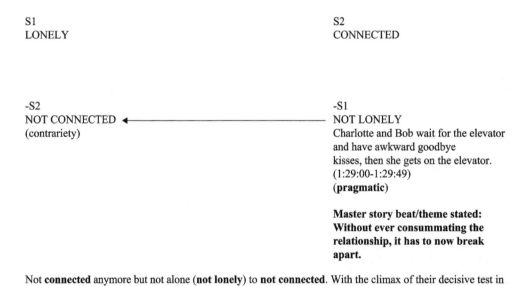

Not **connected** anymore but not alone (**not lonely**) to **not connected**. With the climax of their decisive test in the rearview mirror, there's not much else for them to do. But their glorifying test awaits.

Figure 6.41 Master story beat/theme stated 18—*Lost in Translation.*

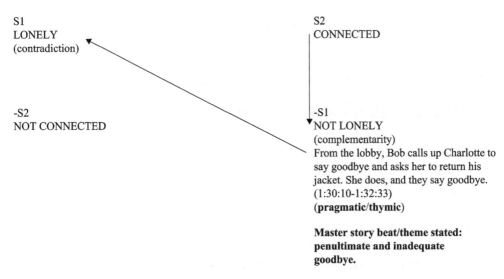

Penultimate goodbye. Near the end, from **connected** to **not lonely** (they are still in each other's midst) anymore but soon to be **lonely** again. The successful completion of the decisive test is past…no glorifying test in sight. They are stuck in a nether world of inaction.

Figure 6.42 Master story beat/theme stated 19—*Lost in Translation.*

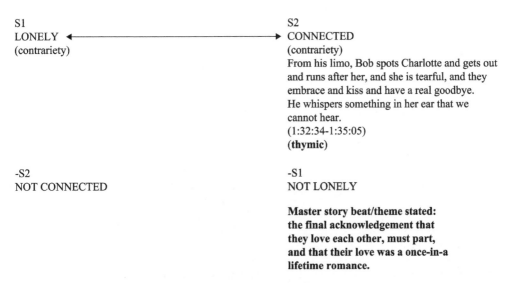

Their glorifying test is in play in this master beat. They are not **lonely**; they are **connected**, but their **connection** in this moment accentuates the pain of their loneliness, hence the dual arrows pointing between the two master poles simultaneously. This is their glorifying test which was delayed a few crucial beats above.

Figure 6.43 Master story beat/theme stated 20—*Lost in Translation.*

Specimen #3—*Get Out*

Contemporary Black Cinema, Horror/ Comedy, Multiple Genres

TITLE: *Get Out*
GENRE: Horror/Comedy
SUBGENRE: Black Cinema
SCREENWRITER: Jordan Peele
DIRECTOR: Jordan Peele
LOG LINE: A Black man is nervous to meet his white girlfriend's family over a weekend, and, when he does, things turn out to be worse than he ever imagined.

The Surface Level—Cataloging Isotopies

Cataloging the isotopies of this masterpiece was instructive, especially in seeing how much of the hidden *truth* of the narrative was pointed towards via the isotopies.

Table 6.29 Isotopies (Objects)—*Get Out*

OBJECTS	
cell phone	broken headlight
white car	cop car
robe	Rose's license and registration
photograph of Black man with balloons	Chris's state ID
photograph of Black woman's pregnant belly in apartment projects with man	rake
	Officer Ryan's shoulder walkie-talkie
photograph of a white person holding a white pit bull on a chain	photo of Jeremy (Rose's little brother)
	Rose's luggage wheelie
photograph of a white kid in a Halloween-type mask	Rose's family photo including grandparents
	candelabras from Bali
mirror	Rose's cell phone
cloth to wipe mirror	photo of Dean's dad in qualifying round of 1936 Berlin Olympics
pastries and doughnuts	
shaving cream	rubber gloves
Canon camera	glasses of iced tea
Chris's laptop	spoon and glass
two takeout coffee cups in a holder	picture of iced tea
Chris's black overnight bag	spilled iced tea
shirt Chris packs	napkin
cell phone	Jeremy's shoulder bag
cigarette	wine glasses
TSA badge	dinner plates
leaping deer (also as ACTOR)	candles
broken mirror on car	carrot cake

deer statue with horns (appears over Rose's
head)
Chris's iPad as laptop
Death Cheetah vs. Matter with Clint 4 poster
teacup on TV screen
manual lawn mower
bingo card poster with Black face on it
stuffed lion toy
buzzing fly
pack of cigarettes
teacup with tea and spoon
Chris's phone with phone charger
maid's mirror
ax and wood for chopping
eyeliner pencil
black cars approaching in motorcade
glasses of wine
walking cane
badminton net, rackets
blind man's cane
wheelchair
mirror in guest room
Chinese food carton
iPhone flash
bingo cards
large photo of Chris on gazebo stage
ukulele
photo of Andre Logan King (Hayworth) and wife
(Philomena)
Chris's shirt
box of photos
random photos of Rose as a kid
photos of Rose with different Black boyfriends
photo of Rose with Georgina as Black
girlfriend
Rose's shoulder bag
badminton racket
Rose's car keys
TSA badge
container with dog food
dog bowl
dog bowls on towel

cameras in Chris's apartment
straps on Chris's hands and legs
chair Chris is strapped into
butterfly cocoon
old TV/communication hub
deer head with antlers
Detective Latoya
bag of nuts
notepad Rod is writing on
pencil
Rod's notes
poker from fireplace
chair arms filled with cotton
Andre Logan King's bloody nose
plastic cone for head for surgery
cotton coming out of ripped chair arms
rubber surgeon gloves
surgeon hat and gown
surgeon mask
candles lighting operating room
box holding brain surgery tools
scalpel
bald head
wheelchair with IV
photos on walls of old establishment people
bloody scalp
metal bucket to discard bloody scalp
surgeon's drill saw
bocce ball
pieces of cotton from Chris's ears
skull top
knife (letter opener)
white glass of milk with black straw
bowl of multicolored cereal
Bing search
photos of NBA players
Rose's earbuds
Rose's iPad computer
knight headpiece
Rose's shotgun
tree Chris smashes into
Rod's TSA car

Table 6.30 Isotopies (Place)—*Get Out*

PLACES	
suburban street	hallway through dining room to back porch
woods off road	back porch
Chris's apartment	living room
bakery	bench by the dock at the lake
elevator of Chris's apartment	stage of gazebo
Chris's front door	tables near gazebo
Chris's bedroom	doorway near back porch
Rose's car	dark wooded area approaching Armitage home
wooded roads to Rose's parents' house	drive circle near Armitage home
outside airport at drop-off/pickup	small storage room in bedroom
off side of road	staircase descending to basement
inside woods	outside airport terminal
Rose's parents' house	Chris's apartment
front porch of Rose's parents' house	basement room ("pre-op prep room")
inside Rose's parents' house hallway	outdoors (Roman on TV)
living room of Rose's parents' house	other outdoor area (Roman on TV)
Armitage kitchen	tree that cocoon is stuck to
Armitage backyard	table with teacup on screen
backyard patio	Detective Latoya's office
dining room	desk area in Chris's apartment
guest bedroom	hospital gown
the sunken place	Jim Hudson's pre-op room
staircase	operating room
front porch at night	operating table
backyard at night	operating tables with monitoring workstation
Missy's study	hallway in basement
black gazebo with black chairs	drive right in front of Armitage house
maid's room through window	young Chris's bedroom
wood-cutting area (help house)	tree Chris smashes into (area near house)
chairs outside gazebo	road where "Grandpa" tackles Chris
area near staircase of Armitage house	road about 100 yards from Armitage house
door looking into maid's room	
Rod's living room	

Table 6.31 Isotopies (Actors)—*Get Out*

ACTORS

Andre Logan King (Hayworth)	Parker Dray
abductor	April Dray
Chris Washington	Philomena King
Rose Armitage	Jim Hudson
leaping deer (also as OBJECT)	David and Marsha Wincott
Sid (Chris's dog)	Ronald and Celia Jeffries
Rod	Hiroki Tanaka
passengers at airport	random people at airport
dying injured deer	Roman Armitage
Officer Ryan	Mrs. Roman Armitage
groundskeeper	Young Rose
Dean Armitage	Young Jesse
Missy Armitage	Young Missy
Georgina	Young Dean
Jeremy	Detective Garcia
party guests	Detective Drake
the Greenes	Detective Latoya
Nelson and Lisa Deets	

Table 6.32 Isotopies (Time/Durativeness)—*Get Out*

TIME/DURATIVENESS

flashback of Chris waiting for his mother
flashback of deer dying
time under hypnosis in the sunken place

States of Being — *Get Out* (First Pass)

- *Andre Hayworth peacefully walking in suburbia.*
- *Chris and Rose kissing.*
- *Andre Hayworth fearfully struggling as he's being abducted.*
- *Chris and Rose laughing about her teasing him that he's jealous over Rod.*
- *Chris expresses it was sexy that Rose defended him against the cop after the deer accident.*
- *Chris and Rose make out after first night at the Armitage house.*
- *Chris observes wounded dying deer.*
- *Chris cries remembering he did nothing to look for his dying mother.*
- *Chris is in the sunken place.*
- *Chris cries falling into the sunken place.*
- *Georgina (maid) crying.*
- *Andre Logan King (Hayworth) talks upbeat about African American experience.*
- *After Chris shoots a flashbulb at Andre Logan King (Hayworth).*
- *Andre Logan King (Hayworth) breaks down and passionately yells "get out" to Chris.*
- *Chris cries about not looking for his mother the night she died.*
- *Chris screams for Rose to give him the keys.*
- *Chris falls into the sunken place.*
- *Chris frightfully tries to escape in pre-op.*
- *Georgina (Mrs. Armitrage) screams and beats up on Chris in car, causing him to crash.*
- *Georgina laughing.*
- *Chris and Rose emotionally vow to leave together and that they love each other.*
- *Detective Latoya seriously listens to Rod discuss how Chris was captured and made into a sex slave.*
- *Chris breaks down trying to strangle Rose.*
- *Rose smiles as Chris strangles her.*

The Master Semiotic Square for *Get Out*

As usual, the challenge is trying to think of the controlling binary opposition terms that will drive the entire analysis. To me, the controlling binary opposition terms most suitable to this movie are: Black/White.

Choosing these terms was simple because in this movie Black people are on the side of good and white people are on the side of evil, and this binary opposition serves various nuances, especially when we add the analysis of the semiotic square of veridiction (discussed later).

So, for now, let's look at the traditional master semiotic square for *Get Out*.

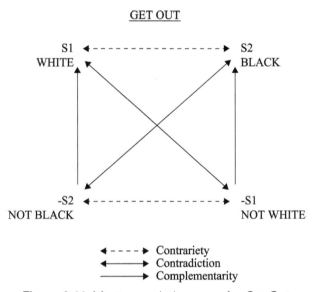

Figure 6.44 Master semiotic square for *Get Out*.

Now it's time to see which term I can associate various isotopies, too. In this movie, a few will switch sides, which is interesting in and of itself. Note: The isotopies are logged onto either side of the controlling binary opposition terms but are not necessarily in direct opposition to each other.

Table 6.33 Isotopies of Objects in binary opposition (based on master semiotic square)—*Get Out*

OBJECTS		
WHITE*	**vs.**	**BLACK**
cell phone		photograph of Black man with
white car		balloons
knight armor headpiece		photograph of Black woman's pregnant belly
pastries and doughnuts		in apartment projects with man

(Continued)

Table 6.33 *Continued*

OBJECTS

WHITE*	vs.	BLACK
photograph of a white person holding a pit bull on chain		photograph of a white kid in a Halloween-type mask
two takeout coffee cups in a holder		mirror
broken mirror on car		cloth to wipe mirror
broken headlight		shaving cream
cop car		Canon camera
Rose's license and registration		Chris's laptop
Chris's state ID		Chris's black overnight bag
Rose's luggage wheelie		shirt Chris packs
rake		cell phone
Officer Ryan's shoulder walkie-talkie		cigarette
photo of Jeremy (Rose's little brother)		TSA badge
Rose's family photo including grandparents		photo of Hayworth and wife (Philomena)
candelabras from Bali		Chris's shirt
Rose's cell phone		container with dog food
photo of Dean's dad in qualifying round of 1936 Berlin Olympics		dog bowl
rubber gloves		dog bowls on towel
glasses of iced tea		cameras in Chris's apartment
spoon and glass		TSA badge
picture of iced tea		Andre Logan King's (Hayworth's) bloody nose
spilled iced tea		cotton coming out of ripped chair arms
napkin		bocce ball
Jeremy's shoulder bag		pieces of cotton from Chris's ears
wine glasses		knife (letter opener)
dinner plates		tree Chris smashes into
candles		Rod's TSA car
carrot cake		Rose's shotgun (switches sides)
deer statue with horns (appears over Rose's head)		Chris's iPad as laptop
Death Cheetah vs. Matter with Clint 4 poster		deer head with antlers (switches sides)
teacup on TV screen		
bingo card poster with black face on it		
stuffed lion toy		
buzzing fly		
pack of cigarettes		
teacup with tea and spoon		
Chris's phone with phone charger		
maid's mirror		
ax and wood for chopping		
eyeliner pencil		
black cars approaching in motorcade		
walking cane		
badminton net, rackets		
blind man's cane		

wheelchair
mirror in guest room
Chinese food carton
iPhone flash
bingo cards
large photo of Chris on gazebo stage
ukulele
box of photos
random photos of Rose as a kid
photos of Rose with different Black boyfriends
photo of Rose with a younger hipper Georgina
    as Black girlfriend
Rose's shoulder bag
badminton racket
Rose's car keys
straps on Chris's hands and legs
chair Chris is strapped into
butterfly cocoon
old TV/communication hub
deer head with antlers
bag of nuts
notepad Rod is writing on
pencil
Rod's notes
poker from fireplace
chair arms filled with cotton
plastic cone for head for surgery
rubber surgeon gloves
surgeon hat and gown
surgeon mask
candles lighting operating room
box holding brain surgery tools
scalpel
bald head
wheelchair with IV
photos on walls of old establishment people
bloody scalp
metal bucket to discard bloody scalp
surgeon's drill saw
skull top
knife (letter opener)
white glass of milk with black straw
bowl of multicolored cereal
Bing search
photos of NBA players
Rose's earbuds
Rose's iPad computer
knight headpiece
Rose's shotgun

---

*From an iconographical standpoint, some objects in this movie mostly point to the "white side" of the spectrum, possessing the flavor of old money, white establishment (badminton, deer head trophies, tea drinking). All of these objects telegraph the meaning of the story, of course, reflecting the power of the controlling binary opposition terms (Black/White) and what lies under the hood of the narrative, which will be revealed.

Table 6.34 Isotopies of Place in binary opposition (based on master semiotic square)—
Get Out

PLACES

WHITE	vs.	BLACK
suburban streets		Chris's apartment
woods off road		elevator of Chris's apartment
bakery		Chris's front door
Rose's car		Chris's bedroom
wooded roads to Rose's parents' house		wooded roads to Rose's parents' house
inside woods (where wounded deer dies)		outside airport at drop-off/pickup
off side of road		
Rose's parents' house		
front porch of Rose's parents' house		
inside Rose's parents' house hallway		
living room of Rose's parents' house		
Missy's office		
Armitage kitchen		
Armitage backyard		
backyard patio		
dining room		
guest bedroom		
the sunken place		
staircase		
front porch at night		
backyard at night		
Missy's study		
black gazebo with black chairs		
maid's room through window		
wood-cutting area (help house)		
chairs outside gazebo		
area near staircase of Armitage house.		
door looking into maid's room		
Rod's living room		
hallway through dining room to back porch		
back porch		
living room		
bench by the dock at the lake		
stage of gazebo		
tables near gazebo		
doorway near back porch		
dark wooded area approaching Armitage home		
drive circle near Armitage home		
small storage room in bedroom		
staircase descending to basement		
outside airport terminal		
Chris's apartment		
basement room ("pre-op prep room")		
outdoors (Roman on TV)		
other outdoor area (Roman on TV)		
Roman outside Armitage house		
tree that cocoon is stuck to		

table with teacup on screen
Detective Latoya's office
desk area in Chris's apartment
kitchen of Armitage house
hospital gown
Jim Hudson's pre-op room
operating room
operating table
operating tables with monitoring workstation
hallway in basement
drive right in front of Armitage house
Young Chris's bedroom
tree Chris smashes into (area near house)
road where "Grandpa" tackles Chris
road about 100 yards from Armitage house

Table 6.35 Isotopies of Actors in binary opposition (based on master semiotic square)—*Get Out*

ACTORS

WHITE	vs.	BLACK
abductor		Andre Hayworth
Rose Armitage		Chris Washington
leaping deer		Sid (Chris's dog)
dying injured deer		Rod
Officer Ryan		passengers at airport
groundskeeper		Officer Ryan (can relate to both sides)
Dean Armitage		Detective Latoya (can relate to both sides)
Missy Armitage		Detective Garcia (can relate to both sides)
Georgina		Detective Drake (can relate to both sides)
Jeremy		random people at airport
party guests		
the Greenes		
Nelson and Lisa Deets		
Parker Dray		
April Dray		
Philomena King		
Jim Hudson		
David and Marsha Wincott		
Ronald and Celia Jeffries		
Hiroki Tanaka		
Roman Armitage		
Mrs. Roman Armitage		
Young Rose		
Young Jesse		
Younger Missy		
Younger Dean		
Detective Latoya		
Detective Garcia		
Detective Drake		

Table 6.36 States of being in binary opposition—*Get Out*[1]

EUPHORIA	vs.	DYSPHORIA
• *Andre Hayworth peacefully walking in suburbia.*		• *Andre Hayworth fearfully struggling as he's being abducted.*
• *Chris and Rose kissing.*		
• *Chris and Rose laughing about her teasing him that he's jealous over Rod.*		• *Panic and distress over hitting the leaping deer.*
• *Chris expresses it was sexy that Rose defended him against the cop after the deer accident.*		• *Chris cries remembering he did not look for his dying mother.*
• *Chris and Rose make out after first night at the beautiful estate.*		• *Chris cries falling into the sunken place.*
• *Georgina laughing.*		• *Georgina (maid) crying.*
• *Andre Logan King (Hayworth) talks upbeat about the African American experience.*		• *After Chris shoots a flashbulb at Andre Logan King (Hayworth), he breaks down and emotionally yells "get out" to Chris.*
• *Chris and Rose emotionally vow to leave together and that they love each other.*		• *Chris cries about not looking for his mother the night she died.*
		• *Chris screams for Rose to give him the keys.*
		• *Chris falls into the sunken place.*
		• *Chris frightfully tries to escape chair in pre-op.*
• *Detective Latoya and colleagues crack up laughing about Rod's sex slave story.*		• *Detective Latoya seriously listens to Rod discuss how Chris was captured and made into a sex slave.*
		• *Jeremy angrily tries to take down Chris.*
		• *Georgina (Mrs. Armitage) screams and beats up on Chris in car causing him to crash.*
• *Rose smiles as Chris strangles her.*		• *Chris breaks down trying to strangle Rose.*

[1]Here are placed states of being on either side and also where appropriate I tried to match with a direct binary opposite on the other side.

The Narrative Level for *Get Out*: The Actantial Narrative Schema (Simple Version)

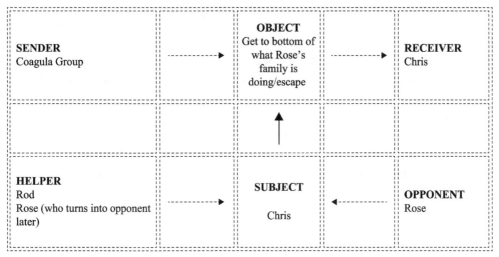

Figure 6.45 Actantial narrative schema semiotic square—*Get Out*.

The Narrative Level for *Get Out*: The Actantial Narrative Schema (Complex Version—The Semiotic Square of Veridiction)

As alluded to earlier, *Get Out* is more complex than our previous specimens because of the appearance vs. reality nature of the story's structure. The complexities of movie stories like *Get Out* are precisely the reason Greimas created a whole other layer to the semiotic analysis, which he called the **semiotic square of veridiction**.

Before I start, allow me to express that while I love all three of my specimen movies, *Get Out* has a dramatic power on its own level not just because of its brilliant (and often hilarious) critique of racism in America. Its genius partially lies in its architecture. Its structure works so well precisely because of the duality between what is actually going on (being) and what seems like is going on (seeming). Greimas talked about this precise situation and provided for it with the additional semiotic square of veridiction.

This additional square is first used in the actantial layer, and renders a binary opposition of being/seeming and added to the other layers (see Figure 6.45) of actants. I apply this additional semiotic square of veridiction to the comprehensive beat map across the board (see Table 6.38). The principle of how this all works underscores a fundamental issue about how we watch and perceive movies in the first place and hence how we break them down. What I mean is, a fiction movie story is a *make-believe* story to begin with. But *Get Out* has a whole other layer of make-believe over the original layer of make-believe that is being presented to us the competent observer. In other words, we're already looking at a make-believe story world (that Chris and we intially see together). Chris is essentially a competent observer in his own world, and we are at first privy to the same level of information as he is. But what he is seeing is also make-believe, and the *truth* of what he is seeing is behind the veneer of surface reality (being vs. seeming) which exists in absolutely a binary opposition.

Because of this multi-layering of reality, the movie forces us as competent observer to piece together what is really going on; therefore, this kind of story becomes very psychologically dynamic, and, in effect, more "real" to our psyches. This technique combines with the mission that the story is on; namely, to give us a glimpse of a Black man's view of the white world and how what he sees isn't what it appears to be. This is pure genius.

That said, the subject of the semiotic square of veridiction is a giant topic, and a full analysis of the tool could fill another book. Therefore, I'm only going to touch on this aspect of the system enough to give you some additional tools to help you break down a movie with the complexity of *Get Out*. In the future, this tool will also help you brainstorm and write your own screenplays that might be similar in architecture to *Get Out*.

The Semiotic Square of Veridiction

Below is a sketch of the semiotic square of veridiction that represents the complex story structure of the kind represented *Get Out* got so right.

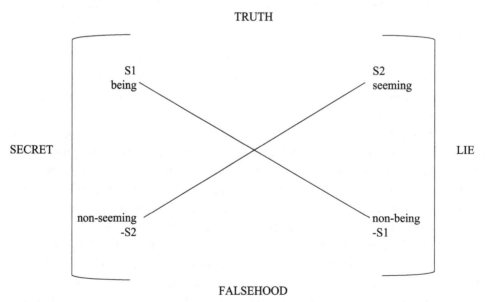

Figure 6.46 The semiotic square of veridiction. Greimas began developing this tool later on in his research, and much work remains to be done with it. But it gets at a very special type of dramatic story: one where things aren't what they appear to be, which is arguably the most powerful kind of story if executed well, as *Get Out* was.

This semiotic square of veridiction is not just four corners of the square of logic that the original semiotic square is based on. It contains a semiotics square in the middle but clearly one of *perception* (being/seeming), etc. For this internal square, S1 is being, S2 is seeming, -S1 is non-being, and -S2 is non-seeming. Then, over that, are four other quadrants *superimposed*. My understanding is that Greimas intended for the semiotic square of veridiction to function primarily on the actantial narrative schema level in a way that can multiply actants, adding binary opposition layers of perception to the original master *six* actants that control all movie story.

Allow me to reiterate what the basic six actants of the actantial narrative schema are:

- sender/receiver
- subject/object
- helper/opponent (anti-subject)

That said, let's look again at the basic actantial narrative schema square of *Get Out*.

To give us some extra breakdown and brainstorming information to study *Get Out* with, I'm going to mainly pull the binary terms from the semiotic square of veridiction above, being/seeming. These two seem to me like they will serve well and cover much of what is going on in architecture of *Get Out*, but I'll use some of the other terms as well from the semiotic square of veridiction in my analysis.

So the original six actants (sender/receiver, subject/object, helper/opponent) have additional actants connected that will have to do with what appears to be going on (seeming) and what *actually* is going on (being), but the difference between the two binary opposition of actants is revealed over time. This architecture feeds directly into the core mechanism of how the movie *Get Out* works, which feeds into the plot's master misdirect.

Let me explain.

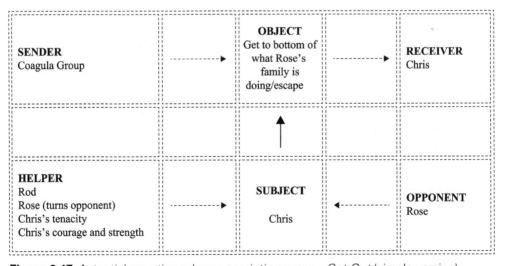

Figure 6.47 Actantial narrative schema semiotic square—*Get Out* (simple version).

Early on, from our perspective as an audience member (competent observer), Rose functions mostly as a helper to Chris, *but* we believe her object (shared with Chris) is to aid Chris in dealing with Rose's racially awkward family and associates and help him diffuse the attendant micro-aggressions hurled at Chris for being Black. But as the movie story evolves *in time*, Rose's family turns into an opponent *but* of an evil nature that is not clear (secret) at first. But for the majority of the movie Rose *seems* like she's still a helper to Chris, first against racism and then against whatever unknown evil might be occurring that he senses and she pretends to sense.

Rose starts as a helper to Chris, dealing with what he thinks is racial awkwardness, then she evolves into a would-be protector (seeming) of Chris dealing with a lurking (secret) evil of her family and associates. Rose will become an opponent to Chris and on a dark sinister level which is revealed later, a life and death struggle. This sinister evil involves Rose's *actual* object (being), which is to enslave Chris. Rose is revealed as a full-blown anti-subject trying to turn Chris into a slave.

Table 6.37 is a simple chart that tracks the basics of these additional actants that we use to look at *Get Out*, and represents a very basic application of the semiotic square of veridiction. A full-scale analysis of this complex tool is beyond the scope of this book, and Greimas was still developing the method at the time of his death. Much remains to be done with this exciting development of narrative semiotics. For our purposes, I'll be using mostly the being/seeming actants when I break down *Get Out* and perhaps a few of the other veridiction actants where appropriate. The main theme to take away from looking at this tool is to understand that sometimes in a movie story things are not as they seem, but in *Get Out* this method is foundational to its architecture and effectiveness.

Table 6.37 Veridiction chart of actants in *Get Out*

ACTOR	VERIDICTION	FUNCTION
Rose	seeming	helper (Chris dealing with family's racial awkwardness)
Rose	being	opponent/anti-subject (to enslave Chris)
Andre	seeming	helper (tries to relax Chris about awkward white people)
Andre (Black man Dre surfacing from the sunken place after phone camera flashes in his eyes)	being	helper (to Chris's eventual goal of saving his own life avoiding slavery)
Georgina (*knowing how to do something*/ Grandma)	seeming	opponent (to Chris discovering the truth)
Georgina (emotional/real Georgina flashes)	being	helper (to Chris sensing the truth of what is really going on)
Walter (*knowing how to do something* Grandpa)	seeming	opponent (to Chris discovering the truth)
Walter (flash from phone camera forces his real Black self to re-emerge and shoot Rose)	being	helper (to save Chris from a life of slavery)

The movie is almost entirely built on the binary opposition of seeming/being, with some use of truth/falsehood, etc. And the entire genius architecture of the movie story is that we (competent observers) pretty much know right away that something is "up" (in a *Stepford Wives* kind of way) early on, especially when we meet the Armitage's Black help (Georgina and Walter) and observe their bizarre behavior.

We suspect at first that Rose's father Dean is just self-consciously awkward about race (as well as their next-day party guests are). When we meet Andre Logan King, the Black man who is married to an older white woman of the group, we first explain it to ourselves (competent observers) that King is merely just an awkward Black man who has been "whitewashed" due to marrying an older white woman. But as the events progress, our sense that something is lurking beneath the façade is inevitable. The misdirect of Rose and her function as a helper is first (seeming) to aid Chris in battling racial awkwardness and then she is later revealed as an anti-subject to Chris (being), who ends up fighting for his life trying to avoid a life of slavery.

Now, as it is with all specimen breakdowns, I like to lay out a foundational canonical narrative schema summary as a "treatment" to help set up the comprehensive beat map, etc. As usual, I'll treat this part of the analysis of the specimen *Get Out* with a basic flow of a story in a narrative syntax and offer both a refresher about the movie's plot for those who might require this data or as a story touchstone for those who might never have seen the movie.

Although for *Get Out* I will be utilizing the semiotic square of veridiction to break down this movie, the canonical narrative schema will *not* consider the additional actants of the semiotic square of veridiction. These will be added later. I believe the canonical narrative schema summary should first represent the movie's story as it *appears* to us (competent observers) in real time in what would be an initial viewing. Hence, the summary for *Get Out* will provide the same foundation that the canonical narrative schema provides for all the specimen movies which will *then* allow for the veridiction tools to be added later in the comprehensive beat map, the logging of the master story beats on the semiotic square, etc.

So for now, let's look at the simple summary of *Get Out*.

A Simple Canonical Narrative Schema Summary—*Get Out*

On a suburban street, a Black man is abducted by an abductor wearing knight headgear, rendered unconscious and thrown into the trunk of a waiting car. In a city, Rose, who is white, buys pastries then shows up to her boyfriend Chris's apartment. Chris and Rose discuss meeting her parents for the weekend and how Chris is self-conscious because he's Black and wonders if they'll accept him. The initial contract is for Rose to facilitate introducing her Black boyfriend Chris to her white family with the goal of wanting the weekend to go smoothly and for Rose's parents to accept their mixed-race relationship and for them to effectively deal with the family's racial "awkwardness."

This goal is a contract between Chris and Rose, set up as a qualifying test to get through the weekend with Rose's white family smoothly, perhaps to set up for a future decisive test of Chris and Rose possibly getting married. (Visiting parents for a weekend can sometimes point in the marriage or the serious commitment direction for couples.) This qualifying test of a smooth weekend with the family will require a *being able to do something*; namely, Chris being able to deal with Rose's lame dad and Rose making it bearable for Chris. She warns Chris that her dad will be awkward about their mixed-race relationship and say things like he'd vote for Obama for a third term if he could.

En route to Rose's parents, the couple hit a leaping deer on the highway, and a cop called to the scene tries to profile Chris (get his ID) despite the fact that Rose was driving. Rose defies the cop and blocks giving the officer Chris's ID information. Chris later remarks this protective behavior was "hot," in that she defended him, implying Rose is continuing to pass the qualifying test of being a protector of Chris from racial scrutiny and will continue to protect him from her family's racial awkwardness over the coming weekend.

When they get to her parent's house Chris must deal with the odd Black help (Walter and Georgina), and Rose's awkward father Dean, who refers to Chris as "my man," reflecting racial awkwardness. Then we meet Rose's weird younger brother Jeremy, who is fascinated by Chris's athletic capabilities in a racially stereotypical way because Chris is Black and athletic. These behaviors are all standard racial micro-aggressions that Chris seems equipped to deal with in his stride. All of these beats are part of the qualifying test for Chris and Rose to endure and tolerate the racial awkwardness of Rose's family for the weekend, which, while off-putting, is seemingly tolerable to Chris for the short term.

However, the entire contract gives hints of shifting for Chris, specifically of him losing control of his psyche when, in the middle of the night, he awakens and meets up with Rose's mother Missy, who offers Chris hypnosis to eliminate his cigarette addiction. As the hypnosis session progresses, Missy talks to Chris about a painful event from his childhood, specifically when he was a young boy and his mother didn't come home one night and young Chris neglected to alert the authorities. It turned out Chris's mother had gotten into a car accident and lay dying on the side of the road while young Chris did nothing. Young Chris might have been able to save her, and his neglecting to call the authorities while she lay dying was a failure of a decisive test on his part to protect his mother and has become an emotional wound ever since.

Missy uses Chris's state of a remorseful memory over this past failure and, with a hypnosis technique, takes over his brain, linking the triggering of the hypnosis to a stirring teacup sound. She taps a teaspoon inside a teacup, and this triggers Chris to fall into a trance and into "the sunken place," a dark psychological region in his mind where he feels as if he's floating in a black void and is powerless and cannot access his body. Although we aren't sure of the nature of Missy's actions, we sense she has executed a qualifying test of some kind that will lead into some as yet unknown greater decisive test for Chris to have to deal with.

A new more horrifying qualifying test of Chris has begun; the story is subtly shifting from surviving the racial awkwardness of Rose's family to something seemingly darker and more life-threatening, but we as competent observers are not sure yet exactly what is going on. Missy has executed perhaps a qualifying test of her own, a *being able to do something*, which is to be able to take over Chris's psyche using an incident in his past and the teacup sound.

The incident of young Chris neglecting to call the police as his mother lay dying can be viewed as a failed decisive test that Chris lives with and serves Missy as an open wound and anchor for her to take control of his brain. During the hypnosis session (which she does to allegedly help Chris quit smoking), Missy gains psychological control of Chris (her *being able to do something*) and sends him to the "sunken place," which we experience visually as him falling to the bottom of a dark abyss and disconnecting from his body, and hence rendered powerless.

Chris awakens as if from a dream. He tells Rose that her mother hypnotized him, and she is annoyed over this. Guests arrive in a black car caravan and are all white, except for a young healthy Black man, Andre Logan King (Hayworth), who's married to an older white woman in the bunch. King is dressed awkwardly (white), and Chris snaps a picture of him, causing King to have a strange reaction. King's nose bleeds, and he seems to have terrible anxiety and screams "get out" to Chris as a warning about something. Whatever is going on, we, the competent observers, can sense it's connected to Missy's hypnosis and "the sunken place," her qualifying test of taking over Chris's psyche earlier, and possibly connected to some future decisive test that we are not aware of yet. Missy gathers up King, and they disappear. Later, Missy returns with King back to "normal," and he apologizes for his behavior and leaves.

This incident causes Chris to think something bad is going on that is way more evil than the original qualifying test he prepared for; namely, of him surviving the racial awkwardness of Rose's family and associates for the weekend. The new survival qualifying test is on as Chris sends the snapped photo of King to his best friend Rod, a TSA officer already suspicious of Rose and her family. Rod discovers that King was named "Dre" and disappeared some time ago, prompting Rod to postulate that the white people Chris is with have a racket whereby they capture healthy Black men and turn them into sex slaves. Chris doesn't buy this but continues to fearfully suspect something bad is happening and can sense he is involved in a situation that will put him into a life-and-death qualifying test, leading to a final decisive test of escaping, which we (competent observers) aren't sure the true nature of but can certainly sense the seriousness of it.

At the lake, Chris emotionally recalls to Rose the incident of failing to save his mother and how Rose is the only person he trusts. He convinces Rose that something bad is going on, and she agrees to escape the family compound with him. Meanwhile, Rose's family and associates are back at the gazebo "auctioning off" Chris in some sort of slavery lottery, which points towards the real contract that Rose's family must have going on, seemingly to enslave Chris, a contract which will constitute a real decisive test, although we don't know what this will be yet but we can sense it (as Rod does).

Chris now launches his new contract to flee Rose's parents' home with Rose before something bad can befall him. The qualifying test will be to deal with her parents one last time and escape, a *being able to do something*; namely, to politely evacuate the house without hurting their feelings. The couple return to the house to pack and make an excuse to leave.

Chris implores Rose to pack and find her car keys. Chris is failing his qualifying test to escape, which will set up a decisive test (he's not sure of what, yet he knows it's linked to his survival). As Rose searches for the car keys, Chris finds a hidden stash of photos of Rose with a series of other Black boyfriends and one which shows Georgina the family maid as Rose's girlfriend, looking young and hip, pointing to evidence that Rose is involved in whatever evil (decisive test of her family) that is afoot. All of these former Black lovers of Rose failed their own decisive test to escape the evil of the family, and Rose is somehow involved.

Chris pleads with Rose to find the car keys so they can escape, and she struggles to find them as Rose's family starts to surround Chris in the living room. Rose reveals she had the keys all along and is on the evil family's side. She is the main deceiver and ensnared Chris into thinking the decisive test was dealing with Rose's family's and associates' micro-aggressions (a master misdirect). The family (including Rose) is doing something evil to the Black people who, over time, have been brought to the house via Rose, as evidenced by the pictures Chris found of her and her lovers. Jeremy starts fighting with Chris, and Missy taps a teacup and causes Chris to become unconscious and collapse, hitting his head as he falls. As he lies unconscious, we see that he has fallen into the "sunken place," which is connected to what will be his real qualifying test of survival, leading to a final decisive test of escaping alive, all of which we can now sense but haven't yet learned the true nature of the ordeal.

Chris wakes up strapped to a chair in the basement, and we now sense his contract has completely shifted to one that will involve his own life-and-death survival. Chris watches a video on a TV in front of him, which explains what is going on: The family is part of the Coagula Group and Dean (a neurosurgeon) has created a procedure which will replace Chris's brain with an old blind white man's brain, that of Jim Hudson, whom Chris talked to briefly at the gathering and learned is a blind photo gallery owner who admired Chris's photography work. We are made to realize that the results of this surgical procedure will be that Chris's psyche will live in the "sunken place" for the rest of his life while Jim's personality will control Chris's body, hence occupying Chris's body as a slave.

Chris now has the contract of needing to escape his fate of having his brain replaced by the old white man's brain. This starts a new qualifying test to see if Chris can get out of the chair. His first *being able to do something* is knowing how to foil the hypnosis triggered by the spoon tapping the teacup when a video of this action appears on the TV that Chris is viewing. He passes out like clockwork. Later, when Jeremy comes to collect Chris for surgery, Chris pretends to be asleep and when his arms are freed, arises, (off camera grabs a bocce ball) and smashes Jeremy on the side of the head. Jeremy collapses and bleeds profusely. Chris pulls cotton out of his ears, signaling it hid the sound of the teacup and he never really went unconscious. His *being able to do something* of the new qualifying test has succeeded, which was to avoid the hypnosis and escape the chair and dungeon where they planned to enslave his body with Jim Hudson's brain.

Chris's decisive test is on and will continue when he confronts other family members seeking to impede his escape in different stages of the remaining narrative. Chris stabs the father, Dr. Dean Armitage, with deer antlers, killing him instantly. Chris runs upstairs, confronts Missy, and they both dive for the hypnosis-triggering teacup. Chris smashes it, prompting Missy to stab his hand with a letter opener, which he in turn uses to slit her throat. Jeremy re-emerges and tries to strangle Chris, and Chris knocks him to the floor and stomps him dead.

The decisive test is still in play; Chris grabs Jeremy's keys and escapes in his car, runs over Georgina and feels bad she's lying dying on the road, reminding him of his mother dying on the side of the road years earlier whom he failed to help (failed decisive test). Despite the fact that Chris is succeeding in this decisive test to escape, he can't help feeling bad for the woman and takes the injured Georgina in the car and drives. Georgina awakens screaming with the angry voice of Grandma Armitage (Rose's grandmother transplanted into Georgina's body), and she viciously yells at Chris and causes him to smash into a tree, killing her.

Rose comes out of the house with a shotgun and shoots at Chris. Walter, the Black groundskeeper controlled by Roses's grandfather's brain, knocks Chris down, and they struggle. Chris shoots a phone flash into Walter's eyes and causes the original Black man (the real Walter) to emerge from his own "sunken place." Walter asks Rose for the shotgun to allow him to shoot Chris himself, and she gives it to him thinking this is her "grandfather" speaking. Walter (the Black man who has briefly emerged from his own "sunken place") shoots Rose and then himself. Rose lies on the floor dying and goes for the gun; Chris takes it away from her. The decisive test is now complete. All parties working against Chris's escape have been killed or subdued.

We now move into a short glorifying test: Chris handling the dying Rose before he can fully escape. Rose is mortally wounded. Chris is in control and, given the violence she led him into, it would be understandable if in anger he just killed her. Chris goes to strangle Rose, who is on the floor dying, and she smiles, hinting that though dying she's pleased because in her racist mind Chris's last final act of violence justifies her actions because he is Black and acting "violent," a racist stereotype of bad Black behavior, and in some ways justifying the entire enterprise of abducting Black men and implanting white brains into them, in her warped mind. But Chris still has enough dignity not to behave violently and decides against killing her, even though she is evil and tried to "kill" him. He cannot bring himself to kill her. This is Chris's glorifying test, which spills over into the short scene when Rod shows up to take him away. Chris has escaped and has maintained his dignity in not killing the woman he was in love with, despite the fact that she tried to kill him and was a violent evil woman.

Comprehensive Beat Map for *Get Out*

Now, let's look at the comprehensive beat map for *Get Out*. As I alluded to earlier, *Get Out* functions on multiple levels, different than the other specimen movies[3] because it deploys more than the typical six actants, and to decode it requires that I apply the semiotic square of veridiction to its breakdowns and analyses.

Get Out presents as a constant game of keeping the competent observer effectively off balance between seeming vs. being in sync with how Chris perceives reality, done in a way that when we learn the *truth* it all makes sense as the antecedents to the reality of what is going on have been masterfully planted. I'll discuss the master story beats/themes stated in detail later, but because they will be presented first as part of the following comprehensive beat map, I'd like to note that, once again, my approach to cataloging master story beats in this specimen breakdown is nuanced and unique. Starting with the comprehensive beat map, you should especially note how the master story beats encompass some of the language of the semiotics square of veridiction as it's impossible to have discussion of the beats of *Get Out* without mentioning this perspective. (Even though as a competent observers first enjoying the movie, we wouldn't be completely cognizant as to the real meaning of all the story beats as they first present to us.) Also of note, states of being have been cataloged earlier but will be treated as part of the regular beat flow so that this specimen analysis can focus on the special tools of the semiotic square of veridiction (being/seeming) without further complications. Rest assured, all the states of being will still be presented in the comprehensive beat map (and master story beats), but they will be reiterated as part of the regular flow of information and not flagged as bold/italics.

---

[3]For the record, *It's a Wonderful Life* can be examined using the semiotic square of veridiction, especially the being/seeming actants. It's structured a little differently in that we the audience are "ahead" of George Bailey in terms of the knowledge of what is really going on.

Table 6.38 Comprehensive beat map—Three specimen movies—Specimen #3—*Get Out*

TIMECODE	BEAT Note: Master story beats/themes stated will be in **bold**.	BEAT TYPE	ACTANTIAL NARRATIVE SCHEMA*	CANONICAL NARRATIVE SCHEMA**
1:18–4:09	An anonymous Black man walks on a suburban street and is followed by a white car and abducted, choked, rendered unconscious, and thrown into the trunk of the car.	PRAGMATIC	The Coagula group captures another Black victim for their transplanting scheme, although the meaning of this will be revealed later; namely, that the Coagula group is an anti-subject to young Black men living in freedom.	The Black man can defeat this abduction but fails (a mini-qualifying test); he is knocked unconscious and subdued.
4:10–5:17	A long shot of trees from a car's perspective as credits run depicts the ride that transports the abducted Black man whom we will later see again.	PRAGMATIC		
5:18–5:59	Chris prepares to shave in his bathroom mirror.	PRAGMATIC	Visiting his girlfriend Rose's family for the weekend is a sender to him a receiver, making him a subject with the object of being found favorable to them given he's Black.	Chris prepares for a contract he thinks is going on (seeming): namely, to win the approval of his girlfriend Rose's family. He has a qualifying test of surviving their racial awkwardness and a very clearly defined *being able to do something*, which is to get through it.

(Continued)

Table 6.38 *Continued*

TIMECODE	BEAT Note: Master story beats/themes stated will be in **bold**.	BEAT TYPE	ACTANTIAL NARRATIVE SCHEMA*	CANONICAL NARRATIVE SCHEMA**
6:00–6:06	Rose looks at pastries in the bakery.	PRAGMATIC COGNITIVE	It's merely a silent cognitive beat that will feed into our perception of Rose as an actant seeming to be a helper who will turn into an anti-subject (being/seeming duality).	Rose (as we'll later learn) is undergoing her own qualifying test to relax Chris to get him to her family's home, so that he doesn't suspect their plans to enslave him (*knowing how to do something*).
6:07–6:11	Chris continues to shave.	PRAGMATIC	The trip to Rose's parents is a sender to Chris the receiver, making him a subject with the object of successfully getting through Rose's parents' weekend. Rose plays helper.	Crosscutting on the couple emphasizes they are preparing for different qualifying tests. Chris thinks it's to get through a weekend with Rose's racially awkward family, and Rose knows it's to capture Chris to enslave his body, but we as competent observers cannot see this yet.
6:12–6:16	Rose looks at pastries and smiles, thinking to herself.	PRAGMATIC COGNITIVE	An unusually internal moment for her character, which will build cumulatively and be clarified later when the being/seeming of the situation (that she is pretending to be a good girlfriend but actually ensnaring him into slavery) is truthfully exposed.	Crosscutting subliminally building the binary opposite qualifying tests; Chris has the one that he thinks he's embarking on (her family approval), and Rose has the one that she knows she's on (ensnaring him into slavery). We the audience keep pace with Chris.

6:17–6:24	Chris shaves and nicks himself.	PRAGMATIC	A mini-qualifying test to shave without cutting himself has failed, but it only goes to underscore Chris's humanness and make us the competent observers aware of his body and red blood humanness.
6:25–6:30	Rose gets out of elevator in Chris's building and turns to go to his apartment.	PRAGMATIC	Crosscutting subliminally building different qualifying tests, Chris's and the "secret" one that Rose is undergoing. She has a robotic vibe to her gait.
6:31–6:58	Chris reviews photos in his camera. Rose knocks on his door, he opens it, they smile and kiss and close the door.	PRAGMATIC	The sexual bond between the couple again furthers the dual qualifying tests (Rose's vs. Chris's, being/seeming) and will further Chris's vulnerability to Rose, a key structural element and the foundation of the movie's brilliant misdirect, which is a classic narrative device aided by the binary opposition actants of being/seeming.
	Rose's sexiness is a helper to her object of relaxing Chris (seeming) so that she can help make him into a slave (being). Chris's attraction to Rose is also a helper to Rose's object of enslaving Chris.		
6:59–8:53	As Chris packs, he asks Rose if she told her parents that he is Black and she makes light of it, saying that despite him being her first Black boyfriend, they won't make an Issue of it and aren't racists.	PRAGMATIC COGNITIVE	The dual qualifying tests are in brilliant display here, feeding perfectly into the master misdirect of Rose, which the movie's genius structure hinges on.

(Continued)

Table 6.38 *Continued*

TIMECODE	BEAT Note: Master story beats/themes stated will be in **bold**.	BEAT TYPE	ACTANTIAL NARRATIVE SCHEMA*	CANONICAL NARRATIVE SCHEMA**
8:54–10:37	Rose drives Chris along wooded roads, and she throws his cigarette out the window.	PRAGMATIC	Rose is seeming to be a helper helping protect Chris against smoking, but her real intent (being) is to preserve his body as a slave vessel so it will have the most worth for her family's goal of enslaving him.	The dual qualifying tests/misdirect deepens. Rose throws out the cigarette seemingly concerned for her lover's health (seeming), and later we learn she's concerned with Chris's body as a slave vessel (being) for the end goal of transplanting a white brain into his body.
	He calls Rod, his best friend (a TSA officer at work), and Rose banters with Rod about how she really wants him instead. Rod issues a warning about not going to a white girl's parents' house, and Chris hangs up.	COGNITIVE	Rod is sender to Chris the receiver by jokingly telling Chris not to go to Rose's parents' house. He is foreshadowing how Chris will be a subject with the object of escaping. Rod is also Chris's primary helper.	
10:38–10:50	As Chris and Rose joke about him being jealous of Rod, a deer leaps across the road and smashes the car.	PRAGMATIC	The deer is a helper/opponent "swing" beat/variable, ingeniously representing the "swing" of how certain actants can go either way (as the coming scene with Officer Ryan will prove). Rose will defy the cop pretending (seeming) to block the cop's racism but actually (being) keeping a record of Chris from being recorded.	The deer accident beat is a variable that is an unplanned qualifying test that will throw Rose's plan off (being). She will have to deal with a *being able to do something*, namely, deal with the cop who is trying to capture Chris's name during the accident report, which would spell trouble for her later when she enslaves Chris and he "disappears."

10:51–12:34	THYMIC	Chris and Rose are freaked out, get out of the car, and Chris goes into the woods to investigate the injured deer.	The deer accident wasn't part of either qualifying test (Chris's imagined one and Rose's real one). It presents an opportunity for a *knowing how to do something*. The thymic beat of Chris and Rose both freaking out is the one time that both parties of the couple experience real emotions together and will subliminally help the competent observer eventually sense the divide between Rose and Chris (being/seeming) all making sense when the actual truth is revealed.
12:35–13:38	PRAGMATIC COGNITIVE	Rose talks to Officer Ryan as Chris contemplates what happened. Officer Ryan asks to see Chris's ID, but Rose tells him that Chris wasn't driving, and the officer backs off. **Master story beat/theme stated: Rose will defend her man against racist cops (but actually is avoiding a record of him having been with her), and this feeds into the misdirect of her intentions to us and to him.**	Officer Ryan poses as an opponent against the union of Chris and Rose by profiling Chris, but it turns out he could've been an unintentional helper to Chris's eventual object (escaping alive) if he had collected Chris's ID, which could've proven useful when Chris would've eventually "disappeared." This deepens the duality of the being/seeming nature of Rose as helper to Chris but really an anti-subject, because she seems progressive and not racist, which helps to separate her out from her racially awkward family, a perception bolstered by her protecting Chris from unwarranted police scrutiny (a lie). Dual qualifying tests of Rose vs. Chris as the misdirect deepens. Rose pretends to protect her man from being racially profiled by a racist cop (seeming); she is eliminating the record of him being there (being).

(Continued)

Table 6.38 *Continued*

TIMECODE	BEAT Note: Master story beats/themes stated will be in **bold**.	BEAT TYPE	ACTANTIAL NARRATIVE SCHEMA*	CANONICAL NARRATIVE SCHEMA**
13:39–13:59	While driving, Chris expresses it was sexy that Rose defended him, and she responds that she is very protective of him.	PRAGMATIC	Rose's pretending to shield Chris from the cop obtaining Chris's info seems like she's a helper to him; he finds it sexy, which is her main helper in luring him into slavery (the actual plot). For now, she is seeming to fight against racism but is in actuality an anti-subject to Chris in that she's trying to lead him into enslavement (being/seeming).	Deepens the dual qualifying tests of Chris vs. Rose while also deepening the Rose misdirect.
14:00–14:26	They pull up to the front of the house and pass the Black groundskeeper raking. Rose checks if Chris is ready to deal with her family.	PRAGMATIC COGNITIVE	Rose pretends to be a helper to get Chris through the weekend (seeming) but is actually preparing to enslave him (being) and is an anti-subject to his ultimate goal to escape and live free. Walter knows what is going on (being) and will appear on the surface to be a Black groundskeeper (seeming).	Deepens the dual qualifying tests of Chris vs. Rose while also deepening the Rose misdirect.

14:27–15:13	Chris and Rose greet the parents at their front door, and they hug Chris. Rose's father refers to Chris with stereotypical cliché Black "street" talk.	PRAGMATIC COGNITIVE	Rose's father is a fake opponent syncing up with her fake intentions of furthering hers and Chris's relationship with Chris, which deepens the Rose misdirect. Rose is enjoined by a family of helpers to the real cause of enslaving Chris. (She will be a helper, too, in getting Chris into the slavery procedure.)	Deepens the dual qualifying tests of Chris vs. Rose and also deepening the Rose misdirect.
15:14–16:00	Rose tells her parents they hit a deer, and Dean (Rose's father) commends Chris for killing a deer as he remarks deer are like rodents and ruin everything. Rose and Missy (Rose's mom) are embarrassed.	PRAGMATIC	The deer is continuing to be a helper in that it prompts Dean to express himself and show his coldheartedness (which should be a clue to Chris indicating something is wrong with these people). Missy is embarrassed (seeming) and appears to be normal. Missy's embarrassment furthers the misdirect that the family is merely awkward and not hiding a slave-making business that they oversee and plan to trap Chris in.	The dual qualifying tests are in play. Chris thinks his qualifying test is to withstand a weekend with weird racist parents. The real qualifying test is from Rose's (and her family's) need to continue to fool Chris that he's dealing with racial awkwardness but in fact being sold into slavery.
16:01–16:35	Dean inquires as to how long Chris and Rose have been dating, again using Black slang. Chris states four months, and Rose corrects him that it's five, and Dean comments that Chris should get used to being corrected, further embarrassing everyone.	PRAGMATIC	The being/seeming duality shifts here in that Dean (Rose's father) is now commiserating with Chris about Rose "correcting" him, pretending to be a helper in the overall object of Chris potentially marrying her (seeming) but really being an anti-subject planning to deceive him in order to enslave him (being).	
16:36–16:42	Dean offers to give Chris a tour, and Rose asks if they can unpack first.	PRAGMATIC		

(Continued)

Table 6.38 *Continued*

TIMECODE	BEAT Note: Master story beats/themes stated will be in **bold**.	BEAT TYPE	ACTANTIAL NARRATIVE SCHEMA*	CANONICAL NARRATIVE SCHEMA**
16:43–17:15	Dean starts the tour and shows Chris family photos, and Chris spies Rose on the couch, and she rolls her eyes at the tour.	PRAGMATIC	The tour causes Rose to appear to be a (seeming) helper to Chris to help him endure her parents, but in reality (being) she is going to work against him (anti-subject) and lead him to enslavement.	Rose's misdirect deepens as she performs in her qualifying test to lull Chris into complacency and eventual slavery.
17:16–17:54	Dean shows Chris a photo of Dean's dad, who was beaten in the qualifier for the 1939 Olympics by Jesse Owens defying Hitler's Aryan race obsession.	PRAGMATIC	Dean is now a helper to his plot of enslaving Chris (and anti-subject to Chris's escape) by seeming to truly expose and oppose anti-racial beliefs but actually being super racist preparing Chris for slavery.	Dean has joined the misdirect, furthering his family's qualifying test to fool, capture, and enslave Chris.
17:55–17:59	Dean shows Chris the basement door that is sealed up due to black mold.	PRAGMATIC		
18:00–18:22	In the kitchen, Chris meets Georgina the maid as Dean explains she has been kept on to keep a part of his mother around, then shows Chris the door to the backyard that he loves.	PRAGMATIC		The misdirect part of the Armitage's qualifying test of enslaving Chris is furthered by showing him the Black "help" that Dean (Rose's father) "kept on" out of pity but in actuality, he enslaved their bodies with the brains of his parents.

Time	Description	Type	Narrative Function	Analysis
18:23–18:40	Dean shows Chris the property and extols the virtues of privacy, and Chris sees Walter (the groundskeeper) and acknowledges him as a Black man subtly.	PRAGMATIC COGNITIVE	Walter (Grandpa) has an awareness of knowing Chris's fate as a future slave and is pretending to be accepting about Chris dating Rose (a seeming helper), but he is furthering his opponent status (being) setting up Chris for enslavement.	Again, the misdirect of Rose's family, manifest in the family's qualifying test of enslaving Chris, is furthered by Dean showing Chris the Black help Dean "kept on" out of pity but actually enslaved.
18:41–19:31	Dean talks about how it's a cliché that he's a white man with Black servants and discusses how he'd vote for Obama for a third term, all of which Chris is laid back about.	PRAGMATIC		This will later connect back to what becomes the real master decisive test of Chris's escape and the real Walter emerging out of the sunken place to shoot Rose and kill himself.
19:32–20:02	Chris and Rose drink iced tea on the porch with Rose's parents. Chris reveals his mother died when he was 11 in a hit and run accident, and Missy clinks a teacup with a spoon. **Master beat/theme stated: establishes the main "hook" into Chris's psyche and giving Missy control of him, linking the emotion of his mother dying to the clinking of the teacup.**	PRAGMATIC COGNITIVE	The full force of the family as anti-subject to Chris's goal to escape alive (being) but seeming to want to help Chris deal with his past.	Here is where the beginning of Chris's real qualifying test occurs in that the fake qualifying test of the weekend being about Chris's racially awkward family (seeming) is replaced by Rose's mother Missy initiating her own qualifying test to enslave Chris (being) via hypnosis, her *being able to do something*, which is taking over his mind and body.
20:03–20:54	Dean questions Chris about his cigarette smoking and then suggests Chris allow Missy to hypnotize him to cure it as she cured Dean's own 15-year cigarette addiction	PRAGMATIC		

(Continued)

Table 6.38 *Continued*

TIMECODE	BEAT Note: Master story beats/themes stated will be in **bold**.	BEAT TYPE	ACTANTIAL NARRATIVE SCHEMA*	CANONICAL NARRATIVE SCHEMA**
20:55–22:02	Dean reveals it's the weekend of their annual family shindig, and Rose protests. Missy reveals that after Dean's father died they wanted to keep the "help" close. Georgina (the maid), pouring tea, has a reaction and spills some. They send her to rest.	PRAGMATIC COGNITIVE THYMIC	The "help" (Georgina and Walter) are key factors in the being/seeming duality by which the entire movie functions. They are actually white people enslaving the bodies of the Black help.	The misdirect of the Armitages; namely, fooling Chris that his qualifying test is to endure racial awkwardness (seeming) when their actual qualifying test will be take control of Chris's psyche to eventually enslave him as they did to their help is showing cracks. The real Black Georgina (from inside) rumbles from the woman's own psyche, momentarily displacing the mind of white Grandma, causing tea to spill. This plants antecedents of what is really going on (being/seeming); namely, that the real qualifying test of the family is to enslave Chris. So, when the *truth* is revealed, the unconscious antecedents will have been presented for a competent observer to piece together.***

Time	Description	Type	Analysis
22:03–22:13	Jeremy (Rose's brother) shows up with a shoulder bag.	PRAGMATIC	Jeremy is a helper to the Armitage family and in his youthful sloppiness gives off the scent of what is really going on (being). (He is an opponent/anti-subject to Chris's ultimate object to escape and live free.)	
22:14–24:07	At dinner, Jeremy recalls how Rose would cut her toenails, suck on them, and store them, then how at a wild party she bit the tongue of a guy who tried to kiss her, making him bleed. Missy goes to get dessert, requesting they clean up their talk.	PRAGMATIC	Much like Dean relating his positive feelings about Rose and Chris killing a deer (revealing him to be cold and savage), Jeremy does the same here. His youthful sloppiness discussing real bad "stories" about Rose, depicting her as disgusting and vicious, suggests that Rose is not as she seems (seeming) but in reality, a monster (being).	
24:08–26:31	Jeremy asks Chris if he's an MMA fan, despite Rose and Dean's objections to the question, to which Chris responds that the sport is too brutal.	PRAGMATIC	The antecedents of what will be revealed about the family's goal to enslave Chris is leaking through Jeremy, who, in his youth, possesses unabashed fascination of Chris as a physical "specimen," hinting at what will be revealed later (being).	Jeremy foreshadows the Armitages' decisive test of finally enslaving Chris as they as a family are many "moves" ahead of Chris and us the competent observers (audience).
	Jeremy switches the subject to street fighting and jujitsu and how it's strategic like chess and about how you should be "a few moves ahead." Jeremy tells Chris that given Chris's genetic makeup, if Chris trained, he would be a beast.	COGNITIVE	More sloppiness by young Jeremy, a sender to us the audience as receivers, building antecedents of the object of Rose's family to enslave Chris but these being cast by Rose as simply racial awkwardness.	
	Jeremy tries to get Chris to stand up and "play" fight, but Missy tells Jeremy to stop, and he responds that he wasn't going to cause Chris harm.	COGNITIVE		

Table 6.38 *Continued*

TIMECODE	BEAT Note: Master story beats/themes stated will be in **bold**.	BEAT TYPE	ACTANTIAL NARRATIVE SCHEMA*	CANONICAL NARRATIVE SCHEMA**
26:32–28:33	Preparing for bed, Rose complains about her family's racist micro-aggressions, and Chris excuses it, saying it's okay.	PRAGMATIC		All deepening Rose's master misdirect—ensuring victory of her real qualifying test (being) and further fooling Chris that his own qualifying test is in conjunction with Rose's (seeming), which is to simply endure the weekend of awkward white people and their racial micro-aggressions.
28:34–28:53	In the middle of the night, Chris lies awake, thinking about the dark woods where the deer died, and slaps a fly.	PRAGMATIC COGNITIVE	This scene reveals a potential helper to Missy, who will hypnotize Chris and seize on his past psychological wounds; namely, his failure to save his mother (evoked by the dying deer), rendering Chris vulnerable to her hypnosis, making the being of what is going on finally starting to be revealed.	The dream enhances Chris's emotional vulnerability as the dying deer calls to mind his dying mother. This becomes the link Missy uses to hook Chris psychologically and hypnotize him, and this vulnerability allows him to be blind to Rose, and her massive misdirect to be so effective and her qualifying test of enslaving him to be succeeding.
28:54–29:29	Chris turns the stuffed lion away from the bed then looks at his pack of cigarettes.	PRAGMATIC COGNITIVE		Turning away the stuffed lion so it's not "looking" at Chris is an indication of the entire misdirect/qualifying test of Rose's family in that there is a being/seeming aspect to everything, and Chris is self-conscious of being "watched" (the lion's gaze) but doesn't know why.

29:30–29:59	Chris, with a sweatshirt on, wanders downstairs in the dark, and, in the background, Georgina walks by.	PRAGMATIC	Georgina will be an Armitage helper almost like a football "safety," competently running a "pattern" in the background just in case needed. The seeming/being binary opposition is in full view as the elderly woman seems very athletic.	
30:00–30:50	Outside, Chris prepares to smoke and sees Walter (the groundskeeper), who runs quickly towards Chris then abruptly turns.	PRAGMATIC	In parallel to Georgina buzzing around if needed, Walter literally runs a pattern depicting his inner Armitage white self as potential helper if needed to enslave Chris.	
30:51–31:16	Chris sees Georgina, with a bug-eye expression, inside at the window, fixing and admiring her hair and face. He goes inside.	COGNITIVE		
31:17–32:51	Chris passes Missy in her study. She warns about his smoking and invites him in. As he sits with her, she stirs her teacup, and they discuss her hypnosis method, and she complains that he shouldn't smoke in front of her daughter.	PRAGMATIC	Missy poses as a helper to Chris to help eliminate his smoking habit via hypnosis, but she is an anti-subject, preserving his body for selling him into slavery (being/seeming). Missy requesting him not to smoke around her daughter in some ways furthers the misdirect of Missy being a helper to the object of Chris and Rose possibly getting married, but it's actually a helper to the cause of enslaving Chris (seeming/being).	The master qualifying test of Rose's family is in full swing to enslave Chris, as Missy has her hypnosis hooks in Chris without him being aware of what is going on. The Armitages have won this important round. Chris is accepting Rose's family (seeming) qualifying test of helping him quit smoking but in reality (being) preparing to enslave him (their real qualifying test).
32:52–33:53	As Missy stirs the teacup, she asks where Chris was when his mother died and asks him to recall the scene, including the rain sounds of that night. He "hears" the rain. She implores that he really "find" the rain sounds.	COGNITIVE	The story of Chris not investigating his mother not coming home is a guilty failure of Chris, and a helper to Missy in her ultimate object to enslave Chris.	The Armitages' qualifying test is almost complete, and they are winning, leading to what will be the decisive test of enslaving Chris via a complex surgical procedure to follow.

(Continued)

Table 6.38 Continued

TIMECODE	BEAT Note: Master story beats/themes stated will be in **bold**.	BEAT TYPE	ACTANTIAL NARRATIVE SCHEMA*	CANONICAL NARRATIVE SCHEMA**
33:54–35:49	Flashback—Chris at age 11 in his room; it's raining; he's watching TV.	COGNITIVE	The story of Chris not seeking his mother is a helper to Missy in her ultimate object to enslave Chris.	Embedded in the story is Chris failing the ultimate decisive test of being a good son by not investigating his mother's not returning home.
	Chris in hypnosis says he "found the rain."	COGNITIVE		Visually, the first phase of the qualifying test of Rose's family to enslave Chris's body is successfully completed. The dual qualifying tests (Rose's family to enslave Chris [being]) vs. the fake one (Chris's need to endure the weekend [seeming]) is not ambiguous anymore; it's clear something evil is afoot. Rose's family's decisive test will be to effectively complete the procedure of implanting a white brain into Chris's body.
	Missy asks where his mom was as Missy stirs teacup.	COGNITIVE		
	Missy accuses Chris of doing nothing when his mother didn't come home that night, and he can't move, learning from Missy he is "paralyzed."	COGNITIVE		
	Missy tells him to sink into the floor, and he "falls through" the chair into a black void.	COGNITIVE		
	Master beat/theme stated: This sequence constitutes a series of beats, leading Chris into the sunken place and taking control of his psyche, setting up the Armitages' master qualifying test of hypnotizing Chris to proceed into the decisive test to enslave Chris via the brain operation procedure.			

35:50–37:11	Chris continues to fall in slow motion into the black void and he sees Missy becoming smaller.	COGNITIVE THYMIC	Clear visual representation of Rose's family's supposed helper status (seeming) is deceptive and that they are opponents to Chris's very life (being).
	Missy looks down at him and tells him he's in a place she refers to as the sunken place.	COGNITIVE THYMIC	
	Chris, crying, is frozen in the chair, and Missy closes his eyelids.	COGNITIVE THYMIC	
	Master story beat/theme stated: The transformation of Chris's enslavement has begun.		
			Visually, it's clear that Chris is emotional about not helping find his mother and cries in his frozen state. This sets up Rose's family's qualifying test to enslave him, which will be later enhanced by Rose's seeming like she's on his side, which will be all that's left of the illusion that Rose is protecting him until she turns on him.
			Missy is winning in her qualifying test, taking over Chris to be able to control him and lead him into slavery (her decisive test).
37:12–37:31	Chris awakens as if from a bad dream and hears his cell beep on the nightstand and discovers it's been disconnected.	PRAGMATIC	Rod is the helper as far as what will become Chris's final object to escape.
37:32–37:43	Chris spies photo Rod took of his dog, and he reconnects the phone.	PRAGMATIC	The qualifying test of whether Rose's family maintains the façade of why he is there must be enough to set him up to be enslaved, but the façade is showing cracks. Chris awakening is as if from a dream is a reset of the misdirect (allowing Rose's *knowing how to do something*, her qualifying test) to be in play again.
37:44–38:00	Chris wanders in the woods and snaps a photo.	PRAGMATIC	Chris's skill at photography helps emphasize our interest in the surface appearance of things, which feeds into the being/seeming dichotomy that the movie's architecture functions on. His photography talent will be a helper in ultimately pushing him to strive to "see," which entails piecing together the true object of Rose's family to enslave him.

(Continued)

Table 6.38 Continued

TIMECODE	BEAT Note: Master story beats/themes stated will be in **bold**.	BEAT TYPE	ACTANTIAL NARRATIVE SCHEMA*	CANONICAL NARRATIVE SCHEMA**
38:01–38:41	Looking outside up at her window, Chris sees Georgina at the mirror, touching her hair, and snaps a photo of her. Georgina senses him and moves away from view.	PRAGMATIC COGNITIVE	Georgina's behavior could be viewed as a helper to Chris, helping him to see through the façade of the family. (being/seeming). But Georgina recovered quickly and didn't reveal that she isn't as she seems (seeming/ being).	
38:41–38:55	Chris snaps more photos and sees Georgina has gone and hears wood chopping and sees Walter working.	PRAGMATIC		
38:56–40:44	Chris meets Walter and comments about Walter working hard and Walter claims he wants to do it and that he knows who Chris is.	PRAGMATIC		
	Walter comments how attractive Rose is and that she is a keeper.	PRAGMATIC		
	Walter apologizes for "scaring" him the night before because he ran hard at him.	PRAGMATIC	Walter, as an Armitage helper, speaks as though he's in favor of Chris and Rose's relationship (seeming to be on Chris's side of enduring the racial micro-aggressions of the weekend) but actually being on the side of enslaving him.	
	Walter asks if the hypnosis worked, as Chris was in Missy's office for some time. He gets back to work, and Chris leaves.	PRAGMATIC		

40:45–40:55	PRAGMATIC	Chris walks away, sniffing his unlit cigarette unfavorably.	Chris loses his appetite for smoking due to Missy's hypnosis, which he thinks is a helper (seeming) to endure Rose's family but is actually a helper to the Armitages' plan to enslave him (being), as he's being fooled as to what the purpose and results of the hypnosis were (being/seeming).
40:56–41:19	PRAGMATIC	Back in their room, Chris tells Rose that her mom hypnotized him during the night, to which Rose apologizes.	The dual qualifying tests (Rose trying to convince Chris all is okay but her real *knowing how to do something* leading him to enslavement) are in play, helping shape Rose's misdirect.
41:20–41:34	PRAGMATIC	Chris relates a dream that he thought he had of being in a hole, and Rose feels bad.	
41:35–42:23	PRAGMATIC	Chris relates his conversation with Walter, that Walter seemed hostile and maybe likes Rose, and Rose jokingly dismisses it.	
42:24–42:40	PRAGMATIC	Rose promises to talk to her dad about it; Chris talks her out of the idea.	This is the second time Rose asked if Chris is ready to have his Blackness awkwardly examined, feeding into the fake qualifying test of enduring the weekend, giving her time to deploy the real qualifying test (auction him and set him up for slavery).
	PRAGMATIC	Chris and Rose see the motorcade of "guests" arriving, and Rose asks Chris if he's ready for it.	All the beats in this sequence pertain to the helper/opponent duality of Rose, who functions under a being/seeming binary opposition to both continue to deceive Chris in thinking (seeming) that she's assisting his handling of her family's micro-aggressions but (being) continuing to prepare to ensnare him into slavery.

(Continued)

Table 6.38 *Continued*

TIMECODE	BEAT Note: Master story beats/themes stated will be in **bold.**	BEAT TYPE	ACTANTIAL NARRATIVE SCHEMA*	CANONICAL NARRATIVE SCHEMA**
42:41–43:35	Guests arrive, and Chris and Rose greet them. Chris and Rose meet the Greenes and Mr. Greene comments on Chris's grip, talks about his professional golfing days, and asks to see Chris's golf form.	PRAGMATIC PRAGMATIC		Fake original Chris/Rose qualifying test deepening (enduring the weekend) with the fake *being able to do something* staged so Chris and Rose "tolerate" the foolish white people's awkwardness with a Black man. At the same time, this strengthens Rose's misdirect to enslave him (the real qualifying test).
43:36–44:03	In the house, Chris and Rose meet Nelson and Lisa, and Lisa feels Chris's arm and asks if "it's better" (implying sex), and Chris and Rose are taken aback.	PRAGMATIC		Fake original Chris/Rose qualifying test deepening (enduring the weekend) with the fake *being able to do something* staged so Chris and Rose "tolerate" the foolish white people's awkwardness with a Black man. At the same time, this strengthens Rose's misdirect to enslave him (the real qualifying test).
44:04–44:22	Chris and Rose talk with Parker and April Dray, with Parker saying the pendulum has swung and how being Black is fashionable. Chris leaves to take pictures.	PRAGMATIC PRAGMATIC		Fake original Chris/Rose qualifying test deepening (enduring the weekend) with the fake *being able to do something* staged so Chris and Rose "tolerate" the foolish white people's awkwardness with a Black man. At the same time, this strengthens Rose's misdirect to enslave him (the real qualifying test).

44:23–44:41	Chris looks through his camera and spies Georgina, talking to Missy on back porch. Missy is handing Georgina drinks to bring inside.	PRAGMATIC	The establishment of Chris as a photographer is a great character trait as he is constantly trying to "see" what is going on and we'll see the *truth* through his eyes.
44:42–44:51	Chris sees Dean talking to a group through his camera, and Dean calls Chris over.	PRAGMATIC	
44:52 45:12	Chris continues looking at the guests through his lens and sees Hayworth (Andre Logan King) getting a drink at the alcohol table.	PRAGMATIC COGNITIVE	
45:13–46:32	Chris talks to Andre Logan King (a young Black man) and senses something is not right about him.	COGNITIVE	Fake original Chris/Rose qualifying test deepening (enduring the weekend) with the fake *being able to do something* staged so Chris and Rose "tolerate" the foolish white people's awkwardness with a Black man. At the same time this strengthens Rose's misdirect to enslave him (the real qualifying test).
	His senior citizen wife Philomena King comes over and comments about Chris and Rose making a great couple.	COGNITIVE	
	As the Kings walk away, Chris extends his hand for a fist bump, which Andre grabs (not understanding the gesture).	COGNITIVE	
46:33–46:45	Chris watches and is puzzled as Andre shows off his very old white man outfit to other senior citizens.	PRAGMATIC	Andre Logan King will be the vehicle by which the seeming/being nature of the actants come clearly into play at once. The whole weekend get-together is staged to merely appear to be about Chris tolerating racial awkwardness by old white people encountering a Black man. This is a helper to the ruse of tricking Chris as to why he's been brought to the Armitage home.

(Continued)

Table 6.38 *Continued*

TIMECODE	BEAT Note: Master story beats/themes stated will be in **bold**.	BEAT TYPE	ACTANTIAL NARRATIVE SCHEMA*	CANONICAL NARRATIVE SCHEMA**
46:46–47:54	At the gazebo, Chris is impressed to meet Jim Hudson, a blind art gallery owner who knows and admires Chris's photographs.	PRAGMATIC	A key moment in that Chris meets who will become the winner of the lottery to enslave Chris's body; namely, Jim Hudson. He is seemingly a helper in the object of Chris enduring the weekend of racial awkwardness and micro-aggressions being himself a photo gallery owner, and complimenting Chris's photography talent.[1]	Rose's qualifying test is strengthened in that Jim Hudson is a welcome "hip" repose from the stock awkwardness of the white people interacting with Rose's Black boyfriend, but Jim is actually furthering the misdirect as well.
47:55–48:26	Jim expresses how he failed as a wilderness photographer and how his genetic disease progressed to blindness, and Chris commiserates.	PRAGMATIC		
48:27–48:50	Chris walks in the house and up the stairs, and the chattering guests all stop talking and cryptically glance upstairs.	PRAGMATIC COGNITIVE	The guests seem like opponents to what will become Chris's object of getting out alive.	
48:51–49:09	In the guest room, Chris finds his phone again disconnected from his charger.	PRAGMATIC		

[1]This being/seeming duality is particularly biting in that all of the other old white people at the gathering only saw Chris's superior physical attributes. But Hudson is aware of Chris's superior artistic makeup as well and still is willing to enslave him.

			The dual qualifying tests are deepening as Rose pretends to disagree that Georgina was bothered by their interracial relationship but mentions she'll talk to her father about it, furthering her misdirect and helping ensure that she wins her qualifying test to help enslave Chris.
49:10–50:19	Rose enters the guest room, and Chris theorizes that Georgina unplugged his phone because she is bothered by Chris and Rose's interracial relationship.	PRAGMATIC	Chris continues to see that racism expressed as micro-aggressions is the problem (seeming) given how he interprets Georgina's actions.
50:20–52:09	Chris talks to Rod on the phone, distressed over how Rose's family treats all Black people as servants.	PRAGMATIC	Chris, seeing how the help are treated as servants (seeming), is a helper to the family attempting to enslave Chris. It's seeming to be ordinary racism of subjugating Blacks that is problematic but not unusual, but they are actually Rose's grandparents (being).
	Chris tells Rod that Missy (Rose's mother) hypnotized him, and Rod responds she wants to make Chris into a sex slave.	PRAGMATIC	Rod has almost figured it out but is missing information and thinks it's about sex slavery (illusion). But Rod's tenacity is a helper to Chris escaping. What he perceives as an illusion also further aids Rose in pretending to be a helper to Chris because Rod's illusion throws Chris off (seeming) from Chris possibly seeing what is really going on (being).

(Continued)

Table 6.38 *Continued*

TIMECODE	BEAT Note: Master story beats/themes stated will be in **bold.**	BEAT TYPE	ACTANTIAL NARRATIVE SCHEMA*	CANONICAL NARRATIVE SCHEMA**
52:10–54:37	Georgina enters the guest room and apologizes for accidentally disconnecting his cell phone.	PRAGMATIC	The façade of Georgina as a helper willing to comply with helping Chris maintain a relationship with Rose (seeming) cracks when the real Georgina rumbles through (being).	
	Chris tells her that he wasn't trying to snitch, which she doesn't understand at first, then reinterprets "snitch" to mean "tattletale."	PRAGMATIC		
	Chris expresses that he gets nervous about being around too many white people, which causes Georgina to get emotional and cry.	PRAGMATIC THYMIC		
	Georgina's crying turns to laughter as she recovers and claims she and Walter are treated like family.	PRAGMATIC		

54:38–56:31	On the porch, Chris meets the other guests and is asked if being Black is an advantage or disadvantage, and he tosses the question to Andre.	PRAGMATIC	Andre (a Coagula helper) quickly turns into a Chris helper due to the flash breaking down his inner psyche, causing his old self to come to the surface. The breakdown of the being/seeming duality by a Black man who formerly inhabited Dre's body (Andre) briefly arises and communicates with Chris to "get out," a true helper.	The dual qualifying tests (Rose's *knowing how to do something*/the real one which is to help enslave Chris vs. the Rose/Chris fake one to survive the micro-aggressions of the weekend) are on display with Chris querying Andre about race issues. Andre appears like a docile "whitewashed" Black man (seeming), but in his being his real self has been buried in the sunken place and comes screaming to the surface.

It's a key transformational beat in terms of giving Chris ammunition to begin to figure out (being) what is going on, and aids Chris in what his new actual decisive test will evolve into; to escape the family home alive. |
| | As Andre is discussing how his experience of being Black has been mostly good, Chris snaps a picture of him and it flashes, causing Andre's nose to bleed and him to scream "get out" to Chris, and he has to be subdued and dragged away screaming in terror.

Master Story Beat/theme stated: The wall between being and seeming has cracked, giving Chris evidence to send to Rod. | PRAGMATIC COGNITIVE THYMIC | | |
56:32–58:02	In the parlor, Dean (Rose's father) explains the flash made Logan have a seizure.	PRAGMATIC	The family restores order, and Andre has returned to being an opponent of Chris's object to survive and returns to being a helper to enslave Chris.	
	Andre appears from the kitchen with Missy and seems calm and back to his old self.	PRAGMATIC		
	Dean announces that they will play bingo, and Rose pulls Chris out of the room for a walk.	PRAGMATIC		

(Continued)

Table 6.38 *Continued*

TIMECODE	BEAT Note: Master story beats/themes stated will be in **bold**.	BEAT TYPE	ACTANTIAL NARRATIVE SCHEMA*	CANONICAL NARRATIVE SCHEMA**
58:03–58:38	At the lake, Chris proclaims to Rose that Andre's reaction wasn't a seizure, and Chris knew the guy who was yelling at him (but not the man *before* the flash disrupted him).	PRAGMATIC COGNITIVE		Rose is now fully (seeming) to play on the side of Chris, but actually enhancing her (being) position to pass her actual Armitage qualifying test of securing Chris for slavery (the procedure).
58:39–58:47	At the gazebo, Dean, as if a conductor, stands and holds his finger up.	PRAGMATIC		The true qualifying test to set up Chris to enslave him has commenced.
58:48–59:08	At the lake, Chris explains to Rose that Rose's mother got in his head and he's thinking a lot of bad things he doesn't want to think about.	PRAGMATIC COGNITIVE THYMIC	Rose's sexiness is a helper to her in her object to enslave Chris (being) as she still pretends to be on his side (seeming).	Chris's ultimate vulnerability (his failure to help his mother who was dying) is what both made him vulnerable to Missy's hypnosis and Rose carrying out her misdirect and setting up to win her decisive test to enslave him.
59:09–59:14	At the gazebo, Dean holds up a finger, and some guests hold up bingo cards marked off.	PRAGMATIC	That Rose's family and friends are just racially awkward is revealed to be an illusion. It's clear something else is going on.	The decisive test for the Coagula group to enslave Chris is about to commence.
59:15–59:48	At the lake, Chris tells Rose that he has to go, and she is annoyed by this and turns away.	PRAGMATIC		

Time	Scene	Modal		
59:49–1:00:40	At the gazebo, next to a portrait of Chris on a stand, Dean leads the guests in a game of silent "bingo," holding up his finger to "call out" numbers, and Jim Hudson wins.	PRAGMATIC	The group are anti-subjects to Chris's desire to be free.	The decisive test for the Coagula group to enslave Chris is about to commence.
1:00:41–1:03:00	At the lake, Chris sadly recalls the night his mom died, how he did nothing when she didn't return home and feels guilty.	COGNITIVE THYMIC	These scenes at the lake are the final beats that emotionally seal Chris in terms of allowing Rose to help her family enslave him by her pretending to be a helper and having sympathy to his need to escape (seeming). This emotionally solidifies her control of him because it also ties Chris and Rose's bond to his remorse for failing the decisive test of saving his mother to his fear of her family's intentions helping to quell Chris's fears. Rose's control as anti-subject (being) to enslave him is complete.	The original duality of the qualifying tests (Rose vs. Chris) is fully at play: Chris's emotions of failing his mother make him vulnerable, and Rose's major move to pretend to side only with Chris by agreeing to return to their home in the city.
	He emotionally tells Rose that she's all he has and isn't leaving her.	THYMIC		
	She tells him that they should go home, and they emotionally proclaim their love for each other.	THYMIC		
1:03:01–1:03:57	Chris and Rose go back to the house, where guests are leaving. Chris walks past Georgina and Walter, who look oddly happy.	COGNITIVE		As audience and competent observers, we can feel the family's decisive test to enslave Chris starting to form and momentum building towards it.
1:03:58–1:04:25	Chris sends the photo of Andre that he snapped to Rod.	PRAGMATIC	Chris's camera and photography skills are a helper to his object of escaping.	Chris has now begun to engage in his own qualifying test to survive. Although he does not completely understand what is going on yet, he is instinctively acting for his survival.

(Continued)

Table 6.38 Continued

TIMECODE	BEAT Note: Master story beats/themes stated will be in **bold**.	BEAT TYPE	ACTANTIAL NARRATIVE SCHEMA*	CANONICAL NARRATIVE SCHEMA**
1:04:26–1:05:09	Rod calls him right back and says that Andre is actually Dre, and Chris recalls him and complains Dre is acting weird, which Rod accounts to him now being a sex slave. **Master story beat/theme stated: Rod the helper has proven to Chris all isn't as it seems, something is going on, he should leave.**	PRAGMATIC	Rod is a helper to Chris's eventual plan to escape.	
1:05:10–1:05:32	Rose comes in the room, and Chris anxiously tells her they have to go immediately, and she leaves to get her bag.	PRAGMATIC		Rose plays out the fake decisive test of having "sided" with Chris (seeming); namely, helping him deal with her family's racial awkwardness and now responding to whatever evil is afoot according to Chris, but she is setting up her real decisive test (being) of finally capturing him for slavery.

Timecode	Description	Type		
1:05:33–1:07:05	Chris sees an open closet and inside finds photos of Rose with many Black boyfriends and one of her and a hipper-looking Georgina.	COGNITIVE	The box of photos are a helper to convince Chris he must escape and that Rose's involvement with the plot of bringing Black men to the family is revealed.	The photos are images of other Black men and Georgina, all of whom failed their decisive test to escape.
1:07:06–1:07:41	Chris tells Rose that he wants the car keys to load bags in the trunk, and she searches for them; he tells her to do it as they move, and they leave the room.	PRAGMATIC		
1:07:42–1:08:08	In the foyer, Chris and Rose are confronted by Jeremy and Missy, both disappointed that he wants to leave. Rose lies and says his dog got sick.	PRAGMATIC	Rose's final pretend is to pretend to be a helper (seeming) to Chris's object to escape but is actually (being) giving her family time to capture and enslave Chris (being).	The full swing of Rose's family's qualifying test to ensnare Chris and enslave his body (decisive test) is in play.
1:08:09–1:08:53	Dean walks near the fire and asks Chris cryptically what Chris wants. Chris retorts that he wants to find the keys, and as Rose keeps looking, Dean rambles about mortality.	PRAGMATIC		The full swing of Rose's family's qualifying test to ensnare Chris and enslave his body (decisive test) is in play.

(Continued)

Table 6.38 *Continued*

TIMECODE	BEAT Note: Master story beats/themes stated will be in **bold.**	BEAT TYPE	ACTANTIAL NARRATIVE SCHEMA*	CANONICAL NARRATIVE SCHEMA**
1:08:54–1:09:43	Jeremy swings at Chris with a badminton racket and upsets Rose, still looking for keys, Chris screams for the keys, and Rose finally reveals that she has them and cannot give them to Chris. **Master story beat/theme stated: While Chris (and Rod) came to suspect that all was not what it seems and the Black people's bodies (being) were somehow not their own, Rose seemed innocent and yet aided key transformations that led Chris into slavery. So this reveal is the final reveal in terms of ending the duality between being (Rose is evil) and seeming (Rose is innocent helping Chris), the essence of the Rose misdirect.**	PRAGMATIC		The finality of Rose's own decisive test (to be the perfect sexual misdirect to fool Chris) is complete, melding into the Armitages' decisive test of enslaving Chris.
1:09:44–1:10:10	Chris tries to escape; Jeremy rushes him with the badminton racket; Missy taps the teacup, causing Chris to pass out and fall back on the floor.	PRAGMATIC	Missy's hypnosis (and teacup) is a helper to the goal of enslaving Chris.	

Timestamp	Description	Category	Notes
1:10:11–1:10:25	Missy directs them all to help Dean take Chris to the basement and that Jeremy "damaged" Chris enough.	PRAGMATIC	
1:10:26–1:11:12	As Jeremy and Dean grab Chris, from his POV he falls into the sunken place, and, as they carry him down the steps, he sees Rose kiss him goodbye and express he was a favorite.	PRAGMATIC	Chris is being carried to the basement to complete the decisive test of enslaving him by implanting Jim Hudson's brain in his body.
1:11:13–1:12:46	Outside the airport terminal leaving his TSA job, Rod calls Chris's cell and gets his outgoing message.	PRAGMATIC	Rod the helper to Chris has been activated, even though he cannot fully see the family's plan. He sees an illusion of a sex slave cult of Black men.
	Rod enters Chris's apartment, feeds the dog, and tries Chris's cell again to no avail.	PRAGMATIC	Rose's family's decisive test is close to commencing. Chris's decisive test to escape will begin soon.
	Rod does an online search for Dre (Andre Logan King) and discovers he's been missing.	PRAGMATIC COGNITIVE	
	Master story beat/theme stated: Rod has a key transformation when he realizes "Dre" (now Andre Logan King) is officially "missing."		
1:12:47–1:13:56	In the basement, Chris awakens with a start, only to discover he's strapped into a chair.	PRAGMATIC	There is no longer any duality between being and seeming of what is going on. The Coagula's decisive test to enslave Chris is about to begin.

(Continued)

Table 6.38 *Continued*

TIMECODE	BEAT Note: Master story beats/themes stated will be in **bold**.	BEAT TYPE	ACTANTIAL NARRATIVE SCHEMA*	CANONICAL NARRATIVE SCHEMA**
1:13:57–1:15:52	Chris, strapped in, watches a video of Roman Armitage discussing how his order has been developing the procedure for years and that Chris was chosen for his genetic advantages. **Master story beat/theme stated:** **Now that the being/seeming split of what is going on has ended via Rose revealing that she is on her family's side aiding in enslaving Chris, the secret/truth is revealed via the video and the secret/truth will further be revealed in Hudson's follow-up video.**	PRAGMATIC	Concerning the family's intentions. They have become anti-subjects to Chris's life.	
1:15:32–1:16:00	A cup of tea and a stirring spoon appear on screen, knocking Chris out again.	PRAGMATIC		

1:16:01–1:18:06	PRAGMATIC	Rod is a helper to Chris yet is lacking complete information, so he postulates an illusion that Rose's family group captures Black men as sex slaves.
In Detective Latoya's office, Rod explains that Chris is missing, shows her the photo of Dre (as Andre Logan King) and postulates the theory that the Armitages have been abducting Blacks and brainwashing them and making them work as sex slaves.		
1:18:07–1:19:15	PRAGMATIC	Rod as a helper to Chris's life sees an illusion of the Coagula group (they capture Black people as sex slaves), which Latoya and her cohorts see as a falsehood.
Two more detectives have joined Detective Latoya, and Rod reiterates his theory that white people are abducting Blacks, brainwashing them and making them sex slaves.		
The detectives crack up laughing, mockingly not believing him.		
Master story beat/theme stated: The detectives in this scene (two black, one Hispanic) don't see what is going on and hence can be seen as "non-white" but *not* Black. It's also Rod realizing that there's no one to turn to.		

(Continued)

Table 6.38 *Continued*

TIMECODE	BEAT Note: Master story beats/themes stated will be in **bold**.	BEAT TYPE	ACTANTIAL NARRATIVE SCHEMA*	CANONICAL NARRATIVE SCHEMA**
1:19:16–1:22:26	Rod writes out a schematic of what might have happened to Chris, but it doesn't add up.	PRAGMATIC COGNITIVE	This represents the binary opposition of Rod almost seeing what is going on with the enslavement of Black men by the Coagula group but not seeing it all and reading it as an illusion.	
	Rod dials Chris's number again, and to his surprise, Rose answers and makes up a story about Chris freaking out and having left. Rod is suspicious and asks which cab company Chris used.	COGNITIVE		
	Rose says that the call is about there being "something" between him and her, and he hangs up. Her family watches her and approves.	PRAGMATIC		
	Master story beat/theme stated: Rod is smart to ask about the cab company that Chris used, detecting the lie. Rose reverts back to her seeming to be on Chris's side but is actually being on the family's side seeking to lure more Blacks to turn them into slaves for white people's brains.			

1:22:27–1:26:02	Chris awakens and watches a video of Jim Hudson, in a hospital gown, talking about what is going to happen to Chris—they will transplant Jim's brain into his body and Chris's psyche will live in the sunken place. Chris recalls the other Black people he recently met, and it makes sense. **Master Story Beat/theme stated: The truth is revealed (truth/ falsehood) of the veridiction square.**	COGNITIVE	Chris now understands what the dichotomy was between being and seeming. Rose seemed to be his helper dealing with the family's racial awkwardness but in reality (being) the family was plotting to enslave him (anti-subjects).	The decisive test of enslaving Chris is almost complete.
1:26:03–1:26:15	Chris discovers cotton in the arms of the chair that he ripped. **Master Story Beat/theme stated: a major turning point in Chris equipping himself to win his decisive test of escaping.**	PRAGMATIC COGNITIVE		Chris's qualifying test, which involves a *being able to do something* (escaping the chair), will set him up for his new and final decisive test—fending off the family and escaping.
1:26:16–1:26:38	The teacup and stirring spoon appear on the TV screen, and Chris protests then is rendered unconscious.	PRAGMATIC		The final decisive test has begun for the Armitage family seeking to enslave Chris. Chris's qualifying test to escape has simultaneously begun.

(Continued)

Table 6.38 *Continued*

TIMECODE	BEAT Note: Master story beats/themes stated will be in **bold.**	BEAT TYPE	ACTANTIAL NARRATIVE SCHEMA*	CANONICAL NARRATIVE SCHEMA**
1:26:39–1:27:01	Dean, in an operating theater in his basement, prepares for surgery as Jim Hudson lies unconscious and waiting on the table.	PRAGMATIC		
1:27:02–1:27:33	Jeremy brings surgical tools, and Dean begins to cut Jim Hudson's scalp.	PRAGMATIC		
1:28:11–1:28:19	Dean begins to cut off the skull of Jim Hudson.	PRAGMATIC		There's a mini-qualifying test at play in that does Dean have the ability to pull off another "transplant" and enslave Chris?

1:28:20–1:29:14	Jeremy opens the straps holding in Chris and turns around to prepare his IV. Chris whacks him in the head with a bocce ball.	PRAGMATIC	Chris has now enjoyed the advantage of the binary opposition of being/seeming. He seemed to be unconscious but in reality was waiting to strike (being).	Chris wins his qualifying test to escape by knocking out Jeremy. His decisive test is on (to fend off the rest of the family and escape).
	Jeremy squirms, and Chris whacks him unconscious.	PRAGMATIC		
	Chris takes out the cotton from the chair from his ears.	PRAGMATIC	The ripped chair and cotton inside were helpers to Chris escaping.	
	Jeremy bleeds profusely.	PRAGMATIC		
	Master story beat/theme stated: Chris is now winning his decisive test, and a series of transformative events will subdue all his opponents.			
1:29:15–1:29:29	Dean removes Hudson's skull and calls for Jeremy and discards it.	PRAGMATIC	Dean's skill as a neurosurgeon is a helper to his object of enslaving Chris with Hudson's brain.	Dean's mini-qualifying test to set up for the procedure to enslave Chris with Hudson's brain is in play.
1:29:30–1:30:12	Dean searches for Jeremy, and Chris surprise-stabs Dean in the throat with the deer antlers, causing Dean to fall to the floor to die, knocking over a candle. A fire starts.	PRAGMATIC	A decoration of white wealth (deer head with antlers) turns into a helper for Chris's escape.	Chris scores again in his decisive test to escape.

(Continued)

Table 6.38 *Continued*

TIMECODE	BEAT Note: Master story beats/themes stated will be in **bold**.	BEAT TYPE	ACTANTIAL NARRATIVE SCHEMA*	CANONICAL NARRATIVE SCHEMA**
1:30:13–1:30:40	Chris comes upstairs, sees Georgina in the kitchen humming and stares her down . . . she runs away.	PRAGMATIC		Chris's decisive test to escape is in play.
1:30:41–1:30:59	Chris sees Missy in the parlor and stares her down. They both spot her teacup, she lunges for it, he sweeps it to the floor and smashes it. **Master story beat/theme stated: Smashing the teacup furthers Chris's escape hopes and is a major blow to Missy being able to control Chris.**	PRAGMATIC		Chris's decisive test to escape is in play. Chris is prevailing in his decisive test to escape.
1:31:00–1:31:36	Chris and Missy again stare each other down, Missy stabs Chris through the hand with a letter opener, and he then slashes her throat with it. **Master story beat/theme stated: Killing Missy pretty much eliminates the weapon of hypnosis and puts Chris one step closer to winning his decisive test.**	PRAGMATIC	Chris's physical strength and endurance is a helper as he's stabbed in the hand but still prevails and kills Missy.	

Time	Scene	Type		
1:31:37–1:32:48	Chris goes to exit house; Jeremy lunges at him, and they struggle, Chris stabs him with the letter opener, kicks him to the ground, then stomps on his head to kill him and grabs his car keys. **Master story beat/theme stated: subduing Jeremy (in classic horror movie fashion, a killed opponent who wasn't really dead and resurrects for a final round).**	PRAGMATIC	Chris's strength is a helper.	Chris is prevailing in his decisive test to escape.
1:32:49–1:33:31	Rose sits in her room with headphones on, eating a bowl of multicolored dry cereal and sipping white milk from a glass, keeping them separate.	PRAGMATIC	Rose's cold detachment is evident as Chris is supposed to be undergoing being turned in a slave. She listens with headphones, which are a helper to Chris's escape plan as she can't hear the commotion of his escaping.	Chris is prevailing in his decisive test to escape. Rose's ritual of segregating multicolored cereal from the white milk is her glorifying test (which will soon unravel) of having captured another Black body to the slavery of a white brain.
1:33:32–1:33:57	Chris drives away in Jeremy's car and smashes into wandering Georgina, which Rose manages to hear despite wearing headphones.	PRAGMATIC		Chris is prevailing in his decisive test to escape.
1:33:58–1:34:28	Chris sees Georgina lying on ground, has flashes of not helping his mother and of Georgina crying earlier and grabs her off the ground.	COGNITIVE	Chris's empathy for wounded Georgina is an opponent to his object of escaping.	Chris briefly stumbles in his execution of his decisive test because of his emotions that make him help Georgina.

(Continued)

Table 6.38 *Continued*

TIMECODE	BEAT Note: Master story beats/themes stated will be in **bold**.	BEAT TYPE	ACTANTIAL NARRATIVE SCHEMA*	CANONICAL NARRATIVE SCHEMA**
1:34:29–1:34:37	Rose comes out with a shotgun and pumps and aims it and watches Chris speed away, commenting that he took her "Grandma."	PRAGMATIC		Rose is trying to kill Chris before he can escape and prevail in his decisive test as her evil position is fully revealed (she has no love towards him).
1:34:38–1:34:59	Georgina awakens and violently screams at Chris and hits him, causing them to smash into a tree and kill Georgina. **Master story beat/theme stated: Another major opponent (Georgina) is taken out but she's revealed in full as "Grandma" (Mrs. Armitage) and beats Chris as he drives, causing her life-ending crash.**	PRAGMATIC	Georgina appeared to be her old self (seeming) but "Grandma" emerged and tries to kill Chris (being).	Chris's brief stumbling in his execution of his decisive test because his emotions that make him help Georgina almost cost him his life.
1:35:00–1:35:18	Chris has survived the crash, but then the car is hit with a shotgun blast.	PRAGMATIC		Rose is trying to kill Chris before he can escape and prevail in his decisive test as her evil position is fully revealed (she has no love towards him).
1:35:19–1:35:39	Rose continues to shoot at Chris, who limps away from the car wreck, and she now encourages "Grandpa," who is running towards the car, to get him.	PRAGMATIC		

1:35:40–1:35:48	"Grandpa" tackles Chris.	PRAGMATIC		
1:35:49–1:36:10	"Grandpa" begins to strangle Chris, who pulls out his phone and shoots a flash into the man's eyes. **Master story beat/theme stated: The flash in Walter's (Grandpa's) eyes resurrects Walter from the sunken place within him.**	PRAGMATIC	Chris's intelligence and training as a photographer are helpers.	
1:36:11–1:36:55	Rose approaches with her gun, but "Grandpa" tells her that he wants to kill Chris himself. He takes her gun and shoots Rose and kills himself. **Master story beat/theme stated: The duality between being/seeming is completely resolved, and the real Walter aided Chris in Chris's decisive test to escape then killed his own body that housed Rose's white grandpa.**	PRAGMATIC	The real Walter emerges (being) from his own sunken place, enough so to shoot Rose and himself. He's briefly a helper to Chris's escape plan but a big one.	Chris's enemies have been handled and he has prevailed in his decisive test to escape.
1:36:56–1:37:07	Chris surveys dead "Grandpa" and Rose.	PRAGMATIC		
1:37:08–1:37:28	Chris sees Rose is still alive on the floor and is reaching for the shotgun, which he grabs away from her.	PRAGMATIC		

(Continued)

Table 6.38 *Continued*

TIMECODE	BEAT Note: Master story beats/themes stated will be in **bold**.	BEAT TYPE	ACTANTIAL NARRATIVE SCHEMA*	CANONICAL NARRATIVE SCHEMA**
1:37:29–1:38:21	As Chris hovers over wounded Rose, who proclaims her love for him, he begins to strangle her, which causes her to smile and makes him stop. **Master story beat/theme stated: Mortally wounded Rose hides behind her seeming to love Chris, and he attempts to strangle her, but stops, avoiding dehumanization despite what preceded, making his glorifying test complete.**	PRAGMATIC COGNITIVE		Chris's glorifying test plays out; namely, despite having every reason to finish off Rose and strangle her, he decides not to. He takes the high ground.
1:38:22–1:39:01	A cop car pulls up, Rose pleads for help and it's Rod, who calls for Chris and takes him away. **Master story beat/theme stated: Once we see Rod, the story is over. The glorifying test will extend through the car ride with Rod as Chris processes what happened.**	PRAGMATIC	Rod is a helper to Chris escaping.	

1:39:02–1:40:35	Chris enters Rod's car, and Rod exclaims that he warned Chris not to go in the house. Chris asks how Rod found him, and Rod attributes it to being a TSA officer and thus "handled" the situation.	PRAGMATIC	Aftermath of the glorifying test continues as Chris processes what happened.
	They pull away and leave Rose to die as she watches them leave.	PRAGMATIC	
1:40:36–1:40:48	Rod drives away with Chris, who contemplates what happened as Rose dies on the ground watching.	PRAGMATIC	Aftermath of glorifying test continues as Chris processes what happened.

* This includes additional language from the semiotic square of veridiction for *Get Out*. What's important to note about how this tool is used is to understand that what the tool traces is how the perception of a competent observer watching the story sees different things over time (being/seeming), etc.

** While the canonical narrative schema summary does not deploy the tools of the semiotic square of veridiction in the treatment, I deploy these terms in the comprehensive beat map because I think it's good to get a sense of how the being/seeming levels apply in this schema, as well as how they pertain to our perception. So in effect, we have a straight-ahead summary in the canonical narrative schema summary without the veridiction tools and in the comprehensive beat map I use the veridiction tools for a contrast. Again, what's important to note about how this tool is used is to understand that what the tool traces is how the perception of a competent observer watching the story sees different things over time (being/seeming), etc.

*** Aristotle's *Poetics* cites this technique, which I call the "anticipated surprise."

Master Story Beats/Themes Stated Cheat Sheet for *Get Out*

Once again, the master story beats/themes stated breakdown for each movie will be unique, and *Get Out* is no exception. In fact, *Get Out* will require additional tools necessitated by the properties of the movie's architecture as the analysis will not benefit from a simple breakdown of master story beats and will require the additional tool of the semiotic square of veridiction to understand how this movie works. For example, as previously stated, *Get Out* is a more complex breakdown than the other two specimens and will deploy the special semiotic square of veridiction that decodes the differences between what we see (seeming) and what is really going on (being), all of which came into consideration when creating master story beats/themes stated for this movie.

For this movie, first off, we need to take a closer look at the anti-subject/antagonist side of the equation and their secret object of enslaving the protagonist Chris. It involves a three-stage transformation process, starting with capturing Chris's psyche, via the hypnosis technique by Missy, and proceeding to the second stage, which is the Coagula group *revealing* the procedure to the strapped-down Chris by Jim Hudson's live video feed from the pre-op room. The third stage (the tragic deed) would be implanting Hudson's brain into Chris's, but this transaction never occurs (as Aristotle's *Poetics* stated, the tragic deed doesn't have to actually occur to have power). This represents the Armitages' master qualifying test (bringing Chris in and setting him up for a transplant of a white person's brain) and decisive test (successfully performing the operation of installing a white person's brain in Chris's body). They have secretly planned all of this, which is hidden to Chris and us the competent observers.

So preceding Chris's being captured by Missy's hypnosis, there is a master misdirect perpetrated by Rose in pretending that the issue with her family (and family's friends) is that they are racially awkward about Black people. Along those lines, a key transformation is when Rose pulls Chris away to the lake, and he gets emotional because he's reminded via the weekend (and hypnosis) that he didn't try and save his missing mother (which is Missy's hook into his soul). At the lake, Chris emotionally professes his love for Rose, and she says it back and decides that she'll leave with him, finalizing her fooling him and ending her qualifying test (melding into the Armitages' master decisive test of enslaving Chris's body via the "procedure"). The next key transformation is when Chris discovers cotton in the arm of the chair and (off screen) stuffs his ears to block the hypnosis noise, then takes out Jeremy, Dean, and Missy, all of which can be seen as part of the same overall "transformation sequence." When he smashes his getaway car into wandering Georgina and then pulls her from the ground (instead of leaving her there), this is a three-part major transformative beat since he had to take her out, but feels bad for her lying on the ground and in trying to save her is betraying his own cause to escape as she then arises, screaming and beating him as he drives, causing him to crash and kill her.

Table 6.39 Master story beats/themes stated—cheat sheet—for *Get Out*

TIMECODE	BEAT	MASTER STORY BEATS/ THEMES STATED*	BEAT TYPE
12:35–13:38	Rose talks to Officer Ryan as Chris contemplates what happened. Officer Ryan asks to see Chris's ID, but Rose tells him that Chris wasn't driving, and the officer backs off.	**Rose will defend her man against racist cops (but actually is avoiding a record of him having been with her) and feeds into the misdirect of her intentions to us and to him.**	PRAGMATIC COGNITIVE
19:32–20:02	Chris and Rose drink iced tea on the porch with Rose's parents. Chris reveals his mother died when he was 11 in a hit-and-run accident, and Missy clinks a glass with a spoon.	**Establishes the main "hook" into Chris's psyche and giving Missy control of him, linking up that emotion of his mother dying to the clinking of the teacup.**	PRAGMATIC COGNITIVE
33:54–35:49	As Missy stirs a teacup, she asks where Chris was when his mother died and asks him to recall the scene, including the rain sounds of that night. He "hears" the rain. She implores him to really "find" the rain sounds. Flashback—Chris at 11 in his room; it's raining; he's watching TV. Chris, in hypnosis, says he "found the rain." Missy asks where his mom was as she stirs teacup. Missy accuses Chris of doing nothing when his mother didn't come home that night, and he can't move, learning from Missy he is "paralyzed." Missy tells him to sink into the floor, and he "falls through the chair" into a black void.	**This sequence constitutes these series of beats all leading Chris into the "sunken place" and taking control of his psyche, setting up the Armitages' master qualifying test of hypnotizing Chris to proceed into the decisive test to enslave Chris via the brain operation procedure.**	COGNITIVE
35:50–37:11	Chris continues to fall in slow motion into the black void, and he sees Missy becoming smaller. Missy looks down at him and tells him that he's in a place that she refers to as the sunken place. Chris, crying, is frozen in the chair, and Missy closes his eyelids.	**The transformation of Chris's enslavement has begun.**	COGNITIVE THYMIC COGNITIVE THYMIC COGNITIVE THYMIC

(Continued)

Table 6.39 *Continued*

TIMECODE	BEAT	MASTER STORY BEATS/ THEMES STATED*	BEAT TYPE
54:38–56:31	As Andre is discussing how his experience of being Black has been mostly good, Chris snaps a picture of him and it flashes, causing Andre's nose to bleed and him to scream "get out" to Chris and having to be subdued and dragged away, screaming in terror.	**The wall between being and seeming has cracked, giving Chris evidence to send to Rod.**	PRAGMATIC COGNITIVE THYMIC
1:04:26–1:05:09	Chris sends the photo of Andre that he snapped to Rod. Rod calls him right back and says that Andre is actually Dre, and Chris recalls him and complains that Dre is acting weird, which Rod attributes to him now being a sex slave.	**Rod the helper has proven to Chris all isn't as it seems, something is going on, he should leave.**	PRAGMATIC
1:08:54–1:09:43	Jeremy swings at Chris with a badminton racket and upsets Rose, still looking for keys. Chris screams for the keys, and Rose finally reveals she has them and cannot give them to Chris.	**While Chris (and Rod) came to suspect all was not what it seems, and that the Black people's bodies (being) were somehow not their own, Rose seemed innocent and yet helped with each key transformation to lead Chris into slavery. So this reveal is the final reveal in terms of ending the duality between being (Rose is evil) and seeming (Rose is innocent helping Chris), the essence of the Rose misdirect.**	PRAGMATIC COGNITIVE THYMIC
1:11:13–1:12:46	Rod does an online search for Dre (Andre) and discovers he's been missing.	**Rod has a key transformation when he realizes "Dre" (now Andre Logan King) is officially "missing."**	PRAGMATIC COGNITIVE
1:13:57–1:15:52	Chris, strapped in, watches a video of Roman Armitage discussing how his order has been developing the procedure for years and Chris was chosen for his genetic advantages.	**Now that the being/seeming split of what is going on has ended via Rose revealing she is on her family's side aiding in enslaving Chris, the secret/ truth is revealed via the video and the secret/truth will further be revealed in Hudson's follow-up video.**	PRAGMATIC

1:18:07–1:19:15	Two more detectives have joined Detective Latoya, and Rod reiterates his theory that white people are abducting Blacks, brainwashing them, and making them, sex slaves. The detectives crack up laughing, mockingly not believing him.	**The detectives in this scene (two Black, one Hispanic) don't see what is going on and hence can be seen as "non-white" but *not* Black. It's also Rod realizing there's no one to turn to.**	PRAGMATIC
1:19:16–1:22:26	Rod dials Chris's number again and to his surprise Rose answers and makes up a story about Chris freaking out and having left. Rod is suspicious and asks which cab company Chris used. Rose says that the call is about there being "something" between him and her, and he hangs up. Her family watches her and approves.	**Rod is smart to ask about the cab company Chris used, detecting the lie. Rose reverts back to her seeming to be on Chris's side but actually is (being) on the family's side seeking to lure more Blacks to turn them into slaves for white people's brains.**	COGNITIVE PRAGMATIC
1:22:27–1:26:02	Chris awakens and watches a video of Jim Hudson, in a hospital gown, talking about what is going to happen to Chris—they will transplant Jim's brain into his body and Chris's psyche will live in the sunken place and Chris recalls the other Black people he recently met and it makes sense.	**The truth is revealed (from the truth/falsehood part of the veridiction square).**	COGNITIVE
1:26:03–1:26:15	Chris discovers cotton in the arms of the chair he ripped.	**A major turning point in Chris equipping himself to win his decisive test of escaping.**	PRAGMATIC COGNITIVE
1:28:20–1:29:14	Jeremy opens the straps holding in Chris and turns around to prepare an IV. Chris whacks him in the head with a bocce ball. Jeremy squirms, and Chris whacks him unconscious. Chris takes out the cotton from the chair from his ears. Jeremy bleeds profusely.	**Chris is now winning his decisive test and a series of transformative events will subdue all his opponents.**	PRAGMATIC
1:30:41–1:30:59	Chris sees Missy in the parlor and stares her down. They both spot her teacup, she lunges for it, and he sweeps it to the floor and smashes it.	**Smashing the teacup furthers Chris winning his decisive test, and is a major blow to Missy being able to control Chris.**	PRAGMATIC
1:31:00–1:31:36	Chris and Missy again stare each other down, Missy stabs Chris through the hand with a letter opener, and he then slashes her throat with it.	**Killing Missy pretty much eliminates the weapon of hypnosis and puts Chris one step closer to winning his decisive test.**	PRAGMATIC

(Continued)

Table 6.39 *Continued*

TIMECODE	BEAT	MASTER STORY BEATS/ THEMES STATED*	BEAT TYPE
1:31:37–1:32:48	Chris goes to exit house; Jeremy lunges at him, they struggle, Chris stabs him with the letter opener, kicks him to the ground, then stomps on his head to kill him and grabs his car keys.	**Subduing Jeremy again (in classic horror movie fashion, a killed opponent wasn't really dead and resurrects for a final round).**	PRAGMATIC
1:34:38–1:34:59	Georgina awakens and violently screams at Chris and hits him, causing them to smash into a tree and kill Georgina.	**Another major opponent (Georgina) is taken out, but she's revealed in full as "Grandma" (Mrs. Armitage) and beats Chris as he drives, causing her life-ending crash.**	PRAGMATIC
1:35:49–1:36:10	"Grandpa" begins to strangle Chris, who pulls out his phone and shoots a flash into the man's eyes.	**The flash in Walter's eyes resurrects Walter from the sunken place within him.**	PRAGMATIC
1:36:11–1:36:55	Rose approaches with her gun, "Grandpa" tells her that he wants to kill Chris himself. He takes the gun and shoots Rose and kills himself.	**The duality between being/ seeming is completely resolved, and the real Walter aided Chris in Chris's decisive test to escape when he emerged from his own "sunken place," shot Rose, then killed his body that housed Rose's white grandpa.**	PRAGMATIC
1:37:29–1:38:21	As Chris hovers over wounded Rose, who proclaims her love for him, he begins to strangle her, which causes her to smile and make him stop.	**Mortally wounded Rose hides behind her seeming to love Chris, and he attempts to strangle her but stops, avoiding complete dehumanization despite what preceded, making his gloryfing test complete.**	PRAGMATIC COGNITIVE
1:38:22–1:40:48	A cop car pulls up, Rose pleads for help, and it's Rod, who calls for Chris and takes him away.	**Once we see Rod, the story is over. The glorifying test will extend through the car ride with Rod as Chris processes what happened.**	PRAGMATIC

* As previously mentioned, the "themes" stated are not always "stated" in the traditional literary sense. But they still function like a theme reverberating through the story. Also, some of the master story beats/themes stated in *Get Out* will deploy additional language of the semiotic square of veridiction where appropriate because this layer of analysis (being vs. seeming) is vital to the architecture of this movie and subsequently rendering a useful breakdown of it.

Using all Four Corners of the Master Semiotic Square to Plot Master Story Beats/Themes Stated—*Get Out*[4]

S1
WHITE
(complementarity)
(12:35-13:38)
Rose talks to Officer Ryan as
Chris contemplates what happened.
Officer Ryan asks to see Chris's ID, but Rose tells him no,
that Chris wasn't driving, and the officer backs off.
(pragmatic/cognitive)

S2
BLACK

-S2
NOT BLACK ◄————————————— NOT WHITE
(contrariety)

-S1
NOT WHITE

Master story beat/theme stated:
Rose will defend her man against racist
cops (but is actually just avoiding a record of
him having been with her) and feeds into
the misdirect of her intentions to us and
to him.

Rose is not **black** but can be viewed here as such in her pretending to defend Chris against being profiled, which is in essence a lie, hence the movement from **not white** to **not black** to **white** (but the movement to **white** is in secret). Rose (being) is trying to enslave Chris, so when she defends him against the racial profiling of Officer Ryan, she is (seeming) to protect Chris, and this beat is a key transformative beat in our (competent observer) and Chris's perception of Rose and her hiding her evil intent to enslave him.

Figure 6.48 Master story beat/theme stated 1—*Get Out.*

---

[4]Language from the semiotic square of veridiction will be used for this collection of story beats as well.

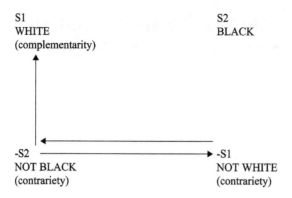

(19:32-20:02)
Chris and Rose drink iced tea on the porch
with Rose's parents. Chris reveals
his mother died when he was age 11 in a hit-
and-run accident, and Missy clinks a glass
with a spoon.
(pragmatic/cognitive)

Master story beat/theme stated:
establishes the main "hook" into Chris's psyche
and giving Missy control of him linking
up that emotion of his mother dying to the
clinking of the teacup.

It's enough to give Missy a "hook" into Chris's brain so she can eventually perform her hypnosis of him.
She's **not black** as in not "**white**" yet (in our perception) but not yet pure evil (**white** in our perception).

Figure 6.49 Master story beat/theme stated 2—*Get Out.*

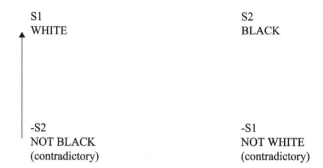

(33:54-35:49)*

- As Missy stirs teacup, she asks where Chris was when his mother died and asks him to recall the scene, including the rain sounds of that night.
- He "hears" the rain. She implores him to really "find" the rain sounds.
- Flashback – Chris at age 11 in his room; it's raining; he's watching TV.
- Chris in hypnosis says he "found the rain."
- As she stirs teacup, Missy asks where his mom was.
- Missy accuses Chris of doing nothing when his mother didn't come home that night, and he can't move, learning from Missy he is "paralyzed."
- Missy tells him to sink into the floor, and he "falls through the chair" into a black void. (**cognitive**)

Master story beat/theme stated:
This sequence constitutes these series
of beats all leading Chris into the
"sunken place" and taking control of his
psyche, setting up the Armitages' master
qualifying test of hypnotizing Chris to
proceed into the decisive test to
enslave Chris via the brain operation procedure.

Here is an instance of Missy as **white**/evil using a mental vulnerability of Chris; namely, his failure to save his mother, as a hook into hypnotizing him. Again, I plot the move from **not black** (and not necessarily evil) to **white** based on what is secret and to be revealed about Missy's motives.

* A collection of many beats as a composite of a master story beat.

Figure 6.50 Master story beat/theme stated 3—*Get Out.* This master story beat is actually a collection of related smaller beats (see above).

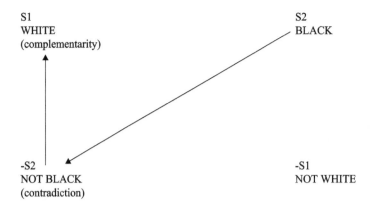

S1
WHITE
(complementarity)

S2
BLACK

-S2
NOT BLACK
(contradiction)

-S1
NOT WHITE

(35:50-37:11)
Chris continues to fall in slow motion into the black void,
and he sees Missy becoming smaller.
(cognitive/thymic)

Missy looks down at him and tells him he's in a place that she refers to as the sunken place.
(cognitive/thymic)

Chris, crying, is frozen in
the chair, and Missy closes his eyelids.
(cognitive/thymic)

Master story beat/theme stated:
The transformation of Chris's
enslavement has begun.

Moves again from **black** to **not black** to **white**, which will plot the trajectory of the story.

Figure 6.51 Master story beat/theme stated 4—*Get Out.*

S1
WHITE

S2
BLACK

-S2
NOT BLACK
(54:38-56:31)

-S1
NOT WHITE
(contrariety)

As Andre is discussing how his experience of being Black
has been mostly good, Chris snaps a picture of him and it
flashes, causing Andre's nose to bleed and him to scream
"get out" to Chris, and Andre must be subdued and dragged
away screaming in terror.
(pragmatic/cognitive/thymic)

Master story beat/theme stated:
The wall between being and
seeming has cracked, giving
Chris evidence to send to Rod.

In essence, Andre (Dre), for a brief instance, is no longer **not black** and moves to **not white**.

Figure 6.52 Master story beat/theme stated 5—*Get Out.*

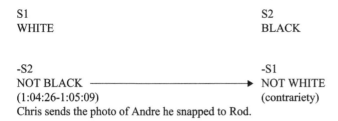

S1
WHITE

S2
BLACK

-S2
NOT BLACK ———————————————→ NOT WHITE
(1:04:26-1:05:09)   (contrariety)
Chris sends the photo of Andre he snapped to Rod.

-S1
NOT WHITE
(contrariety)

Rod calls him right back and says that Andre is actually Dre,
and Chris recalls him and complains that Dre is acting weird,
which Rod accounts to him now being a sex slave.
(**pragmatic**)

Master story beat/theme stated:
Rod the helper has proven to
Chris that all isn't as it seems, something
is going on, he should leave.

This movement is Rod sensing what is going on and calling into question Andre Logan King's being **not black** but is essentially **not white**. This again connects to the being/seeming dichotomy.

Figure 6.53 Master story beat/theme stated 6—*Get Out*.

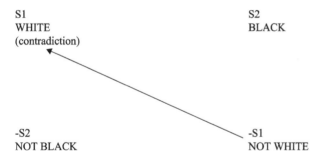

S1
WHITE
(contradiction)

S2
BLACK

-S2
NOT BLACK

-S1
NOT WHITE

(1:08:54-1:09:43)
Jeremy swings at Chris with a badminton racket and
upsets Rose still looking for keys. Chris
screams for the keys, and Rose finally reveals she
has them and cannot give them to Chris.
(**pragmatic/cognitive/thymic**)

Master story beat/theme stated:
While Chris (and Rod) came
to suspect all was not what
it seems, and the Black people's bodies
(being) were not their own, Rose seemed
innocent and yet helped with each key
transformation to lead Chris into slavery.
So this reveal is the final reveal in terms of
ending the duality between being (Rose is evil) and
seeming (Rose is innocent helping Chris), the
essence of the Rose misdirect.

Until now, Rose might have been viewed as being on Chris's side (**not white**), but she is clearly opposed to him and quickly comes out as **white**.

Figure 6.54 Master story beat/theme stated 7—*Get Out*.

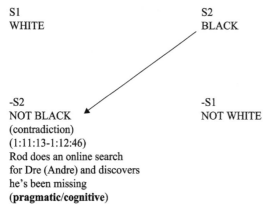

S1
WHITE

S2
BLACK

-S2
NOT BLACK
(contradiction)
(1:11:13-1:12:46)
Rod does an online search
for Dre (Andre) and discovers
he's been missing
(**pragmatic/cognitive**)

-S1
NOT WHITE

Master story beat/theme stated:
Rod has a key transformation when he
realizes "Dre" (now Andre Logan King)
is officially "missing."

Rod "senses" what is going on but doesn't have the complete picture. He senses Dre is not "**black**" anymore but doesn't completely understand that his body has been taken over by a white brain. Hence for this master story beat I have the movement from **black** to **not black**.

Figure 6.55 Master story beat/theme stated 8—*Get Out.*

S1
WHITE

S2
BLACK

-S2
NOT BLACK
(complementarity)

-S1
NOT WHITE

1:13:57-1:15:52
Chris, strapped in, watches a video of
Roman Armitage discussing how
his order has been developing the
procedure for years, and Chris was chosen for
his genetic advantages.
(**pragmatic**)

Master story beat/theme stated:
Now that the being/seeming split of what
is going on has ended via Rose revealing
she is on her family's side aiding in
enslaving Chris, the secret/truth is revealed
via the video and the secret/truth will
further be revealed in Hudson's
follow-up video.

I consider this movement (Jim Hudson's brain implanted into Chris's body) from **white** to **not black** in that Jim will no longer be in essence white but not black. Chris can be seen as starting out **white** because he had a white girlfriend and was duped by her into slavery (**white** but will not be **black** either (**not black**)).

Figure 6.56 Master story beat/theme stated 9—*Get Out.*

S1
WHITE

S2
BLACK

-S2
NOT BLACK ⟵———————————————— NOT WHITE
(contrariety)

-S1
NOT WHITE

(1:18:07-1:19:15)
Two more detectives have joined Detective Latoya, and
Rod reiterates his theory that white people are abducting
Blacks, brainwashing them, and making them sex slaves.
The detectives crack up laughing, mockingly not believing him.
(**pragmatic**)

Master story beat/theme stated:
The detectives in this scene (two Black,
one Hispanic) don't see what is
going on and hence can be seen as
"non-white" but not black. It's also Rod
realizing there's no one to turn to.

Since the scene consists of two **blacks**, one Hispanic (**not white**) but they don't see what is going on, you can
say they are **not black**, hence the movement from **not white** to **not black**.

Figure 6.57 Master story beat/theme stated 10—*Get Out*.

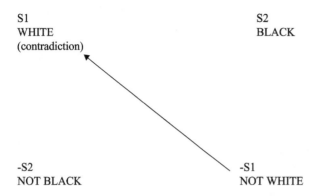

S1
WHITE
(contradiction)

S2
BLACK

-S2
NOT BLACK

-S1
NOT WHITE

1:19:16-1:22:26
Rod dials Chris's number again, and, to his surprise, Rose
answers and makes up a story about Chris freaking out
and having left. Rod is suspicious and asks which cab
company Chris used.
(**cognitive**)

Rose says that the call is about there being "something"
between him and her, and he hangs up. Her family
watches her and approves.
(**pragmatic**)

Master story beat/theme stated:
Rod is smart to ask about the cab company
Chris used, detecting the lie. Rose
reverts back to her seeming to be
on Chris's side but actually is (being) on
the family's side seeking to lure more
Blacks to turn them into slaves for
white people's brains.

It can be said that Rose moves from pretending to be **not white** (on Chris's side) to **white** (trying to lure
Rod into slavery).

Figure 6.58 Master story beat/theme stated 11—*Get Out.*

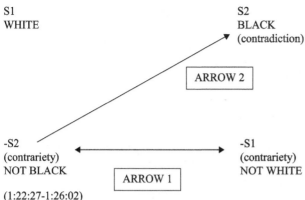

S1
WHITE

S2
BLACK
(contradiction)

ARROW 2

-S2
(contrariety)
NOT BLACK

-S1
(contrariety)
NOT WHITE

ARROW 1

(1:22:27-1:26:02)
Chris awakens and watches a video of Jim Hudson, in
a hospital gown, talking about what is going to
happen to Chris – they will transplant Jim's brain into his
body, and Chris's psyche will live in the sunken place.
Chris recalls the other Black people he recently met and
it makes sense.
(**cognitive**)

Master story beat/theme stated:
the truth is revealed (from the truth/falsehood
part of the veridiction square).

The central conflict is afoot, which will ultimately render Chris neither **black** (**not black**) or (**not white**)
once an invader (Jim Hudson) is implanted in his body and takes over. [ARROW 1]

(1:26:03-1:26:15)
Chris discovers cotton in the arms of the chair that he ripped.
(**pragmatic/cognitive**)

Master story beat/theme stated:
a major turning point in Chris equipping
himself to win his decisive test of
escaping.

Because Chris was so entrusting of Rose, he was duped and had limited vision and, in essence, was **not**
black temporarily, which translates as capable of fighting for and protecting himself. With this one move
of blocking the hypnosis signal via the cotton in his ears, he becomes fully **black**. [ARROW 2]

Figure 6.59 Master story beat/theme stated 12—*Get Out*. Each of the two beat directional
arrows will be annotated (see above) as this is a complex master beat.

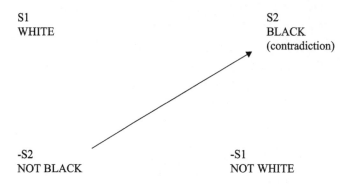

(1:28:20-1:29:14)
Jeremy opens the straps holding in Chris and turns
around to prepare an IV. Chris whacks him in the head
with a bocce ball.
(pragmatic)

Jeremy squirms, and Chris whacks him unconscious.
(pragmatic)

Chris takes out the cotton from the chair from his ears.
(pragmatic)

Jeremy bleeds profusely.
(pragmatic)

Master story beat/theme stated:
Chris is now winning his decisive
test and a series of transformative
events will subdue all his opponents.

Chris, who because of being in love with Rose had sidestepped his "blackness," which in essence made
him vulnerable, is now able to move from **not black** to **black** and save himself through wit and ingenuity
(blocking his ears).

Figure 6.60 Master story beat/theme stated 13—*Get Out.* There are four separate
moments to this beat.

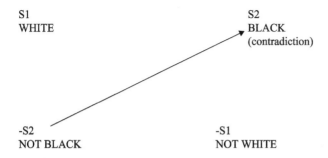

1:30:41-1:30:59
Chris sees Missy in the parlor, stares her down. They both spot her teacup, she lunges for it, he sweeps it to the floor and smashes it.
(pragmatic)

Master story beat/theme stated:
Smashing the teacup furthers Chris
winning his decisive test,
and is a major blow to Missy
being able to control Chris.

1:31:00-1:31:36
Chris and Missy again stare each other down, Missy stabs Chris through the hand with a letter opener, and he then slashes her throat with it.
(pragmatic)

Master story beat/theme stated:
Killing Missy pretty much eliminates
the weapon of hypnosis and puts
Chris one step closer to winning his
decisive test.

In both master story beats/themes stated, Chris has moved from being duped (**not black**) to **black**, capable of completely counteracting the (**white**) evil.

Figure 6.61 Master story beat/theme stated 14—*Get Out.*

1:31:37-1:32:48
Chris goes to exit house; Jeremy lunges at him.
They struggle, Chris stabs him with the letter opener,
kicks him to the ground, then stomps on his head to
kill him and grabs his car keys.
(**pragmatic**)

Master story beat/theme stated:
subduing Jeremy again (in classic horror
movie fashion, a killed opponent wasn't
really dead and resurrects for a final round).

Chris, no longer under the spell of Rose and the hypnosis of Missy which rendered him **not black** and powerless, moves to **black**, rendering him completely capable of counteracting the (**white**) evil.

Figure 6.62 Master story beat/theme stated 15—*Get Out.*

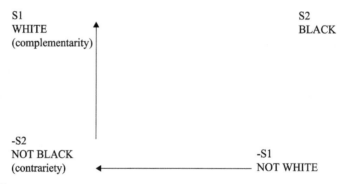

(1:34:38-1:34:59)
Georgina awakens and violently screams
at Chris and hits him, causing them to smash into a
tree and kill Georgina.
(**pragmatic**)

Master story beat/theme stated:
Another major opponent (Georgina)
is taken out, but she's revealed in full
as "Grandma" (Mrs. Armitage) and
beats Chris as he drives, causing her life-ending crash.

Georgina (who is **not white** but **not black** and possessed by the brain of Rose's grandmother) moves from **not white** to **not black** to **white** as the evil spirit of the **white** woman totally controls her until she's killed. (Hence the movement from **not white** to **not black** to **white**.)

Figure 6.63 Master story beat/theme stated 16—*Get Out.*

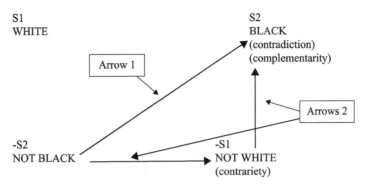

(1:35:49–1:36:10.)
"Grandpa" begins to strangle Chris, who pulls out his
phone and shoots a flash into his eyes.
(pragmatic)

**Master story beat/theme stated: The flash in Walter's
eyes resurrects Walter from the sunken place within
him. [ARROW 1]**

The camera flash at Walter has instantly transformed him
from **not black** (controlled by a white brain) to **black**
(himself as Walter again briefly) (ARROW 1)

(1:36:11–1:36:55)
Rose approaches with her gun, "Grandpa" tells her that he
wants to kill Chris himself, and he takes her gun and shoots
Rose and kills himself.
(pragmatic)

**Master story beat/theme stated: The duality between
being/seeming is completely resolved and the real
Walter aided Chris in Chris's decisive test to escape
when he emerged from his own "sunken place," shot
Rose, then killed his body that housed Rose's white
"Grandpa."**

Walter has briefly emerged to take over his body and through his actions of killing Rose and finally the body
that Grandpa Armitage has enslaved moves from **not black** to **not white** to **black** (ARROWS 2) in that he
was **not black** (had been enslaved by a **white** man's brain), not really **white** (still seeming **black**) to **black**,
making him capable of conquering evil.

Figure 6.64 Master story beats/themes stated 17—*Get Out.* Note: This is a complex
illustration examining two master story beats/themes stated with multiple arrows on the
semiotic square.

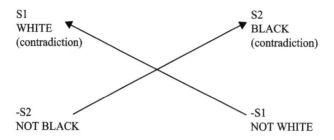

(1:37:29 -1:38:21)
As Chris hovers over wounded Rose, who proclaims her
love for him, he begins to strangle her, which causes her
to smile and makes him stop.
(**pragmatic/cognitive**)

**Master story beat/theme stated: Mortally wounded
Rose hides behind her seeming to love Chris, and he
attempts to strangle her but stops, avoiding complete
dehumanization despite what preceded, making his
glorifying test complete.**

The movement here is best described for Rose from **not white** to **white** in that she is lying and again
pretending to be **not white** but attempting to trick him (**white**). Chris's final transformation has taken him
from **not black** (not capable of protecting himself) to **black**, and he has triumphed and not allowed the
horrible treatment he underwent to dehumanize him enough to strangle wounded Rose.

Figure 6.65 Master story beat/theme stated 18—*Get Out.*

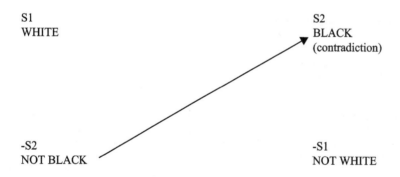

1:38:22 -1:40:48
A cop car pulls up.
Rose pleads for help, and it's Rod, who calls for Chris and takes him away.
(**pragmatic**)

**Master story beat/theme stated: Once
we see Rod, the story is over. The
glorifying test will extend through the
car ride with Rod as Chris processes
what happened.**

Chris has defeated the evil, and Rod will take him to safety, and again we can plot the move
from **not black** (blinded by Rose) to **black**, capable of fighting evil.

Figure 6.66 Master story beat/theme stated 19—*Get Out.*

7

Demonstration of Using the Tools to Develop a Feature Screenplay

Through the Night

Next up, I will demonstrate setting myself up to write a feature film screenplay by using various tools of my *Semiotics for Screenwriters* system and then transplanting some of the results onto Final Draft's Beat Board and Outline Editor. This will include me writing a speculative comprehensive beat map; plotting master story beats on all four corners of the story's controlling master semiotic square; brainstorming elements in search of isotopies; brainstorming states of being and an actantial narrative schema for the story; and, finally, providing a canonical narrative schema summary and a few scenes from the potential demo screenplay. Master story beats/themes stated will be included, speculatively of course, but since I'm not breaking down a specimen movie, I don't feel the need to use a "cheat sheet." You could create one for your original screenplay, of course. Remember that themes will evolve and "develop" as you go along.

Begin Wherever in Your Writing Process that You Want!

I can't emphasize this concept enough: the *Semiotics for Screenwriters* system is meant to serve your writing process anywhere in your writing workflow, be it at the early brainstorming stage of writing, after a vomit draft has been sketched, or even if you are revising a final rewrite and need semiotics to "tweak" aspects of your story. And everything in between. This system is not, I repeat, *not* meant to give you a bunch of restrictive rules that you must follow in order to execute a screenplay. The system provides tools to train your brain to think deeply about movie stories you love, to stimulate your imagination and guide your writing processes.

As you'll see, the outcome of this demonstration will give me tools that will *prepare* me to write a screenplay. When I eventually use them to finish the screenplay, I will discover depth and character development, but for now the materials that this method affords me is an extreme road map (comprehensive beat map) and deep thought into my story, themes, etc. I will provide the first few scenes, including one of a master story beat, so that you'll get to see a "final outcome" (at least a few pages of it). This is why the comprehensive beat map is aptly named; it's a map of a journey just the way you would map out a plan to drive cross-country. The map gives you direction, but the adventure will develop in the trip.

That said, allow me to begin.

Log Line Creation

For this demo script, entitled *Through the Night*, I started with a story idea and some script pages. Taking these and following the semiotics workflow (brainstorming elements in search of isotopies and sketching out a canonical narrative schema summary, etc.), I then came up with a log line:

> *Through the Night*
> **Log line:** An actor whose New York-based experimental theater is on the verge of closing seeks to appease his youngest member, who is a ticket-selling machine and wishes to "hang out all night in the city" as it's alleged the theater troupe did years ago, according to their published memoir *Theater in the Margins*.

This log line is clearly for an independent film, and that's fine; the *Semiotics for Screenwriters* system can develop any kind of movie. This idea is what I call a hangout movie, meaning the characters just "hang out" throughout the story as emotions are experienced and character arcs are manifested. It's a "slice of life" kind of story, so to speak.

But don't be fooled. This kind of story is difficult to pull off because the conflict must be internalized, and it's held together *thematically* more so than by mere dramatic/narrative syntax.

Find a Compatible Specimen Movie to Break Down as a Model

For *Through the Night*, I'm using *Lost in Translation* as a master specimen because it has similarities to how I envision *Through the Night* going, and because we went through it in this book.

Brainstorm on Elements as Potential Isotopies

Now I will brainstorm on the random isotopies of *Lost in Translation* and take notes of any random elements that percolate up when I think about my story in terms of isotopies (elements that will eventually yield narrative intent).

Below is a collection of elements that I brainstormed, which were raw at first, then I went back to my breakdown of *Lost in Translation* and further enhanced them.

Note: When I eventually wrote the components for my movie, I did *not* use all of the elements that I brainstormed as isotopies. But brainstorming elements helped immensely because as I wrote the canonical narrative schema, the elements that would become isotopies would reveal themselves from the massive pile and slip in to become part of the story. And the contrast of what elements were used in contrast to elements that were not used helped me to further envision my story. Remember, a key benefit of brainstorming elements against a master specimen movie is that you hold the narrative intent of the isotopies of the master specimen in your brain and are constantly reminded of them as you write your own movie.

Table 7.1 Raw elements of Actors, Objects, Place (pre-isotopies)—*Through the Night* (demo)

ACTORS	OBJECTS	PLACES
Justin (55)	pens	backstage
Sue (52)	*Theater in the Margins*	side of stage
Emily (58)	memoir	outside of theater
Casey (53)	diary	theater lobby
Madison (25)	love letters	inside Ubers
Clarke (65)	keys to apartment	Justin's home in Wisconsin
landlord (70)	character shoes	Central Park ball fields
Madison's Boss (50) *	props from show	streets around theater
Tom Boring (45)**	eviction notice	Central Park reservoir walk
Jill Boring (45)	**Justin's daughter's school**	apartment near theater
Justin's son (7)	**science project**	benches of Central Park
Justin's daughter (9)	**text from Justin's wife showing**	**billboard buildings of Times**
young female customer (25)	**his son's baseball game**	**Square NYC.**
tourists in park	cot that Justin sleeps in	**outside Madison's hotel**
unhoused man	the hotel room	**window**
unhoused woman	trees of Central Park	streets en route to Madison's
furniture store executive	**Emily's backpack**	hotel
	Justin's Apple watch	side door of The Metropolitan
	cell phones	Museum of Art
	email of appointment for	Emily's bookstore
	sub teaching	

* Items in **bold** are elements that never made it into the final draft of the canonical narrative schema summary, the comprehensive beat map, or the final treatment.

** I included actor ages (Tom Boring (45)) because this is a speculative screenplay and the age provides a quick visual reference for a reader to be able to get a glimpse of the actor the same as I would do if I were writing the actual screenplay.

Table 7.2 Raw elements pre-isotopies (Time/Durativeness, Events)—*Through the Night* (demo)

TIME/DURATIVENESS	EVENTS
right before a show opening	closing night
during a show	**fundraising night***
after a show late into	**kid's school science fair**
Friday night	
Saturday morning	
Saturday afternoon	
Saturday night	
Sunday morning	
Sunday afternoon	
Sunday night	
Monday morning	

* Items in **bold** are elements that never made it into the final draft of the canonical narrative schema summary, the comprehensive beat map or the final treatment (the final story documents).

Create a Master Semiotic Square

Using the semiotic square from *Lost in Translation* was a place to start in order to try and invent an original one for my demo story *Through the Night*. *Lost in Translation* may *not* be the perfect specimen to model given my story line, but specimen movies are not broken down for the purpose of having our own screenplays blindly copied off of them; we break down classic movies to give us a general snapshot of the structural architecture of a great movie using semiotics. The knowledge that we cull from them will include how the specimen is held together, the what and why of how it works, and then we can use this knowledge as a touchpoint point of departure to start our own brainstorming and writing process.

For example, I first off noticed how *Lost in Translation* is paced. It's slow, and the movie allows for a lot of time spent with each of the two main characters so that when they come together, it's special. The lovers spend a fair amount of time apart from each other, and this is weaved in and around the times that they do interact with each other. This downtime allows for the interaction time to be more exciting in terms of how we, the competent observer, feel about their coming together. This architecture provides for a dialectic between lonely and connected in *Lost in Translation* and can be used (albeit differently) in my speculative movie story *Through the Night*. The primary difference I realized is that in *Lost in Translation* the primary romance is between a male and female. In *Through the Night*, there is also a traditional chaste romance at the center of the story (between Justin and Emily), but their love story is also within the context of bonding as part of a family of the theater troupe, so the storyline is different. But the dynamics are similar.

Also, I realize from breaking down *Lost in Translation* that another reason it works so well is it makes the respective marriages of the two lovers dysfunctional enough so that you root for them to fall in love, but there still exists enough of a real marriage for each couple that provides the perfect amount of "risk" for the lovers to form a *sexually* romantic union. In other words, you root for the chaste love story as long as it stays chaste, and the architecture to achieve this very difficult mini-genre (chaste romance) is brilliantly achieved in *Lost in Translation*. My semiotics breakdown of the movie helped me understand this delicate structure.

Lonely/connected as controlling binary opposition terms perfectly depicts the dramatic journey of the two protagonists in *Lost in Translation*, but my original movie's plot might be a little different if only because most of the time in my movie the characters are together (not lonely). But as we know from the plotting of the master story beats onto all four corners of the master semiotic square, there can be a lot of nuances within these definitions of terms.

In other words, the lonely/connected vibe can permeate the entire movie that I'm writing but in different ways, and I found different opportunities to color the narrative with traces of loneliness. Also, these controlling binary opposition terms represent a pole that the narrative structure moves along on throughout the story, since the good friends of the theater troupe can be lonely, not connected, etc., even when together.

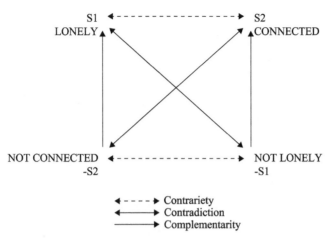

Figure 7.1 Master semiotic square—*Through the Night* (demo). I deployed the master semiotic square from *Lost in Translation*. While not a perfect match for *Through the Night,* it will suffice and offer enough of an overall framework for my brainstorming.

Also note: While there are individual relationships between my characters, my story is more of a family dynamic, resulting in more of a group protagonist.

Mapping Raw Elements as Potential "Isotopies" to Either Side of the Controlling Terms of Master Semiotic Square

First up, I map brainstormed elements as potential isotopies to either side of my master binary opposition terms using standard semantic categories (objects, place, time, events, actors).

Table 7.3 Raw elements (Objects) (pre-isotopies) mapped to key binary opposition terms of master semiotic square—*Through the Night* (demo)

OBJECTS

LONELY	vs	CONNECTED
love letters[*]		*Theater in the Margins* memoir
Justin's Apple watch[*]		diary
email of appointment for sub teaching[*]		keys to apartment[*]
eviction notice[*]		props from show[*]
text from Justin's wife showing son playing baseball[*]		prop bag[*]
		cot that Justin sleeps in
		trees of Central Park
		Emily's backpack[*]
		cell phones

[*] Elements that never made it into the final story documents.

Table 7.4 Raw elements (Place) (pre-isotopies) mapped to key binary opposition terms of master semiotic square—*Through the Night* (demo)

PLACES

LONELY	vs.	CONNECTED
Justin's home in Wisconsin		backstage
billboard buildings of Times Square*		side of stage
New York City inside Ubers		outside of theater
outside Madison's hotel window*		theater lobby
Central Park ball fields		inside Emily's car
		acting class*
		Central Park ball fields
		streets around theater*
		Central Park reservoir walk
		apartment near theater*
		benches of Central Park
		streets en route to Madison's hotel
		side door of The Metropolitan Museum of Art
		Emily's bookstore

Table 7.5 Raw elements (Actors) (pre-isotopies) mapped to key binary opposition terms of master semiotic square—*Through the Night* (demo)

ACTORS

LONELY	vs.	CONNECTED
Sue (52)		Emily (58)
landlord (70)		Casey (53)
Tom Boring (45)		Justin (55)
Jill Boring (45)		Madison (25)
Justin's son		Clarke (65)
Justin's daughter		young female customer (25)
tourists in park		
Unhoused people		
Madison's Boss (50)*		

* Element that never made it into the final story documents.

Table 7.6 Raw elements (Time/Durativeness) (pre-isotopies) mapped to key binary opposition terms of master semiotic square—*Through the Night* (demo)

TIME/DURATIVENESS

LONELY	vs.	CONNECTED
Friday evening		right before a show opening
Saturday morning		during a show
Sunday morning		after a show late into the night
Monday morning		Friday night
		Saturday afternoon
		Saturday night
		Sunday afternoon
		Sunday night

Brainstorm Elements In Search of Isotopies in Additional Categories

The additional categories where I can find binary opposition can be Men vs. Women, Humans vs. Animal, Day vs. Night, etc., and then I proceeded to map the *elements* in search of isotopies to new semantic categories.

Table 7.7 Raw elements (pre-isotopies) in binary opposition (other semantic categories)—*Through the Night* (demo)

PEOPLE		
MEN	**vs.**	**WOMEN**
Justin		Sue
Clarke		Emily
Tom Boring		Casey
landlord		Madison
Madison's Boss*		

* Element that never made it into the final story documents.

Table 7.8 Raw elements (pre-isotopies) in binary opposition (other semantic categories)—*Through the Night* (demo)

SEXUAL ORIENTATION		
STRAIGHT	**vs.**	**BISEXUAL**
Justin		Emily
Clarke		Madison
Casey		young female customer

Through the Night—States of Being (Possible)

Next up, I'll brainstorm possible states of being. First of all, let me reiterate, in my semiotics system, states of being are examined both on the surface level of story *and* the narrative level for reasons I disclosed earlier. After studying and meditating on the states of being information culled from *Lost in Translation*, I have brainstormed possible states of being that I can use for *Through the Night* story first in a raw sense (pre-isotopy), then will try and move them to either side of a dysphoria/euphoria table.

This part of the brainstorming ensures that I'm building an *emotional life* of the characters or at least the *potential* for one. As it is with *all* brainstorming of elements in search of potential isotopies, some will be used, some won't. The ones that don't get used will help point in the direction of what the story actually is. When I slotted in the states of being into the comprehensive beat map, I ended up using many of the ones that I initially conjured up. Lastly, this brainstormed list doesn't include *all* the states of being that I eventually charted in my comprehensive beat map. I invented others as I went along in the development process. Again, as with all things concerning this semiotics system … the purpose of brainstorming is to think and get guidance and direction on your story.

States of Being — *Through the Night*

- *Madison cries about feeling like her engagement is off.*
- *Justin is exhilarated that the troupe has a full house for a show.*
- *The troupe is excited that Madison sold 40 tickets to Saturday's show.*
- *Justin is stressed out that his wife Sue gives him an ultimatum about having to get a job and earn money.*
- *Justin pushes back on Emily when she asks about a microscope she got his daughter for Christmas and Emily is hurt and withdraws.*
- *Justin is saddened because Emily has really grown apart from him and was his best friend.*
- *Justin comes to realize that he can't save the theater and keep it going.*
- *Madison is frustrated that she has to go to a waitressing job on Saturday.**
- *Justin and the troupe take Madison to the Central Park ball fields and sit around and play bongos and chant as they did in the old days according to the memoir.*
- *Justin and Madison stay up late and watch video recordings of some of Justin's old plays in the apartment in the city that they crash at.**
- *Madison relates how she's afraid of not going to law school and failing in life, and she feels like her fiancé isn't coming back.*
- *Madison is exhilarated that they are going to Central Park.*
- *Madison watches Justin's son's baseball game and really enjoys it.**
- *Clarke is sad and cries when he tells his friends that he has terminal cancer.*
- *Clarke becomes completely okay with dying and wants to have a good time.*
- *The rest of the group cries with Clarke when they find out he has cancer, but he is not sad.*
- *The group has a session of chanting and meditation and are unable to seemingly convince Clarke of his immortality as he doesn't care.*
- *Justin is sad that he must part from Emily at the end of the closing weekend.*
- *Madison cries as she feels like she has failed to save the theater.*
- *Justin tells Emily that he loves her and she is the love of his life, to which she gets sarcastic about.*
- *Emily is sad to say goodbye to Madison, who decides to go to law school anyway.*

* States of being that did not make it into the final story.

Now I move the states of being on either side of a euphoria/dysphoria table. At first, I move obvious ones into either side of the binary table without regard for trying to think of specific binary opposition for each beat.

Table 7.9 States of being—first sort—binary opposition categories

DYSPHORIA	vs.	EUPHORIA
• Madison cries about feeling like her engagement is off. • Justin is saddened because Emily has really grown apart from him and was his best friend. • Madison is frustrated that she has to go to a waitressing job on Saturday. * • Justin is exhilarated that they have an audience. • Justin comes to realize that he can't save the theater and keep it going. • Justin is able to take Madison through some of the paces he went through to write his plays like wandering around Central Park at night. • Madison relates how she's afraid of not going to law school and failing in life and she feels like her boyfriend isn't working out. • Clarke is sad and cries when he tells his friends that he has terminal cancer. • The rest of the group cries with Clarke when they find out he has cancer. • Madison cries as she feels that she has failed to save the theater. • Justin is sad that he must part from Emily at the end of the closing weekend. • Emily is sad to say goodbye to Madison, who decides to go to law school anyway.		• Justin and Madison stay up and watch some video recordings of Justin's old plays in the apartment in the city they crash at. * • Madison is exhilarated that they are going to Central Park. • Madison watches Justin's son's baseball game and really enjoys it. * • The group has a session of chanting and meditation and are able to convince Clarke of his immortality. • Justin tells Emily that he loves her and she is the love of his life, to which she gets sarcastic about.

* States of being which did not make it into the final story.

Now I will try and use some states of being and see if they have direct binary opposition counterparts. From doing this part of the process, I also created *additional* states of being that made it into the final story. Note: I only used a few of the original brainstormed states of being in this table because these were the ones that suggested *direct* binary oppositions.

Table 7.10 States of being with direct binary oppositions

DYSPHORIA	vs.	EUPHORIA
• Madison cries about feeling like her relationship with her fiancé is failing.		• Madison tells Emily that she is in love with her. *
• Justin is sad that he feels Emily doesn't love him anymore.		• Madison tells Emily that she is in love with her. *
• Justin is saddened because Emily has really grown apart from him and was his best friend.		• Justin has a good time hanging out and talking to Clarke in the hotel late at night. *
• Justin is sad thinking about losing Clarke.		• Clarke is completely okay with dying to the point where Justin is fascinated. *

(Continued)

Table 7.10 *Continued*

DYSPHORIA	vs.	EUPHORIA
• Madison is afraid about not going to law school.		• Madison is happy that she has put going to law school on hold when she sells out the house. *
• Madison cries as she feels that she has failed to save the theater.		• Madison is exhilarated that they are going to Central Park.
• Justin is sad to say goodbye to Emily. *		• Justin is happy to see Emily when he comes back to the city.

*New additions based on brainstorming states of being as binary oppositions that were added *and* put it into the final story.

Actantial Narrative Schema

Now I'll brainstorm for the actantial semiotic square. I looked at all the components, including the actantial narrative schema for *Lost in Translation* as a guideline because in doing so I'm reminded that what makes the lonely/connected dialectic of the protagonists enhanced is their alone downtime. To render this all useful for me to brainstorm my original screenplay, I set up lonely/connected as my controlling binary opposition terms. Then I brainstorm for my original movie *Through the Night* (Figure 7.3). Many of these actants added below (Figure 7.3) were added as a result of looking at the schema for *Lost in Translation* (Figure 7.2).

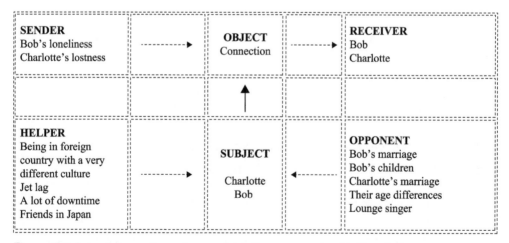

Figure 7.2 Actantial narrative schema semiotic square—*Lost in Translation*.

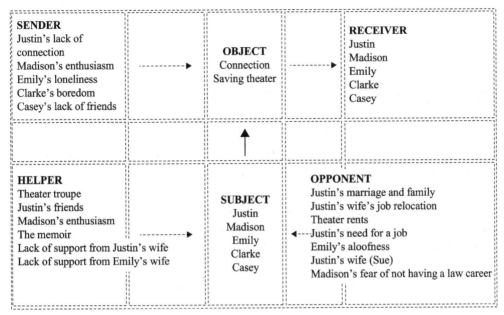

Figure 7.3 Actantial Narrative Schema Semiotic Square—*Through the Night* (demo).

Canonical Narrative Schema Summary (Speculative)

Now comes one of my favorite parts of the process, whereby I take all of the preceding breakdown and brainstorming work I've done and gather it all as information and fashion a canonical narrative schema summary treatment. This becomes my first attempt at creating a flowing narrative syntax that looks more like a traditional "treatment," albeit written using semiotics terms. Note, this is a speculative summary for a potential spec script, so obviously it won't have the full development and pristine architecture that the three masterpieces I broke down already do. But that's not an issue because the purpose of doing all of this breakdown and brainstorming work is to give us tools to draft out our feature screenplay with. It's a map for a *potential* journey.

For this phase of the process, I don't worry if I don't know exactly where the story is going yet, but there are considerations that the canonical narrative schema uncover that are very valuable to writing the actual screenplay. It's probably the schema I return to most when I want to understand the dramatic structure of the story and how it moves in time.

Remember, the canonical narrative schema is the first time that you get the feeling of a narrative syntax of the story. For me, it's important to work out all the details of this schema's very important master tests, even if in doing so I can sometimes *overkill* on using them. I tend to like outlining the major "contract" and the three major related tests of the story and then perhaps think of *some* of the subsequent "minor" contracts and related tests as microcosms that might run throughout the story, help flesh it out, and connect everything back to the main contract and the three master tests. Mapping out the master canonical narrative schemas is important since these contracts and tests should be defined at an early point in the brainstorming and writing process, even if I have to continually go back and update them after working on the comprehensive beat map and thereby discovering more about the architecture of this very important schema and subsequently the entire story and screenplay.

The Canonical Narrative Schema Summary—*Through the Night*[1]

Justin has a contract to figure out how to make a living alongside his wife to help support their two kids and has his first qualifying test start (unknowingly to him) while he and his wife are hosting Tom and Jill Boring for dinner in their Wisconsin home. The Borings are high school teachers, and Justin's wife Sue works as a telemarketer and wants Justin to get a substitute teaching job at their school so he can help with the bills.

Justin has a *being able to do something*, which is to bond with the Borings so they'll help him get teaching work, a *being able to do something* he isn't even aware of, which will take him through a qualifying test of networking with the Borings, setting up a decisive test he doesn't want; namely, acquiring and maintaining a substitute teaching job. But the dinner is awkward; Justin is hostile to the couple, whom he can't relate to, especially when he tries to tell them about his experimental theater troupe in New York, The Marginal Theater Company, which he still runs. The Borings do their best to try and relate to Justin and say they love theater and saw *Frozen* on Broadway as proof, all, of course, to Justin's chagrin as he's somewhat a snob.

Later in bed, Sue gives Justin an ultimatum: either he earns an income or she's divorcing him. She's very cold. His contract is to make a living to help support his family. The qualifying test of bonding with the Borings so they will help him has somewhat failed (at least in his mind), but he can re-attempt his qualifying test and attempt to be hired as a substitute teacher, feeding into a would-be decisive test to hold the job successfully and contribute to the family income. Justin can't sleep because he's stressed out over the ultimatum. He tells Sue that his theater lost its lease, and he's going back to New York one last time to shut down the theater for good.

Justin flies to New York (as he often does on weekends when there are productions of his theater's plays running), intent on shutting down the theater and returning to Wisconsin to earn a living teaching, forgetting about his New York life. He meets up with Emily, his co-theater runner/partner in crime, best friend, old flame, etc. He meets her at the used bookstore in Manhattan where she works. He witnesses a young female customer bringing up Justin and Emily's old out-of-print theater memoir entitled *Theater in the Margins* to the counter to purchase after Emily signs it. The young female customer flirts with Emily. Seeing the enthusiasm that a young person has for his troupe via the memoir causes Justin to get the idea he can stay in New York and move in with Emily, who has recently separated from her wife. When Justin brings up the idea, he promises Emily that he views their relationship as platonic and insists they are still best friends. This is a new contract, for

---

[1]Regarding writing an original canonical narrative schema summary for an original script, it can tend to be longer, closer to an actual treatment, as it is an opportunity to work out a lot of story beats in a connected narrative syntax, to later be plotted on a comprehensive beat map, etc.

Justin to move in with Emily and have them live together successfully (a decisive test). Of course, the qualifying test will play out this weekend as Justin has a *being able to do something*/a *knowing how to do something*, which is prove to Emily they still get along and can live together, and he is capable of earning money in New York.

On the subway to the theater, Emily chats about a play that she is writing and how she is stuck with where to go with it. Justin doesn't have any ideas. They laugh about things past, and there is a real affection for each other. Emily asks about Justin's daughter Emma, whom she has grown attached to having no kids of her own. She asks about a microscope that she gave Emma for Christmas because Emma had expressed to Emily an interest in becoming a doctor. Justin tells her that his wife Sue is freaked out by the expensive gift-giving that Emily bestows on his daughter. This hurts Emily, who is also suspicious that Sue doesn't like Emily interacting so much with Emma because Emily is bisexual and might influence her (Sue is more conservative). Emily gets withdrawn. She seems as though she will be unreachable for the rest of his weekend trip because Justin hurt her feelings. The qualifying test to bond with Emily enough so that he can move in is failing. A contract is established for Justin to get Emily to open up to him again, which sets up a new *being able to do something* (a new mini-qualifying test).

Justin and Emily arrive at the theater and meet the landlord, who is showing the space to furniture chain executives, who plan on moving in when Justin and his theater troupe move out this coming Monday. Justin says they can still afford the space, but the landlord doesn't believe that Justin's theater can pay rent anymore. The troupe would need to sell 100 tickets this closing weekend to pay back rent and stay open. Justin tells Emily that he will tell the rest of the troupe that the theater has to shut down, and he begins to mentally prepare for this discussion. Meanwhile, the rest of the troupe, consisting of Madison (25), Clarke (65), and Casey (53), are preparing to put on the evening's show, a play Justin wrote called *A Homeless Woman Dies in the Woods*, a mostly one-woman show that Madison stars in along with Clarke, who makes several appearances. The play is experimental and nihilistic as all the troupe's plays are, à la theater of the absurd, Samuel Beckett, Ionesco, etc.

Justin came to New York this weekend with the original contract of shutting down the theater (a qualifying test), to set up his decisive test to go back to Wisconsin and find employment, but it has shifted to a new contract of keeping the theater alive. This becomes possible now because the newest member of the troupe, Madison, has sold 40 tickets to Saturday's show (a new qualifying test) through her NYU alumni network and plans to sell a lot more for Sunday's show, which can actually pay the one month's back rent (a decisive test) to convince the landlord not to kick the troupe out and save the theater. Madison is young and incredibly enthusiastic and willing to pound the phones on the closing weekend mornings to sell tickets. But there is a catch; she read Justin and Emily's memoir, which a small press published 30 years ago, as well. It's ancient history except for the wonkiest theater students. Madison found it in a used book bin for two dollars, read it several times, and this led her to Justin and Emily's theater troupe. This memoir gives her courage and context for the new mini-qualifying test to sell enough tickets to pay the troupe's back bills (a *being able to do something*) and the mini-decisive test to convince the landlord to not kick them out, which will feed into Justin's new greater decisive test to move in with

Emily and earn a living so he can stay in New York. The memoir documents how (albeit 30 years ago) on closing weekends, the troupe would hang out all night in the city, mostly in Central Park, and drink, smoke pot, sometimes do drugs, meet all kinds of crazy people, and have strange experiences, many of which became the basis of their original plays that they put on in the theater, including the one running now.

Madison has reread the memoir and assumes the troupe will be carrying on this ritual of hanging out all night as it's a closing weekend. She wants to party in a similar fashion with the current albeit older members of her troupe. But it's been decades since they behaved that way. Besides, Justin and the rest of the troupe are in their fifties and sixties, are old and cranky, and don't want to hang out all night. They want to do the show and go home and sleep, as has been their ritual for many years now. Justin feels that Madison might be their last hope of turning the theater around since she is a ticket-selling machine. She plans to pound the phones Saturday and Sunday morning to sell the remaining 60 tickets for the weekend's final three shows. This could pay one month of back rent and keep the dream of keeping the theater alive a little bit more until Justin can "figure out" what to do. Justin convinces the rest of the troupe (friends for decades) to hang out in the city with Madison this weekend and give her the full "hanging out experience." They agree to do this, much to their chagrin, but they are loyal to Justin and the theater company.

Madison has rented a hotel room for them to all crash in, and Justin devises a plan to get her drunk so she'll just pass out in the hotel, and they won't have to hang out outside and can all just crash in the hotel room. In fact, concerning the new contract (to save the theater), Madison has already passed a qualifying test, which is selling a lot of tickets for Saturday night's show, but it renders Justin and the troupe in need of passing a new qualifying test of satisfying Madison's craving to fulfill the "hang out" ritual prescribed in the troupe's memoir (a *being able to do something*). Emily gets the idea that she is going to try and seduce Madison so the younger woman will be even more inclined to sell tickets and stay part of the troupe. Justin is suspicious of Emily's motivations and thinks she just likes Madison, who has a lot of energy, and is very attractive.

On the way to the hotel, Emily and Madison talk and really begin to bond and "hit it off," and it seems like romantic sparks are flying. Madison knows a lot about Emily and Justin's past romantic relationship because it's all documented in the memoir as are aspects of their psychological makeup and vulnerabilities. Emily and Madison walk and talk, and Justin, Clarke, and Casey walk behind them, observing them bantering. Justin, who loves Emily, is getting a little jealous.

Clarke was supposed to retire from his post office job but hasn't yet, and Justin is annoyed with him because Justin himself spent a lot of time helping Clarke make that decision, getting him financially prepared, and talking him through all the variables of retirement, etc. Clarke's wife left him twenty years ago, and Justin helped him get through this stressful time. Justin and Clarke had plans to travel together and go skiing, hiking, etc. Now those plans are on hold since Clarke is still working his job. Justin then gets a call from his wife Sue. Sue is opposed to Justin hanging out all night with the troupe, and Justin tells her of his plan to merely get Madison drunk so that she'll just fall asleep. Sue thinks that's an even worse idea. Justin pretends he gets cut off and hangs up and shuts off his phone.

While walking to the hotel, Madison banters with Emily, and sparks are flying. Madison encounters unhoused people on the street and gives one money and tries to get his story, perhaps to get inspiration to write with. Her doing this attracts other unhoused people, who start following the troupe then eventually fall away and are gone. While in the hotel, Madison gets word from her fiancé that he is ending their engagement because she is not going to law school and is not holding up her end of their "bargain" (he's going to medical school). Madison breaks down. She takes a shower, and the troupe feels bad for her and decides to appease her and give her the "full experience" of hanging out all night on a closing weekend although they would prefer staying in the nice hotel room. Madison comes out of the shower and is delighted to hear they will hang out all night, and then gives them all THC-laced "gummy bears" that will get them high. They take the gummies and smoke pot, preparing to leave for Central Park.

The contract to give Madison the full experience of hanging out all night on a closing weekend with the troupe presents a *being able to do something* of giving her a satisfying "hanging out experience" that leads to a qualifying test, which will take place on the first night of the closing weekend, Friday night. The *being able to do something* is to show Madison a real "hang out" first night. Justin calls back Sue (his wife), who again is cold and dismissive of the troupe's plan to hang out, and again tries to encourage him not to do it. Justin says he wants to do it for Madison because she's heartbroken that her fiancé dumped her. Sue presses to find out if he's really trying to save the theater instead of shutting it down as promised, and he doesn't answer. She makes him promise to Zoom into their son's science fair the next morning, he hesitates, and she hangs up on him. Justin has forsaken his original contract, shutting the theater down (his qualifying test) to fulfill the decisive test of getting the substitute teaching job through the Borings so that he may become a real contributor to his family's income. But now Justin's own personal newfangled qualifying test has evolved into getting through the first night of hanging out to fulfill the decisive test of hanging out all weekend for Madison and giving her the full experience, the one that she has fantasized about via the troupe's memoir. Justin views Madison's enthusiasm as a way of saving the theater. Also, Justin and the troupe feel for Madison in her pain caused by her broken engagement, and they want to give her a great "hanging out" weekend.

The troupe get high, eat gummies, and take Ubers to Central Park. Madison, who rides with Justin and Emily, talks about how, when the troupe did hang out, mostly in Central Park, they chanted ritualistically to the void of the universe, and she thinks that they are going to do this sort of thing again that night. Justin and Emily are reluctant and almost embarrassed of their quirky youthful behavior. They were wild college students back in the day, singing out to the trees, the universe, etc. And they were very high. This documented behavior also relates to the kind of theater they make, experimental theater. Madison begins to probe more about Justin and Emily, including about their past love relationship, which is long over but was documented in the memoir. Justin and Emily blow it off, but we sense there is still some pain there, which is also putting tension on Justin's qualifying test of bonding with Emily, a bonding that he seeks so she'll let him move in with her (his decisive test of figuring out how to come back to New York).

The troupe gets to the park, and on the way in Madison and the theater troupe have become very high. They walk around the reservoir, and Madison approaches unhoused people, hoping to coax them to participate in the ritual hanging out and perhaps even shake a story out of them. After all, Madison remarks, their current play is *A Homeless Woman Dies in the Woods*, so it follows that she is interested in talking to more unhoused people as research and possible inspiration.

The troupe continues to the ball fields but pass through a rocky area of the park. Madison stops and remarks that, according to the memoir, this is where something magical happened and that is where something needs to be recited per "tradition." Justin, Emily, and Clarke are clueless. Madison seems disappointed that they don't even know their own traditions. Suddenly, Casey remembers what Madison is referring to and recites a few related sentences from the memoir (to everyone's surprise). The rest of the troupe chimes in half-heartedly, the "ritual" picks up momentum, and Madison is happy. This remembrance of a ritual chant documented in the memoir became a mini-qualifying test that Casey stepped up and performed well in. They proceed onto the ball fields, and Clarke remarks, "Nothing magical just happened," and Justin comments, "And nothing magical happened back then either. Except that we made it home alive." They high-five each other.

The troupe members walk to the ball fields, some lamenting about the nice comfortable hotel room awaiting them. They sit and look at each other without much to say. They smoke more pot, and Madison is disappointed because it's written in the memoir that they used to play bongos to accompany their odd rituals of chanting to the void of the universe to help inspire them. The troupe members look at each other, "Bongos . . . chanting? But no one has bongos?" To compensate, Casey pulls out a bongo "app" on her iPhone and begins to play. Someone else finds a tambourine app and another a recorder app, and they all play but it's not coordinated music. Madison wants them all to chant, but they don't know any of the old chants. The qualifying test of this old ritualistic behavior is very "theatrical" and pertains to the kind of avant-garde theater that they used to make, which was very dark and nihilistic but the product of youthful creative energy. They used to chant to the dark void of the universe, almost in a "mocking" kind of way. But it was fun then because they were young and could mock death as they had their whole lives ahead of them. But they are now actually old and facing mortality, so it's not so much fun anymore. The troupe doesn't remember any chants, and Madison doesn't really know any of them, so the qualifying test to give her a good "hang out" time to feed into the decisive test of a satisfying full "hang out closing weekend" is failing. It's an awkward moment.

Then, once again, Casey saves the day and remembers all of the chants and starts to recite them (another mini-qualifying test aced by Casey). It triggers Madison to be able to also remember and recite the chants, and the rest of the group chimes in, somewhat clumsily. Casey has solved the *being able to do something/knowing how to do something*, which is give Madison a great "hanging out all night" experience as prescribed in the memoir (the current qualifying test of the troupe) feeding into the troupe's decisive test of saving the theater (which is now connected to Madison having a great closing weekend "hang out experience"). During this ritual, Justin is sitting next to Emily and holds her hand

and experiences a connection with her as she chants and seems beautiful to him. She smiles back to him, and it seems like perhaps they have ignited their love affair again.

The ritual grows into a round-robin for each troupe member to talk about whatever they want to talk about, pitch an idea for a play, offer up an artistic observation, life observations, etc. It's a "holding court" kind of bonding. They criticize movies, plays, and their general boredom with contemporary entertainment. The evening is uplifting, and Madison proclaims she is not afraid of forsaking going to law school anymore and wants a life of the theater. Emily proclaims that she's going through with her divorce. Justin says that he's not going to go back to Wisconsin and will try and convince his wife and kids to move to New York, which sounds delusional to everyone. Casey merely states that she's getting another cat. Clarke has been quiet but when prompted announces that he has terminal cancer and is done with treatments and wants to commit assisted suicide with their help after Sunday's final show. This comes right after a barrage of theatrical nihilistic chants that they just executed to appease Madison (like the old days as prescribed in their memoir). Clarke's news shocks everyone, especially Justin, who thought he was pretty close to Clarke, but Clarke never told him (or anyone in the group). The troupe is freaked out, hug him and each other, cry, etc.

After serious discussion and debate, the group agrees to assist Clarke in his suicide, but it's very overwhelming to them emotionally, especially for young Madison, who has befriended Clarke as an older uncle figure during the course of the current production. Now, a new clear decisive test has been laid out: to effectively be able to send Clarke off with a great final weekend and simultaneously satisfy Madison with the "hanging out all night ritual" on a closing weekend, satisfying her craving. Of course, this is a decisive test that exists in the shadows of the more immediate decisive test regarding Justin and his marriage, and the ultimatum that Sue (his wife) put on him; namely, that he shuts down the theater, leaves New York for good and goes back to Wisconsin and gets substitute teaching work and earns a living, or else she's leaving him and taking the kids. However, as we have learned, Justin is now trying to make a final go of staying in New York by convincing Emily that he can live with her successfully (his new qualifying test), which depends on him proving that he can support himself in New York. But the whole plan seems half-baked.

The troupe returns back to the hotel. Madison is crashing and suddenly relates that she is scared about not going to law school and fears losing her fiancé. The troupe convince her to just to go to sleep. She takes one of the beds in the room, and Emily "volunteers" to sleep in her bed as well to "comfort" her. Justin rolls his eyes and pulls out a cot. Clarke gets the other bed, and Casey agrees to sleep on the floor on pillows. Later in the night, it seems to Justin that Emily and Madison are under the covers fooling around, but it's dark and shadowy and he tries to really see but can only imagine. Regardless, he is jealous but keeps these feelings to himself and returns to sleep.

Some time later, Justin wakes up, goes into the hotel room's bathroom, and talks to Sue on Zoom. He tells her about Clarke, but she doesn't care . . . she's done with Justin and his theater troupe and hangs up. Later still, in the middle of the night, Justin and Emily can't sleep. Justin gets up and covers Clarke's feet, then he and Emily go outside for a "vape." Justin still has a qualifying test to undergo with Emily; namely, to see if he's able to get her to open up to him again so that he can broach moving in with her. Emily has withdrawn from him because he had criticized her for spending too much on his daughter's Christmas gifts. This qualifying test of bonding with Emily can potentially lead into the decisive test of Justin being allowed to move in with Emily, and give him a new start in New York, and also restart their relationship, even if it's just a deep friendship. He misses her a lot. He is able to talk about the experience that they just had in Central Park, holding hands and chanting, which he alludes made them feel very close. She smiles warmly.

Justin tries to probe Emily about their own relationship, and she is sarcastic and dismissive because they are both married although her marriage is in separation and his is on the rocks. He asks her about her feelings for Madison, and Emily is almost defensive after having probably just made love to her, but Justin is not sure because the room was dark and Emily and Madison were under the covers. Justin brings up moving in with Emily again, paying half the bills since her wife has moved out. Emily mocks him because she doesn't believe he can earn enough to pay half the bills. He feels bad about this but still thinks they can live together even if it's platonically. He tells her that she is his favorite person on earth, and he just wants to hang out with her. Emily thinks they are too old to just "hang out" and he asks, "Why do we have to stop hanging out? Is it a law?" Emily states that she thinks this is unhealthy given they are both married. Justin then discloses he's jealous of her relationship with Madison, which Emily dismisses, denying she's even having one. He said he saw them fooling around under the covers. She says that he's crazy and she's merely flirting with Madison to convince her to stay with the troupe and sell tickets. Justin doesn't buy it. Justin's qualifying test of bonding with Emily (for the decisive test of moving in with her) is failing, and as a result he's not sure if he wants to continue the theater. As they continue to talk more about life, Emily breaks down, expressing complete discontent that she has failed at everything in life (love, career, etc.). Justin holds her and comforts her. She admires him because even though he should feel "even worse" about his own lot in life he doesn't and is stoic. But though Emily has become more vulnerable to Justin, he doesn't feel connected to her.

SATURDAY

The next day, the troupe has breakfast at the hotel (Madison's treat), and most of them are suspicious of Clarke's upbeat attitude given that he has just announced he is dying. They think he might have had a psychotic break. They do Saturday's show and, because Madison sold 40 tickets to Saturday's show, it goes well, and the group is happy. The weekend will be a qualifying test for the decisive test of whether Justin can really move in with Emily and make a go of it as well as a continuing qualifying test to give Madison a satisfying closing weekend so she'll stay with the troupe and sell tickets. They all also want to give Clarke a great send-off.

Clarke's announcement of his terminal illness and his desire to commit suicide with them makes Justin's own needs to move in with Emily seem superficial. Clarke was a staple of the group, prompting uncertainty of what will happen to the troupe when he's gone. Also, Justin returning to NYC would involve convincing Emily he can pay rent to live in her apartment, a *being able to do something* in that regard. And Emily is still hurt by him pushing back on her for wanting to continue a strong relationship with Emma, Justin's daughter. Emily continues developing her romantic relationship with

Madison, riding in the car with her and holding hands with her as Justin watches and is jealous. The troupe again takes THC-laced gummy bears that Madison supplies. They then proceed to go to Central Park in order to have another night out.

Walking into Central Park, the troupe is high and act out, running on park benches, bantering, interacting with some visitors, etc., but all in a harmless way. As they continue their animated antic-filled approach to the ball fields, Madison brings up the idea that, in accordance with the troupe's memoir, they visit the adjacent Metropolitan Museum of Art where, as the memoir states, the troupe used to be let in a side door by a hip security guard Neville. Neville would proceed to let them hang out all night in the empty museum in the presence of the Egyptian sarcophaguses with the lights out in an effort to "scare themselves" and laugh in the face of death. There the troupe would meditate and work through their fears of the void and then turn around and use some of this experience and energy to write nihilistic experimental plays which would be produced in their theater, ones like *A Homeless Woman Dies in the Woods* that they are currently wrapping up.

Justin and Emily are against the idea, especially given Clarke's situation, but Clarke is crazily stoic and wants to do it. Emily and Justin postulate that Clarke might be in shock, not completely "with it," and in denial about his terminal condition, but he seems resigned to dying and not suffering and having a great final weekend. The qualifying test of giving Madison another night towards the decisive test of the full "hanging out experience" weekend *and* Clarke a great send-off is still in play. Madison is being amped up with her desire to follow what is laid out in the memoir, which now includes hanging out in the museum at night. But Clarke's request for the troupe presiding over his assisted suicide has given color to the qualifying test of another successful night in the closing weekend, setting up the decisive test of giving Madison a great "hang out closing weekend" and Clarke aid in his suicide on Sunday night.

The troupe starts tripping heavily on the unregulated gummies and learn from Madison that she bought them on the streets (not in a store), and the troupe gets fearful because the gummies could be laced with fentanyl. Clarke calms them down. They hang out on the ball fields and chant and laugh and talk. Justin, who holds Emily's hand (who in turn is focused on Madison and holding *her* hand), asks Emily if she thinks he could move in with her, and she doesn't respond.

The troupe walk to the museum side door to investigate if they can convince Neville (the old guard) to let them in and discover that Neville is not working there anymore. A new guard, Marissa (35), has replaced him, and she is tough, no-nonsense, and not interested in the troupe's nostalgia. Marissa also informs the troupe that Neville, the old guard that used to let them in, has retired and is sick. The troupe walks away, but Justin and Emily run back to Marissa and tell her the situation with Clarke's terminal illness. Marissa is moved but says that she can't do anything. But as they walk away again, Marissa feels bad and calls out that she knows Neville and, though he's old, he does occasionally fill in and she will try and get him to come in for the midnight shift. She tells them to come back at midnight. Allowing the troupe to hang out in the museum at night would help fulfill the qualifying test of giving Madison another great night in the closing weekend, feeding into a successful decisive test of a great "hanging out" experience *and* of giving Clarke a successful decisive test of a great send-off, achieving what would be a combined successful decisive test completed for Madison, the troupe, and Clarke. Justin also realizes if he can successfully pull this all off, combined with selling enough tickets to pay their bills, it can enhance his chances of moving in with Emily (his qualifying test of bonding with her) to set up his decisive test of moving back to New York.

The troupe goes back to the ball fields of Central Park to wait until midnight, and they have another ritualistic night of talking, chanting, dancing, etc., and have a great time, all part of the qualifying test to give Madison a real "hang out experience" and Clarke a great send-off. There are some odd unhoused people who come up to them and interact with the troupe, and one gets a little aggressive with Casey, but the troupe gets him to leave. They try and convince Clarke of his immortality based on their own old mythology, twisted science, etc., but he doesn't care about immortality. He's very stoic. As fun as the night is, they haven't yet had any experiences worthy of writing a new play about, which would be the ultimate score for Madison and her feeling like she had a great "hanging out" closing weekend (her decisive test), and Madison mentions this fact.

Midnight comes, and they all go back to the museum, and Neville has shown up but seems very sick. He's in a wheelchair with oxygen. But he remembers the troupe and embraces them and lets them into the museum. The troupe is in the empty museum at night and are very high from the gummies (and pot). They take their seats, and he shuts the lights off so that the room is illuminated merely by exit lights. Everything is in shadows. They see the ancient Egyptian coffins and are somewhat freaked out, but Clarke is stoic and calms them down. They sit in the middle of the room and hold hands and are silent. Madison begins to cry for Clarke, and Emily holds her hand. Emily holds Justin's hand, too, and he feels very connected to her again. Madison wants them to chant to help Clarke, but Justin can't bring himself to do it, it all seems too real. "Chanting to the void" has taken on too much meaning now that Clarke is really dying, and they sit there silently. Casey initiates a chant that she remembers about addressing the void of the universe, and they are reluctant to join in. But then Clarke joins in, and they all do, and eventually they all start to laugh. Neville watches it all. They move to leave, and Neville says a final goodbye to them given his days on earth are numbered as well.

They go back to the ball fields to fulfill another part of the ritual that they used to do years ago, which is to sit in the presence of the tall park trees and communicate with them because they believe trees are immortal and this ritual somehow will help ensure their own immortality. They were obviously young and very high a lot when the memoir was written, and Madison is going to make sure that they fulfill her dream of going through a ritual closing weekend with them (their decisive test) with each of the final evenings representing qualifying tests. Due to the power of the unregulated gummies, they start to hallucinate ghosts and get scared.

They return to the hotel in Ubers. Justin sits in the front of one, and Emily and Madison in the back, where they make out as Justin has to watch via the rearview mirror. They go to the hotel and learn that Madison has booked *another* room just for her and Emily, and

Justin is jealous but deals with it. He, Casey, and Clarke go into their room and hang out and talk. Justin is impressed that Clarke is incredibly stoic about death and doesn't believe in an afterlife, etc.

Later in the night, Justin gets a key from the front desk and sneaks into Madison and Emily's room, and it's dark and again watches in shadows what *might* be Emily and Madison fooling around under the blankets, but he's not sure. He slips back out again and goes into his room, but Clarke catches him coming in and Justin is crying and he is embarrassed. Justin and Clarke go to the roof and hang out and talk about their lives, about death, etc. Clarke is fearless; Justin is very impressed by Clarke's stoicism in the face of death. Clarke grills Justin about his feelings for Emily, which makes Justin fully realize that he's still in love with Emily. Justin finally admits it and asks Clarke if he thinks there is any hope of her returning his feelings, and Clarke tells him he doesn't know. Clarke tells him that he thinks Justin has been a great friend to him over the years. Meanwhile, back in Madison and Emily's room, Madison tells Emily that she is in love with her.

Later, Emily comes into Justin's room and claims that she can't sleep, and she and Justin go out and have a vape (smoke). Outside, they talk about new ideas for Emily's experimental play, and Justin helps her figure out how to finish it, and she is grateful. She seems to warm up a little bit to him, and perhaps his qualifying test to ingratiate himself to her again, enough so he can broach the idea of moving in with her (his decisive test), has succeeded. But he is obsessed with her "fling" with Madison, which she dismisses. He tries to take it to the next level and tells her that he still loves her and thinks about her all the time. She doesn't respond. He asks her if she's falling in love with Madison, and she smiles and doesn't respond. He asks her to recall the times that he and she would hang out on the beach in Staten Island and make love, talk, find inspiration, etc. Emily suggests that they go there right now, and she orders an Uber to take them there. On the car ride over, he talks to his wife on Zoom and gets an update about how the Borings told her that they are still willing to help him get a teaching job. He is silent. She hangs up on him.

Justin and Emily arrive at the Staten Island beach and walk around and reminisce a little bit. With the glow of the Verrazzano-Narrows Bridge in the background, Justin looks at the beautiful illuminated beach and remembers how he used to be brimming with creativity and ideas when, years ago, he and Emily would visit this very spot and brainstorm plays, make love, talk, laugh, sleep, etc. But now Justin realizes he has nothing left to say artistically. He's done creating theater. He's done being a playwright and a theater runner. He is completely bankrupt as a writer and artist. Though he has passed the qualifying test of ingratiating himself to Emily enough so that she'll consider letting him move back and support himself in NYC (his new decisive test), it's ironic because Justin no longer wants it anymore. He's decided to leave the theater and go back to Wisconsin, and he no longer needs to move in with Emily. He still must shut down the theater and give Clarke a send-off and oversee his assisted suicide. Emily now seems sad that he might not be moving in, but says she is determined to keep the theater going and will work with Madison to do so. Justin is convinced she is in love with her. Emily just smiles and doesn't respond, which annoys Justin. They go back to the hotel to sleep.

SUNDAY

Sunday arrives, and Madison hasn't sold the 60 extra tickets (the decisive test of the troupe being able to stay in the theater space), so the landlord wants them to start clearing out the space by Monday morning as their lease has expired. Emily wants to keep the theater going as her love for Madison has inspired her to do so. The Sunday matinee show only sold four tickets, and everyone is bummed out. For lunch, the troupe orders pizza per Clarke's request, and they eat and have fun and laugh and start figuring out what to throw out, etc. Clarke eats the pizza although he's not supposed to, and he gets sick but shrugs it off and doesn't want to get morose. He's incredibly stoic. The furniture store people show up and begin doing measurements. Justin gets angry and yells at them and throws them out and then feels bad and chases them outside and apologizes to them outside the theater. The troupe have been partying through the closing weekend and are exhausted and fall asleep on stage.

Meanwhile, an audio technician was called in to fix a digital tape "loop" that is used in the show and has not been working correctly. As she fixes it, it plays loudly on the stage speakers. The loop consists of voiceovers that are haunting and bleak, and as the troupe listens, the voices seem odd even to themselves who created the play. It is as if the troupe members are actually listening to themselves for the first time, hearing what they do theatrically and getting to experience who they are more objectively than ever before. Justin gets on another Zoom call with his wife, and she complains as she shows him a video of his son's science fair that he missed, and he complains that seeing it on Zoom is inadequate. She states that he doesn't seem committed to shutting down the theater, part of his original contract to do so he can go back to Wisconsin to earn a living, which would feed into a qualifying test of landing a teaching job and finally flow into a decisive test of earning/ maintaining a job for the family. This goal (contract) is brought back to the forefront of his mind. But first he has to close off the last show.

For the final Sunday night show, Madison hasn't sold *any* tickets, and it's Clarke's last show ever, and she feels bad. The troupe wants the final show to go on no matter what, but they feel bad it would be to an empty house. The troupe believes that you cannot stage a play without *any* audience at all. So Madison goes out on the streets and winds up bringing in two unhoused people to sit in the audience so that at least it's not an empty house for the final performance. They do the last run of *A Homeless Woman Dies in the Woods* to the two unhoused people as audience members. One unhoused man laughs at everything, almost manically so, but the unhoused woman has a negative reaction, which progresses as the play develops, and she finally violently charges the stage and starts choking Madison. The other troupe members have to fight her off and wind up destroying some of the stage set in the struggle. The final show is interrupted and then shut down before it can be completed. Madison is completely shaken up, and the unhoused people are escorted out by the police, whom Justin called to the scene. The theater is finished.

The troupe eat gummies and clean up and then Uber it to Central Park after the final Sunday night show, but Madison is visibly shaken up from the assault by the unhoused woman and starts texting her ex-fiancé hoping he'll respond. Emily is concerned that she's losing Madison and tries to talk to her as they approach the park, but Madison seems distant. Justin is distressed about how things went down but feels bad that Emily is obsessed with Madison. The troupe go to the park and traipse onto the ball fields but avoid any unhoused people who approach them. They sit around and prepare for Clarke's suicide. Clarke, who has been stoic all along, now feels some fear, and Justin tells him that he doesn't have to do it. He can go to the hospital, have more treatments, etc. Whatever he decides, they will be there for Clarke throughout the entire end process.

Clarke regains his composure and decides to take his "medicine" to commit suicide, and the troupe does a ritualistic chant as he drinks the lethal dose of medication, falls asleep, and dies. Casey calls the ambulance and reports the situation and the EMTs come as well as the police, and, after watching a video Clarke made to explain his assisted suicide, take away his body and exonerate his friends.

Madison decides that she's seen enough of the "theater life" and has effectively gotten it "out of her system" and will go to law school and reunite with her fiancé, and is leaving the troupe. Her fiancé comes and meets her right outside the park in a BMW, and Madison gets in his car to go away on vacation, and she says goodbye to Emily and is gone forever. Emily is heartbroken as she had fallen for Madison, which she finally admits to Justin. Justin had already figured out that he is creatively dead, and he and Emily cannot recapture what they had, so he decides to return home and take the substitute teaching job. The troupe has succeeded in the decisive test to give Madison a real "hanging out all night" experience and giving Clarke a great final send-off, but Justin has failed in finding meaning by way of continuing to be an inspired playwright/director with the troupe, which leads into him losing his desire to move in with Emily and stay in New York. He returns to his original contract of shutting down the theater (his qualifying test for his wife) and preparing to move back and be a substitute teacher so he can contribute to his family's income (his ultimate decisive test).

Justin sees that there is a late flight to Wisconsin that he can get on, and Emily and Casey agree to clean out the theater later. Casey goes home, and Emily says goodbye to Justin, whose Uber arrives to take him to the airport. Emily admits that she still loves Justin, but she cannot be with him because she wants to give her marriage a chance. She encourages him to do the same, to give his own marriage a chance, at least for his kids. They embrace, and he gets into his Uber. He cries on the way to the airport. This is his glorifying test.

Table 7.11 Comprehensive beat map*—*Through the Night* (demo)**

BEAT	BEAT TYPE	ACTANTIAL NARRATIVE SCHEMA	CANONICAL NARRATIVE SCHEMA
Justin and Sue have dinner with Tom and Jill Boring, who discuss their populist theater taste, which annoys Justin, who has been running a failing experimental theater in NYC. He's a total theater geek.	PRAGMATIC	Having dinner with the Borings is a sender to Justin the receiver, reminding him he's the subject with the object of maintaining more interesting social interactions with his real friends, his theater troupe in New York.	Sue has a contract initiated in that she wants to get Justin a job substitute teaching so he can contribute to the household income, and the Borings are a means to do so since they teach at the local elementary school. The qualifying test will be if Justin is able to make the deal with them to meet about teaching, and the decisive test will be if he can hold down the job.
Justin is bored by the Borings because they have such mainstream taste in theater and he can't relate to them at all although he tries.	PRAGMATIC	The dinner is a sender to Justin the receiver, making Justin the subject with object of longing for his New York theater friends. The Borings are opponents to Justin's plans to stay connected to New York.	Unbeknown to Justin, this is a mini-qualifying test to see if Justin can relate to the Borings and make friends with them because Sue, his wife, is desperate for friends and for them to take Justin seriously as a substitute teacher. Justin has an unknown *being able to do something* (played out in a qualifying test), which is to ingratiate himself to the Borings enough so they'll get him a teaching job. He fails it, at least from his own perspective in that he wants nothing to do with them or the job.
Sue expresses to the Borings that Justin is interested in substitute teaching which he at first denies then Sue glares angrily at him. The Borings light up because they are teachers in the local elementary school and can "get him in." Justin goes to deal with a fight in the den where the Boring's meathead son Carl has Justin's daughter into a headlock. When Justin tries to break it up, Carl headlocks him, and they crash into his bookshelves.	PRAGMATIC COGNITIVE	The fight that Justin breaks up (pulling the Boring's kid off his daughter) is a sender to Justin the receiver, making him the subject with the object of not pursuing a friendship with them again.	Justin is failing his qualifying test of landing a substitute teaching job through the Borings, setting up the decisive test, which would be he gets the job and holds it.

As the Borings are leaving, Justin tells them that the only reason they were invited over is Sue wants them to hook him up with a substitute teaching job.	PRAGMATIC COGNITIVE		Justin has failed his qualifying test in his wife Sue's eyes (trying to ingratiate himself to the couple so they'll get him a teaching job), which him holding would would be a decisive test.
Later in bed, Justin and Sue fight about him flying to New York this weekend (as he often does) as it's getting expensive. He proclaims that he is finally going to shut the theater down. **Master story beat/theme stated: Justin expresses that he is ready to shut down the theater.**	PRAGMATIC	Justin's responsibility to his family is a sender to Justin the receiver, making him the subject with the object of getting a job and shutting the New York theater. The prospect of a dull life living outside of New York is an opponent to Justin wanting to stay in Wisconsin.	Justin proclaims he's going to shut down the theater, a *being able to do something*, which is a qualifying test to fulfill his duties as a father, and become a producer for his family.
Emily works at a bookstore and is dealing with a customer who is seeking a Broadway coffee table book. Justin shows up from the flight, wheeling his luggage, and watches the cash register. A young female customer brings up a used copy of Justin and Emily's memoir *Theater in the Margins* and flirts with Emily. Justin realizes the theater (and his New York life) has some worth, and he decides he wants to come back to New York and live with Emily.	PRAGMATIC	The memoir *Theater in the Margins* is a sender to the young female customer (the receiver), making her a subject with the object of meeting Emily and flirting with her. It's also rich documenation of the troupe's earlier life together that will serve as a helper to Justin's object of moving back to New York.	

(Continued)

Table 7.11 *Continued*

BEAT	BEAT TYPE	ACTANTIAL NARRATIVE SCHEMA	CANONICAL NARRATIVE SCHEMA
Emily and Justin ride the subway to the theater, and they bond and laugh and have fun again. She tells him about a new play that she is writing and is stuck about, and he doesn't have any way to help her. He tells her that he's leaving Wisconsin and moving back to New York, hoping his wife and kids will follow him. He has decided to live there again, and he wants to move in with Emily to get established. Emily asks about Justin's daughter Emma (9), whom she has grown attached to, and gave her a microscope since Emma once expressed wanting to be doctor. Justin reveals that his wife Sue was freaked out by the expensive gift. ***Justin pushes back on Emily when she asks about a microscope that she got his daughter for Christmas, and Emily is hurt and withdraws.***	PRAGMATIC COGNITIVE	Justin's response about Sue feeling Emily "freaked out" by giving Emma such an expensive gift is a sender to Emily the receiver, making her come to terms with her place in Emma's life. Emily becomes a subject with the object of minding her own business and staying out of Emma's life (Justin's daughter), realizing she has to let it go. This hurts Emily very much and sets up a tense dynamic that will be maintained throughout much of story until the end. That Emily wants to be meaningful in Emma's life is an opponent to keeping Justin and Emily's friendship going and an opponent to Justin's plans to move back to New York.	Justin now has a new contract, which is that he wants to move in with Emily, and support himself and live with her. But he has a new qualifying test to get through, which is to reingratiate himself to Emily. Because he hurt her regarding his request that she back off with showering his daughter with gifts, she's colder and more aloof to Justin. He will execute a series of qualifying tests *being able to do something(s)* that will include getting Emily to trust him again during this weekend. This will set up a possible decisive test of him moving back in with Emily and proving he can support himself in New York.

They get to the theater and encounter the landlord, who has just shown the theater to a furniture store chain executive. It's clear that the landlord is giving the theater space to the store and Justin and his troupe must be out by Monday (it's Friday). Justin tells the landlord that he can still pay the bills, but the landlord doesn't believe him. Inside, Justin and Emily meet up with the rest of the troupe members, Casey, Clarke, and Madison, who are preparing the final performances of the current show *A Homeless Woman Dies in the Woods*, a play that Justin wrote. Justin prepares to tell the troupe that they lost their lease and this weekend's shows will be their final shows.	PRAGMATIC COGNITIVE	Losing their lease is a sender to Justin the receiver, who is a subject with the object of telling the troupe the theater is being shut down the following Monday. The landlord is an opponent to the troupe keeping their theater open.	Justin is grappling with his original qualifying test to shut the theater down to appease his wife and go back to Wisconsin and earn a living.
As Justin is telling Casey, Clarke, and Madison the theater is closing, Emily rushes into the room excited because they sold 40 tickets for tomorrow's show (Saturday), which can help pay the back rent they owe. It turns out the "new kid," Madison, sold the tickets to her network of NYU theater alumni and plans on selling a lot more for Sunday's two shows. ***The troupe is excited that Madison sold 40 tickets to Saturday's show.*** **Master beat/theme stated: Because of Madison selling tickets, the troupe is closer to keeping the theater open, which is at the heart of the troupe's long deep friendship and their ability to continually hang out together.**	PRAGMATIC	Madison's success selling tickets and her drive to sell more is a sender to Justin and Emily, the receivers, who are now subjects with the object of using Madison to sell enough to pay the back rent and save the theater. Madison's enthusiasm is a helper.	A new decisive test of whether the troupe can sell another 100 tickets for Sunday and pay their back rent owed is launched. In essence, each show and subsequent number of tickets sold is a qualifying test with a *being able to do something*, which is sell as many tickets as they can for each show and then sell 100 tickets for the Sunday night show (the decisive test to keep the theater open).

(Continued)

Table 7.11 *Continued*

BEAT	BEAT TYPE	ACTANTIAL NARRATIVE SCHEMA	CANONICAL NARRATIVE SCHEMA
As they plan to go home for the evening, Madison announces that she thought they were going to hang out all night the way they do every night of a closing weekend according to the memoir that Justin and Emily wrote that documents the troupe's early days (30 years ago). They wrote that on closing weekends they'd stay out all night in the city and encounter all kinds of people and have strange experiences. Some of these encounters would become the basis of their original plays. It is all outlined in the memoir that Justin and Emily published.	PRAGMATIC	The memoir is a sender to Madison the receiver, making her the subject with the object of experiencing hanging out all night on a closing weekend with her theater troupe. Conversely, Madison's desire to hang out all night is a sender to the troupe as receivers, who are subjects with the object of giving Madison a great "hang out" weekend. The age of the troupe's members is an opponent to the plan to stay out all night, but Madison's enthusiasm is a helper.	Madison is setting up hanging out all night with theater troupe as a qualifying test to see if they can give her a part of the complete closing weekend experience of adventure as promised in their memoir (the decisive test), and this first night qualifying test entails a *being able to do something,* which is give Madison a fun hanging out first night of the closing weekend.
Justin and Emily have a mini-conference about Madison and her desire to hang out all night. They wish to appease her and follow through on this to keep her motivated to sell tickets Saturday and Sunday morning since Madison seems hell-bent on having these adventures.	COGNITIVE	Madison's desire to hang out all night is a sender to Justin and Emily, making them the subjects with the objects of appeasing her so that she will keep selling tickets and maybe they will retain a slight chance of the theater staying in business. Again, their age is an opponent because they are too tired to want to hang out all night.	Same as above.

Justin convinces the troupe to hang out all night with Madison while Madison is in the bathroom getting changed. When she returns, they announce their plans to hang out all night to Madison, who is exhilarated.		Justin's enthusiasm to keep selling tickets is a reason to give Madison a sender to the troupe as receivers making them the subjects with the object of appeasing Madison.	The first qualifying test of staying out the first night of the closing weekend is in play. The decisive test will be the group hanging out all night for the entire weekend for Madison.
Madison rented a hotel for them all to crash, which is a luxury. The troupe walks to it, Madison banters with Emily, and there's sexual chemistry between them. It seems as though Emily is trying to seduce Madison so that she'll keep selling tickets. Justin trails behind with Casey and Clarke and tells them *his* plans to buy wine and get Madison drunk so she'll just pass out in the hotel room.	PRAGMATIC	Emily's desire to keep Madison engaged in selling tickets is a sender to herself the receiver, and she is a subject with the object of seducing Madison. Emily's attractiveness and Madison's fascination with her is a helper.	This is a mini-qualifying test of Emily's to see if she can seduce Madison to keep her on the stick about selling tickets.
Watching Emily and Madison "hit it off" makes Justin jealous because he still likes Emily. Justin, Clarke, and Casey trail Emily and Madison, and ***Justin is saddened because Emily has really grown apart from him and was his best friend.***	PRAGMATIC	Emily and Madison becoming romantically involved is a sender to Justin the receiver, making him the subject with the object of figuring out a way of impressing Emily and winning her back.	Madison's enthusiasm to hang out all night sets up a mini-qualifying test to see if the troupe can get her drunk so she falls asleep and forgets about hanging out.
Justin and Clarke talk about Clarke deciding *not to* retire from the post office as they had discussed. Justin is mad because he spent a lot of time with Clarke on the decision.	PRAGMATIC		
Sue calls Justin's cell. Justin drops behind the group and talks to Sue. She is opposed to him crashing in Madison's hotel room, and Justin tells her the plan to get Madison drunk and put her to sleep, a plan Sue dislikes even more.	PRAGMATIC		

(Continued)

Table 7.11 *Continued*

BEAT	BEAT TYPE	ACTANTIAL NARRATIVE SCHEMA	CANONICAL NARRATIVE SCHEMA
En route to the hotel, Madison gives money to an unhoused man and wants to hear his story, but the wad of bills she pulls out attracts other unhoused people, who start following the troupe but then fall away and are gone.	PRAGMATIC	Madison's desire to have the hanging out all-night adventure is a sender to her the receiver as she tries to pry out of the unhoused man something interesting to write a play about. She becomes the subject with the object of prying a story out of the unhoused man.	The qualifying test of fulfilling Madison's hanging out adventure experience develops with her talking to the unhoused man and trying to pull him into the experience of hanging out all night.
In the hotel room, the troupe members sit around and drink wine, then Madison goes to the bathroom to talk privately to her fiancé on her cell phone.	PRAGMATIC		
Madison, returning to the group, cries about feeling like her engagement is off since her fiancé just broke up with her because she is not upholding her end of the pact that they made, which involved her going to law school and him going to medical school. Justin responds by pouring her wine to drown her sorrows, wanting to get her drunk so she'll fall asleep and not want to hang out all night. **Master story beat/theme stated: Madison has a broken engagement and is sad and now really needs the bonding with the group.**	PRAGMATIC THYMIC	Justin's desire to get Madison drunk is a sender to Madison the receiver, making him the subject with the object of putting her to sleep so the troupe doesn't have to go out all night. Madison's ability to absorb drugs and alcohol is an opponent.	The desire to give Madison the full experience of hanging out all night with the theater troupe is enhanced now by her being sad that her fiancé dumped her. The qualifying test, which will encompass hanging out this Saturday night in Central Park, now has more meaning for all involved given this news.

Madison goes to take a shower to alleviate her suffering, and the troupe decides they must appease her and follow through on hanging out because now they feel bad for her. **Madison is exhilarated they are going to Central Park.** Justin calls his wife, and she protests his plan to hang out all night and crash in Madison's hotel room to appease Madison, with the supposedly new reason that Madison is sad because she's heartbroken. Sue thinks he is just trying to save the theater. She asks him to promise to Zoom in to their son's science fair the next morning. He hesitates, and before he can answer, she hangs up.	PRAGMATIC	Madison's sadness that her fiancé dumped her is a sender to Justin and Emily as receivers to now really show her a good time not only so she'll sell tickets but because they care about her and she's now "one of theirs" . . . she is "family."	Justin, Emily, Clarke, and Casey now have a "pact" and contract to really show Madison a good time. The qualifying test will be the first night out, including enduring the effects of the marijuana gummy bears. The decisive test will be if Madison has a satisfying hanging out all night for the entire weekend experience with the troupe. During the phone call, Sue reminds Justin of his original contract, to shut the theater (his original qualifying test) and come back and get a teaching job (decisive test).
The troupe gets high and eats gummies that Madison supplies. They take two Ubers and meet up in Central Park and begin walking in via the 59th Street entrance. Madison rides with Justin and Emily, and Madison talks of how when the troupe used to hang out and chant to the void of the universe. Madison thinks they will be doing this sort of thing again. Madison references Justin and Emily's past romantic relationship, as per the memoir, while Madison is endearing herself to Emily romantically herself.	PRAGMATIC	Madison's youthful enthusiasm and beauty is a sender to Emily the receiver, making her a subject with the object of pursuing Madison romantically.	The qualifying test of giving Madison a fun adventure in Central Park at night has officially moved outside, a marker that it has begun. Emily has taken on a new qualifying test of making Madison fall in love with her so that Madison will perhaps become Emily's new long-term romantic partner although Emily pretends that she is just trying to cajole Madison into remaining enthusiastic about selling more tickets (decisive test). This puts strain on Justin's qualifying test to be able to endear himself to Emily so she'll let him move in with her and restart his New York life (decisive test).

(Continued)

Table 7.11 *Continued*

BEAT	BEAT TYPE	ACTANTIAL NARRATIVE SCHEMA	CANONICAL NARRATIVE SCHEMA
They go into the park and encounter odd people who are just hanging out and don't want to talk. Madison tries to talk to them and draw them out, but they are just weird.	PRAGMATIC	The random people that the troupe met going into Central Park are not interested in participating in Madison's adventure. They are opponents to her object of having the full "hanging out" adventure.	The qualifying test of giving Madison a fun adventure in Central Park at night has officially moved outside, a marker that it has begun.
They get to the reservoir and walk around it and are excited. Madison talks to everybody and anybody who will talk to her, but they have no interest in talking to her.	PRAGMATIC	The random people that the troupe met going into Central Park are not interested in participating in Madison's adventure. They are opponents to her object of having the full "hanging out" adventure.	The qualifying test of giving Madison a "hang out experience" is in play. We may begin to sense that the decisive test to it all will be whether the hang out weekend turns into viable material for a new play or not.
They get to a rocky area and Madison stops and says that according to the theater's memoir this is where something magical happened. It involves some sort of chant that is written in the memoir but no one knows what it is. Madison seems disappointed and suddenly Casey recites the chant (and knows it well to everyone's surprise), and it's a chant to the empty universe. The rest of the troupe fumbles with it but chimes in and Madison joins in and is happy. **Master story beat/theme stated: Casey is very connected to the memoir and the troupe's past and helps the rest of the troupe feel connected again with hopes of saving the troupe.**	PRAGMATIC COGNITIVE	Madison's desire to have the full adventurous hanging out all night experience on the closing weekend is a sender to herself the receiver and is failing. She is becoming disappointed in the group's inability to play along and beginning to realize she is a fool. Casey has become the receiver to Madison's desire to have the complete hanging out adventure, so Casey has become the subject with the object of picking up the slack of showing Madison a good time. Casey's memory is a helper.	The first qualifying test of giving Madison a satisfying hanging out all night experience is failing because no one remembers the chant. The first qualifying test (a first great hang out night) that would feed into an overall decisive test of a great closing weekend "hang out experience" is now succeeding in that Casey picks up the ball and is able to play along with Madison in a way that satisfies her.

The troupe members get to the Central Park ball fields and sit on the grass in a circle. Madison pulls out pot, and they start smoking and getting really stoned and really talking.	PRAGMATIC COGNITIVE	The troupe's shared interactions is a sender to the troupe as receiver, helping them to feel bonded and they become a subject with an object of restoring their glory days of unity and comradery. Their age and attendant cynicism are opponents.	The qualifying test of Madison's first adventure hanging out all night is in play.
According to the memoir, the troupe members are supposed to play bongo drums to help them in their ritualistic chant. So Casey plays bongo "apps" on her iPhone, and others join in with iPhone instruments. They start chanting to the universe and specifically the trees to embrace these elements as part of the ebb and flow of life and death.	PRAGMATIC COGNITIVE	Casey is a helper to the object of giving Madison a great "hanging out experience".	" . . "
Madison says that now she's not scared to forsake law school and is prepared to live a life of the theater. Emily says that she's leaving her wife. Justin says that he's not going back to Wisconsin; he's going to stay and build a life in New York and call for his wife and kids. Casey states meekly that she's getting another cat.	PRAGMATIC COGNITIVE	" . . "	" . . "

(Continued)

Table 7.11 *Continued*

BEAT	BEAT TYPE	ACTANTIAL NARRATIVE SCHEMA	CANONICAL NARRATIVE SCHEMA
Clarke tells the group that he's terminally ill and dying of cancer. They are freaked out. But Clarke isn't . . . he accepts it as nature taking its course. The rest of the group is crying and freaked out by Clarke's announcement that he is dying, and Clarke is almost puzzled. He's incredibly stoic and completely unafraid. ***The rest of the group cries with Clarke when they find out he has cancer, but he is not sad.*** Clarke informs the group that he wants them to assist him in commiting suicide. **Master story beat/theme stated: Clarke announcing his terminal illness and his wish to commit assisted suicide with the troupe in the park on Sunday night gives the hanging out aspects of their nights greater importance, depth, and meaning, making them more inclined to want to stay together.**	PRAGMATIC COGNITIVE THYMIC	Clarke's announcement that he's terminally ill and dying is a sender to the rest of the troupe as receiver, making them the subjects with the object of ensuring Clarke has a good final weekend. But the seriousness of Clarke's condition is an opponent to this object in the minds of the rest of the troupe. Clarke stating that he wants to commit suicide with the group in the park on Sunday night is a sender to the rest of the troupe as receiver, making them subjects with the object of giving him his wish, assisting in his suicide and giving him a great send-off.	A new contract is initiated in that these troupe members now have a want/need/ desire to give Clarke a great send-off and aid in his suicide. This dovetails with the qualifying test to give Madison a fun night out (and an ultimate closing weekend, their decisive test).

Back at the hotel, all get into beds. Emily and Madison get into one of the two beds. Clarke takes the other bed. Justin gets the cot, and Casey sleeps on the floor on pillows. *Madison relates how she's afraid of not going to law school and failing in life and how she feels like her fiancé isn't coming back.* Justin talks to Sue in the bathroom privately and tells her about Clarke, but she doesn't care. She's done with Justin and his troupe and hangs up.	PRAGMATIC		Justin still has his own qualifying test with Emily to see if he can reingratiate himself to her so she'll let him move back with her so he can restart his New York (a decisive test) life, but it's not going well. She's still mad he pushed back on her giving his daughter too expensive a gift. He is also miserably failing to execute his initial contract of come to New York, shut down the theater, and go back home to his family and get a job.
It's the middle of the night, and in the dark room, Justin can make out that Emily and Madison are making love under the covers.	PRAGMATIC	Justin getting a glimpse in shadows of Emily and Madison being intimate is a sender to him the receiver, making him the subject with the object of Emily, longing for her even more. Madison's youthful beauty is an opponent to Justin reconnecting romantically to Emily.	
Later, Justin is looking at Clarke asleep in his bed, stares at him, and covers his feet. Emily is also up.	PRAGMATIC		
Justin and Emily hang out outside, and she smokes her electronic cigarette, and they talk about how they are going to proceed with carrying out Clarke's desire to commit assisted suicide. She seems guarded with Justin since he hurt her by pushing back on her giving his daughter gifts.	PRAGMATIC	Justin's appeal to their deep long-standing friendship is a sender to Emily the receiver, making her the subject with the object of wanting to now reconnect to Justin more. Her anger with him for pushing back on her gift-giving to Emma (his daughter) is an opponent as is her marriage.	Justin's qualifying test to see if he can get Emily to warm up to him again is in play as he wants to move in with her and restart a New York life (decisive test).

(Continued)

Table 7.11 *Continued*

BEAT	BEAT TYPE	ACTANTIAL NARRATIVE SCHEMA	CANONICAL NARRATIVE SCHEMA
Justin then probes Emily about their own relationship and if she still has any feelings for him. She thinks he's nuts given that he's married with kids; she's married too.	PRAGMATIC COGNITIVE THYMIC		Justin's qualifying test to see if he can get Emily to warm up to him again is in play as he wants to move in with her and restart a New York life (decisive test).
Justin queries Emily about how she would feel if he moved back. She doesn't have a response. Justin asks Emily if she's "falling" for Madison; she denies it. Emily "breaks" down because she feels she has failed in life, and Justin comforts her.	COGNITIVE THYMIC	Justin's feelings for Emily is a sender to himself the receiver, making him the subject with the object of convincing Emily to get over her grievances about him and ultimately let him move in with her and share expenses. Her deep (hidden) love for him is a helper.	The qualifying test of whether Justin can figure out how to build a new life in New York is in play (decisive test), and he has a *being able to do something*, which is figure out how to convince Emily to let him stay with her even though she barely wants to talk to him at this point.
SATURDAY The next day, the group has breakfast together. Clarke seems very upbeat and positive, and the rest of the troupe is suspicious of his positive attitude towards dying. They suspect he is in complete denial and has had a psychotic break.	PRAGMATIC COGNITIVE		
They perform Saturday's show to 40 people in attendance, which is a big crowd for this troupe, and the audience has a great response which causes them all to get emotional.	THYMIC		

The troupe all take THC gummies again but from another source that Madison never tried before. The night goes on, and Madison wants to go to Central Park to hang out but this time try and get into The Metropolitan Museum of Art through a side door as the troupe did years ago aided by a night guard named Neville, who let them in and allowed them sit in the dark with the Egyptian sarcophaguses to "scare themselves" and laugh in the face of death and the "void." This kind of experience was often the subject of their experimental theater shows.	PRAGMATIC	Madison's desire to hang out in the museum after it closes is a sender to the rest of the troupe as receiver, making them the subjects with the object of appeasing her. Clarke has the desire as well but for different reasons (he has a different object).	A new mini-qualifying test is in play, which is whether they will be able to get into the museum at night and have a quiet meditation session in the dark. The *being able to do something* is to convince the guard to help them. This all feeds into the decisive test to give Madison and Clarke a great "hang out" closing weekend.
They start tripping out on the gummies and go to the side door of the museum and the old guard is not there; it's young female guard Marissa, who is not amused by them. Emily and Justin tell her about the situation with Clarke; she is unmoved. They walk away disappointed.	PRAGMATIC	" . . . "	The troupe is failing the qualifying test of getting into the museum at night that Madison and now Clarke want in an effort to match the earlier experiences of hanging out all night documented in the troupe memoir.
Marissa calls them back and says she knows the old guard Neville, who fills in from time to time, and will call him and try to get him for the midnight shift. She tells the troupe to return at midnight.	PRAGMATIC	Casey was a receiver to the sender of Madison and Clarke wanting to get into the museum at night and Casey is also a sender to Marissa.	Casey alone has helped the troupe pass the qualifying test of getting them into the museum, setting up for the decisive test of showing Madison a good time hanging out and giving Clarke a great final send-off closing weekend. The *being able to do something* involves convincing Marissa to let them in.

(Continued)

Table 7.11 *Continued*

BEAT	BEAT TYPE	ACTANTIAL NARRATIVE SCHEMA	CANONICAL NARRATIVE SCHEMA
The troupe members go to the ball fields to hang out again, take out the bongo apps and app flutes, and have another ritualistic meeting in the presence of the trees because they used to believe that the trees "perceived them," at least according to their memoir. Some odd unhoused people approach them, and one gets aggressive with Casey, but the other troupe members are able to get him to back off. **The group has a session of chanting and meditation and are seemingly unable to convince Clarke of his immortality as he doesn't care.** The troupe haven't yet had any experiences of "hanging out through the night" that constitute grounds to write a new play about.	PRAGMATIC	The unhoused people, one of whom gets aggressive with the troupe, is an opponent to the troupe's desire to hang out all night. The troupe's determination though is a helper.	The dual decisive test of providing Madison with a great hanging out weekend and giving Clarke a great send-off is in play, which will be built towards by performing in the qualifying tests of each individual night of the closing weekend leading up to the final night of hanging out, Sunday night.
The troupe members go to the side door of the museum and meet Neville, the museum guard from the past, who proceeds to let them inside the museum. He is very old and seemingly on his last leg. He has an oxygen tank and is dying of a terminal illness, too. But he came to the museum via Marissa's prompting to help them out.	PRAGMATIC		

They tell Neville what they are doing, and he's okay with it. He sees Clarke and the condition he is in and instinctively hugs him.	PRAGMATIC COGNITIVE	The qualifying test is in play along with a *being able to do something*, which involves whether they accomplish having a great night in the museum, feeding into the decisive test of giving Clarke a great send-off weekend and Madison a fulfilling closing "hanging out all night" weekend experience.
They go into the Egyptian sarcophagus room, and the guard turns the lights out. Neville participates in the ritual and gets very emotional in contrast to Clarke staying stoic.	PRAGMATIC	
Justin and Madison hold Emily's hands. Madison wants to chant but can't do it because she's self conscious about Clarke and his condition. **Master story beat/theme stated: Emily is in love with Madison, and Justin is in love with Emily, and they quietly hold hands together trying to help set up Clarke for death.** Justin can't bring himself to administer the final chant to the void; it's taken on too much *real* meaning as Clarke is really dying. Justin is emotional over Clarke, and Casey steps in and knows the chant by heart and proceeds to continue uttering it for the ritual.	COGNITIVE THYMIC	Justin's failure to recite the chant is a sender to Casey the receiver, who is the subject with the object of carrying on the tradition of the troupe for Madison's and Clarke's sake. Her memory is a helper.
Clarke seems completely fearless in the face of impending death. A tear rolls down Madison's face. Neville says goodbye to the group and walks away. Due to the power of the gummies, the troupe members start to hallucinate visions of ghosts. They get scared, but then Marissa comes back and turns the lights on, which snaps them out of it. She promptly escorts them out of the museum.	THYMIC	

(Continued)

Table 7.11 *Continued*

BEAT	BEAT TYPE	ACTANTIAL NARRATIVE SCHEMA	CANONICAL NARRATIVE SCHEMA
The troupe goes back to the hotel in Ubers; Madison and Emily in the back of one with Justin in the front. He watches them make out and is jealous.	THYMIC		
Back at the hotel, the troupe learns that Madison reveals that she got a second room, and Emily goes with her to sleep with her there. Justin, Clarke, and Casey hang out, talk about life and Clarke's condition, and remark about how he is so stoic.	PRAGMATIC	Their sleeplessness is a sender to them as receivers making them the subjects with the object of going out and finding something to do.	There is a new contract emerging; namely, will Justin and Emily, who were once lovers and still have feelings for each other, be able to figure out how to make their relationship "fit" with everything else that is going on. The qualifying test of Justin *being able to do something* and endear himself to Emily again is taking somewhat of a romantic urgency.
Later, Justin gets a key from the front desk and sneaks into Madison's room. Emily and Madison are asleep in each other's arms. He leaves embarrassed.			

	COGNITIVE THYMIC		
Justin comes back into the room crying because he's jealous but feels self-conscious and petty about it when he runs into Clarke. Justin and Clarke go outside on the hotel roof-deck and sit and talk. Clarke seems completely resigned to death and dying and has dealt with non-existence and the void. That's why he kept working. He didn't want anything to change. Clarke is completely okay with it. Justin is upset but tries to acts stoic. **Master story beat/theme stated: Justin has an intense moment of bonding and friendship with Clarke. He realizes he's losing his friend and recognizes the power of the depth of their friendship, and, due to Clark's stoicism, feels both fearless and yet powerless.**			
	PRAGMATIC		
Madison tells Emily that she is in love with her. Later, Emily sneaks into Justin's room and says she can't sleep and suggests they go outside for a smoke (vape). Outside, Justin and Emily talk about new ideas for Emily's experimental play that she is struggling with, and he figures out a way that she can finish it and she is grateful. She is warming up again to him. Emily asks him if he has gotten any ideas for writing a new play based on the weekend, especially given Clarke's impending suicide. She suggests they go somewhere for inspiration. This is a sign that perhaps she is reconsidering being in a relationship with him or at least considering allowing him to move in.			

(Continued)

Table 7.11 *Continued*

BEAT	BEAT TYPE	ACTANTIAL NARRATIVE SCHEMA	CANONICAL NARRATIVE SCHEMA
Emily orders an Uber, and she and Justin get in and travel to South Beach. En route, Sue Zooms Justin to tell him that the Borings are still willing to get him a substitute teaching job. They arrive at South Beach, Staten Island, get out of the Uber, and walk around and reminisce.		Sue's haranguing Justin is an opponent to his desire to stay in New York and restart his life there.	Justin had forgotten about his original contract of getting a job back in Wisconsin, especially the qualifying test of closing his theater and ingratiating himself to the Borings so they'll deliver his decisive test (a viable teaching job), and this all comes to the forefront of his psyche again.
Justin now realizes that he has nothing left to say and gets very emotional about it. They take the Uber back to the hotel to go to sleep. Emily announces to Justin that she will keep the theater going anyway with Madison. **Master story beat/theme stated: Justin has been hiding from himself the fact that his artistic life has been running dry, and now he's come face-to-face with the reality that he has nothing left to say.**	COGNITIVE THYMIC	The atmosphere of the beach at night is a sender to Justin the receiver, making him a subject with the object of shutting the theater since realizing he has to grow up and has nothing left to say anymore. This becomes an anti-subject to his desire to stay in New York and restart his theater life there.	Going to the beach late at night used to serve as a source of inspiration. Returning to it now can serve as a mini-qualifying test to see if it still inspires them, but it doesn't. It merely reminds Justin he has nothing left to say. Though Emily finally seems responsive to him and expresses openness to perhaps him moving in with her to restart his New York life, he doesn't have the will for it anymore.

SUNDAY Sunday's matinee is a disappointment. They haven't sold the 60 tickets for the two Sunday shows. In fact, they've sold only four tickets for the matinee and zero for the last one. It's not looking good in terms of having enough ticket revenue to pay their back rent. They are starting to come to terms with having to dissolve the theater and move out Monday morning. Madison cries as she feels that she has failed. **Master story beat/theme stated: Madison has failed to save the theater and has remorse and doesn't like the pain of the theater life.**	THYMIC	Failure to sell enough tickets to pay their bills is an opponent to the cause of keeping the theater open, and even though Justin is resigned to closing it, Emily still has the object of wanting to keep it going. Her love of Madison is now a helper to this cause.	The decisive test to save the theater has failed (they only sold two tickets for the final show).
Backstage before Sunday evening's show, Madison has ordered in pizza for everybody, and they eat and have fun and laugh. They realize it's Clarke's last meal. He eats the pizza even though he's not supposed to, and he gets sick and throws up but then sloughs it off and is not going to get depressed. He is unbelievably stoic.	PRAGMATIC COGNITIVE	Clarke's stoicism is a sender to the rest of the troupe as receiver to not be so afraid of death, making them a subject with the object of optimism to get him through his final day.	
The furniture store executives come to do more measurements, and Justin gets into an argument with them, gets mad, and throws them out. He then feels bad and goes after them to apologize.	PRAGMATIC	The presence of the furniture store executives is a sender to Justin the receiver, making him the subject with the object of protecting his theater.	The qualifying test to sell enough tickets to save the theater has failed.

(Continued)

Table 7.11 *Continued*

BEAT	BEAT TYPE	ACTANTIAL NARRATIVE SCHEMA	CANONICAL NARRATIVE SCHEMA
The troupe members have been partying and staying up so much that they sleep on stage in between Sunday's matinee and the Sunday night show.	PRAGMATIC		
As they sleep, an audio technician comes in to fix the audio loop of the voices that is playback during the show, causing an odd sounding looping to go on . . . that eventually wakes everybody up. The audio loop seems odd even to the troupe and causes them to reflect.	PRAGMATIC	The audio loop of the vocal playback becomes a sender to the troupe members as receivers, making them the subject with the object of moving on from the theater they built.	
Sue Zooms Justin, rants at him for missing their son's science fair via Zoom, and shows him a video clip of it. She's mad that he made no attempt and it seems like he's not shutting the theater and hangs up on him.	PRAGMATIC	Madison now is a helper to the object of giving Clarke a final good performance and at least have some audience.	Justin's original master qualifying test to shut the theater (to set him up for his decisive test of going back to Wisconsin and providing for his family there) is in play.
Madison goes out and finds an unhoused man and woman and offers them food and booze if they come to see the show so the troupe does not have to perform their last show ever without any audience.	PRAGMATIC		

The show, which involves Madison ranting as an unhoused woman dying in the woods, having delusions, and hearing voices, causes Madison to become self-conscious because there are real unhoused people in the audience.	COGNITIVE		
The unhoused man watches the final performance of *A Homeless Woman Dies in the Woods* and laughs incongruously at the show, apparently not getting the tragic seriousness of it.	PRAGMATIC COGNITIVE		
The unhoused woman watching the show starts to rant back at the show, behavior which starts to get disruptive and interferes with the play.	PRAGMATIC	The unhoused man and woman's "reactions" to the troupe's final performance is a sender to the troupe as receiver, making the troupe the subject with the object of just getting through their final show. The unhoused man and woman are also opponents to the troupe's desire to keep the theater alive.	There is a mini-qualifying test of having their last performance be meaningful with an audience, which entails a *being able to do something*, to "play through" the rants and reactions of the unhoused man and woman who have been recruited to be the audience.
The unhoused woman's ranting is odd in that she seems almost triggered by the play. Eventually the woman marches on stage and starts having a fight with Madison, which shuts the whole show down. The woman angrily tears up the set. It is bedlam, and the oddly powerful unhoused woman almost kills Madison. **Master story beat/theme stated: It's a scary moment for Madison as the unhoused woman has a lot of strength and power and almost kills Madison.**	PRAGMATIC COGNITIVE THYMIC	The final performance of the play is a sender to the unhoused woman the receiver, who for some reason has a violent reaction to the play, and she's the subject with the object of killing Madison, an action which is halted after the woman engages in a struggle with the troupe.	The troupe has failed the qualifying test of having the theater deliver a compete final performance, which undermines the group's desire to properly execute the decisive test of providing Madison and Clarke with a great final night of a "hanging out" send-off.

(Continued)

Table 7.11 Continued

BEAT	BEAT TYPE	ACTANTIAL NARRATIVE SCHEMA	CANONICAL NARRATIVE SCHEMA
The troupe gathers outside, and Clarke says he's ready for his final night and has his medicine for his assisted suicide all ready. The group eats gummies supplied by Madison.	PRAGMATIC		The decisive test of giving Clarke a good send-off is in play. Also, the decisive test of trying to hand off the theater to Madison, who originally said she was determined to carry on the tradition in a new location, has failed given her heart is no longer in being a troupe member.
The group gets Ubers to Central Park.	PRAGMATIC		
Justin rides with Emily and Madison in the back seat. Madison is visibly shaken by the attack from the unhoused woman and starts texting her ex-fiancé.	THYMIC		
The group goes to the ball fields and prepares for Clarke's suicide. Clarke, who has been stoic all along, feels some fear, and Justin says he'll stay in the hospital with Clarke if he wants to continue treatment. Either way, they are there for him. Clarke decides to go through with the assisted suicide.	PRAGMATIC COGNITIVE	Clarke's impending death makes his "soul" a sender to the void of the universe, which is the receiver making the universe the subject with the object of quietly, painlessly snuffing him out.	A glorifying test (in terms of Clarke's suicide) is the cold meaningless universe overseeing Clarke's death remains unmoved yet in this action Clarke remains stoic in the face of his own end.
Clarke takes the medicine and dies. The surviving members call the ambulance and the police, and the troupe shows the police a video Clarke had made explaining what he did. **Master story beat/theme stated: Clarke has bravely met his end and the troupe could not save him. They realize this.**	COGNITIVE	Clarke's death is a sender to the troupe as receivers, making them the subjects with the objects of wanting to move on from their theater.	

(Continued)

Madison is "breaking up" with Emily, who gets very emotional. Justin is trying not to listen but can't help it. Madison announces that she's going to law school and marrying her fiancé. He comes and takes Madison away. **Master story beat/theme stated: Emily met her fate due to her falling for a much younger woman.**	COGNITIVE THYMIC		Emily's decisive test of keeping Madison in a relationship has failed.
The next morning, Justin, Emily, and Casey clean out the theater. Casey leaves, and Justin has to get an Uber to the airport. Emily proclaims she'll finish cleaning the theater. Right before Justin's Uber arrives, Emily says goodbye to Justin and admits that she still loves him and he could move in with her. He states it's too late and they should both give their marriages a chance, in his case at least for the kids. **Master beat/theme stated: Justin now spends what he knows will be his last moments with Emily since he's going to return home and not come back to New York.**	PRAGMATIC COGNITIVE THYMIC	The combined events including failing to save the theater, Clarke's death, and Madison dumping Emily, act as a sender to Justin and Emily, the receivers, making them subjects with the object of wanting to move on to new lives. For Justin, this means to return home and make his life with his family work.	Justin's qualifying test of connecting to Emily enough so she will let him try moving in with her (decisive test) has failed.

Table 7.11 *Continued*

BEAT	BEAT TYPE	ACTANTIAL NARRATIVE SCHEMA	CANONICAL NARRATIVE SCHEMA
The Uber pulls up, Emily and Justin embrace, Justin gets in and goes to the airport.			The glorifying test (which is still connected to the glorying test of Clarke dying stoically in the face of the cold meaningless universe) manifests here in that Justin still feels a lot of emotion for Emily as he departs. She feels it as well.

* Guesstimating timecode is speculative and not necessary when writing an original script, especially in the planning stage as here. But you can add approximate timecode if you like with the knowledge that a minute of screen time adds up to about one page (if the page is correctly formatted, etc.).

** There will be some instances of the states of being that were originally developed via brainstorming here just so you can see how they might function in a speculative work. But because this is a speculative original story, I limited how many I used and opted for using more straight-ahead language in the beat map and in the master story beats to focus you on how to use all these tools when developing an original work.

Master Story Beats/Themes Stated Plotted on Master Semiotic Square For Demo Script *Through the Night*[2]

Now, using the master semiotic square, I'll brainstorm master story beats and transformation based on the *values* the story has.[3] Once again, these master story beats will be very simple. I won't be stating themes in a traditional literary fashion. Nevertheless, it's important to recognize that these master story beats will feel like a theme is in play whenever they arise in a movie, especially when they represent your subjects moving towards or away from their primary objects as determined by the controlling binary opposition terms (lonely/connected in this case) of the story's master semiotic square.

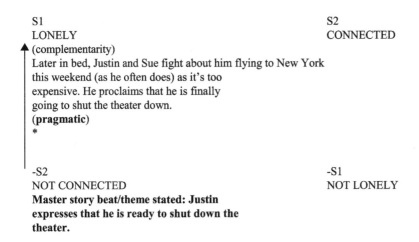

S1
LONELY
(complementarity)
Later in bed, Justin and Sue fight about him flying to New York this weekend (as he often does) as it's too expensive. He proclaims that he is finally going to shut the theater down.
(**pragmatic**)
*

S2
CONNECTED

-S2
NOT CONNECTED
Master story beat/theme stated: Justin expresses that he is ready to shut down the theater.

-S1
NOT LONELY

This sets up the foundation of the loneliness that Justin is going to experience because in one fell swoop he would have to cut off from New York and his theater friends forever and do a job he hates and live in a place he hates. The movement goes from **not connected**, which he feels in his marriage, to specifically feeling **lonely** about having to close the theater and lose his friends there as well.

* When creating master beats for an original script, timecode will be conspicuously omitted since it's all speculative at this point, and there's not much benefit guestimating how much time each beat will use.

Figure 7.4 Master story beat/theme stated 1—*Through the Night* (demo).

---

[2] I tend to skip over the master story beat/themes stated "cheat sheet" because I believe that tool is derived from an existing movie we're studying and breaking down, not an original work. That said, feel free to create one just to get a feeling for how the collection of what you deem as your master story beats adds up.
[3] If you find that brainstorming transformations off the master semiotic square forces you to rethink master story beats/themes stated, the comprehensive beat map, or any part of the components of the story, go back and tweak the related documents to reflect what this part of the process has revealed to you. (You will find that just executing this part of the breakdown will inform your scene writing as it will give you a handle on theme, tone, transformations, values, etc.)

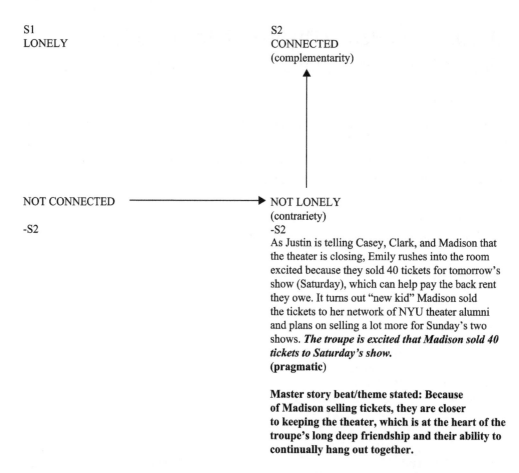

S1
LONELY

S2
CONNECTED
(complementarity)

NOT CONNECTED ⟶ NOT LONELY
(contrariety)

-S2

-S2

As Justin is telling Casey, Clark, and Madison that
the theater is closing, Emily rushes into the room
excited because they sold 40 tickets for tomorrow's
show (Saturday), which can help pay the back rent
they owe. It turns out "new kid" Madison sold
the tickets to her network of NYU theater alumni
and plans on selling a lot more for Sunday's two
shows. *The troupe is excited that Madison sold 40
tickets to Saturday's show.*
(pragmatic)

**Master story beat/theme stated: Because
of Madison selling tickets, they are closer
to keeping the theater, which is at the heart of the
troupe's long deep friendship and their ability to
continually hang out together.**

While Madison's breakthrough of ticket sale stardom isn't exactly the deep shared connection (**not
connected**) that Justin longs for, just hanging out with the troupe is enough to feel **not lonely** and the
event of selling out the house for Saturday (tomorrow's show) actually makes Justin and the troupe feel
connected again. Hence the movement.

Figure 7.5 Master story beat/theme stated 2—*Through the Night* (demo).

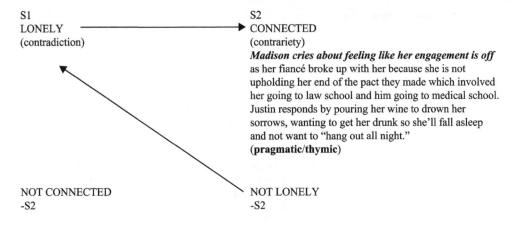

S1
LONELY
(contradiction)

S2
CONNECTED
(contrariety)
Madison cries about feeling like her engagement is off
as her fiancé broke up with her because she is not
upholding her end of the pact they made which involved
her going to law school and him going to medical school.
Justin responds by pouring her wine to drown her
sorrows, wanting to get her drunk so she'll fall asleep
and not want to "hang out all night."
(pragmatic/thymic)

NOT CONNECTED
-S2

NOT LONELY
-S2

**Master story beat/theme stated: Madison has a
broken engagement and is sad and now really
needs the bonding with the group.**

Madison starts feeling **not lonely** because she has the superficial comradery of the troupe, but when she
discovers her engagement is broken, she is sad and **lonely**, and the group comforts her and makes her feel
better, which makes her feel very **connected**.

Figure 7.6 Master story beat/theme stated 3—*Through the Night* (demo).

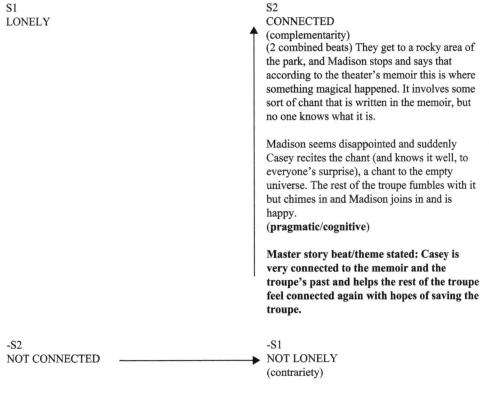

S1
LONELY

S2
CONNECTED
(complementarity)
(2 combined beats) They get to a rocky area of
the park, and Madison stops and says that
according to the theater's memoir this is where
something magical happened. It involves some
sort of chant that is written in the memoir, but
no one knows what it is.

Madison seems disappointed and suddenly
Casey recites the chant (and knows it well, to
everyone's surprise), a chant to the empty
universe. The rest of the troupe fumbles with it
but chimes in and Madison joins in and is
happy.
(pragmatic/cognitive)

**Master story beat/theme stated: Casey is
very connected to the memoir and the
troupe's past and helps the rest of the troupe
feel connected again with hopes of saving the
troupe.**

-S2
NOT CONNECTED

-S1
NOT LONELY
(contrariety)

Casey, who despite being with her old troupe always felt a little ignored and the odd girl out being with her
old friends, feels **not connected** but not completely **lonely** either (**not lonely**). But she traverses to feeling
not lonely because she was able to recall and recite some of the memoir, which makes her a hero for the
moment and makes her (and the troupe) feel very **connected**.

Figure 7.7 Master story beat/theme stated 4—*Through the Night* (demo).

S1
LONELY ◄──────────────────────────► S2
(contrariety)   CONNECTED (multiple beats)
                                       (complementarity)
                                       Clarke tells the group that he's terminally ill and dying
                                       of cancer. It throws the group. They are freaked out. But
                                       Clarke isn't…he accepts it as nature taking its course.

                                       The rest of the group are crying and freaked out by
                                       Clarke's announcement that he is dying, and Clarke is
                                       almost puzzled. He's incredibly stoic and completely
                                       unafraid.

                                       The rest of the group cries with Clarke when they find
                                       out he has cancer, but he is not sad.

                                       Clarke informs the group he wants them to assist him in
                                       committing suicide.
                                       (pragmatic/cognitive/thymic)

                                       Master story beat/theme stated: Clarke announcing
                                       his terminal illness and his wish to commit assisted
                                       suicide with them in the park on Sunday night gives
                                       the hanging out aspects of their nights greater
                                       importance, depth, and meaning, making them more
                                       inclined to want to stay together.

-S2   -S1
NOT CONNECTED   NOT LONELY

Clarke announcing his terminal illness and his wish to commit assisted suicide with the group has the ironic
effect of making them both go from **not lonely** to **connected** because the depth of feeling and emotion that
his announcement has charged them with moves them from a more superficial sense of each other (**not**
lonely) to an immediate and deep sense of friendship (**connected**).

But this feeling of connection is short-lived, and the movement is to the self-awareness that they cannot save
their friend and they are ultimately mortal and will die alone (**connected** to **lonely**).

Figure 7.8 Master story beat/theme stated 5—*Through the Night* (demo).

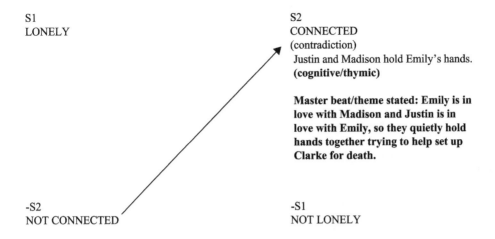

S1
LONELY

S2
CONNECTED
(contradiction)
Justin and Madison hold Emily's hands.
(cognitive/thymic)

**Master beat/theme stated: Emily is in
love with Madison and Justin is in
love with Emily, so they quietly hold
hands together trying to help set up
Clarke for death.**

-S2
NOT CONNECTED

-S1
NOT LONELY

Even though their troupe and friendship is fading, there is a feeling of deep connection as they sit in the
room of ancient coffins through the night. They started from **not connected** (going through the motions of
the final night with Clarke in the museum) to a magical feeling of silent deep connection (**connected**) even
though they will disperse after this night.

Figure 7.9 Master story beat/theme stated 6—*Through the Night* (demo).

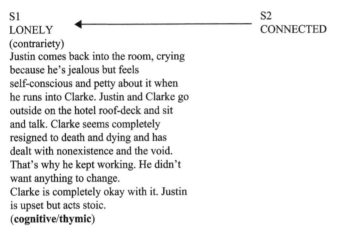

S1
LONELY
(contrariety)
Justin comes back into the room, crying
because he's jealous but feels
self-conscious and petty about it when
he runs into Clarke. Justin and Clarke go
outside on the hotel roof-deck and sit
and talk. Clarke seems completely
resigned to death and dying and has
dealt with nonexistence and the void.
That's why he kept working. He didn't
want anything to change.
Clarke is completely okay with it. Justin
is upset but acts stoic.
(cognitive/thymic)

**Master story beat/theme stated:
Justin has an intense moment of
bonding and friendship with Clarke
and realizes he's losing his friend and
recognizes the power of the depth of
their friendship and because of
Clark's stoicism feels both fearless
and yet powerless.**

S2
CONNECTED

-S2
NOT CONNECTED

-S1
NOT LONELY

Justin talking deeply with Clarke about his impending death and Clarke's utter stoicism about it is moving
and really deepens their friendship and contributes to Justin's feeling of being **connected**. But at the same
time, Justin is powerless to save Clarke and knows he'll be without him and thus feels very **lonely** in the
universe. This again repeats the movement pattern brought on by Clarke announcing his imminent suicide
from **connected** to **lonely**, because it makes Justin feel very alone and powerless since he can't lean on
Clarke anymore.

Figure 7.10 Master story beat/theme stated 7—*Through the Night* (demo).

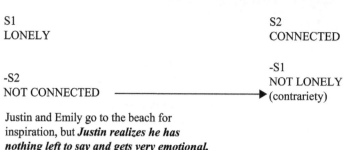

S1
LONELY

S2
CONNECTED

-S1
NOT LONELY
(contrariety)

-S2
NOT CONNECTED

Justin and Emily go to the beach for inspiration, but ***Justin realizes he has nothing left to say and gets very emotional.*** They get an Uber to go back to the hotel. **(cognitive/thymic)**

Master story beat/theme stated: Justin has been hiding from himself the fact that his artistic life has been running dry, and now he's come face-to-face with the reality that he has nothing left to say.

Justin has been having difficulty reaching Emily and isn't feeling connected (**not connected**), but she is starting to open up to him a little bit and he feels **not lonely**. His relationship with her always provided artistic inspiration to him, but she found the relationship draining and left him to marry her current wife (whom she is now separated from).

Figure 7.11 Master story beat/theme stated 8—*Through the Night* (demo).

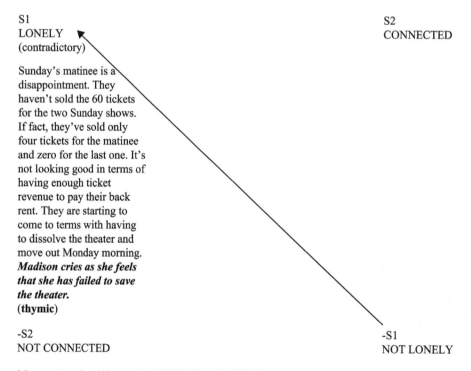

S1
LONELY
(contradictory)

S2
CONNECTED

Sunday's matinee is a disappointment. They haven't sold the 60 tickets for the two Sunday shows. If fact, they've sold only four tickets for the matinee and zero for the last one. It's not looking good in terms of having enough ticket revenue to pay their back rent. They are starting to come to terms with having to dissolve the theater and move out Monday morning. ***Madison cries as she feels that she has failed to save the theater.*** **(thymic)**

-S2
NOT CONNECTED

-S1
NOT LONELY

Master story beat/theme stated: Madison has failed to save the theater and has remorse and doesn't like the pain of the theater life.

She now feels no **connection** to her cohorts because she is embarrassed and feels like she failed everyone, despite their denying this. Since ultimately her relationship with the troupe has been fun but not altogether too deep, the movement here will be tracked as **not lonely** to **lonely** as she feels very alone and inadequate not being able to save the theater.

Figure 7.12 Master story beat/theme stated 9—*Through the Night* (demo).

S1
LONELY
(contrariety) ◄─────────────────────── CONNECTED   S2

The unhoused woman ranting is odd in that she seems almost triggered by the stage play and eventually she marches on stage and starts having a fight with Madison which shuts the whole show down and she tears up the set and it is bedlam and the oddly powerful unhoused woman almost kills Madison.
(pragmatic/cognitive/thymic)

Master story beat/theme stated: It's a scary moment for Madison as the unhoused woman has a lot of strength and power and almost kills Madison

-S2
NOT CONNECTED   -S1
NOT LONELY

The whole experience of the theater crumbles for Madison; she felt very **connected** to something bigger than herself (the theater, acting, the troupe via the play) but now she moves from **connected** to **lonely**, amplified by the destruction of the stage sets and almost loss of her life, which all makes her feel very **lonely**.

Figure 7.13 Master story beat/theme stated 10—*Through the Night* (demo).

S1
LONELY ◄─────────────────────── CONNECTED   S2
(contrariety)
Clarke takes the medicine and dies. They call the ambulance and the police and show the police the video Clarke had made explaining what he did.
(cognitive)

Master story beat/theme stated: Clarke has bravely met his end, and the troupe could not save him. They realize this.

-S2
NOT CONNECTED   -S1
NOT LONELY

Clarke's death makes the ultimate loneliness set in, seeming to move from ultimate connection when they were helping him die, hence the movement from **connected** to **lonely** because they have a shared sense of feeling lost.

Figure 7.14 Master story beat/theme stated 11—*Through the Night* (demo).

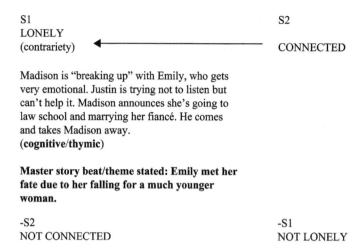

S1
LONELY
(contrariety)

S2
CONNECTED

Madison is "breaking up" with Emily, who gets
very emotional. Justin is trying not to listen but
can't help it. Madison announces she's going to
law school and marrying her fiancé. He comes
and takes Madison away.
(cognitive/thymic)

**Master story beat/theme stated: Emily met her
fate due to her falling for a much younger
woman.**

-S2
NOT CONNECTED

-S1
NOT LONELY

Emily still had complete hope in her and Madison being together, and it's an extreme change for her to learn
that Madison was just having fun and doesn't love her as much as she loves Madison. Emily's thought is that
they were very much **connected** but in reality were not and hence moved from **connected** to **lonely** quickly,
almost in a reversal (reversal of fortune).

Figure 7.15 Master story beat/theme stated 12—*Through the Night* (demo).

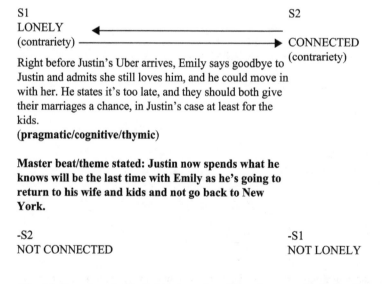

S1
LONELY
(contrariety)

S2
CONNECTED
(contrariety)

Right before Justin's Uber arrives, Emily says goodbye to
Justin and admits she still loves him, and he could move in
with her. He states it's too late, and they should both give
their marriages a chance, in Justin's case at least for the
kids.
(pragmatic/cognitive/thymic)

**Master beat/theme stated: Justin now spends what he
knows will be the last time with Emily as he's going to
return to his wife and kids and not go back to New
York.**

-S2
NOT CONNECTED

-S1
NOT LONELY

After Madison departs, Emily is more vulnerable and open to Justin. Emily spends the night holding him
because she's sad and it goes from **lonely** to **connected** and back to **lonely**.

Figure 7.16 Master story beat/theme stated 13—*Through the Night* (demo).

Screenplay Scene Developed for a Master Story Beat for *Through the Night* (Includes Master Story Beat 1)

```
ESTABLISHING SHOT - SUBURBAN HOUSE - NIGHT

CRICKETS CHIRP.


INT. SUBURBAN HOUSE - NIGHT

Having dinner are JUSTIN LAKE (55), SUE LAKE (54), TOM and
JOAN BORING (40s).

Justin seems as if he doesn't want to be there. His wife Sue
makes eye contact with him, "Don't be a jerk."

There is long awkward silence.

                    JOAN
          It's so nice for you to have us
          over. We don't know many other
          couples in the neighborhood.

                    SUE
          Same.

The SOUND OF KIDS playing in a side room is evident.

                    JOAN
          And it seems like the kids are
          getting along.

O.C. WE HEAR A LIGHT SMASHING.

                    JUSTIN
              (yells)
          Kids! Everybody okay?

                    CHARLOTTE (O.C.)
          We're fine dad.

There is a pause and the couples reset.

                    TOM
          So Joan tells me you fly back to
          New York every weekend.

                    JUSTIN
          *Some* weekends. Unless there's no
          show.

                    JOAN
          Show! Right. You're into Broadway
          plays or something.

                    JUSTIN
          Or something.

                    SUE
          Justin runs an off-
```

Figure 7.17 Demo of a scene from original screenplay *Through the Night* developed using the semiotics system leading up to and through master story beat 1.

2.

                    JUSTIN
                (clarifying)
          Not exactly Broadway. More off
          Broadway.

                    SUE
          You left out a couple of offs
          there.

                    TOM
          What do the "offs" mean?

                    SUE
          It means nobody sees the plays!

Sue, Tom and Joan laugh. Justin frowns.

                    SUE (CONT'D)
                (feels bad)
          It's about the size of the theater.
          The more offs the smaller.

                    JUSTIN
          That's not exactly accurate.

                    TOM
                (detecting tension)
          Oh.
                (siding with Sue)
          Riiight!

                    JOAN
          So how big is an off off theater?

                    SUE
          More like off off off off *off*
          theater you mean.

Joan looks at her oddly.

                    JUSTIN
                (angrily holds up two
                 fingers)
          Two offs! Two!

They look taken aback by his testiness. Justin tries to
smooth it out.

                    JUSTIN (CONT'D)
          It's not just about the size.

Tom holds a finger in the air, ("I'll solve it") and looks it
up on his iPhone and reads.

                    TOM
                (reading iPhone)
          The "offs" usually but not always
          pertain to the size of the theater.

                    JOAN
          So your theater must be small.

Figure 7.17 *Continued.*

                                                          3.

                    TOM
          Right. But size doesn't matter.

He laughs loudly at his own bad joke. Joan is embarrassed and
tries to cover.

                    JOAN
          We love plays. Whenever we go to
          New York we go to at least one.
          Last Christmas we saw *Frozen*.

Justin rolls his eyes.

                    SUE
               (trying)
          Oh. How was it?

                    JOAN
          It started good. Then Carl, he's
          our oldest, he didn't understand it
          was a live show ya know. He thought
          he was ya know at the movies -- and
          that he was free to yell at the
          screen.

                    JUSTIN
          Stage. There was no screen.

                    JOAN
          Right. You know what I mean. He
          confused the stage with the screen.
          And yelled at it. The way kids do.

                    JUSTIN
          My kids don't yell at the screen.
          Or the stage.

Sue looks at him sternly for being negative. There is silence
and tension. Sue tries to break it.

                    SUE
          Was it a good show?

                    JOAN
               (shrugs)
          Don't know. Carl kept yelling and
          disrupted the show. We were asked
          to leave. They refunded us.

Justin looks horrified. There is a pause.

                    TOM
          So what do you do Justin?

                    JUSTIN
          What do you mean "do?"

                    TOM
          I mean for a living.

Figure 7.17 *Continued.*

4.

                    JUSTIN
          I run a Ponzi scheme.

                    TOM
          Can I get in on it?

He laughs again at his own joke.

                    TOM (CONT'D)
          That theater in New York can't be
          your living.

                    JUSTIN
          I'm a leech. I mooch off my wife
          who is actually a grown up.

                    SUE
             (embarrassed)
          Justin is considering doing
          substitute teaching work. He just
          got his teaching license.

                    JUSTIN
          Which means the system has failed.

                    TOM
          Oh why didn't you say so!

                    JOAN
          You know we're both teachers at
          P.S. 22.

                    SUE
             (she knew)
          Really! Wow. That is great. What a
          coincidence.
             (to Justin)
          Isn't that great Justin?

                    JOAN
          We're always looking for
          substitutes.

                    JUSTIN
          There's a reason for that.

                    JOAN
          Why don't you meet me during my
          break on Monday, between eleven
          thirty-five and eleven fifty and
          we'll get you into the system.

                    JUSTIN
          You have your break times down to
          minutes?

                    SUE
          That would be great. Thanks!
             (to Justin)
          Isn't that great honey?

Figure 7.17 *Continued.*

5.

                    JUSTIN
          But I have this thing about
          children.

                    JOAN
          What thing?

                    JUSTIN
          I hate them.

There is an awkward silence. Sue looks scared like he blew
it. Suddenly Joan and Tom start laughing like he was kidding.

                    JOAN
          How can you hate them? They're
          great. So kind -- and well behaved.
          "Ms. Boring is the pandemic over?
          Ms. Boring can I go to the
          bathroom?"

Justin looks at them and is horrified. Suddenly O.C. Justin's
daughter SCREAMS.

KID'S ROOM - SAME

Justin runs into the room to find the Boring's MEATHEAD
SON(12) has Justin's daughter CHARLOTTE(10) in a headlock in
a play wrestle. She is scared.

                    JUSTIN
          Stop it. You're gonna hurt her.

The Meathead Son doesn't stop. Justin tries to pry them apart
and the Meathead Son then grabs Justin and puts *him* in a
headlock. Justin then picks the Meathead Son up and he
smashes Justin against the bookshelf and books fall on them.

INT. SUBURBAN HOUSE - AT FRONT DOOR - NIGHT

The Borings are saying goodbye. Justin has a laceration on
his neck and is rubbing his shoulder. They shake hands.

                    TOM
          Sorry about your shelves.

                    SUE
          That's okay. It's just Justin's old
          theater books. We were looking to
          get rid of them anyway.

                    JUSTIN
          We were?

                    JOAN
          So come by the school at eleven
          thirty-five on Monday. We'll get
          you hooked up with substitute work.

                    TOM
          She's very connected at P.S. 22.

Figure 7.17 *Continued.*

                         SUE
          We had a great time.

                         JOAN
          So did we.

                         TOM
                    (to Justin)
          Off off off off off off off we go!

They go to leave. Justin holds the door open to get a last
word in.

                         JUSTIN
          You know that Sue doesn't really
          like you two, right?

REACTION SHOT: THE BORINGS FROWN

                         JUSTIN (CONT'D)
          She just invited you over so she
          could beg you to get me a job as a
          substitute teacher.

Tom and Joan look at him frozen. Then they crack up like it's
another joke, Tom points at him, "funny guy."

They leave and Sue waves a friendly, "goodbye." She closes
the door and her entire demeanor changes. She is livid.

                         SUE
          What was that?

                         JUSTIN
          What?

Sue starts cleaning up.

                         SUE
          What you said about me inviting
          them over just to beg them for a
          job for you?

                         JUSTIN
          But it's true right?

She doesn't answer.

                         JUSTIN (CONT'D)
          It's true. Right?

                         SUE
          I thought we agreed -- we never
          ever ever tell friends the truth.

                         JUSTIN
          Then they're not friends.

                         SUE
          That's not the point.

Figure 7.17 *Continued.*

7.

                    JUSTIN
          Then what is the point?

Sue grabs the dirty dishes and carries them in her arms to
the kitchen and throws them into the sink where they CRASH.
She is mad and starts doing dishes loudly. Justin tries to
negotiate.

                    JUSTIN (CONT'D)
          We just spent three excruciating
          hours with, I'm not making this up,
          Tom and Joan Boring.

Sue angrily washes dishes.

                    JUSTIN (CONT'D)
          And how is it when I try to talk
          about theater she brings up *Frozen*?

Sue ignores him.

                    JUSTIN (CONT'D)
          They didn't show any real interest
          in our lives.

                    SUE
          Your life. Did you show any real
          interest in *their* lives?

                    JUSTIN
          There's nothing there.

                    SUE
          You're not so fascinating.

                    JUSTIN
          I know -- I'm boring too. But my
          boringness is more interesting than
          theirs.

                    SUE
          Yeah well my boringness is I'm
          chained to my desk for eight hours
          a day and they are the first couple
          that showed any interest in being
          friends.

                    JUSTIN
          Why does every fight we have end up
          having to do with your job?

                    SUE
          Because it's time you got one of
          your own! And they are connected in
          the school system here.

                    JUSTIN
          Yeah but I don't want to become
          him. He scared me. He spent --
               (looks at phone)
                    (MORE)

Figure 7.17 *Continued.*

                    JUSTIN (CONT'D)
-- I clocked it at twenty one
minutes -- talking about fire ants
and weed killer.

                    SUE
So. Fire ants and weed killer are
important.

                    JUSTIN
To the gardener they are. If I
become a substitute teacher they'll
cut my brain out and I'll talk
about fire ants and weed killer
too.

                    SUE
Why do you have to be such a snob?

                    JUSTIN
Me not liking to talk about fire
ants and weed killer doesn't make
me a snob.

                    SUE
I'm telling you -- you're a snob.

                    JUSTIN
I'm not a snob.

                    SUE
What, you're mad our guests weren't
interested in Samuel Beckett?

                    JUSTIN
Yes!

                    SUE
Snob.

                    JUSTIN
     (talks to dog in dog bed)
Coco do you think I'm snob?

                    COCO
Woof!

                    SUE
You see!

                    JUSTIN
I thought we determined that Coco's
single "woof" answers could be
interpreted as a yes or no
depending on the context.

                    SUE
Sounded like a "yes."

Figure 7.17 *Continued.*

9.

                    JUSTIN
          It did I'll give you that.
              (to dog)
          Thanks traitor.

                    COCO
          Woof!

                    JUSTIN
          Yeah. See who sneaks you scraps.

Coco stares at him.

INT. BEDROOM - NIGHT

It's later in the evening. Justin and Sue are lying in bed
reading. Sue is reading a novel. Justin is reading a giant
biography of Bertolt Brecht.

                    JUSTIN (CONT'D)
          Oh, right -- make sure you set the
          alarm for six because you have to
          drive me to the airport.

                    SUE
          Seriously? I have a meeting at
          eight tomorrow morning.

                    JUSTIN
          You know you drive me to the
          airport every Friday I'm going to
          New York.

                    SUE
          Can't you take the bus?

                    JUSTIN
          The bus? This bus system sucks! I'd
          have to leave now to make it.

                    SUE
          So. Miss a week of the theater. We
          can use the money we save in
          airfare.

                    JUSTIN
          Again with the money.

                    SUE
          It's getting really expensive ya
          know -- you running back and forth
          to New York.

                    JUSTIN
          I'm the executive director of the
          theater. I have to be there.

                    SUE
          But you're not in this show. And
          Emily can run the house.

Figure 7.17 *Continued.*

10

> JUSTIN
> Run the house *and* the show?

> SUE
> Yes. Why not? There's never any
> audience. What's the big deal?

> JUSTIN
> There's been audiences.

> SUE
> Years ago. Come on Justin -- your
> theater is dead -- face it.

> JUSTIN
> I faced it. Many times. Remember? I
> even wrote a play about it -- *Get
> Up On Stage! We Out Number You!*

> SUE
> We lost ten grand on it.

> JUSTIN
> It was money from my inheritance.
> And ten grand is nothing in
> theater.

> SUE
> It takes me three months to clear
> ten grand.

> JUSTIN
> So *that's* what this is about? You
> working like a dog to pay the bills
> and me just flying off to New York
> to run a theater where nobody goes
> to shows and it's costing us money.

> SUE
> Something like that.

> JUSTIN
> Well -- I have good news for you.

He sits up.

> JUSTIN (CONT'D)
> We lost our lease.

> SUE
> Oh no -- really? Why didn't you
> tell me. What happened?

> JUSTIN
> We don't sell tickets anymore.
> We're behind two months rent.

> SUE
> (disappointed)
> Tap into your inheritance again.

Figure 7.17 *Continued.*

11.

```
                JUSTIN
    We need it for retirement.

                SUE
    I'll never retire. I'm going to
    work until I'm embalmed. Spend it
    on the theater.

                JUSTIN
    No. I can't. No more! I'm gonna man
    up and shut it down and move back
    here and be a substitute.
         (bad taste in mouth)
    Blech!

                SUE
    I think it will be fun.

                JUSTIN
    Fun is not the goal. Survival is.

                SUE
    I think you'll have fun.

                JUSTIN
    I'll do it under one condition.

                SUE
    What?

                JUSTIN
    If I'm a substitute teacher and I
    start talking about fire ants and
    weed killer you have to kill me.

                SUE
    Done! You didn't even have to ask.

He frowns at her suspiciously.
```

Figure 7.17 *Continued.*

8

Using Final Draft Beat Board and Outline Editor with the Semiotics Tools

Creating a Final Draft Beat Board Outline Using *Lost in Translation* as Specimen

The following is a sample of laying out beats for *Lost in Translation* on Final Draft's Beat Board and Outline Editor (see Figures 8.1 to 8.2).

Note: Before I placed the beats on the Beat Board I went ahead and took the added step of creating simple names for each of the beats while in Final Draft as a way to recall what the nature of each beat was. This is a first step *before* I placed the beats onto the Outline Editor. This way I can use this specimen movie breakdown as a pivot off which to write my own script or at least get an overall sense of where things in my specimen movie lay out as a guidepost.

For this demonstration I started by placing my breakdown of *Lost in Translation* onto the Beat Board and then invented names for the beats as Final Draft provides a structure by which to do so. This step of course is optional, but I find it helps.

Using Final Draft with Comprehensive Beat Map for Writing Original Screenplay *Through the Night* (Demo)

Take the comprehensive beat map you invented for your original screenplay (as I have done as a demo) and drop it onto the Final Draft Beat Board (see Figures 8.3 to 8.5).

You can continue to map your entire set of beats from the comprehensive beat map onto the Beat Board Outline which can be viewed in some ways as a "timeline." Setting this up in advance of writing your own script can help guide you as you write.

Finally, you can have your specimen movie breakdown "running" in the background (in Figure 8.4 in Outline 1) as a reference for you to drop your original screenplay comprehensive beat map against.

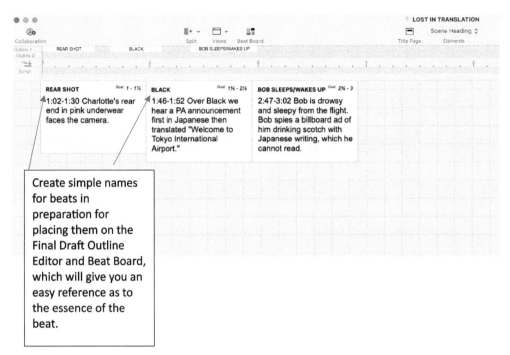

Create simple names for beats in preparation for placing them on the Final Draft Outline Editor and Beat Board, which will give you an easy reference as to the essence of the beat.

Figure 8.1 Using Final Draft Beat Board with the semiotics tools 1. These chunks were derived directly from *Lost in Translation*'s comprehensive beat map. I gave the beats "names" at this stage such as BLACK, BOB SLEEPS/WAKES UP because Final Draft Beat Board affords me the opportunity to do so.

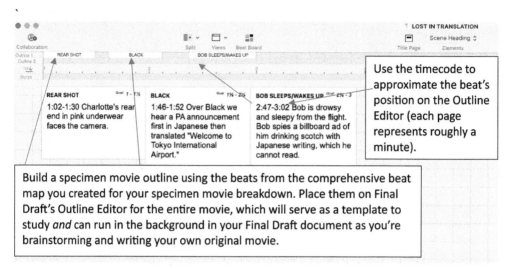

Build a specimen movie outline using the beats from the comprehensive beat map you created for your specimen movie breakdown. Place them on Final Draft's Outline Editor for the entire movie, which will serve as a template to study *and* can run in the background in your Final Draft document as you're brainstorming and writing your own original movie.

Figure 8.2 Using Final Draft with the semiotics tools 2. The next phase is for me to take the beats and drop them onto the Outline Editor.

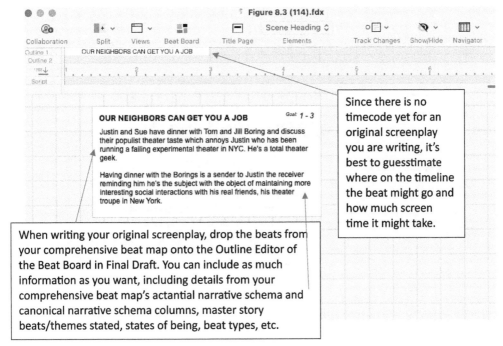

Figure 8.3 Using Final Draft with the semiotics tools 3—*Through the Night* (demo).

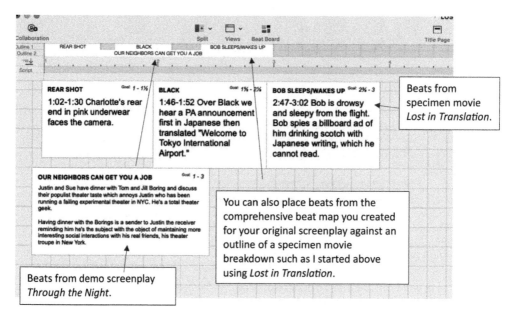

Figure 8.4 Using Final Draft with semiotics tools 4—*Through the Night* (demo).

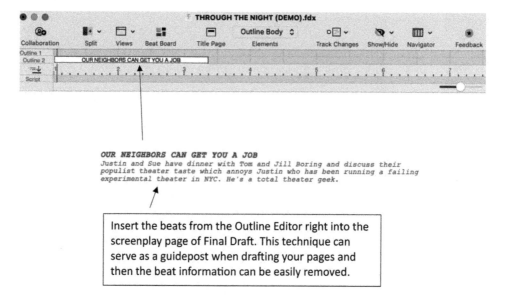

Figure 8.5 Using Final Draft with semiotics tools 5—*Through the Night* (demo).

Closing Thoughts

As I attempt to close out this study, I wanted to thank you for taking this semiotics journey with me. I realize it's a lot of information and many of these tools are brand new to you. I invite you to learn them and use them in whatever way you see fit. What I have laid out is what works for me; however, I'm sure over time my understanding of what to do with the tools will evolve. I hope to try and keep the community of writers who enjoy this kind of work updated, and I'd love to hear your thoughts on new ways to use the tools.

The last thought I'd like to leave with you is: You are very capable of writing solid work if you take the time to break down specimen movies you love, study them very deeply, and train your brain. Be well and as always . . . keep writing!

Bibliography

Greimas, A. J. (1966), *Sémantique Structurale*, Paris: Larousse.

Greimas, A. J. (1987), *On Meaning: Selected Writings in Semiotic Theory*, University of Minnesota Press.

Greimas, A. J. and J. Courtés (1982), *Semiotics and Language: An Analytical Dictionary*, Indiana University Press.

Martin, B. and F. Ringham, (2000), *Dictionary of Semiotics*, London and New York: Cassell.

McKee, R. (1997), *Story: Substance, Structure, Style, and the Principles of Screenwriting*, Harper Collins.

Propp, V. (1968), *Morphology of the Folktale*, ed. L. A. Wagner, trans. L. Scott, University of Texas Press.

Saussure, F. de (2011), *Course in General Linguistics*, Columbia University Press.

Snyder, Blake (2005), *Save the Cat! The Last Book on Screenwriting You'll Ever Need*, Studio City, CA: Michael Wiese Productions.

Tierno, M. (2002), *Aristotle's Poetics for Screenwriters*, Hachette Books.

Vogler, C. (2020), *The Writer's Journey – 25th Anniversary Edition: Mythic Structure for Writers* (4th Edition), Studio City, CA: Michael Wiese Productions.

Glossary of Terms

Actant: An action force or function in a story that usually adds up to an actor (character) but not always. Sometimes can be inanimate (a tornado in *The Wizard of Oz*).

Actantial Narrative Schema: The system derived from the much more complex system of narratemes by Vladimir Propp, whereby A. J. Greimas took the 31 commonly occurring actants in any story (helper, hero, etc.) and reduced them down to six actants in binary opposition: sender/receiver, subject/object, helper/opponent (anti-subject).

Anti-Subject: The actant that diametrically opposes the subject in terms of the desire/want/quest for an object.

Being able to do something/Knowing how to do something: In the narrative level (namely the Canonical Narrative Schema), once a subject is in pursuit of an action of want/desire/need, there will be a qualifying test that will lead to a decisive test (which determines if the object is obtained or not). The qualifying test is meant to develop some sort of competency (a *being able to do something* or a *knowing how to do something*) that will prepare or *qualify* the subject to partake in the decisive test.

Binary Opposition: The fundamental principle that narrative semiotics is built on; namely, that you only can perceive of things because of their opposites. You know of evil because of good, life because of death, up because of down. This is the very rudiment of the structuralist system the narrative semiotics derives from but (as this study will show) it's much more complex.

Canonical Narrative Schema: As a canon looks at any body of story within a given system, culture, or collection, the Canonical Narrative Schema looks at the overlying principles that apply to all stories, including that they contain a contract, a qualifying test, a decisive test, and a glorifying test.

Cognitive Beat: There are three primary beats that occur on the narrative level. The first is a cognitive beat which is where something significant happens in the brain of an actor where they realize, learn, or know something.

Competent Observer: Instead of a "target audience," semiotics postulates a competent observer who must have the "competency" to bring together the meaning in the binary oppositions and structures of the narrative.

Complementarity: In the semiotic square, which is based on classical logic, the complementary pairs of terms are like each other but not exactly alike thereby giving an opportunity to create variations of terms/meanings/ideas while still adhering to the master semiotic square.

Contract: Part of the Canonical Narrative Schema whereby something happens that creates a need/want/desire in a subject (for an object) and the pursuit of said object is established by a contract.

Contradiction: Yet another term within the semiotic square which again uses the structure of classical logic and allows to have direct opposition of terms/words/ideas/meanings with differences/nuances providing for more depth of narrative choices.

Contrariety: At the top left and right of the semiotic square, you have the master binary opposition terms and they relate to each other in pure contrariety (life vs. death, etc.). The bottom left and right terms of the semiotic square are also contrariety terms, but they are contrarieties of contradictions (non-life vs. non-death, etc.).

Decisive Test: The climactic "test" of the Canonical Narrative Schema whereby it's decided if the subject came into conjunction with their object of desire (does Dorothy in *The Wizard of Oz* get to go home?).

Dysphoria: To track the "emotional life" of actors (characters), semiotics uses a term known as "states of being" (emotional states of character). To be able to log the states of being in a movie in binary opposition, we use the two contrary terms "dysphoria" and "euphoria." Dysphoria is the negative emotional feelings an actor experiences.

Elements: Before a word, concept, idea, etc. can become an "isotopy" (a narrative particle), we first call it an element because sometimes we'll generate elements that won't suggest a "narrative intent" and therefore will never become an isotopy.

Euphoria: The binary opposite of dysphoria (see Dysphoria).

Function: Actants are said to be "functions" within a story which can be deemed as action "forces" that *can* be represented by actors/characters but it's the more abstract way of stating this.

Generative Trajectory: Narrative semiotics postulates that there are multiple levels of "meaning" in a story and the generative trajectory tracks these levels, how they are stacked up, and how they relate to one another. They are: the surface level of story (the things of story that communicate to us); the "narrative level" (which is the overall structure of story); and the deep level of meaning (which is the thematic level).

Glorifying Test: The final of the three tests of the Canonical Narrative Schema which can be said to correlate to the denouement of drama whereby the subject (protagonist) experiences whatever they will experience from either having come into conjunction with their object or not. It's not exactly a "contest" the way the other two (Qualifying/Decisive) tests are.

Helper: One of the three pairs of actants in the Actantial Narrative Schema that comes to "help" the subject in quest for their object (the Tin Man in *The Wizard of Oz* is a helper to Dorothy trying to get to Oz and get home).

Isotopies: Plural of Isotopy (see below).

Isotopy: The single most reducible particle of story that shows "narrative intent."

Narrative Intent: A term used to talk about how isotopies that shape a narrative point toward a story even in their elementary states.

Object: One of the three pairs of actants and part of the subject/object binary opposition which states that once a sender sends to a receiver, creating a need/want/desire for an object, a subject is "created."

Opponent: One of the three pairs of actants (helper/opponent) and is the one that opposes the subject in quest of their object. It can be any actant that opposes the subject regardless of the motivation. Not to be confused with an anti-subject who diametrically opposes the subject in pursuit of an object.

Pragmatic Beat: Of the three beats (pragmatic/cognitive/thymic), the pragmatic beat is the name for the basic action without any necessarily psychological component as the other two. Most beats are pragmatic beats.

Qualifying Test: One of the three "tests" of the Canonical Narrative Schema and is a "preparation test" to qualify to participate in the decisive test (the climatic test). It can be one scene or a whole act and appear in different manifestations in the movie.

Receiver: Part of the three pairs of actants in the Actantial Narrative Schema. The receiver is opposed to the sender as a sender sends to a receiver and begins a story contract. In addition to the master story being expressed using the concept of sender and receiver, individual scenes in a movie can be expressed using sender and receiver in a microcosm way.

Semiotic Square: Using classical logic, the semiotic square represents a visual representation of all meaning using terms of binary opposition and their corollaries.

Semiotic Square of Veridiction: A more complex semiotic square which has a layer of perception to analyze works where all isn't what it seems. Detective films tend to utilize this kind of analysis.

Sender: One of the three actants in the Actantial Narrative Schema. A sender sends to a receiver initiating a need/want/desire for an object (which creates a subject).

States of Being: Terms for the emotional life of an actor which can exist on the surface level (isotopic level) and the narrative level and be analyzed using the binary terms of euphoria and dysphoria.

Subject: One of the three pairs of actants (subject/object) whereby a sender sends to a receiver and creates a need/want/desire for a subject to obtain an object.

Surface Level (Figurative Level): The level of meaning where the "things" of a story are communicated to us by what we see and hear.

The Deep Level of Meaning: The thematic level of story whereby transformations for subjects in a story are tracked, meaning they come in conjunction with their object (or disjunction) of value and themes are stated based on this.

The Narrative Level: The level of story where the syntax (what follows what) is played out, including the working out of the Actantial Narrative Schema and the three pairs of actants (sender/receiver, subject/object, helper/opponent [anti-subject]), and the Canonical Narrative Schema which includes the contract (a want for an object is established) and the three tests that determine if the subject will obtain or not obtain it (the qualifying test, the decisive test, the glorifying test).

Thymic Beat: One of the three beats of the narrative level and correlates to "states of being." The thymic beat is a strong emotional beat for an actor (character).

Index